Rush
Limbaugh
and the
Conservative
Media
Establishment

ECHO CHAMBER

KATHLEEN HALL JAMIESON

JOSEPH N. CAPPELLA

OXFORD
UNIVERSITY PRESS

OXFORD
UNIVERSITY PRESS

Oxford University Press, Inc., publishes works that further
Oxford University's objective of excellence
in research, scholarship, and education.

Oxford   New York
Auckland   Cape Town   Dar es Salaam   Hong Kong   Karachi
Kuala Lumpur   Madrid   Melbourne   Mexico City   Nairobi
New Delhi   Shanghai   Taipei   Toronto

With offices in
Argentina   Austria   Brazil   Chile   Czech Republic   France   Greece
Guatemala   Hungary   Italy   Japan   Poland   Portugal   Singapore
South Korea   Switzerland   Thailand   Turkey   Ukraine   Vietnam

Copyright © 2008 by Kathleen Hall Jamieson and Joseph N. Cappella

Published by Oxford University Press, Inc.
198 Madison Avenue, New York, NY 10016

www.oup.com

First issued as an Oxford University Press paperback, 2010

Oxford is a registered trademark of Oxford University Press

Library of Congress Cataloging-in-Publication Data
Jamieson, Kathleen Hall.
Echo chamber : Rush Limbaugh and the conservative media establishment /
Kathleen Hall Jamieson, Joseph N. Cappella.
p.   cm.
Includes bibliographical references and index.
ISBN 978-0-19-539860-1 (pbk.)
1. Limbaugh, Rush H.   2. Journalism—Objectivity—United States.
3. Conservatism—United States.   I. Cappella, Joseph N.   II. Title.
PN1991.4.L48J36 2008
302.230973—dc22
2008003855

1 2 3 4 5 6 7 8 9
Printed in the United States of America
on acid-free paper

Contents

s we were putting the finishing touches on this manuscript, political happenstance offered up a test of one of our central arguments.
Our analysis of the conservative media establishment suggested that if Rush
Limbaugh, the editorial pages of the *Wall Street Journal,* and key players on
Fox News were confronted by a serious Republican presidential contender
whose proposals and past deviated from Reagan doctrine, they would marshal against the candidacy.

After a year of speculation about the prospects of presidential candidates
John McCain, Mitt Romney, Rudy Giuliani, and Fred Thompson, the emergence late in 2007 of Mike Huckabee, a telegenic former preacher and governor of Arkansas, as a serious Republican contender upended conventional
wisdom. In conservative circles, surprise at Huckabee's rise was overlaid with
concern about the ideological inclinations of the charismatic former Baptist
minister. Specifically, some worried that beneath his socially conservative,
antiabortion, anti–gay marriage veneer beat the heart of a social liberal and
foreign policy moderate. If so, Huckabee's candidacy constituted a betrayal
of Reagan conservatism.

As Huckabee surged in Iowa polls, the media voices on which we focus
in this book, including Rush Limbaugh, Fox News's Sean Hannity and Chris
Wallace, and editorial page writers at the *Wall Street Journal*, moved to the fore
to test the Arkansan's adherence to the Reagan catechism. On his nationally
syndicated radio show, Limbaugh concluded that there is "a lot of liberalism"
and not "a lot of Reaganism" in Huckabee (December 21, 2007). Among
Limbaugh's issues with the telegenic former preacher was his embrace of
the notion that the United States should strive to be well regarded in the
world community, a seeming repudiation of the muscular foreign policy of
presidents Ronald Reagan and George W. Bush.[1] On the *Journal's* website,
OpinionJournal.com's editor James Taranto raised concerns about the same
article that riled the talk radio host and also attacked the governor's social
policies with the suggestion that Huckabee's health care proposals smacked
of nannyism. Rounding out the critique, on the *Wall Street Journal's* editorial

pages, Kim Strassel challenged Huckabee's economic conservatism by noting that Huckabee's record as Arkansas governor revealed him to be "ambivalent about tax increases."[2]

Key players in the Fox News family weighed in as well. In an interview with Huckabee, Fox's conservative host Sean Hannity challenged him on his prison commutation and pardon policies (December 11, 2007). Fox's *Hannity and Colmes* also featured a former Arkansas journalist who averred that Huckabee's claim to be a conservative was belied by his gubernatorial record (December 26, 2007).

Lest the political establishment miss the importance of the concerns expressed by such media powerhouses as Limbaugh, others in the conservative media served up reminders. When an anonymous Huckabee aide characterized Limbaugh's critique of him as the Washington-dictated views of an "entertainer," Fox News empaneled four experts who informed listeners that a candidate who risked Limbaugh's wrath would pay a political price. Meanwhile the impact of Limbaugh's opinion was magnified by the *New York Times,* which reported that the talk radio leader had accused Huckabee of "practicing 'identity politics' (as an evangelical) and conservative apostasy." Limbaugh "told his listeners that Mr. Huckabee is 'not even anywhere near conservative,'" the *Times* reported.[3]

The day before Iowans caucused, Limbaugh informed his audience: "Governor Huckabee supports open borders and amnesty. . . . His position allows for all kinds of taxpayer aid to the children of illegals. . . . He said to the legislature of Arkansas, 'Send me any tax increase, send it up here.' . . . Conservatism, ladies and gentlemen, true conservatism balances budgets by cutting government, not by raising taxes. Governor Huckabee is opposed to school choice, and he said we should treat dictators and terrorists with the Golden Rule" (January 2, 2008). One of Limbaugh's conclusions moved onto cable when Fox News's bottom-of-the-screen ticker carried Limbaugh's pronouncement to the Fox audience on the eve of the caucus: "Governor Huckabee who might be a fine man and is a great Christian is not a conservative" (January 2, 2008).

The morning after Huckabee topped the Republican field in the Iowa caucuses, an op-ed in the *Journal* proclaimed, "Mike Huckabee's New Deal: More God, More Government." Featured in the piece were Huckabee's gubernatorial record of support for free health insurance for children and the working poor, his opposition to school choice and vouchers, and his support for an increase in the minimum wage. He "pleased teachers' unions" said the author and "satisfied labor."[4] On the day New Hampshirites voted in their primary, another essay on the editorial pages of the *Journal* attacked the centerpiece of Huckabee's economic platform, a flat tax on consumption labeled the Fair Tax.[5]

In an election year with a surfeit of debates, a Fox News–sponsored candidate matchup was the first to directly challenge Huckabee's conservatism. In that debate of January 10, 2008, the first after the New Hampshire primary, moderator Chris Wallace raised a question unasked by moderators who had hosted the earlier MSNBC, CNN, and ABC debates: "Governor Huckabee, in your 10 years running Arkansas, you raised taxes. They were higher at the end of your 10 years than they were at the beginning by hundreds of millions of dollars, and you increased the size of government." The implication that Huckabee is either a hypocrite or a heretic lurks just beneath the surface of the question Wallace then asked: "Is that your idea of change, to be a big government Republican president?" (South Carolina, January 10, 2008). On the day Michiganders went to the polls in their Republican primary, Rush Limbaugh's conclusion was categorical: "If either of these guys (Huckabee or Arizona senator John McCain) gets the nomination, it's going to destroy the Republican Party" (January 15, 2008).

In the country's earliest years, the process of assessing a person's fitness for the presidency was superintended by the nation's property-owning elites; in later times, party leaders claimed that role. Today, in Republican circles, the conservative opinion media shoulder part of that function. As we will show later, by so doing, they helped undercut the presidential primary aspirations of conservative columnist and author Pat Buchanan in 1996 and of Arizona senator John McCain in 2000. Vetting Republican candidates seeking their party's nomination is one of the functions of conservative media we explore in this book. But it is not the only one.

––––––

As the Huckabee illustration suggests, we believe that Rush Limbaugh, Fox News, and the opinion pages of the *Wall Street Journal* constitute a conservative media establishment. We don't expect readers to find that claim either novel or in need of extensive documentation. In a world in which Fox's owner Rupert Murdoch has recently purchased the *Wall Street Journal* and in which Limbaugh's is the most popular political talk radio program, Fox the most watched cable network, and the *Journal* the second most read paper in the country, we instead see our goal as understanding how these outlets make sense of politics for their audiences and fathoming what their success means for the Republican Party and the democratic process. In this book we analyze the ways Limbaugh, Fox, and the editorial pages of the country's major conservative newspaper both have protected Reagan conservatism across a more than decade-long period and insulated their audiences from political persuasion from Democrats and the "liberal media."

Specifically, we argue that these conservative media create a self-protective enclave hospitable to conservative beliefs. This safe haven reinforces the views of these outlets' like-minded audience members, helps them maintain ideological coherence, protects them from counterpersuasion, reinforces conservative values and dispositions, holds Republican candidates and leaders accountable to conservative ideals, tightens their audience's ties to the Republican Party, and distances listeners, readers, and viewers from "liberals," in general, and Democrats, in particular. It also enwraps them in a world in which facts supportive of Democratic claims are contested and those consistent with conservative ones championed. To explore the implications of the emergence of popular, commercially viable conservative opinion media, we ask what happens when conservative partisan outlets attract a large audience of the like-minded and make it possible for them to gather information and opinions about politics within a protective shelter from which they emerge holding polarized attitudes about Democrats and armored against discrepant information.

To set the premise of the book's central argument in place, we open with chapters showing that Limbaugh, the opinion pages of the *Wall Street Journal* (often James Taranto), and key players on Fox News (including Brit Hume, Sean Hannity, and Carl Cameron) adopt similar lines of argument, shared evidence, and common tactical approaches in their defense of conservatism and their attack on its opponents. In the process, we identify one overarching defining argument characterizing the content of these three outlets: the "liberal" media are both biased against conservatives and liberal and, as a result, untrustworthy. In the first two chapters, we prepare for the argument of the book with case examples that show how the conservative opinion media deploy a common vocabulary, build unique knowledge and interpretation, and polarize by distancing their audience from Democratic actions and positions.

Throughout the book we illustrate the ways these conservative voices portray themselves as the reliable, trustworthy alternative to mainstream media, while at the same time attacking "liberals" and dismissing or reframing information that undercuts conservative leaders or causes. In the process, they challenge the credibility of news outlets such as the *New York Times* and NBC, CBS, MSNBC, and CNN. The decibel level of this critique rises when the information or interpretation that the "mainstream media" offer is problematic for conservatives; unsurprisingly, these conservatives feature the work of the mainstream when it advances the conservative cause. This reframing builds the audience for conservative media by inviting it to turn to conservative outlets for reliable information and protects its members from Democratic views when they immerse themselves in the stream of the "liberal media" or view counterattitudinal information in such venues as presidential debates. Framing the mainstream media as liberal also ensures that the differences between liberals and conservatives are regularly featured, a move that creates cohesion within the conservative audience.

Our exploration of the conservative media's indictment of "liberal media" is set for us in a context in which scholarly efforts to isolate mainstream media bias have largely come up empty. A meta-analysis of 59 studies found no bias in newspapers and measurable but insignificant biases in news magazines and television news, with slightly more statements by Republicans in magazines and slightly more by Democrats on television.[6] The more media bias is discussed, the more people believe it exists, regardless of whether the news at the moment favors Republicans or Democrats,[7] a finding that could help explain why those in the audience of the conservative opinion media who repeatedly hear or read this claim are more likely to believe it. Another factor shaping conservatives' conviction that the media are liberal may be what scholars term the "hostile media phenomenon." Viewers are prone to detect and feature instances in which reporting seems to support an opposing ideology while not noticing the bias that favors their preferred position. These explanations aside, none of these studies examines one specific claim that conservative opinion media make—which is that the mainstream employs a double standard.[8]

The conservative opinion hosts underscore the notion that the mainstream media use a double standard that systematically disadvantages conservatives and their beliefs. To advance this notion, the conservative outlets feature instances of bias on the other side. This process builds a storehouse of evidence available to conservatives when challenged about their beliefs. Moreover, the audience can call on this information to buffer itself from claims detrimental to the conservative cause. These media outlets also enwrap conservatives and conservatism in positive emotion and tie negative feelings both to the mainstream media and to conservatism's adversaries.

Binding these dissimilar media figures and venues into a conservative media establishment is their embrace of the tenets of Reagan conservatism. The *Wall Street Journal* is the founding member in the club on which we focus. Long before the California governor emerged on the national scene, the *Journal* had championed the economic views that would come to be known as Reaganomics. The *Journal* had also been in the vanguard challenging Franklin Roosevelt's New Deal. Since that time, the *Journal's* editorials had rejected Roosevelt's social and economic policies while at the same time arguing for tax cuts and against government intervention, regulation, and expansion of social programs. The editorial pages of the *Journal* carry a consistent view of the history of the battle against liberalism. In that account, Roosevelt's policies failed to lift the country from the depression, for example. Reagan not only embraced these views but also embodied the free market philosophy espoused by the *Journal,* among others.

Those in search of a conservative presidential icon have few modern choices because Dwight Eisenhower and Richard Nixon's social policies were more centrist than conservative. Indeed, Nixon violated conservative doctrine by advocating wage and price controls, increasing governmental regulation of the environment, and supporting a health care reform proposal that made Bill Clinton's 1993–94 effort seem moderate by comparison. By contrast, Reagan governed from the right. Harking back to Reagan's time also permits conservatives to rally behind the philosophy of a personable and successful two-term president who was reelected in a landslide and who, unlike Nixon, left office in good standing with the American people. In addition, if one hopes to hold a voting coalition together, invoking the name of the president who originally assembled it makes strategic sense.

The conservatives on whom we focus champion a version of the past that asserts that Reagan conservatism succeeded where Franklin Roosevelt's liberalism failed. Specifically, Reagan's growth-producing military and economic policies saved the economy from destructive "liberal" taxation and sent the communist enemy into a death spiral. Conservatives are at war with what they call the liberal media in part because, they argue, it is an elite transmission belt that perverts the public's understanding of conservatism's successes and proffers a false account of liberalism's record.

This commitment to the Gipper's brand of conservatism means that Limbaugh, Hannity, and the *Journal*'s editorial pages take exception to moves by Republican leaders that expand the role of the federal government in education, increase spending on social programs, or initiate new "entitlements" such as the prescription drug benefit. This adherence to Reagan conservatism ensures that these outlets will reinforce a common set of presuppositions, a redundancy that heightens the impact of their underlying message. It guarantees as well that they protect an interpretation of Reagan conservatism that argues that the period 1980–88 vindicated Reagan's defense buildup, tax cuts, and assaults on regulation.

The conservative opinion media carry the Reaganesque message to an audience disposed to accept it. Magnifying the political importance of the three aforementioned outlets is the fact that their audiences are filled with voters indispensable to Republican victory. Where both Fox and Limbaugh attract an audience tilted toward economically anxious middle-class males from churchgoing households and southerners, the *Journal* addresses the party's business base.

The relationship between Limbaugh, in particular, and his audience harks back to an earlier age. By attracting this audience and engaging it in extended communication about the merits of conservatism and the dangers inherent in liberalism and in the "liberal" media, the conservative media perform functions once associated with party leaders. In this role, they reinforce a set of coherent rhetorical frames that empower their audiences to act as conservative opinion leaders, and enable Limbaugh in particular to mobilize party members for action, hold the Republican Party and its leaders accountable, and occasionally help screen candidates for the party's nomination. In a world in which the party identification of some shifts with the political tides, one byproduct of either listening to Limbaugh or watching Fox News or doing both may be an increased adherence to the Republican Party and with it a protection from the influences that might encourage alliance with or votes for Democrats. This phenomenon provides a floor of support for a faltering Republican president and a base of loyal voters likely to back the Republican Party nominee even when the Democrats have nominated an appealing centrist or a third-party candidate claims to be the bona fide conservative in the race.

Both Fox and Limbaugh insulate their audiences from persuasion by Democrats by offering opinion and evidence that make Democratic views seem alien and unpalatable. From 2004 survey data, we surmise that increasingly, Limbaugh's audience, which once paid more attention to mainstream broadcast and cable news than did others of similar education and income, is now less likely to turn to such sources, and more likely to turn to the second player in our analysis, Fox News. In other words, we suggest that those Rush listeners who are also Fox viewers are now better able to confine themselves in an insulating, protective media space filled with reassuring information and opinion. This space cushions already held beliefs. It also inculcates frames of interpretation that blunt the persuasive power of antagonistic views.

We do not suggest, however, that Limbaugh's audience ignores or boycotts other media.[9] The shift of Limbaugh's audience toward Fox is a tendency, not a mass exodus. What exposure to conservative media does, we argue, is increase the likelihood that what its audiences take from the mainstream (as it is generally termed) is that which is compatible with their conservative ideology. We find the same protective effect for Democratic claims and corresponding rejection of Republican ones among both CNN viewers and among those who turn their radio dials to National Public Radio (NPR).

In the final third of the book, we turn to the possible effects of the conservative opinion media establishment. We show, for example, that Limbaugh's audience differs both from nonlistening conservatives and from the public at large in the kind of knowledge it holds and in its interpretation of political information. His audience also interprets political information and political events in a way that is both systematic and consistent with Limbaugh's rhetoric. This creates for his listeners a polarized view of political phenomena. Because our data are drawn in the main from surveys, in most cases the method we employ opens two alternative explanations: either he has produced this effect directly, or his message draws in audiences and reinforces their dispositions. It may of course do both. Where we have experimental data, it often supports the former interpretation without excluding the latter.

Limbaugh's and Fox's message also distances his audience from Democrats and the mainstream media. In the 2004 National Annenberg Election Survey (NAES 2004), we find evidence that their audiences hold distorted perceptions of the positions of Democrat John Kerry, just as audiences for CNN and for NPR hold distorted perceptions of Republican stands. Overall audiences for Fox and Rush were more likely than nonviewers and nonlisteners of similar ideological disposition and education to embrace Republican campaign messages and reject Democratic ones.

In the final chapter we ask what all of this suggests about the future of partisan media of both the Left and the Right. At the same time, we examine concerns about the impact of partisan media on public deliberation and democracy.

To make our case, we draw on analysis of the content of these media as well as survey and experimental data. Some of the limitations of the evidence we offer in this book are the byproduct of its history and the history of the media we are studying. Although Rush Limbaugh made his national radio debut in 1988, he didn't attract our attention until 1994. In March of that year, the talk radio host raised red flags in the mainstream media and among Democrats with his announcement on air that Clinton White House confidant Vince Foster "was murdered." A subsequent inquiry concluded that Foster had killed himself.

The following November, under the leadership of Newt Gingrich, the Republicans took the House of Representatives, a turnover that put them in power for the first time in 40 years. In the wake of that revolution, Republican leaders called Limbaugh a "majority maker" and named him an honorary member of the freshman class of the 104th Congress. Gingrich's former press secretary, Tony Blankley, recalls, "After Newt, Rush was the single most important person in securing a Republican majority in the House of Representatives."[10]

Our interest in media effects in politics prompted us to study the content and impact of political talk radio in general and his program in particular in the context of the 1996 presidential campaign. As testimonials about Limbaugh's influence mounted, so, too, did concern in the mainstream media about this supposedly new force in American politics. We expanded our study to ask how well what these traditional media sources said about political talk radio matched its actual content.

In a preliminary report on that study, coauthored with our colleague media systems scholar Joe Turow and issued in August 1996, we concluded: "Press reports of talk radio suggest that it typically offers a discordant perhaps dangerous discourse that is intolerant and histrionic, unmindful of evidence, classically propagandistic." That conclusion was not supported by our content analysis of actual shows. "While the language of call-in political talk radio is less civil than the discourse of national party leaders," we reported, "the segments mentioned in articles on talk radio are not typical of the hosts quoted, nor are they representative of the political talk radio shows with the largest audiences."[11] In other words, at least some in the mainstream seemed to be vilifying the upstart medium.

Just as we came late to the realization that Rush Limbaugh had become a force in politics, we were tardy in studying a parallel phenomenon emerging in cable. Although Fox had been around since 1996, it wasn't until 2000 that the Fox audience became large enough to isolate in our surveys. By 2000, the similarities between its content and that of Rush Limbaugh's radio show could not be missed. Our interest was heightened by two moments in reporting on the 2000 presidential campaign: first, Fox scooped the other networks with a report that as a younger man Bush had been charged with "driving under the influence"; second, Fox was the first network to call the 2000 presidential election for Governor George W. Bush, a call made with a Bush relative in the Fox decision process.

In our focus on the news, we neglected the most long-lived of the conservative media establishment, the opinion pages of the newspaper that spawned supply-side economics, the *Wall Street Journal*. Our reason was straightforward. Although sizable for a newspaper, this paper's audience is too small to isolate in the surveys our early work relied on. Not until we fielded the massive NAES in 2000 were we able to study a large enough population to isolate *Journal* readers. This history means that in some parts of the book we focus exclusively on understanding Rush Limbaugh's program and its possible effects, and in others we bring in data about Fox News and the *Journal*.

To address the specific questions we concentrate on in this book, we draw on rhetorical analyses of the content of the media outlets, supplemented by surveys, experiments, and content analysis conducted in 1994–2005. We include a brief summary of the surveys and have posted questionnaires and statistical backup for our reported analysis on the Annenberg Public Policy Center website (www.annenbergpublicpolicycenter.org/echochamber/). This website includes original data, questionnaires, and statistical analyses that will allow our more technically oriented readers to view past results, reproduce our analyses, or conduct new ones.[12]

The experimental and survey work from 1996 was supported by grants from the Carnegie Corporation of New York and the Ford Foundation. The 2000, 2004, and 2008 NAES surveys were made possible by funding from the Annenberg Foundation. And a sabbatical at CASBS freed Kathleen's time to complete this manuscript.

Backing our work on this project were teams of Annenberg graduate and undergraduate students. In the early years of the project, Melinda Schwenk and Joe Borrell played particularly important roles. In the middle years, Kate Kenski and Danna Young did the same. In more recent times, at odd hours, during holidays and weekends, Bruce Hardy and Jeffrey Gottfried did the heavy lifting with good humor and without complaint. Throughout, Josh Gesell, Miriam White, and Jackie Dunn valiantly chased down obscure references. We continue to miss Josh, whose death last spring left a chasm in the social fabric of the Annenberg Public Policy Center.

We are indebted as well to our Oxford editor, David McBride, and the Oxford back office team for ensuring that our second coauthored OUP book made it past the charts and tables and into print.

For more reasons than we can or should put in a preface, we are grateful to the spouses who found us in college and have stayed with us into years filled with salmon, bluefish, calamari in red sauce, and Rush Limbaugh. To Bob Jamieson and Elena Cappella, we dedicate this book.

Echo Chamber

How the Conservative Opinion Media Attack
the Democratic Opposition

Rush Limbaugh, Fox News, and the editorial page of the *Wall Street Journal* are part of a larger phenomenon. In 1982, there "was the *New York Post*...[and]...the *Washington Times*.... There was no alternative media, except small conservative publications: *National Review, Commentary,* the *American Spectator, Human Events*. There was nothing else," *New York Post* editor and columnist John Podhoretz told Limbaugh in the spring of 2004. "There was no you. There was no talk radio. There was no News-Max. There was no Internet. There was no Fox news channel.... And now these views have a voice, they have a place to go."[1] Speaking of the rise of right-of-center talk radio and websites as well as Fox, conservative organizer Paul Weyrich noted in fall 2003, "There are 1,500 conservative radio talk show hosts.... You have Fox News. You have the Internet, where all the successful sites are conservative. The ability to reach people with our point of view is like nothing we have ever seen before!"[2]

The result was palpable anxiety in Democratic circles. In December 2002, for example, the Democratic Party's 2000 presidential nominee, Al Gore, identified Limbaugh, Fox News, and the *Washington Times* as "part and parcel of the Republican Party." In an interview in the *New York Observer,* Gore argued that "most of the media [have] been slow to recognize the pervasive impact of this fifth column in their ranks that is, day after day, injecting the daily Republican talking points into the definition of what's objective as stated by the news media as a whole....Something will start at the Republican National Committee, inside the building, and it will explode the next day on the right-wing talk-show network and on Fox News and in the newspapers that play this game."[3] Gore was not the only Democratic leader to take on the conservative opinion media. In stump speeches delivered in the 2004 Democratic primaries, former Vermont governor (and current head of the Democratic National Committee) Howard Dean repeatedly declared that the American flag does not belong to Rush Limbaugh.

In this book, we explore the implications of the emergence of mass-audience, ideologically coherent, conservative opinion media by focusing on the content of three conservative media outlets: the *Wall Street Journal* editorial page, two programs on Fox News, and Limbaugh's radio show. Each has an internet presence. Taken together, these communication channels constitute important venues for reinforcing the tenets and values of Reagan conservatism. In the pages that follow, we show that for their audiences, these conservative outlets marginalize mainstream media and minimize their effects. At the same time, we suggest that both Fox and Limbaugh insulate their audiences from persuasion by Democrats by building up a body of opinion and evidence that makes Democratic views seem alien and unpalatable. Moreover, we show that Limbaugh's audience, which once paid more attention to mainstream broadcast media than others of similar education and income, is increasingly less likely to turn to such sources and more likely to turn to the second player in our analysis, Fox News. In other words, we argue that the conservative media have developed the capacity to wrap their audience in an insulating media enclave of information and opinion.

It is not our purpose to determine whether what is generally known as the "mainstream" media, consisting of major dailies such as the *New York Times* and *Washington Post*, major broadcast outlets such as ABC, CBS, and NBC, and cable networks such as MSNBC and CNN, are indeed "liberal," as the conservative media suggest. Nor, with a few exceptions, do we examine the effects the mainstream media have on their audiences. (For practical purposes, the past decades of scholarship and the findings that are central to our understanding of mass media have been based on a study of the mainstream.)

Our goal is not to provide an exhaustive analysis of all of the conservative media on the scene or to determine the origins of the messages found in the conservative media. As a result, we will not assess the notion, advanced by media commentator Tim Cuprisin of the *Milwaukee Journal Sentinel*, that there is a "Republican transmission belt: the right-wing radical blogs to Rush Limbaugh's radio show to Fox News and then into the headlines."[4]

There is nothing novel in our starting assumption that these three outlets are conservative. Nor will anyone be surprised by the argument that they share common lines of argument. We see our contribution here as an analysis of how they function across a decade-long period and a theoretically driven grounding from which to understand their possible effects.

In this chapter and the next, we introduce the notion that conservative opinion media are an important part of the political landscape. To make this case, we develop two case studies, one involving the 2004 Democratic presidential nominee, John Kerry, and the other a prominent Republican,

Mississippi senator Trent Lott. We do this to illustrate the ways Fox News, Limbaugh, and the print and web editorial pages of the *Wall Street Journal* play both offense and defense in service of conservative objectives. As these case studies will suggest, the big three reinforce each other's conservative messages in ways that distinguish them from the other major broadcast media, CBS, NBC, ABC, CNN, MSNBC, and major print outlets such as the *Washington Post* and *New York Times*.

Our task in this chapter is exploring the ways the three outlets on which we focus undercut conservatism's opponents. To do so, we begin with a 2004 exchange between those supporting the incumbent, Republican President George W. Bush, and those on the side of the presumptive Democratic Party presidential nominee, Senator John Kerry, about a supposed remark by Kerry at a town hall event in Florida on March 8, 2004. There, news reports indicated, the presumptive Democratic Party nominee said, "I've met 'foreign' leaders who can't go out and say it all publicly, but boy they look at you and say, you gotta win this, you gotta beat this guy, we need a new policy, things like that." After listening again to his audiotape more than a week after his first account, the pool reporter responsible for reporting the original remark, Patrick Healey of the *Boston Globe*, reported that Kerry had said not "foreign leaders," but "more leaders." Had this journalistic blunder created a firestorm of controversy around a Republican Party nominee, the conservative opinion leaders would have minimized the damage to their candidate by crying "media bias." The Democrats didn't have a comparable argument in their arsenal.

Both before and after Healey corrected the record, representatives of the Bush administration demanded names. On *Fox News Sunday* with Chris Wallace, Secretary of State Colin Powell said, "I don't know what foreign leaders Senator Kerry is talking about. It's an easy charge, an easy assertion to make, but if he feels that's [an] important assertion to make, he ought to list names. If he can't list names, then perhaps he ought to find something else to talk about." A White House statement insisted, "If Senator Kerry is going to say he has support from foreign leaders, he needs to be straightforward with the American people and state who they are.... Or the only conclusion one can draw is he's making it up to attack the president." In response to a reporter's question, President Bush said on March 16, "If you're going to make an accusation in the course of a presidential campaign, you ought to back it up with facts."

Our story continues at a March 15, 2004, rally in Pennsylvania, where a questioner named Cedric Brown confronted the presumptive Democratic standard-bearer. Brown, a Vietnam War vet, insisted that the senator reveal the names of the foreign leaders who wanted to help him "overthrow" the Bush presidency. He also suggested that Kerry was a liar and articulated an assumption earlier advanced by Limbaugh that the supposed meeting may have been with the head of North Korea. The back-and-forth between Kerry and Brown took about eight minutes.

Using media treatment of that exchange as a case study, in this chapter we will illustrate the conservative opinion media on the attack. Specifically, we will argue that the frames employed in hard news stories by Fox and ABC News differed in significant ways, with the Fox News report markedly more hostile to Kerry and ABC tilting in the other direction. In addition, we will argue that conservative media opinion leaders aggressively disparaged the Kerry statement. Specifically, taken together, Limbaugh, Hannity, and the *Wall Street Journal*'s opinion pages marshaled four strategies to marginalize Kerry and undercut his perceived acceptability as a candidate for president: extreme hypotheticals, ridicule, challenges to character, and association with strong negative emotion.

The media covered the controversy through three sets of competing frames, as follows. (1) Whereas both the mainstream broadcast and conservative Fox focused on the Kerry-Bush conflict, Fox also created an anti-Kerry frame. (2) While mainstream broadcast focused exclusively on the conflict and its strategic intent, Fox concentrated in addition on the Kerry-Brown exchange over Brown's political affiliation and past votes. (3) Whereas mainstream print cast Kerry as restrained and civil in tone and Brown as yelling, conservative opinion leaders indicted Kerry's temperament by describing him as "yelling" and "thuggish." We will discuss each set of frames in turn.

In the next chapter, we compare non-news conservative opinion media to opinion comments in mainstream outlets; here we open by contrasting a hard news story on ABC with one on Fox. We do so to suggest that in news, the difference between the traditional broadcast networks and Fox is one of framing.

Competing Frames 1

MAINSTREAM FRAME: KERRY AND BUSH FIGHT ABOUT CREDIBILITY

Frames focus on some facets of a story and not others, invite the audience to accept some assumptions over others, and imply some questions while ignoring others. Among the frames that dominate reporting on politics are those centered on strategy and conflict. When employing the strategy frame, reporters usually ask, who's ahead and why? In its more obvious form, strategic framing is found in stories accounting for horse race results in polls. A subtler manifestation of the strategy structure divorces the "underdog" from direct contact with strong verbs by casting him as "trying" to accomplish objectives or as struggling or foundering. Instead of concentrating on the substantive differences revealed by attack and response, the conflict frame features attack and response in order to explore the strategic intent of the exchange.[5]

In reports on the Kerry-Republican back-and-forth over the "foreign" leader remark, CBS and ABC brought different information but not different frames into relief. We concentrate on ABC's story here because the CBS report is a synopsis provided to viewers by the anchor, not a full-blown report.

The CBS synthesis invites viewers to ask: Should Kerry name names? Is Kerry's refusal warranted? Is the White House justified in suggesting that Kerry is lying? "In the presidential campaign, Bush campaign operatives in the White House today stopped just short of calling Senator John Kerry a liar for saying that some foreign leaders hope he defeats President Bush in November," said CBS anchor Dan Rather. "Senator Kerry says he won't identify the leaders because it would betray their confidences. But White House spokesman Scott McClellan said that if Kerry won't name names, it must be because he is, and I quote, 'making it up.'"[6] By sandwiching the Kerry position between an opening and closing statement focused on the Bush perspective, this CBS piece creates a net advantage for the Republicans.

Since ABC was the only mainstream broadcast network to air a reporter's hard news story on the Kerry exchange on March 15, we will compare its hard news stories to that on Fox.

Linda Douglass's story on ABC invited viewers to ask the same questions as did the CBS report but suggested others as well: Who is more truthful, Kerry or Bush? Is the Bush campaign attacking Kerry to deflect attention from its own record? Has the Bush administration deceived the public about and silenced a government official over the true cost of the prescription drug benefit?

The structure and content of the ABC piece were dictated by its thesis: "the campaign seems to be all about credibility." Consistent with that notion, the ABC report showed each side assaulting the truthfulness of the other. The story featured two attacks: the Republican one on Kerry's credibility for his refusal to name the names of the foreign leaders with whom he allegedly spoke, and Kerry's charge that the Bush administration had silenced a government official who was trying to reveal the true cost of the Bush prescription drug plan.

Anchoring the March 15 nightly news, Elizabeth Vargas opened by noting: "The issue today was credibility. The White House made the extraordinary accusation that John Kerry might be dishonest. It is yet another sign of how intensely both sides of this campaign intend to fight." She then handed off to Douglass, who presented and commented on clips of Kerry making statements.

DOUGLASS (*voice-over*): The White House charged today that John Kerry may have been lying when he suggested to contributors that foreign leaders support his campaign. He said, "I've met more leaders who can't go out and say it all publicly, but boy, they look at you and say, you gotta win this, you gotta beat this guy." Yesterday, a Bush supporter demanded to know which foreign leaders he was talking about.

KERRY: *I have had conversations with a number of leaders in the course of the last two years up until the present moment. And I am not going to betray the confidences of those conversations.*

DOUGLASS (*voice-over*): Today, President Bush's spokesman challenged Kerry to back up his claim or, quote, "the only conclusion is that he's making it up to attack the president of the United States." Kerry side-stepped the questions.

DOUGLASS (*off-camera*): The White House accuses you of making it up, Senator.

KERRY: *They're trying to change the subject from jobs, health care, the environment, Social Security. They don't have a campaign, so they are trying to divert it.*

DOUGLASS (*off camera*): Kerry is determined not to give ground in the war over who is most truthful. Today, his campaign released a list of what it called false statements by the White House.

DOUGLASS (*voice-over*): The Senator pointed to reports that the administration concealed the true cost of the Medicare prescription drug bill. A government expert says he was ordered not to release the information.

KERRY: *He was told to be quiet. He was threatened by the administration with the possible retribution that would come if he didn't. There is no place for silencing the truth.*

DOUGLASS (*voice-over*): Seven months before the election, the campaign seems to be all about credibility. Linda Douglass, ABC News, Washington.[7]

FOX FRAME: KERRY LACKS CREDIBILITY

Opening the March 15, 2004, *Special Report with Brit Hume,* on Fox, Hume forecast the news story to come later in the newscast not by summarizing Kerry's justification or his counterattack on the truthfulness of the Bush administration but by saying, "John Kerry still won't say who those foreign leaders were, whom he claims are back—who he claims are backing him for president."

In the hard news segment Hume forecast, Fox's Carl Cameron focused on the attack-counterattack Kerry initiated over the adequacy of funding for first responders to disasters and terrorist attacks, on the Bush-Kerry attack-counterattack over "foreign leaders," and on the exchange between Kerry and Cedric Brown. In a story that opened with Kerry "battered for refusing to name foreign leaders" and closed with Republican accusations that Kerry was making things up, Cameron reported as follows. (Kerry, Colin Powell, and Cedric Brown were shown on screen making their statements after Cameron introduced them.)

> CAMERON: Battered for refusing to name foreign leaders that he claims want President Bush defeated, John Kerry tried to get back on offense accusing the administration of underfunding first responders in a speech to the nation's largest firefighters' union.
> KERRY: *This administration has given our homeland security efforts short shrift.*
> CAMERON: Kerry renewed a claim that few Americans believe, according to the polls, that the president deliberately underfunded national security to cut taxes for rich cronies.
> KERRY: *This administration has put a tax giveaway for the very wealthiest of our nation over making sure that we do all that we can to win the war on terror here at home.*
> CAMERON: Outraged, Republicans call it hypocrisy and accused Kerry of voting against the troops, when he opposed the $87 billion to stabilize and complete the post-Saddam Iraq war. Undaunted, Kerry seemed to link last week's attacks in Madrid to what he sees as the president's security failings.
> KERRY: *This administration is big on bluster and is short on action. But as we saw again last week in Spain, real action is what we need.*
> CAMERON: Camp Kerry quickly said the senator does not blame Spain or the U.S. for the attacks on Madrid, but that Kerry would do more than President Bush to improve security and U.S. international relations.
> KERRY: *He pushed away our allies at a time when we needed them the most.*
> CAMERON: Republicans now deride Kerry as a quote "international man of mystery," for his various un-backed-up charges recently, particularly—refusing to name foreign leaders that Kerry claims want President Bush out. Secretary of State Powell weighed in yesterday on *Fox News Sunday*.
> POWELL: *He ought to list some names. If he can't list names, then perhaps he should find something else to talk about.*

CAMERON: Kerry kept the mystery going at a Pennsylvania town hall meeting, when he told a demanding voter that it was, quote, "none of his business" what Kerry was discussing with still nameless foreign leaders.

KERRY: *And I'm not going to betray the confidences of those conversations, but I have had conversations with leaders. I've also had friends of mine who've met with leaders. As recently as this past week I've heard from a couple of leaders. I'm not going to tell you who they are because that would betray their position.*

CAMERON: Then Kerry upped the ante, claiming unnamed U.S. business leaders overseas want Bush out too.

KERRY: *There are business people...*

CAMERON: Kerry is a finger pointer and as he angrily stabbed the air, he tried to turn the table on his inquisitors.

KERRY: *What are you? Are you a registered Republican? Are you a Republican? You answer the question. That's not an answer. Did you vote for George Bush?*

QUESTIONER CEDRIC BROWN: *I voted for George Bush.*

KERRY: *Thank you.*

CAMERON: The man did say "Yes." Today White House spokesman... accused Kerry of lying, saying that if he doesn't name the foreign leaders, quote, "The only conclusion one can draw is that Kerry is making it up to attack the president."[8]

The strategic frames of Fox and ABC differ. On Fox, Kerry is cast as "battered" and on the strategic defensive. (He "*tried* to get back on offense"; "He *tried* to turn the table on his inquisitors" [emphasis added].) By contrast, ABC situates Kerry as a contender who is "determined not to give ground in the war over who is most truthful." On Fox, Kerry's attack on Bush is portrayed as an attempt "to get back on offense," whereas the Bush response is portrayed as motivated by outrage.

Overall, whereas the Fox piece focuses on Kerry's credibility, ABC concentrates on charges and countercharges about the relative truthfulness of Bush and Kerry. Whereas Douglass attributes claims about truth or falsity to a campaign ("Today, his campaign released a list of *what it called* false statements by the White House" [emphasis added]), Cameron invites the inference that Kerry's answer is unbelievable (his charges are "un-backed-up"). Cameron also questions Kerry's credibility with the statement "Kerry renewed a claim that few Americans believe, according to the polls."

But if the Fox piece disadvantages Kerry, the ABC piece advantages him. Although in Douglass's piece, each side is questioning the other's truthfulness, Vargas leads into the story by tagging only the Bush attack as an "extraordinary" accusation. Yet each side has made a strong attack on the truthfulness of the other. In the ABC segment, Kerry has accused the Bush administration of "silencing the truth," and the Bush representative has accused Kerry of "making it up to attack the president." In addition, Douglass devotes more time in her piece to Kerry's charge than the Bush campaign's attacks.

By contrast, Cameron ignores Kerry's counterattack on Bush's truthfulness and, after quoting the Bush campaign's ridiculing label for Kerry, "International Man of Mystery," reinforces the label in his own voice by saying "Kerry kept the mystery going." Without mentioning the source, Cameron has embraced the label being offered to the media by the Republican National Committee.

Competing Frames 2: Mainstream Omission of Kerry-Brown Exchange; Conservative Focus on It

Frames make some features of an event more salient and omit others. The second framing difference between mainstream broadcast and Fox is one of omission. Whereas the mainstream focused on Kerry's statement and Bush's response, Fox included as well the Kerry-Brown exchange about Brown's past votes.

Kerry's question about Brown's past votes was nowhere to be seen in mainstream broadcast network evening news. By contrast, Brown was featured in Cameron's Fox report and hosted in other Fox venues as well. Brown's only interviews on national television occurred on Tuesday, March 16, when he appeared twice on Fox, first in the morning on *Fox and Friends* and then on *Hannity and Colmes*. The Fox questioners were sympathetic to Brown. Hannity, for example, presupposes that Kerry was deceiving Brown:

HANNITY: I don't think John Kerry was being honest with you. Do you think he was being honest with you?
BROWN: He didn't appear to be honest. He refused to answer my question. [9]

In the Fox interviews, Brown portrayed the Massachusetts senator's "attack" as "unfortunate" and called for a congressional investigation into Kerry's supposed meetings with foreign leaders. While talking with Hannity, Brown stated, "I think Senator Kerry betrayed our country. And he needs to answer for that."

Although he was ignored by mainstream broadcast, Brown was interviewed by mainstream print. The *Washington Post*, for example, noted, "Afterward, Brown, who described himself as a small-business owner and a graduate of West Point, said, 'If he's lying about something so simple as this, you have to wonder whether President Kerry would be an honest person.

I wanted to give him an opportunity to defend his lie. He gave a non answer, which tells me he's lying.' "[10]

Both network accounts are selective. After all, ABC ignores the exchanges between Brown and Kerry. By contrast, Fox's Cameron omits all of Brown's extreme statements and ignores the Kerry counterattack on Bush's truthfulness. We are not arguing that the Fox frame is selective and ABC's is not, but rather that one pattern of selection disadvantages Kerry whereas the other advantages him.

Ignoring the mainstream print accounts, the conservative opinion media charged that by ignoring Kerry's questioning of Brown's voting history, mainstream news reporters revealed their liberal bias. As we argue in chapter 2, beliefs that the mainstream media are liberal, employ a double standard, and are systematically biased against conservatives are commonplace in conservative circles in general and in the conservative opinion media in particular. The evidence? In his hard news segment, *Fox News's* Cameron included both Kerry's statements about not disclosing names and the exchange with the questioner, while mainstream broadcasts ignored the second. In response, the conservative commentators on Fox, conservative talk radio, and WSJ.com focused like lasers on the final moments of the exchange as evidence of both Kerry's character flaws and media bias.

On his nationally syndicated talk radio show, Limbaugh asks, "Can you imagine if Bush asked a person in a town meeting, 'Did you vote for Bill Clinton? Did you vote for Al Gore?' Can you imagine what the press would do to George Bush?" Writing at WSJ.com, James Taranto acknowledges print coverage but takes media coverage in general to task for not focusing on the final Kerry-Brown exchange: "News reports noted that Kerry had told the voter his putative contacts with 'foreign leaders' were 'none of your business,' but ignored Kerry's thuggish interrogation of the voter, which we saw when Fox News Channel aired the footage last night. Rush Limbaugh has the transcript."[11]

Competing Frames 3: Conservative and Mainstream Characterizations of Kerry's Manner Differ

Because a candidate's temperament or character matter to voters, campaigns attribute positive affect or emotion to their contender and negative emotion to the opponent. When they characterize a candidate's demeanor in ways that violate an audience's sense of social norms, news accounts create a context for such judgments. The characterizations of Kerry's exchange are dramatically different in the conservative and mainstream accounts we are focusing on here. As we will show, the alternative verbs, adverbs, and adjectives used to characterize Kerry and Brown's speech are markedly different. And whereas the mainstream print media set Kerry's speech in the context of Brown's behavior and questions, conservative opinion leaders omitted them.

THE CONTEXT

In their description of the context of the Kerry-Brown exchange mainstream print reporters were on the same page. The *Washington Post* noted that Kerry "was repeatedly called 'a liar' during the public forum by a heckler, Cedric Brown, who interrupted Kerry's comments on health care, education and the economy to raise questions about the assertion of foreign endorsements. Under questioning by Kerry, Brown described himself as a Bush supporter."[12] According to an account in the *Los Angeles Times*, the questioner, Cedric Brown, "abruptly" stood up and interrupted the candidate, saying " 'Recently, you said you met with foreign leaders. They wanted to help you overthrow the Bush presidency and his administration.' As the audience booed and shouted him down, Brown yelled, 'I want an answer!' " "Kerry," the *Times* reported, "quieted the crowd. 'Shh, everybody, please, no, no, no,' he said. 'This is democracy; this is the way it works. This is fine; I have no problem with it.' "[13]

"The town meeting was contentious at times," the Associated Press reported, "with 52-year-old Cedric Brown repeatedly pressing the candidate to name the foreign leaders whom Kerry has said are backing his campaign. 'Were they people like the president of North Korea?' asked Brown. 'I'm not going to betray a private conversation with anybody,' Kerry said. As the crowd of several hundred people began to mutter and boo, Kerry added, 'That's none of your business.' "[14]

In these accounts, Kerry's questioning of the questioner is set in the context of Brown's interruption, inflammatory charges (e.g., "they wanted to help you overthrow the Bush presidency"), and verbal attacks on Kerry (e.g., repeatedly calling him a liar). Unlike the *Los Angeles Times* and *Washington Post* accounts, Limbaugh, Taranto, and Hannity and Cameron on Fox severed Kerry's response from that context.

THE CHARACTERIZATIONS

In mainstream print, it was Brown, not Kerry, who reportedly yelled, a fact that might be attributed to the fact that Brown did not have a microphone. While failing to detail the nature, tone, or manner of Brown's questions,

Limbaugh, Hannity, and Taranto freely characterize Kerry's response in ways that differ from the independently gathered descriptions in mainstream print. Cameron on Fox terms Kerry's response as "angrily stabbing." Kerry's comments were labeled "thuggish" (Taranto, in WSJ.com), as "yelling" (Hannity), and as "browbeating" (Limbaugh) by the conservatives. By contrast, in the *Houston Chronicle,* for example, Brown was described as a heckler and Kerry as "somewhat rattled."[15] The *New York Times* described the exchange as "volatile." In the *Los Angeles Times* account, Brown "yells." None of the mainstream print reporters described Kerry as yelling. Reporting for the *Los Angeles Times*, Matea Gold instead described Kerry's manner as "calm but firm."[16]

The conservative opinion media's characterization differs as well from that of the hard news account on the Fox News website, which noted (March 16, 2004):

> While on the campaign trail Sunday, Kerry got questioned by someone at a town hall meeting in Bethlehem, Pa., about his relationship with foreign leaders and the comments he made about him ousting Bush.
>
> Cedric Brown implied in his question that Kerry was "meeting with foreign leaders to overthrow Bush" and then said to Kerry: "You lied to us."
>
> "I haven't met with foreign leaders for any overthrow purpose," Kerry responded. "I never said that. What I said was, that I have heard from people who are leaders elsewhere in the world, who don't appreciate the Bush administration approach and would love to see a change in the leadership of the United States."
>
> At times, the crowd booed the man and shouted for him to sit down. *Kerry responded by keeping the crowd calm and continuing the exchange, asking Brown about his party affiliation and whether he voted for Bush.* (emphasis added)

Beyond Framing: Marginalizing Kerry

The differences between the mainstream and Limbaugh, Hannity, and Taranto extend beyond the use of dissimilar frames. As this controversy played out, conservative opinion media also marginalized Kerry by employing extreme hypotheticals, deploying ridicule, interpreting his rhetoric as evidence of a character or temperamental flaw, and tying him to strong negative emotion.

SETTING UP AN EXTREME HYPOTHETICAL

Demonstrating the different levels of restraint shown in the arguments of the *Journal*'s editors and those of Limbaugh (as well as of Sean Hannity and WSJ.com opinion writer Taranto), Limbaugh echoed the *Journal*'s request that Kerry name names but added the suggestion that the leaders Kerry has been speaking with were heads of enemy states. In so doing, Limbaugh also advanced a notion that if articulated by a Republican officeholder would have elicited immediate controversy. Specifically, he said he thought he knew the identity of the foreign leaders Kerry had been speaking to, and added: "And regardless of who they are, let's name some names. Bashar Assad in Syria, Kim Jong II in North Korea" (March 17, 2004). The assertion was ridiculous on its face, and Limbaugh undoubtedly knew it was. Underlying Limbaugh's trope is the assumption that any leader who would criticize U.S. policy must be an enemy of the country.

Importantly, introduction of the names of villainous foreign leaders exemplifies a rhetorical function that Limbaugh and the conservative opinion hosts serve for the Republican Party: expanding the range of attack by marking out extreme positions that by comparison make the official position of the Republican candidate or party leaders seem moderate. At the same time, if some in Limbaugh's audience take the allegation of actual talks with heads of outlaw states seriously, as Brown appeared to, then the association reinforces, if it does not actually shape, that person's view that Kerry's dispositions are extreme and disqualify him from serious consideration as a presidential contender.

Even if the audience knew that Limbaugh's hypothetical was implausible, the hedge he implied in "regardless of who they are" linked Kerry with disreputable individuals. Finally, without saying so explicitly, the hypothetical implied that Kerry was either naïve or disloyal to the country's interests. Throughout the 2004 campaign, the conservative opinion talkers disassociated Kerry from the United States, making it more plausible for the organization calling itself Swift Boat Veterans for Truth (SBVT) ultimately to air an ad charging that he "gave aid and comfort to the enemy" during the Vietnam War. Aid and comfort is, of course, the definition of treason. Indeed, the link to Kerry's anti–Vietnam War protests was precisely the one Brown made in the interviews he gave, explaining that he was motivated to question Kerry by his experience as a Vietnam vet who was spat on after returning home from that war. Like the justification of the charge made by SBVT, this rationale created a coherent explanation for an attack on Kerry: the attackers are cast as motivated not by partisanship but instead by a need to right a wrong done them and others like them by Kerry's anti–Vietnam War protests.

RIDICULE

In this controversy, the conservative media also employed a second recurrent tactic: ridicule. In WSJ.com, James Taranto (March 16, 2004) noted that on eBay, "someone is auctioning off an Imaginary Foreign Leader Endorsement." In the endorsement, the word "lie" is freely used.

> Have you ever been caught in a lie while running for President of the United States? If you want to make a current president jealous, look better in front of your political buddies who have real foreign relations experience, or if you are just a liar who got called out on your bogus campaign lies, this is the auction for you!!! I'll pretend I am the leader of a foreign nation that supports your candidacy for President of the United States until the elections in November. . . . Shipping/Handling charge for this item is $15.00, we only ship to Massachusetts.[17]

The next day, on March 17, 2004, Brit Hume brought the same information to Fox viewers.

> Speaking of Kerry, while administration officials demand he name the "foreign leaders" that allegedly told him they endorse his candidacy, at least two—"foreign leader endorsements" have been put up for sale on eBay . . . as parodies. One insists "if you want to make a current president jealous . . . or if you are just a liar who got caught out on your bogus campaign lies, this is the auction for you." . . . Bids for this endorsement reached more than $15,000, but eBay has since taken it down. An endorsement from the "duly elected supreme leader of . . . Bogusonia" is still up for grabs, with the highest bid standing at $2.75.[18]

Extreme hypotheticals and ridicule increase the likelihood that listeners will see Democratic leaders as more distant from the middle of the political spectrum than they actually are. In addition, because the hypotheticals are speculative, Limbaugh can disassociate from them if his use of them proves controversial. Later, we will explore survey data suggesting that the attentive audience for conservative media marginalizes Democrats. An audience is of course less receptive to persuasion from sources that have been discredited in these ways.

QUESTIONING KERRY'S CHARACTER AND TEMPERAMENT

The Bush campaign's rhetoric focused on Kerry's honesty. If he won't name names, he must have made up the conversations with "foreign" leaders. The conservative media played out this logic by speculating about the identity of the foreign leaders and by reinforcing the Bush argument by auctioning off endorsements by foreign leaders.

A *Wall Street Journal* editorial backed the administration's request that Kerry name names and insinuated that if Kerry were indeed talking with foreign leaders, it must be to make promises not shared with the American people. "Who are these foreign leaders, and what is Mr. Kerry privately saying that makes them so enthusiastic about his candidacy?" it asked. "What 'new policy' is he sharing with them that he isn't sharing with Americans?"[19]

Later we will argue that conservative media provide coherent, consistent interpretations of the meanings of events that reinforce the political worldview of their audiences. Underlying these moves are the assumptions that Democrats are untrustworthy, unstable, and arrogant. The implication of the Bush attack saying that Kerry may be making up exchanges with foreign leaders pivots on trustworthiness, for example.

Consistent with this notion, James Taranto in WSJ.com, Sean Hannity on Fox News, and Limbaugh on his nationally syndicated talk radio show characterized the final Kerry-Brown interaction as an indictment of Kerry's temperament. Writing in WSJ.com the next afternoon, Taranto observed, "'That's none of your business' is more polite than '*You sit down!*' But it's breathtakingly arrogant for Kerry to assert his putative promises to foreign leaders to change America's policies are none of the voters' business."[20]

Like Taranto, on *Hannity and Colmes,* Hannity likened Kerry to Howard Dean, former governor of Vermont and one-time front-runner who had unexpectedly stumbled in the 2004 primaries after a series of behaviors that were ridiculed by the conservative media. During Hannity's interview with Brown, he said, "You remember when Howard Dean said 'Now you sit down, you've had your say.' Your incident with him reminded me of that."[21] Kerry's comment, Limbaugh suggested, was equivalent to that of Dean. "Kerry did a Dean." Dean had ordered an audience member "Sit down!" when he perceived that that person had gotten out of line. "So there's Kerry browbeating a participant," Limbaugh said, "and the guy Howard Dean browbeat was a Bush voter. The press tarred and feathered Dean, beat up, said he was mental, said he was unstable." The imputed double standard is here claimed to be manifest in differential treatment of two Democrats.

TYING KERRY TO STRONG NEGATIVE EMOTION

Limbaugh moved on to an extreme interpretation of the Democratic senator's intent in questioning Brown's past vote. Here Limbaugh's derisive tone matched his splenetic content. According to Limbaugh, Kerry was telling

Cedric Brown, "'I'm Senator Kerry. You're nothing but human debris. You challenge my word? Well, screw the hell out of you. You vote for Bush? I thought so, you SOB." To the extreme position (Kerry has betrayed his country by talking with enemy heads of state and is a liar) and ridicule (Kerry should buy an endorsement from a foreign leader on the internet), Limbaugh now attached negative emotion toward Kerry on Brown's (and the listener's) behalf. If Kerry thinks that anyone who questions him is "human debris," what must he think of Limbaugh, Limbaugh's listeners, and those who support President Bush?

———

The roughly eight-minute encounter between Kerry and Brown produced two very different foci. In the hard news piece on *Fox News,* Kerry's truthfulness was at issue; on ABC, each candidate was attacking the truthfulness of the other in an attempt to undercut his credibility. Meanwhile, across the conservative opinion media, a complementary message tailored to each medium's audience was advanced. The *Journal*'s editorial page raised such rhetorical questions as Who are these foreign leaders, Why are they enthusiastic about his candidacy, What promises has he made to them? Meanwhile, Hannity on Fox, Taranto in WSJ.com, and Limbaugh on radio framed the Kerry-Brown exchange to suggest that Brown's questions were appropriate and Kerry's manner and response were not. And in caustic, primal language, Limbaugh disparaged Kerry as contemptuous of Brown and all who voted for Bush in 2000.[22]

The exchange between Brown and Kerry occurred in the envelope of a larger controversy. In both instances, the frames and interpretations offered by the conservative media underscored the Republican message and undercut the Democratic one.

The Feedback Loop

Throughout the book, we will show the feedback loop created between Republican leaders and conservative media. Here we see it as well. By the end of the week, the vice president had picked up the talk radio refrain. The Fox News website reported:

At a fund-raiser in Phoenix on Sunday, Vice President Dick Cheney noted Cedric Brown's question and Kerry's response to the man: "That's none of your business."

"But it is our business when a candidate for president claims the political endorsement of foreign leaders," Cheney said at the fund-raiser for Rep. Rick Renzi, R-Ariz., on Monday. "At the very least, we have a right to know what he is saying to them that makes them so supportive of his candidacy."[23]

The reporting of the Kerry statement about "leaders" and the exchange with Brown illustrate the conservative media on the attack. In so doing, they laid down assumptions about the character and temperament of the presumptive Democratic nominee on which the Republican candidates could build. In the process, they reinforced the notion that embrace of the Democratic ideology or candidates was unjustifiable and contemptuous behavior, and media accounts that seemed to justify the actions of the Democratic Party nominee were inaccurate.

Our examination of the conservative media's treatment of the Brown-Kerry exchange shows them playing offense. Specifically, they created coherent attacks against the Democrats by expanding the extremes of the discourse, ridiculing the Democratic contender, impugning his character, and attaching strong negative emotion to the audience's experience of him. As this example suggests, in subsequent chapters we will explore how the conservative media work to marginalize the mainstream media and minimize their effects while distancing their conservative audience from Democratic views and providing lines of argument and evidence to solidify that audience's embrace of conservative ones. Attacking is one side of a two-sided process. As we illustrate in chapter 2, what we call the conservative media establishment also protects conservatism from attack.

How the Conservative Opinion Media Defend Conservatism

The conservative media's defensive dexterity was on display in the complementary rhetoric that emerged from Limbaugh, the *Wall Street Journal*'s opinion pages, and Fox discussants to protect the Republican Party and the Republican president when one of their own, Mississippi Republican Trent Lott, uttered what some would characterize as an infelicitous phrase and others as a self–indicting revelation while praising his elderly colleague Strom Thurmond on his hundredth birthday. Woven throughout this case study is a line of argument we showed at play in the Kerry-Brown case in chapter 1: the "liberal" media employ a double standard. We also suggested that the conservative opinion media try to discredit their opponents by rhetorical framing, deploying extreme hypotheticals, using ridicule, attacking character, and engendering negative emotion. Here we examine a complementary move that embraces these strategies while turning the tables. Specifically, we argue that after the conservative media defended conservatism from being tainted by Lott's ill-chosen language and inept self-defense, they pivoted to turn defense into attack by charging the Democrats with a breach similar to Lott's. Taken together, the case studies in our first two chapters prefigure the themes of this book by suggesting the ways the conservative opinion media build a base of supportive knowledge, push perceptions of their opponents to the extreme, replay common arguments in defense and attack, and insulate their followers from counterpersuasion.

By speaking in one voice and reinforcing each others' arguments, what we call the conservative media establishment (see chapter 5, section entitled "What Do We Mean by 'Echo Chamber,'" for clarification of this term) helped the Republican Party navigate its way through what could have been a self-destructive episode in December 2002 when the maladroit comments of its presumptive Senate leader, Trent Lott, seemed to endorse segregation. As we will show, in April 2004, the same media turned the tables on the Democrats by prompting a prominent Democrat to apologize for a statement conservative commentators viewed as similar to the one that had precipitated the decision by Lott to end his candidacy for the position of Senate majority leader more than a year earlier.

By shifting control of the Senate to the Republicans, the November 2002 elections paved the way for a return of Trent Lott as Senate majority leader. On December 20, Lott issued a statement saying that he would not seek that post "in the interest of pursuing the best possible agenda for the future of the country." Between the first moment and the second, the conservative media shaped a coherent message for the Republican Party and its leader, President George W. Bush.

At issue in Lott's decision was a statement he made on December 5, 2002, at a celebration of the one-hundredth birthday of Strom Thurmond, South Carolina Republican senator and former 1948 Dixiecrat presidential contender. "I want to say this about my state," Lott said. "When Strom Thurmond ran for president, we voted for him. We're proud of it. And if the rest of the country would have followed our lead, we wouldn't have had all these problems over all these years either." Despite the fact that his remarks were carried on C-SPAN and the audience for the birthday celebration was filled with reporters, those in attendance failed to perceive their newsworthiness. An Internet blogger, Josh Marshall of Talkingpointsmemo.com, brought Lott's comments to media attention the day after the event.

As news interest in Lott's remark mounted, historians and journalists scrambled to recover news clips and historical records of the 1948 Thurmond campaign. "We stand for the segregation of the races and the racial integrity of each race," said the States' Rights Party platform in 1948, "the constitutional right to choose one's associates; to accept private employment without governmental interference."[1] "Thurmond, then governor of South Carolina," noted the *Washington Post*,

> was the presidential nominee of the breakaway Dixiecrat Party in 1948. He carried Mississippi, Alabama, Louisiana and his home state. He declared during his campaign against Democrat Harry S. Truman, who supported civil rights legislation, and Republican Thomas Dewey: "All the laws of Washington and all the bayonets of the Army cannot force the Negro into our homes, our schools, our churches."[2]

Lott's seeming endorsement of a segregationist campaign created problems both for George W. Bush and the party he led. In 2000, Bush—then the Republican governor of Texas—had been elected president after campaigning as a "compassionate conservative" whose appeal to moderates was premised in part on his outreach to African Americans and Hispanics. The political value of the African-American and Hispanic vote was high. In an interview Tim Russert, host of NBC's *Meet the Press*, quoted a passage from a leaked memo to President Bush from his pollster, Matthew Dowd, stating: "If you get the same percentage of black, Hispanic and white votes in 2004 as you did in 2000, you'd lose the election in 2004 by three million votes." According to Russert, the changed outcome would be a function of "changing demographics."[3] "Mr. Lott played right into the hands of opponents who are eager to paint the Republican Party's Southern ascendancy as nothing more than old-fashioned bigotry," noted an editorial in the *Wall Street Journal*.[4]

The importance of appealing to African Americans and Hispanics was demonstrated in the general election of 2004. Data from the 2000 NAES show that in the fall of 2000, only 34 percent of Hispanic men supported George W. Bush over Al Gore, but in 2004, 46 percent did. The Republicans improved their percent of the African American vote as well in 2004.

Nor could President George W. Bush and the Republican Party afford to alienate those, particularly moderate Republican women, who find intolerance anathema. In 2004 Bush, in fact, gained most of his vote margin over his Democratic challenger by drawing an increased number of votes from white, married women.[5] As political analyst Stu Rothenberg explained, "The risk they have with the Trent Lott fiasco is that they turn off swing white voters, moderate, even conservative voters who don't want to be associated with a party that they deem to be intolerant."[6]

Just as embracing Lott was freighted with political consequences, so, too, was repudiating him. If southern conservatives believed that the Mississippi senator was the victim of political correctness run wild, they might both rally to his defense and blame those who failed to do so. In short, in the absence of political cover, there was political risk for Bush in condemning Thurmond and distancing himself from the remarks of a loyal party leader from the South, the secure geographic base of the Republican Party. The conservative opinion media provided that cover.

These complexities fueled the newsworthiness of the contest over Lott's future. On December 7, the *Washington Post* reported:

> Lott's office played down the significance of the senator's remarks. Spokesman Ron Bonjean issued a two-sentence statement: "Senator Lott's remarks were intended to pay tribute to a remarkable man who led a remarkable life. To read anything more into these comments is wrong."
>
> Bonjean declined to explain what Lott meant when he said the country would not have had "all these problems" if the rest of the nation had followed Mississippi's lead and elected Thurmond in 1948.[7]

The story in the *Post* suggested that the birthday remarks were not the isolated comments of a person paying tribute to an elderly friend.

In 1998 and 1999, Lott was criticized after disclosures that he had been a speaker at meetings of the Council of Conservative Citizens, an organization formed to succeed the segregationist white Citizens' Councils of the 1960s. In a 1992 speech in Greenwood, Mississippi, Lott told CCC members: "The people in this room stand for the right principles and the right philosophy. Let's take it in the right direction, and our children will be the beneficiaries."[8]

Black leaders responded to Lott's birthday remarks with comments that ranged from disbelief to outrage. "I could not believe he was saying what he said," noted John Lewis (D. Ga.) in the *Washington Post*.[9] "It sends a chilling message to all people,"[10] reported Elijah Cummings (D. Md.), a member of the Congressional Black Caucus.

Within two days, Lott had begun trying to explain his way out of the dilemma his words had created for him and his party. On December 9, he said, "A poor choice of words conveyed to some that I embraced the discarded policies of the past."

In the following days, the *Journal*'s editorials and op-ed pages joined Fox's Sean Hannity and Brit Hume as well as Limbaugh and Hannity on talk radio to guide the Republican Party through the dilemma into which Lott's remarks had cast it. They collectively did this by distancing the party from Lott's message, undercutting the assumption that it is opposed to civil rights or racist, attacking the Democrats for their past civil rights failures, excoriating the mainstream media for employing a double standard in their discussions of Lott, and ultimately signaling that Lott had broken from conservative orthodoxy and should step aside. In the process, they buffered conservatives from attack, bolstered their audience's disposition to argue the conservative case, and guided the incumbent president through the complications posed both by Lott's remarks and his subsequent apologies.

Distancing the Republican Party from Lott's Message

The first challenge Lott's statement posed for the Republicans in power was straightforward. It ran counter to the message of incorporation on which the incumbent president had won and opened his party to attack by Democrats bent on regaining control of the Congress and the presidency.

The conservative opinion media responded by distancing the party from Lott's message. On December 9, both Taranto and Limbaugh disavowed Lott's statement in no uncertain terms. Noting that Democrats were "indignant" and Republicans "mortified," Taranto explained: "Thurmond, of course, ran in 1948 as a segregationist and carried Alabama, Louisiana and South Carolina along with Mississippi." Taranto then disagreed with Lott's claim that the country would have been better off had it voted with the states that supported Thurmond in 1948. "If the rest of the country had followed the lead of these four states, we'd have had a lot bigger problems than we did."

On December 10, Limbaugh made a statement that was widely quoted in mainstream media: "What Lott said is utterly indefensible and stupid. I don't even want to explain it." Less frequently reported was his next statement: "Yes, there's a double standard on this stuff. But you have to take this into account before you open your stupid mouth." By featuring it on his website (RushLimbaugh.com), Limbaugh invited the mainstream media to quote him. Occasionally, reporters and commentators indicated that that was in fact where they found the statement. " 'What Lott said is utterly indefensible and stupid.' Limbaugh said in a quote you can find at rush-limbaugh.com," wrote Tim Cuprisin in the *Milwaukee Journal Sentinel* on December 12.[11]

One sign of Limbaugh's influence is that it was his remark and not that of Hannity or those in the *Weekly Standard* or the *Wall Street Journal* that attracted mainstream media attention. The press took Limbaugh's statements as a signal of conservative rejection of Lott's remarks. "Even Rush Limbaugh, the conservative talk-show host," wrote the *Financial Times* of London on December 13, "was sharply critical of Mr. Lott: 'What Lott said is utterly indefensible and stupid. I don't even want to attempt to explain or defend it.' "[12] That paper's statement assumes that Limbaugh would ordinarily try to explain or defend the remarks of a Republican leader of the Senate. If even he will not defend Lott's remarks ("Even Rush Limbaugh"), then Lott is in trouble with his own party's faithful.

Democrats quickly used Limbaugh's statement to highlight broad dissatisfaction with Lott's comment. On CNN on December 13, Congressman Harold Ford (D. Tenn.) challenged the notion that African American members of Congress were the only ones voicing concern. "Rush Limbaugh and the Family Research Council and I think hundreds of thousands, if not millions, of Americans of all different backgrounds are offended by what Senator Lott said."[13]

Limbaugh and the *Journal* editorial page expressed similar sentiments. In an unsigned editorial on December 10, the *Journal* argued:

Plainly America would not have been well served by the triumph of the segregationist Dixiecrats at a moment when the civil rights movement was coming into its own. Such a reading gives short shrift not only to the black struggle for equality, but also to the history of both Mr. Thurmond and the GOP. Mr. Lott played right into the hands of opponents who are eager to paint the Republican Party's Southern ascendancy as nothing more than old-fashioned bigotry.[14]

As Lott began the process of apologizing, the conservative media provided a running commentary on the inadequacy of his attempts. Writing on WSJ.com, Taranto quoted Lott's statement "A poor choice of words conveyed to some the impression that I embraced the discarded policies of the past.... Nothing could be further from the truth, and I apologize to anyone who was offended."

"Lott's apology is adequate," notes Taranto, "but his explanation is not.... The only way to take it [Lott's original statement] as anything other than an expression of nostalgia for segregation is to assume that Lott was ignorant of what Strom Thurmond (and Lott's state, or rather its white citizens) stood for in 1948. That's just not plausible."

Taranto also worried: "Lott could be endangering the GOP's majority in the Senate." On Fox, Brit Hume said, "it seems to me the problem is he describes the policy as discarded, not discredited."[15]

PREPARING THE BASE TO COUNTERARGUE

Throughout this controversy, Limbaugh's rhetoric illustrates the way he crafts a coherent posture from which to argue a conservative position. Instead of defending Lott, Limbaugh argued that the Democratic attack on the Mississippi senator was hypocritical and mainstream media coverage showed that conservatives are held to a higher standard than others, a continuous refrain confirming the supposed liberal bias of the mainstream news media.

As evidence of a "double standard," in the following days Limbaugh pointed out a number of things. First, Democratic senator Robert Byrd, a former Klansman, held a leadership position in his party and was not condemned when he made "comments about white n-words." Second, Democrats had greater guilt for segregation than Republicans but bore less accountability for it. For example, "Al Gore's father voted against the Civil Rights Act in 1964 as a senator from Tennessee." Third, Democrats have used insensitive language and not suffered the criticism or penalties being suggested for Lott.

Specifically, "we can't forget Fritz Hollings and his comments about African Americans being cannibals."

On *Hannity and Colmes* that evening, Hannity was on the same page. He condemned the "double standard" Democrats employed, indicted Al Gore for not criticizing his own father, "who in the most important vote of his life, was nowhere to be found for the Civil Rights Act of '64," suggested that "segregation is the legacy of the Democratic Party," and castigated former president Bill Clinton for praising J. William Fulbright, former senator from Arkansas, "a known segregationist." "He gave him the Presidential Medal of Freedom Award, a known segregationist, one of 19 senators who issued a statement entitled 'The Southern Manifesto,' condemning the '54 Supreme Court decision of Brown versus Board of Education." Finally, like Limbaugh, he noted that "Fritz Hollings also referred to African leaders . . . as cannibals."

On that show, Hannity asked Democrats who were raising questions about Lott to condemn Clinton as well. Unlike Limbaugh, who cast the argument in an ironic tone, Hannity was prosecutorial, as the following exchange illustrates. On December 11, his guest was African American member of Congress Gregory Meeks (D. N.Y.):

HANNITY: Did you support Jesse Jackson for president?

MEEKS: Yes I did.

HANNITY: Jesse Jackson has admitted to spitting in white people's food. Jesse Jackson used the term "Hymie Town." Why would you support a man who did all that? Spitting in white people's food because they're white? Spitting in white people's food?

Later after repeating his case against Fulbright, Hannity asked: "Do you condemn Bill Clinton for what he said. . . . Do you condemn Bill Clinton for calling this segregationist a visionary, a humanitarian, my mentor, a remarkable man, presidential freedom, this past October. Do you condemn it?"

MEEKS: Again, Sean—

HANNITY: Yes or no?

MEEKS: We're talking about a person who's elected—

HANNITY: Bill Clinton was president.

MEEKS: We're talking about an individual—

HANNITY: He gave the award as president.

MEEKS: Bill Clinton was no segregationist. We're talking about a man who is elected and will be the most powerful man in the U.S. Senate.

HANNITY: Bill Clinton was the president.

MEEKS: And, what we're also talking about is a repetitive statement—

HANNITY: I'm going to give you one other opportunity. Clinton praised this guy twice. That is all about politics. I want to know, you answer yes or no, will you condemn Bill Clinton for calling that segregationist a remarkable man in October?

MEEKS: This is not about Bill Clinton. This is about Trent Lott.

HANNITY: It's about your double standard—

(*cross talk*)

MEEKS: Did you forgive Jesse Jackson? You keep talking about it.

COLMES: We've got to go.

MEEKS: This is about Trent Lott.

COLMES: By the way, Bill Clinton also in his comments about Fulbright said "I disagreed with him vehemently about a number of things over [the] years." He mentioned that as part of those statements.[16]

For Hannity's like-minded viewers, the Democratic representative's refusal to condemn Clinton and Jackson confirms the existence of the double standard.[17]

On December 11, Fox's Brit Hume introduced the double standard frame into a question to his panelists, asking

about the argument that's made that this is a double standard in play. That Bob Byrd can use the dreaded and utterly inappropriate n-word, as it happens on an interview on *Fox News Sunday,* and while there's a brief kerfuffle about it, it goes away. And he remains a senior figure among the Democrats in the Senate, not a member of the leadership. Well not the leader but a leader, and this former member of the Klan, Bob Byrd.

At this point a panelist responded, "But that's the crucial difference, he's not the leader. I think it's OK for a senator to make a gaffe of this proportion, but not the leader."[18]

Because *Hannity and Colmes* pairs conservative Hannity with liberal Alan Colmes, its format lends itself to introduction of evidence supportive of the Democratic position on issues framed from only a conservative point of view by Limbaugh and Hannity's radio shows. Accordingly, it is Colmes who dismisses Hannity's and Limbaugh's Clinton-Fulbright analogy by offering additional evidence of what Clinton actually said in paying tribute to Fulbright. According to Colmes, Clinton said, " 'I admired him, I liked him. There were occasions when we disagreed. I loved arguing with him.' " To fracture the analogy, Colmes then added, "That is not the same thing as what Trent Lott did."[19]

To blunt the possibility of the Lott controversy tainting the Republican Party, the conservative media repeated the fact that prominent Democrats opposed major pieces of civil rights legislation and argued that the Republican Party was the true champion of civil rights. "Now before all you Democrats get hepped up on this," Limbaugh noted, "remember that Al Gore's dad, Albert Arnold Gore Sr. did indeed oppose the Civil Rights Act (Dec. 9, 2002)."

"Remember," noted Limbaugh, "that Senator Robert Byrd, the man Democrats elected Senate President Pro Tem...was not only a member of the Ku Klux Klan but was paid to recruit new members." In this context, a Democratic attack on the Republican Party because of Lott's statement is hypocritical. "This is not to defend Trent Lott, but when you're going to be all high and mighty and claim somebody should resign for impropriety, you'd better not be dirty yourself."

Limbaugh used this cascade of evidence to validate one of the arguments on which the conservative opinion media pivot. Conservatives were criticized for behavior ignored or forgiven in "liberals"; the Democrats glorying in Lott's misery and generalizing his sentiments to the Republican Party were employing a "double standard." "I'm not trying to excuse Lott here in any way but there's a double standard here that gives the impression that Republicans are inclined toward racism when the fact of the matter is the segregationists in the United States Senate are [sic] Democrats," said Limbaugh. The enumerated list included Sam Ervin, Al Gore Sr., and J. William Fulbright. To it Limbaugh added, "Wallace, Maddox, Connor—all segregationists, all Democrats" (December 12). It was not Republicans who should be ashamed of being allied with the party of Trent Lott and Strom Thurmond, but rather Democrats who castigated Republicans while effacing their disreputable past. Indeed, Republicans should feel justifiable pride in their party, notes Limbaugh, because from Lincoln's Emancipation onward, "we've been fighting for equality and judging people as individuals rather than members of groups ever since."

A *Journal* editorial made a similar argument:

> For one irony here is that the Civil Rights Act of 1964 would never have been possible without Republican leadership. Not only was that legislation a personal victory for Everett Dirksen, then Senate Minority leader, Republicans in both the House and Senate supported the measure in far greater percentages than Democrats. Only six GOP Senators voted against the act, compared with 21 Democrats.[20]

Also writing in the *Journal*, John Fund stressed the same point:

The landmark 1964 Civil Rights legislation, as historians have noted, could not have passed without lopsided support by Republicans. Twenty-one Senate Democrats voted against the bill, but only six Republicans voted nay—although one of them was Barry Goldwater, the party's presidential standard-bearer that year, who opposed it on libertarian rather than racial grounds.[21]

Limbaugh reiterated that Republicans, not Democrats, pioneered civil rights legislation. "In 1969 Nixon—not JFK or LBJ—was the first to implement federal policies designed to guarantee minority hiring to combat racial inequalities." "Incidentally," Limbaugh added, "Nixon won 30% of the black vote in 1960" (December 16, 2002). Here Limbaugh was jumping from the Nixon presidency in 1969 back to 1960 to cite the black vote. Missing from the account is the fact that the major civil rights legislation of the 1960s was initiated by Lyndon Johnson. In 1964, Republican nominee Barry Goldwater flew across the United States to return to the nation's capitol to vote against the Civil Rights Act. Whereas Limbaugh ordinarily divides the world into liberals and conservatives, he now parsed it into Democrats and Republicans. The reason was strategic. Although Republicans provided proportionately more support for the Civil Rights Act than Democrats, conservatives in both parties opposed it.

Limbaugh continued on to say that Nixon "was the first U.S. government official to meet with Dr. Martin Luther King Jr. Compare that to the Kennedys who wiretapped Dr. King's telephone. Compare that to the liberal record on school vouchers" (December 16, 2002).[22] Limbaugh concluded: "let's embrace this legacy and stop accepting this racist label as fact."

This is a compartmentalized rhetoric. Ordinarily, the talk show host would not track affirmative action to a Republican president and speak favorably about it. However, in an attempt to rebut charges about the Republican past, this is a viable rebuttal point. Confronted with a December 18 *Washington Post* story on a split in the White House over the position it should take on an affirmative action case pending before the Supreme Court, Limbaugh returned to home ground. "Affirmative action is wrong. Saying it isn't quotas is semantics and newspeak at its worst. You're counting people up based on their race, gender or creed. That's a quota." He adds, "Affirmative action is nothing more than reverse discrimination."

Even after Lott had said he would not seek the leader position, Limbaugh continued to expand on his original lines of attack on Democrats. There is not "one black in the House Democratic leadership" said the radio host the following January 8.

Having outlined the case for Democratic hypocrisy and a media double standard, Limbaugh moved on to argue that neither Lott nor the Republican Party was racist. The arguments about a double standard and hypocrisy were then woven into that larger theme. "If Lott were racist, we'd have known it by now," declared Limbaugh on his web page (December 12). The line of argument is "know them by their deeds." "Is there legislation that Lott has sponsored, backed or supported that indicates he's a racist?" asks Limbaugh. If so, it "would have come out long ago."

Limbaugh's rhetoric showed an awareness that he risked being cited as an apologist for Lott. He repeatedly closed off that interpretation with such disclaimers as "I'm not trying to excuse Lott here in any way." During the Lott contretemps, Limbaugh was also more cautious in his use of evidence about Bill Clinton than he otherwise would be. "Since Bill Clinton didn't specifically say he supported the segregationism of Fulbright or his record, we can't hold Clinton to the standard even though the guy was his mentor." Note the change from November 11, 2001, when, speaking of Arkansas governor Orval Faubus and Arkansas senator J. William Fulbright, Limbaugh said, "they didn't want white people and black people living together.... Had they lived during the time of the founding, Bill Clinton's idols would have been enthusiastic slaveholders.... These are the guys that Bill Clinton is running around taking leadership ideas from" (November 11, 2001).

In an interview with Lott on his radio show, Hannity, too, argued that Lott's remarks should not be misconstrued as racist. Lott labeled his own words "poorly chosen and insensitive" (December 11). He also said that he did not "accept those policies of the past at all." "It was certainly not intended to endorse his [Thurmond's] segregationist policies that he might have been advocating or was advocating 54 years ago," noted Lott. "Right," responded Hannity. As late as December 19, Limbaugh was noting that he wanted to meet anyone who thinks Lott was actually "desiring to return to the days of segregation in America."

Later, we will argue that the conservative opinion media work to create an out-group identity for Democrats and liberals and an in-group identity for conservatives. We also suggest that these conservative media serve the interests of the Republican Party by reinforcing the relationship between core constituencies and conservatism. Both moves were on display in the Lott controversy when Limbaugh reinforced the notion that the (solid Republican) South is not racist. Specifically, Limbaugh blunted the notion that the South in general and Mississippi were less tolerant than the rest of the country. To support that claim, he offered his listeners a piece of evidence that could be used to rebut the offending charge. "Where do you find more black elected officials? From the South or from the elitist enlightened northeast and upper Midwest?" he asked (December 16, 2002). Evoking central elements involved in creating an in-group identity, Limbaugh reminded listeners: "We cannot leave it to the left and the Democrats to (A): explain history, and (B) define us. They're trying to demonize the modern South as part of their effort. It's not fair," says Limbaugh. He drew his evidence for demonization of the South from a statement by a scholar (presumably part of the liberal elite) and from two articles in what he calls the liberal media. The first was a George Mason University professor's statement that the Republican Party "is as much the party of Thurmond as it is the party of Lincoln." Second were a column in the *Washington Post* by E. J. Dionne entitled "The Party of Lincoln or Lott" and a *New York Times* story by Adam Clymer entitled "The GOP's 40 Years of Juggling on Race."

Finally, having armed his conservative listeners to argue the case, Limbaugh warned them that they must both respond to charges that the party is racist and at the same time avoid piling on Lott. "These accusations have not been responded to. There have been people trying to pile on the accusations of Lott just to save themselves from being lumped in with him or because they think he's a weak leader. "But," he cautioned, shifting to second person, "someone will be next, and it could be your favorite guy or it could even be you" (December 13, 2002).

POLICING THE REPUBLICAN STRATEGY

On December 10, Limbaugh tasked President Bush with playing an agenda-setting role in arbitrating the Lott controversy and predicted that Bush would do so. "I think the saving grace of Trent Lott here is going to be George W. Bush. Actually, I think the agenda here is going to be propelled by the White House as it should be, by the way." What the White House should do Limbaugh did not say.

Seven days after Lott's praise of Thurmond and two days after the *Journal's* call for an apology and Limbaugh's declaration that Lott's statement was stupid, on December 12, Bush declared that Lott's remarks "do not reflect the spirit of our country" and noted that "any suggestion that the segregated past was acceptable or positive is offensive." "Senator Lott has apologized and rightly so. Every day that our nation was segregated was a day our nation was unfaithful to our founding ideals."[23]

However, whereas the *Journal* and Limbaugh had not taken a position one way or the other on whether Lott should resign, through his spokesperson,

Ari Fleischer, Bush said he "does not think that Sen. Lott should resign." News accounts relayed this signal to audiences. "Senate Republican Leader Trent Lott's troubles grew today when President Bush himself joined the critical chorus," noted Dan Rather on *CBS Nightly News*, "However, the president indicated he does not think that Lott should be removed from his position of power."[24] A chorus from Republican media helped shift that position to an agnostic one in which Bush placed Lott's future in the hands of the Senate Republicans.

PROTECTING CONSERVATISM FROM LOTT

When Lott's effort to save his position mutated into an embrace of principles hostile to those of the conservative media establishment, they turned on him in unison. The transition occurred 11 days after Thurmond's birthday party, when Lott, appearing on Black Entertainment Network, expressed his regret at having voted against a national holiday commemorating the life of Martin Luther King Jr., voiced support for affirmative action "across the board," and said, "I'm part of a region and the history that has not always done what it's supposed to have done." "The society that I was born into," said Lott, "was wrong and wicked. I didn't create it and I didn't even understand it for many, many years."

Lott had now moved beyond conservative rhetoric advanced by the editorial page of the *Journal*, as well as Limbaugh and Hannity, on three grounds. Each argued that there was as much if not more racism in the North than in the South; each opposed the Martin Luther King Jr. holiday on the grounds that the cost in economic productivity was too high;[25] and each opposed affirmative action.

The conservative media were uniform in their negative appraisal of Lott's appearance on Black Entertainment Network the night before. Limbaugh accused Lott of switching parties. "Lott came out for affirmative action.... Instead of saying that both Democrats and Republicans opposed a national holiday [for King] because it costs the government money, Lott claimed that he didn't know much about King until recently." "Is that not sick?" asked Limbaugh. He also labeled "B.S." Lott's claim that "he didn't know of Dr. King's accomplishments until recently" (December 17, 2002). On his website's posting for paid subscribers, Limbaugh included the statement "Trent Lott would vote for a Rodney King holiday. He'd vote for a Don King holiday. He'd vote for a Burger King holiday if that's what it took, folks" (December 17, 2002). Lott had become the target of tactics Limbaugh ordinarily reserves for Democrats: use of extreme hypotheticals and ridicule.

Nor did the *Journal* applaud Lott's performance. On WSJ.com, Taranto indicted Lott for "embracing the entire liberal agenda on race." "In doing so he implicitly endorses the smear that the only way not to be a 'racist' is to embrace 'affirmative action' and other such policies."[26] On December 18, Shelby Steele, a research fellow at the Hoover Institution, sounded a similar note in a *Journal* op-ed:

> A vacuum of white guilt as wide as the Grand Canyon has opened in him, and he will never again see civil rights, welfare, judgeships or education with a clear eye. He will now live in a territory of irony where his redemption will be purchased through support for racialist social reforms that make a virtue of the same segregationist spirit that has now brought him low.[27]

On Fox News (December 17), Brit Hume framed the exchange in political terms, asking "What about the promises Lott is making in search of forgiveness?" For Hume these included Lott's apparent willingness to "back an affirmative action agenda." The Fox anchor then asked: "Does that make him more or less attractive to his Republican colleagues?" *Special Report with Brit Hume* regular Mort Kondracke answered: "A lot of conservatives have been worried that Lott would bend so far over backward that he wouldn't be credible." Another regular, *Weekly Standard* editor Fred Barnes, added: "He looks silly."

As the conservative media backlash was building against Lott, an ABC News–*Washington Post* poll reported that 6 out of 10 Americans thought Lott should step down as majority leader. Three-quarters of Democrats and three-quarters of African Americans held that view, as did one out of three Republicans. On Wednesday, December 18, Lott recalls in his autobiography, "Governor Jeb Bush of Florida invited his favorite reporters into his historic Tallahassee office and told them that my remarks were beginning to politically damage the Republican Party as a whole. Jeb didn't say I should quit, but he might as well have."[28]

In his autobiography, Lott argues that had Bush not facilitated his removal he would have been able to take and hold the position of majority leader. Bush's sentiments at the time were telegraphed through the media in comments such as this one:

> President Bush has decided not to intervene to save Sen. Trent Lott (Miss.) after concluding he has become an albatross to the party and no longer has any chance of surviving as Republican majority leader, administration sources said yesterday. "The president is allowing

the process to work itself out in a way that will seem natural and doesn't have a lot of fingerprints on it," a senior Republican official said. "When the inevitable happens, the president can be in a position where he hasn't coerced the process but also hasn't stood by someone who will create problems."[29]

Lott's failure to put his ill-chosen words behind him was rhetorical as well as ideological. He had abandoned what Limbaugh sees as the principled rhetoric that opposes additional holidays on economic grounds and put in its place a rhetoric Limbaugh finds unbelievable. Instead of both supporting the Republican agenda to help African Americans and challenging the assumptions of "the conventional, nanny-state, you-can't-compete African American agenda of the left with things like school vouchers and enterprise zones," Lott "joined so-called liberals like Ted Kennedy."

BLUNTING DEMOCRATS' ATTEMPTS TO TAKE ADVANTAGE OF THE LOTT COMMENT

As Lott was struggling to move his candidacy for the leader's position off life support, on December 18 former president Bill Clinton suggested: "I think what they [Republicans] are really upset about is that he made public their strategy." Limbaugh counterattacked the next day, saying that "the NAACP sued him [Clinton] because he didn't enforce the Voting Rights Act." That morning, writing in WSJ.com, Taranto noted, "Clinton was at his vicious, nakedly partisan worst yesterday as he weighed in on the Trent Lott matter. He dismissed GOP criticism of Lott, implying that all Republicans are really racists at heart."[30]

Early in the controversy, the *Journal*'s op-ed page teed up an argument against Lott as leader without explicitly calling for him to step aside. In an opinion piece entitled "The Weakest Link," John Fund noted in the December 12 *Journal*, "If the Republican congressional leadership—which includes stars such as Senate Whip Mitch McConnell and House Speaker Dennis Hastert—were contestants on the *Weakest Link*, you can bet who they'd vote off first."[31] On December 13, the *Journal* followed up with an "outlook and review" piece carrying the subtitle "He [Lott] must ask if he's still the best leader for the GOP."

The first extended, explicit call for Lott to step aside in the three outlets we are studying occurred not as an editorial but as an op-ed in the *Journal*. On December 14 John McWhorter, senior fellow at the Manhattan Institute, associate professor of linguistics at the University of California, Berkeley, and, importantly, an African American, made the case against Lott as majority leader, concluding: "Republicans, black Americans and our country would be better off without Mr. Lott as majority leader."[32]

The next day, the second-ranking Republican in the Senate, Don Nickles (R. Okla.), called for a vote on Lott as majority leader. Senator Chuck Hagel (R. Neb.) urged his colleagues to conference to either "re-confirm their confidence in Senator Trent Lott's leadership or select a new leader."

On *Fox News Sunday* (December 15, 2002), *Weekly Standard* editor Bill Kristol argued that Lott should step aside:

> Well, I'd like to see him gone. . . . Some of us think that this comment is—however much he apologizes—the apology tour is even more offensive in a certain sense. No one wants him to grovel or to apologize. I don't think he's personally a bigoted man. I think he lacks an understanding of the last five decades of American history. That comment reflected such a lack of understanding.
>
> And I don't think he's the best person to lead the Republicans in the Senate for the next two years. I don't think most people in the White House think he's the best person now to lead the Republicans in the Senate for the next two years.[33]

Piece by piece, the *Journal*'s talent pool built the case that Lott should not serve as majority leader. In the *Journal* on December 19, John Fund wrote: "Conservatives are outraged at the damage Mr. Lott has caused to their efforts to reach out to minority communities and advocate principled race-neutral policies. Mr. Lott's outrageous pandering to his critics has only stoked the anger and disappointment. Bill Clinton survived, but Trent Lott is no Bill Clinton."[34]

On December 20, with Republicans scheduled to meet January 6 to decide whether Lott would be their Senate leader, Peggy Noonan, an analyst on Fox, a columnist for the *Journal,* and a former staffer to Presidents Reagan and George H. W. Bush, minced no words in a column in the *Journal.*

> It would have been good if he had resigned this week. Maybe he will over the holidays. But it would be best for the Republican Party—and the country—if Republican senators were utterly brutal and fired him before then. If they do not move before Jan. 6th they certainly must fire him as leader on that date. And when they do they should read a brief statement explaining what they did and why they did it. And then they should speak no more, and go back to work.[35]

The same day, Lott announced that he would step aside.

CASTING THE LOTT CONTROVERSY
AS A VICTORY FOR BUSH

The day before Christmas, *Journal* columnist Thomas Bray translated Lott's demise into credit for President Bush. "Chalk up another huge victory for George W. Bush. In helping to push Trent Lott out of the Republican leadership, he exhibited the same refreshing moral clarity that he has already shown on the foreign front." The praise came attached to the hope that the president would file an appropriate brief in the "University of Michigan racial-preference cases, which the Supreme Court is expected to decide next spring."[36]

WARNING DEMOCRATS THAT EXPLOITATION OF LOTT'S
COMMENTS WOULD CARRY A COST

To ward off Democratic use of the Lott incident, a December 28 editorial in the *Journal* asked, "Want to purge racists? How about Robert Byrd?" The piece then built the same case Limbaugh had made against Byrd throughout the controversy. Interestingly, as the *Journal* noted, the comment for which both indicted Byrd was uttered on Fox News. "Only last year Mr. Byrd told Fox News that 'there are white niggers. I've seen a lot of white niggers in my time, if you want to use that word. But we all—we all—we just need to work together to make our country a better country and I—I'd just as soon quit talking about it so much.'"

Media Differences in Treatment of the Lott Controversy

The conservative and mainstream media differed in their treatment of Lott in two ways. First, the lines of argument developed by the *Journal's* opinion writers, Limbaugh, and Hannity on Fox differed from those quoted in the nonconservative media. Second, where the mainstream was preoccupied with whether Lott would stand for the position of leader or not, the conservative media focused on creating a rhetoric that ensured that the Republican Party and its incumbent president would not be harmed by the Lott statements, regardless of outcome, and focused as well on making a case that the sins of Democrats exceeded those of the true party of civil rights, the Republican Party.

Republican statements quoted in the mainstream press did not lay out comparable Democratic moments or argue that the media were imposing a double standard. Instead, the few statements that did not address the comments about whether Lott should stay or go as leader can be parsed into three categories.

> *Lott's comment isn't racist.* Rep J. C. Watts (R. Okla.) stated, "I think he went too far. I think he probably wishes that he would have chosen a different set of words, but I don't think that it implies racism in any way."[37]
>
> *Lott's apologies should be accepted.* For example, Senator Rick Santorum (R. Pa.) said: "These words had meanings. And he's been held accountable for them. And he's apologized for them. And I think it's time to move on."[38]
>
> *The attacks on Lott are overkill.* Pat Buchanan, former Republican presidential candidate, noted: "They are beating this man to death in what I think is one of the ugliest mob lynchings I've seen in my life in Washington."[39]

Neither CBS nor NBC nightly news quoted someone employing a dominant argument advanced by the conservative media establishment: that the Democratic attack on Lott was hypocritical and media coverage of it was based on an anticonservative double standard. Nor was the Robert Byrd example employed on either. The reason is simple. The object of network news scrutiny is the controversy, not its media framing.

The Rhetorical Superstructure

To summarize, as the Lott controversy percolated, the *Journal's* opinion writers, various commentators—Sean Hannity on Fox and Limbaugh on radio—served as rhetorical leaders for the Republican Party. In the process, they licensed the statement by Bush rejecting Lott's seeming nostalgia for Thurmond's segregationist presidential bid. Before Bush took a stand, Limbaugh, the *Journal,* and the *Weekly Standard* had. By doing so, they protected Bush from an attack from the Right for not supporting a conservative southerner and, by easing Lott out, denied Democrats a useful line of attack in the 2004 elections.

The conservative media framed the controversy by casting Lott's statement as unacceptable but not a sign that Lott or Republicans were racists. Throughout, Limbaugh offered two overarching frames: the Republican Party is the party of real civil rights, and the Democrats are the beneficiaries and Republicans the victims of a media-abetted double standard.

In support of the view that the party of Lincoln championed civil rights, Limbaugh made the case that Republican support for school vouchers and enterprise zones indicated a strong commitment to the well-being of African Americans. When Lott defected from conservative orthodoxy by supporting affirmative action and said that he regretted opposing a national holiday honoring Martin Luther King Jr., Limbaugh acted in his role as conservator of conservatism by tagging Lott as a Democrat and castigating him for implying that there was something illegitimate about the traditional conservative positions on those issues.

Limbaugh argued that it was the party of Lincoln, not the Democratic Party, that passed the major civil rights legislation of the 1960s. In the process, Limbaugh featured some and ignored other evidence—such as the vote by Republican Party nominee Barry Goldwater in 1964 against the Civil Rights Act.

Limbaugh, the *Journal,* and Hannity on Fox also argued that a double standard was being applied and that the Democrats were hypocrites who had within their own ranks a former recruiter for the Klan. Throughout the controversy over Lott, it was Limbaugh and the *Journal* that offered an ongoing, coherent rhetoric that disassociated the party from Lott's remarks and, when Lott abandoned orthodox conservative rhetoric, from Lott himself. The latter move implied that Lott would have great difficulty serving as majority leader. At the same time, the conservative media establishment helped guide the Republican Party through the morass.

The rhetoric of the conservative media about Lott's gaffe and subsequent transgression provided listeners and readers with an identity: we are not racists but a party that made civil rights possible. It also offered cues that the audience could reject Lott's statement without conceding that it either revealed racism on Lott's part or represented the views of the party. For those so inclined, these outlets modeled arguments with evidence with which they could enter debates about Lott (party of civil rights, attacks are double standard) and a rhetorical model that consistently disapproved of Lott's statement while lodging evidence that Democrats had said worse without penalty. In the process, a pantheon of Democratic villains was featured: the Klan recruiter Robert Byrd, Clinton's segregationist mentors, Faubus and Fulbright, the father for whom Al Gore was named who opposed the Civil Rights Act, even Bill Clinton, who was sued to enforce the Voting Rights Act. Whereas these villains were guilty of deeds, Lott had simply spoken words that none of the conservative media opinion leaders believed had any correspondence to his legislative actions or personal life. In the process of constructing this rhetorical superstructure, the conservative opinion media in general and Limbaugh and the *Journal* in particular sheltered their audiences from persuasion and armed them to frame, defend, and attack from a coherent conservative perspective. In short, they created what we will call a conservative knowledge enclave. The process is an ongoing one. Even with the Lott issue resolved, the conservative media continued to police the media environment for evidence to reinforce their interpretation of that affair.

Turning the Tables

The argument that the media and liberals employ a double standard is not an incidental weapon in the conservative arsenal. Unsurprisingly, then, the conservative media's focus on former Klan member Senator Robert Byrd did not end with the termination of the Lott controversy. In January 2004, Limbaugh told his listeners that he had found an "amazing sound bite from the PBS Martin Luther King documentary 'Citizen King.'" He then played a tape of Byrd saying in March 1968 ("four years after the Civil Rights Act" was passed):

> Martin Luther King fled the scene. He took to his heels and disappeared, leaving it to others to cope with the destructive forces he had helped to unleash. And I hope that well-meaning Negro leaders and individuals within the Negro community in Washington will now take a new look at this man who gets other people into trouble and then takes off like a scared rabbit.

"Whoa!" said Limbaugh. "This is Robert Byrd, former member of the Ku Klux Klan in 1968. He's now the dean of all Democrats in the Senate. He's the Democratic Party's elder statesman."

The focus on Byrd was revived in April 2004 when Hannity, Limbaugh, and Fox hosts turned the critique liberals had used against Lott against Democratic senator Chris Dodd (D. Conn.) over remarks he had made about Robert Byrd. By praising a segregationist of his own party, Dodd had committed the same offense as Lott. Consistent with the notion that a double standard is employed against conservatives, there was no liberal outcry at Dodd's breach.

The occasion occurred on April 1, 2004, when the Connecticut senator paid tribute to Senator Robert Byrd, who had just cast a vote in the Senate that brought the total of votes he had cast there over the years to 17,000. In the course of his remarks, Dodd said, "Robert C. Byrd would have been right at the founding of this country. You would have been in the leadership crafting the constitution. You would have been right during the great conflict of civil war in this nation."

On April 5, James Taranto led the charge in WSJ.com:

> Given that Byrd is a former member of the Ku Klux Klan, blogger Gary Farber writes, "this is Trent Lott all over again." Back in December 2002, CNN reported that Dodd had weighed in on Lott's objectionable comments about Sen. Strom Thurmond:
>
> "If Tom Daschle or another Democratic leader were to have made similar statements, the reaction would have been very swift," Dodd said. "I don't think several hours would have gone by without there being an almost unanimous call for the leader to step aside."[40]
>
> Dodd isn't part of the Democratic leadership, so he has nothing to step aside from—but still, an apology might be in order.[41]

Limbaugh followed suit on April 7 by reminding listeners of Dodd's statement during the Lott controversy. But unlike Taranto, called for Dodd's resignation. "Hey," said the talk show host, "let's throw this back at 'em. Because Christopher Dodd has just defined the terms for his own resignation." He also raised the issue of hypocrisy. "The Democrats are hardly audible on this. You cannot hear them, the Democrats aren't saying much."

Where was the mainstream media in all this? The same night, Brit Hume noted on his "Political Grapevine," "Speaking of Dodd's remarks, you'd have a hard time knowing about them from the major media. CNN, *USA Today,* the *New York Times*, and the *Washington Post* have ignored the story. Even the largest newspaper in Dodd's home state, the *Hartford Courant,* hasn't said a word. So far, only the Capitol Hill newspaper *Roll Call* has published the story."[42] Early the next week, Dodd apologized.

The next night, April 8, on Fox's *Hannity and Colmes,* Hannity underscored Byrd's past as a member of the Klan, reminded viewers that Lott was "demoted" for his remarks, and asked: "Well, what should happen to Senator Dodd?" According to Hannity, neither Lott nor Dodd was a racist. "I think both guys were trying to say something nice about older colleagues." But because Dodd "was the first to scream and yell and jump up and down and make a political issue out of it [Lott]....the standard should be applied to him....Otherwise, he's a hypocrite."[43]

———

The cases we have explored in the first two chapters show the ways the three media outlets attack, in the first case, and defend, in the second, using consistent and complementary rhetorical strategies. Embedded in this rhetorical repertoire are two all-purpose lines of argument that can be deployed in virtually any situation.

First, as they are ideologically biased, the "liberal media" cannot be trusted to convey what is happening in politics or faithfully represent conservatives and conservatism. Second, liberals cover up their own versions of the very abuses for which they attack conservatives. The first line of argument insulates the audience from information found in the mainstream media when it disadvantages the conservative cause. The second provides evidence to rebut charges against conservatives and sets the grounds from which to counterattack.

Conservative Opinion Media:
The Players

We have grouped Limbaugh's talk show, the editorial pages of the *Wall Street Journal,* and the two programs on Fox News not because they are conjoined triplets separated at birth but because they are cousins with a shared commitment to Reagan conservatism, a common ideological ancestry, and a network of related kin. In the next chapter, we explore their ideological underpinnings, and here their network of connections. Without attempting to exhaust the connections that bind them, let us note a few. Fox chief executive and chairman Roger Ailes produced Limbaugh's short-lived television program. Former Fox analyst John Fund helped author Limbaugh's best seller *The Way Things Ought to Be,* has served on the *Journal*'s editorial board, and writes the weekly "Political Diary" for WSJ.com. Before signing on as press secretary to President George W. Bush, Tony Snow both was featured on Fox and subbed for Limbaugh while Limbaugh was in rehab for addiction to narcotic pain killers. Both Limbaugh and Ailes have written opinion pieces for the *Journal.*

The networks of people that tie Fox's personnel to the *Journal* are also closely linked. In the Fox talent pool is former *Journal* op-ed editor David Asman, as well as Reagan and George H. W. Bush speechwriter and contributing *Journal* editor Peggy Noonan. Fox is also linked to the *Weekly Standard.* Fred Barnes, known with Mort Kondracke as one of the two anchors on Fox's *Beltway Boys,* is executive editor of that Murdoch-financed publication. In 2005, Fox News announced that it would broadcast the *Journal Editorial Report.*

Just as influential representatives of the mainstream media have ties to Democratic politics, the resumes of those at Fox and the *Journal* tend to carry Republican credentials. Whereas CNN, NBC/MSNBC, and ABC have drawn high-level talent from the Democrats, Fox has done the same from the GOP. Tom Johnson, past president of CNN, was an advisor to Democratic president Lyndon Johnson, as was Bill Moyers of PBS; both Tim Russert and

Chris Matthews of NBC/MSNBC have worked in Democratic politics, and ABC's George Stephanopoulos is a former Clinton aide.

By contrast, Fox's Roger Ailes advised presidents Nixon, Reagan, and G. H. W. Bush, and Tony Snow was a press secretary for President George W. Bush. Fox's Monica Crowley worked for Nixon; Jim Pinkerton did the same for Reagan and G. H. W. Bush. Former Speaker of the House Newt Gingrich is a frequent Fox guest.

Although more conservative than liberal hosts are found on Fox, neither Fox nor CNN nor MSNBC are without representatives from across the aisle. Among those with left-of-center views on Fox are Alan Colmes, Greta Van Susteren, and former Dukakis campaign manager Susan Estrich. A number of defectors from the Democratic fold also are Fox regulars, including former Clinton advisor Dick Morris and former Georgia senator Zell Miller, a Democrat turned Bush champion.

Nor are conservatives found only on Fox. On MSNBC, former Republican member of Congress Joe Scarborough for a time hosted his own evening show and now has a morning slot. Tucker Carlson superintended a prime-time show on MSNBC. Glenn Beck, who reports that he was during "the Reagan Administration...absolutely a Republican" but is "much more of a Libertarian than anything else,"[1] has had a regular program on the Headline News channel since May 2006. Importantly, this means that when cable viewers, remote control in hand, turn from a conservative program to sample something on another network, the newly chosen program may be another conservative political show. This fact means that when they feature conservative hosts, CNN and MSNBC solicit Fox viewers. The same pattern is possible for cross-channel network shifting among shows with liberal hosts.

Some of the conservative media share a financial godfather. Media titan Rupert Murdoch, head of Fox's owner, News Corporation, has built a media empire on the realization that there is commercial value in creating media outlets that tilt to the right. In late July 2007, Murdoch secured a deal with the Bancroft family, owners of Dow Jones and Company, to purchase that company and with it the *Wall Street Journal,* a move that made him the owner of two of the three players on which we focus in this book.

The power of cross-promotion on Fox and the conservative talk radio shows to sell books by conservatives was on display in January 2003 when Murdoch-owned HarperCollins acquired the rights to a memoir by Justice Clarence Thomas, a conservative, for an advance of 1.5 million dollars. In negotiations, Justice Thomas promised promotion by the conservative media. "Editors who met with Justice Thomas said he also expected politics to influence the book's promotion," reported the *New York Times.* "He told potential publishers that he expected strong support for his book from conservative commentators, and especially from his friend Rush Limbaugh. In 1994, Justice Thomas performed Mr. Limbaugh's third wedding, and he told editors that Mr. Limbaugh planned to read the book aloud over the air."[2]

True to Thomas's forecast, on the launch date of *My Grandfather's Son,* Limbaugh interviewed Thomas on his radio show (October 1, 2007). Throughout the weekend before the interview, Limbaugh's website announced the event, and the *Hannity and Colmes* website did the same for Hannity's interview with Thomas the following day. RushLimbaugh.com also posted the promotional statement "Buy It Now: *My Grandfather's Son*—Clarence Thomas."

In an interview with Hannity, conservative talk radio host (and Watergate conspirator) G. Gordon Liddy noted the benefits of promotion by the conservative media. "I recall my book first came out, first program I did was your show. And it went to number one. So they [talk radio listeners] do act. And I've had similar experiences from my show. But they act in normal responsible ways. They'll buy a book. They'll go and vote a particular way if you persuade them."[3]

From the *National Review,* the *American Spectator,* and *Human Events* to the *Weekly Standard,* the *Washington Times, Commentary,* and *Public Interest,* there are of course many conservative and neoconservative media outlets. Columnists George Will and Fox regular Cal Thomas are read in newspapers throughout the country. The entire genre of political talk radio is dominated by those of conservative bent. (Within radio, Christian programming is a powerful force sustaining social conservatism. For that audience, James Dobson's *Focus on the Family* is a particularly important player. During much of our study, so, too, were Jerry Falwell's *Old Time Gospel Hour* and Pat Robertson's *700 Club*). Although these media can be seen as part of the conservative opinion media, examining their relationships, content, and influence is beyond the scope of this book because their individual audiences are too small to isolate in surveys.)

Before arguing in the next chapter that the media players on which we focus are ideological soul mates, we here briefly outline their origins and influence.

Rush Limbaugh

Political talk radio emerged in force in the United States in the 1990s. In 1990, talk/news radio was exceeded only by the contemporary music format in its reach in the top 75 markets.[4] By fall 1994, news/talk was the nation's most popular format.[5] Talk radio is profitable. According to then Federal Communications Commission chairman Reed Hundt, it produced "one out of every $7 that broadcasters earned in radio in 1993."[6] The demand for political talk in this medium was driven in part by demographics. Older listeners tend to prefer that format to music. The baby boomers are, in other words, a natural constituency for talk radio.[7]

Political talk was the answer to an AM station owner's prayers. Since stations were designed to locate their audiences in the places in which most lived in the 1940s and 1950s, AM outlets had trouble reaching those outside the urban core. The FM stations set up in the 1960s and 1970s set their sights on the desirable suburban markets. A second blow to AM stations came in the 1970s and 1980s when the clearer signal and stereo sound of FM radio made it the preferred outlet for music. As a result, AM stations foundered. "The mass exodus of listeners from AM to FM over the last 20 years," wrote *Broadcasting* in August 1990, "has left some 5000-plus stations scrambling to keep from being in the red—or, worse yet, going dark."[8] Talk radio was a savior of AM.

Changing technology made national talk radio viable. When syndicated talk shows had to be sent by copper wire over phone lines, as they did until the mid-1980s, the audio quality was too poor to carry long programs. Another prohibitive factor was the cost of linking stations by phone lines. The satellite dish changed all that. Stations now receive broadcast quality from anywhere in the country. Broadcasting over the internet increased access. Among other things, the new technology made it possible for local hosts to "link several stations together into an 'instant network.'"[9]

Although national syndication was technologically easy to accomplish by the early 1990s, attracting large audiences in major markets was not. Among political talk radio hosts in that period, only Limbaugh was consistently aired in the major markets.

A change in broadcast regulation was a final gift to the AM stations in search of a new identity and audience. The doctrine had required that broadcasters provide a reasonable opportunity for the presentation of opposing views on controversial public issues. In 1985, the Federal Communications Commission concluded that the fairness doctrine, in place since 1949, was no longer needed.[10] A federal appeals court concurred in 1989.[11] When Congress added the doctrine to the Communications Act, President Reagan vetoed it. Congress failed to override the veto.

The end of the fairness doctrine paved the way for talk radio as we know it today. Neither hosts nor stations currently have an obligation to provide balance or to open their programs to those of competing views. Stung by the effectiveness of conservative political talk radio (which played a role in torpedoing immigration legislation in 2007), some Democrats, including Illinois senator Dick Durbin and his Massachusetts colleague John Kerry, began talking about reviving the fairness doctrine, a move that talk hosts characterized as the "Hush Rush" movement. "I can tell you that a restored Fairness Doctrine will only do one thing," observed talk radio and cable host Glenn Beck, "and that is put AM radio out of business essentially."[12]

Political talk radio is an editorial page writ long. Newspapers editorialize, house op-ed pages, and label some forms of news "interpretation." The rest is supposedly straight news. (Increasingly, interpretation characterizes "straight news" as well, a point well argued by Harvard political scientist Thomas Patterson.)[13] By analogy, political talk radio is a newspaper filled with editorials.

Practically since the launch of his show, Limbaugh has been the top-rated political radio host in the nation. Media reports place his listenership at between 13.5 and 20 million listeners. In 2004, *Talkers* magazine set Limbaugh's audience at 14.75 million and Sean Hannity's at 13 million.[14] To place Limbaugh's audience in perspective, an Annenberg survey in the fall of 2003 found that more than 2 in 10 Americans (26%) listened to NPR every week; 1 in 10 said the same about Limbaugh (10%).[15]

Limbaugh also publishes what he describes as the most read political newsletter in the country, has written two best-selling books, and produces a website that streams his radio show and amplifies its message with specially packaged material available only to paid subscribers.

The person who styles himself El Rushbo is credited by Republicans with helping their party recapture the House of Representatives in 1994. "Rush Limbaugh did not take his direction from us," reported Republican House leader Tom DeLay; "he was the standard by which we ran. [He] was setting the standard for conservative thought."[16] "In 1993 and 1994, he was the salvation of the conservative movement. Every day Rush Limbaugh would give us our marching orders, if you would," recalls conservative marketing guru Richard Viguerie.[17] As noted in the preface, in 1994 the Republicans in the House named Limbaugh an honorary member of their class.

Conservatives acknowledge Limbaugh's role as party leader.[18] In that capacity, he has ready access to and provides a national audience for Republicans of whom he approves. Their willingness to be guests on his show testifies to his influence. In one interview, Limbaugh and Vice President Cheney bore witness to their membership in a mutual admiration society. Limbaugh punctuated the interview with statements of agreement, including "Exactly" and "Amen." "That's an excellent point you make," he interjected at one point. At the end of an interview, Cheney sent Limbaugh a valentine of his own, announcing, "Great to talk to you, as always. Love your show.... You do great work" (September 13 2002).

Fox News

Just as changes in technology facilitated the rise of conservative political talk radio, the proliferation of cable channels paved the way for Fox. Ted Turner's launch of a 24-hour cable news channel, CNN, in 1980 meant that viewers no longer had to turn to an all-news radio station or wait until early evening to tune in to network news broadcasts. News was now available when the audience wanted it.

Equally important, breaking news could now be covered live throughout the day and evening without interrupting soap operas or prime-time dramas. In its first decade, CNN established the importance of the function it served. It was the only network on "live" on January 28, 1986, when the space shuttle *Challenger* exploded. In the summer of 1989, CNN's coverage of student protests in Tiananmen Square, Beijing, riveted audience attention on the ongoing struggle of the Chinese to democratize their country.[19]

Twenty-four-hour news-focused cable was also a natural home for politics. Important political speeches could be run in whole or part. Political discussion programs could be slated to capitalize on the presence of an interested audience.

Like CNN, the Fox News channel, which began operating October 7, 1996, was billed as "a 24-hour general news service." Launched with 17 million homes in 1996, by 2000 Fox was available in more than 54 million households. In 2003, that number exceeded 80 million.

First at CNBC and then at Fox, Roger Ailes, who in 2003 was named *Broadcast and Cable*'s "journalist of the year," transplanted some of the important characteristics of talk radio to cable. Both Alan Colmes and Sean Hannity began their media careers as popular talk radio hosts, for example. But unlike CNN, Fox News set its sights on attracting an audience of conservatives with content more hospitable to right-of-center views than mainstream media. Fox's efforts to attract conservatives were effective. A 2004 Pew Center for the People and the Press survey found that 22% of those in the United States get most of their news from Fox. Of these, 46% identified themselves as conservatives, and 32% as moderates.[20] (We treat selective partisan exposure to ideological channels of communication in chapter 6.)

Fox's rise was meteoric. When we closed our collection of survey data in 2005, Fox News had a higher average number of viewers than any of the other cable outlets. Although its audience declined in 2006 (as did the audiences for CNN and MSNBC), in that year Fox still consistently led its competitors in the ratings. In December 2004, Nielsen figures showed that "Fox averaged 1.67 million viewers in primetime compared with CNN's 855,000, MSNBC's 374,000, Headline News' 212,000 and CNBC's 161,000."[21] The two Fox programs we focus on each did well. *Hannity and Colmes* averaged 2,297,000 viewers, and *Special Report with Brit Hume* 1,763,000. Fox's daily average audience was larger than CNN's for the first time in January 2002.[22] In late 2004, Fox's "total Day average of 1,210,000 viewers was up 56% versus November 2003, beating CNN, MSNBC, and CNBC's combined average of 1,001,000 viewers."[23]

In 2004, large audiences were drawn to Fox's political coverage. Of that year's general election, noted the *New York Times,*

> Fox News clobbered the other cable news networks, its 8.1 million viewers more than tripling its own election night prime-time performance in 2000. NBC, ABC and CBS, on the other hand, lost millions of viewers this year, according to Nielsen Media Research. And Fox News actually came closer to CBS in the ratings than CNN did to Fox News.[24]

At the time, media commentators argued that the success of Fox and conservative talk radio signaled a change in the media culture of the United States. An article in *Television Week* noted:

> We have seen in the past year the rise of the Fox News Channel, founded only in 1996, as one of the most important news media in our culture.... Fox has engaged an ever larger audience that is amazingly loyal to the FNC brand.... Fox News, in combination with a network of conservative talk radio commentators, has changed the way many Americans process news—despite or maybe because of the adamant opposition of numerous intellectuals, journalists, celebrities and others who still can't believe what has happened.[25]

Although the network includes liberals on its shows, with few exceptions, the hosts tilt right. Whereas until the demise of *Crossfire,* CNN balanced liberal Paul Begala with conservative Tucker Carlson, Fox's *Beltway Boys* features a hardline conservative, Fred Barnes, and a moderate conservative, Mort Kondrake. *Fox News Watch* panelist Cal Thomas, a respected conservative columnist syndicated in more than 550 newspapers, hosted his own show on Fox until mid-2005. And in the matchup between the verbally aggressive Sean Hannity and the mild-mannered Alan Colmes, Hannity's is the dominant voice.

Nor is it true that the conservatives featured in the conservative media find their home exclusively within its boundaries. For example, Cal Thomas coauthors a regular exchange with Bob Beckle in *USA Today*. And beginning in January 2008, Fox commentator William Kristol, who also edits the *Weekly Standard,* joined the op-ed page of the *New York Times* under a one-year contract.[26]

Conservative assumptions are more likely to go unchallenged on Fox's talk shows than on CNN's, and liberals are more likely to be required to defend their premises. The opposite is true on CNN. As we suggested in our opening chapters, on the panels on the *Special Report with Brit Hume*, presumption resides with the conservative argument; the liberal carries the burden of proof. Consistent with that view, Cal Thomas, Fox analyst and host, notes, "Only Fox treats patriotism as something other than a sickness. Only Fox thinks America is a better country than its critics say. Only Fox thinks capitalism is good and not something for which an apology is necessary. Only Fox sees the world in tones other than moral equivalency."[27]

Unlike Limbaugh's radio show or the *Journal*'s editorial page, Fox promises that it is fair, balanced, and unafraid. Balance is achieved by simply inviting liberal guests—not by ensuring that their ideas will receive comparable time. The notion of different amounts of access is important, because we know that in highly controlled settings, mere exposure to signs and symbols produces a preference for them.[28] In more realistic contexts, consistent repeated exposure and disproportionate exposure to one point of view can produce effects consistent with the message. An audience that gravitates primarily to conservative sources whose message is consistent and repetitive is more susceptible to reinforcement and persuasion than an audience exposed to alternative points of view in approximately equal amounts.

The conservative claim that Fox is unbiased because it is "fair and balanced" is made with a wink and a nod.[29] "Conservatives will almost always defend Fox's claim to be 'fair and balanced,'" writes conservative direct mail consultant Richard Viguerie, "but they find it hard to do so without a smirk or smile on their face.... They proudly want to claim Fox as one of their own—it's one of the movement's great success stories."[30] Writing in 2003, Robert L. Bartley, emeritus editor of the *Journal,* acknowledged that Fox's slogan "We report, you decide" was a "pretense." He noted: "Even more importantly, the amazing success of Roger Ailes at Fox News has provided a meaningful alternative to the Left-establishment slant of the major networks," and "His news is no more tilted to the right than theirs has been tilted to the left, and there's no reason for him to drop his 'we report, you decide' pretense until they drop theirs."[31]

Although much of its issue agenda is identical to that of CNN, Fox's agenda includes issues the other networks ignore. Under the headline "Out-Foxing the Experts: Asking Everyone Tough Questions Doesn't Make a Network Conservative," former Limbaugh support writer and former Fox news analyst John Fund has written in his "Political Diary" on WSJ.com (February 9, 2001):

> There is no question that Fox gives conservatives *at least* equal time and often reports stories—such as Jesse Jackson's curious finances or the missing e-mails at the Clinton White House—that other networks ignore. But if Fox appears to be further to the right, it is precisely because other cable outlets have given short shrift to conservatives and their views. I'm sure there have been times when Fox spent less time on GOP scandals than other networks, but it also was the very first network to report details of George W. Bush's hidden DUI incident last November.[32] (emphasis added)

When the same issues are treated, the assumptions that frame the pieces and the voices heard within it may differ as well. Brian Anderson wrote in the *Journal*:

> Watch Fox for just a few hours, and you encounter a conservative presence unlike anything on television. Where CBS and CNN would lead a news item about an impending execution with a candlelight vigil of death-penalty protesters, for instance, at Fox "it is de rigeur that we put in the lead why that person is being executed," senior vice president for news John Moody noted.... Fox viewers will see Republican politicians and conservative pundits sought out for meaningful quotations, skepticism voiced about environmentalist doomsaying, religion treated with respect, pro-life views given airtime—and much else they'd never find on other networks.[33]

Because Fox is perceived to be conservative, it took flak when it was the first network to call the election of 2000 for George W. Bush. Bush's first cousin, John Ellis, employed by Fox as an election analyst in 2000, was in touch with the Bush family throughout election night. Also raising criticism from other media was the revelation in Bob Woodward's *Bush at War* that Fox chair Roger Ailes sent President Bush a memo shortly after 9/11 urging him to attack Afghanistan.[34]

A prominent Fox host believes that the network shapes the attitudes of its viewers. Referring to the 2002 election, Fox's Brit Hume informed radio host Don Imus, "People watch us and take their electoral cues from us. No one should doubt the influence of Fox News in these matters."[35] Fox is influential in part because Republicans in power treat it as if it is. Newt Gingrich, for example, told media analyst Ken Auletta, "If I go on the Fox network, no question that people in the Administration see that." The conservative cable network may be affecting journalism as well. In the spring of 2005, an Annenberg survey of 673 mainstream journalists—owners and executives, editors and producers, and staff reporters—found a belief that Fox has influenced the way broadcasters cover the news, as well as how others present the news on the air.[36]

In this survey, a majority of 673 journalists surveyed (51%) with a margin of error of ±4% stated that Fox News had influenced the way other broadcasters covered the news. Anecdotal evidence for a Fox effect on journalism surfaced when "CNN's war correspondent, Christiane Amanpour, was

TABLE 3.1

TO WHAT EXTENT, IF AT ALL, HAS THE SUCCESS OF THE
FOX NEWS CHANNEL INFLUENCED THE WAY OTHER BROAD-
CASTERS **PRESENT** THE NEWS—TO A GREAT EXTENT, MODERATE
EXTENT, SMALL EXTENT, OR NOT AT ALL? (UNWEIGHTED DATA)

Journalists	
Great extent	18%
Moderate extent	39
Small extent	25
Not at all	8
Don't know	7
Refused	2

TO WHAT EXTENT, IF AT ALL, HAS THE SUCCESS OF THE
FOX NEWS CHANNEL INFLUENCED THE WAY OTHER BROAD-
CASTERS **COVER** THE NEWS—TO A GREAT EXTENT, MODERATE
EXTENT, SMALL EXTENT, OR NOT AT ALL? (UNWEIGHTED DATA)

Journalists	
Great extent	14%
Moderate extent	37
Small extent	29
Not at all	11
Don't know	7
Refused	3

critical of her own network for not asking enough questions about WMD. She attributed it to the competition for ratings with Fox, which had an inside track to top administration officials."[37]

The Wall Street Journal's *Opinion Pages*

In existence for more than a century, the *Wall Street Journal* is a major U.S. media institution. A four-page paper in 1889, the *Journal* passed the 1 million subscription mark in 1966.[38] With 2,106,744 subscribers in 2004, the *Journal* had the second largest subscription base in the country. Only *USA Today* was larger. The circulation of most U.S. papers slipped in 2004; the *Journal*'s rose by more than 15,000, an increase attributable in part to a jump in the number of online paid subscribers.[39] At the time of its purchase by Murdoch in 2007, the *Journal* had 2.1 million subscribers to the *New York Times*'s 1.1 million.[40] The *Journal*'s success on the web was noteworthy as well. In August 2007, its publisher predicted: "WSJ.com will soon reach the milestone of one million paying subscribers.... Some 40% of print subscribers have access to the online *Journal*, double the proportion of two years ago.... This past quarter the unit of Dow Jones that includes the Journal had an increase of more than 30% in operating income."[41]

Our study focuses on the editorial pages of the *Journal*—*and not its news content. There is no scholarly consensus about the ideological tilt of the Journal's news pages*. One 2005 study found that the *Journal*'s news pages are the second most "right leaning" of a sample of those of more than 400 newspapers in the United States. Ideological tendency was assessed by the news pages' use of phrases describing social and political issues that were more likely to be employed by Republicans than Democrats in Congress. That study excluded the opinion pages of the *Journal*.[42] A smaller study that used criteria for ideological tendency such as mentions of left- and right-leaning think tanks identified the *Journal* as one of the most liberal newspapers.[43]

At the time of the sale to Murdoch, the *Economist* described the *Journal* as "not really one newspaper but two—a newspaper and a highly opinionated conservative magazine." "Hitherto," noted the article, "it has succeeded in drawing a line between them." The same article characterized the *Journal* as "the gold standard of business reporting" and called its op-ed pages "the Bible of American conservatism."[44] With the sale pending, *Journal* publisher L. Gordon Crovitz reminded readers that Murdoch and the Bancrofts agreed with the statement in the Dow Jones Code of Conduct that "Opinions represent only the applicable publication's own editorial philosophies centered around the core principle of 'free people and free markets.' "[45]

Drawing on the reputation and intellectual resources of the *Journal*, Murdoch planned to boost the impact of his Fox Business Network, which was launched in October 2007 as a competitor to CNBC and Bloomberg Television. So highly regarded are the news pages of the *Journal* that its competitor, the *New York Times*, editorialized against the Murdoch purchase, noting that the *Journal* "produces a balanced and trustworthy news report that is required reading for corporate and political leaders around the world."[46] Protesters from the liberal activist group Moveon.org responded to the sale by assembling outside the headquarters of Dow Jones to distribute parodic headlines supposedly revealing " 'the type of unreliable, partisan information businesspeople can expect from the news pages of the *Journal* under Rupert Murdoch.' "[47]

Beginning in 2000, the *Journal* offered a sampling of its editorial page content and some materials generated specifically for the web at no cost on a website called Opinion.Journal.com; complete versions of the editorial pages were available by paid subscription at wsj.com/opinion. After the purchase of the *Journal* by Murdoch, in January 2008 that division ended when the two sites merged to become a nonsubscription online site with full access to *Journal* opinion. Important for our purposes is that fact that the newly merged site includes clips from the *Journal's* weekly Fox cable program the *Journal Editorial Report*.

For 30 years, Bob Bartley led the opinion pages of the *Journal*. When President George W. Bush awarded him the Presidential Medal of Freedom, the citation read "Robert L. Bartley is one of the most influential journalists in American history." Hume, Hannity, and Limbaugh embrace the assumptions of Reagan conservatism; the *Journal's* editorial page helped create them. For example, *Journal* editorial writer Jude Wanniski introduced fiscal conservatives to supply-side economics in the 1970s. Also appearing on the opinion pages of the *Journal* in those early years were supply-siders Arthur Laffer and Robert Mundell. The case that cutting taxes and government spending would trigger economic growth was proclaimed on December 11, 1974, in the *Journal* in what Godfrey Hodgson terms "the "supply-side manifesto." "With lower taxes," the piece argued," it is more attractive to invest and more attractive to work; demand is increased, but so is supply."[48] Here was a defining premise of what would become known as Reaganomics. Elaborated in Wanniski's 1978 book, *The Way the World Works: How Economies Fail—and Succeed*,[49] supply-side economics and attacks on the capital gains tax grounded the editorial philosophy of the *Journal*. The notion carried with it strategic implications for the way Republicans could win elections. Economic analyst Alan Murray observed, "Twenty-five years ago, Jude Wanniski, a former editorial writer for the *Journal* and self-appointed high priest for the supply-side movement...argued Democrats were winning elections by playing Santa with government-spending programs, while Republicans were losing them by being responsible and focusing on deficits."[50] The statement indicates how important the editorial page of the *Journal* was in fueling the Reagan revolution while also explaining the political rationale behind the Republican embrace of supply-side economics.

Just as the *Journal* led the way to Reaganomics, so, too, it championed the premises that would justify welfare reform in the 1990s. In 1984, Charles Murray published a provocative attack on liberal social welfare policy arguing that instead of alleviating poverty, the welfare state was fostering it. *Losing Ground: American Social Policy, 1950–1980* was a frontal attack on the assumptions and policies spawned by the New Deal and Lyndon Johnson's Great Society programs. In *Losing Ground*, Murray called for the abolition of programs ranging from Medicaid, Aid to Families with Dependent Children (AFDC), and unemployment insurance to workers' compensation.[51] Although Reagan cut the rate of increase of some social programs, overall Murray's call produced few practical outcomes during the Gipper's time in office.

In October 1993, Murray narrowed his target in an argument in the *Journal* that the funding of out-of-wedlock births through the welfare system encouraged a practice that should be discouraged. His prescriptions were clear:

> End all economic support for single mothers. The AFDC (Aid to Families with Dependent Children) payment goes to zero. Single mothers are not eligible for subsidized housing or for food stamps. An assortment of other subsidies and in-kind benefits disappear....From society's perspective, to have a baby that you cannot care for yourself is profoundly irresponsible, and the government will no longer subsidize it."[52]

Importantly, Murray's argument framed the issue as one affecting both the black and white community. "But the black story, however dismaying, is old news. The new trend that threatens the U.S. is white illegitimacy."

The election of a Republican-controlled House in 1994 provided the votes to ensure that the promise Clinton had made in 1992 "to end welfare as we know it" was translated into law before the 1996 elections. Gingrich has called welfare reform "the most successful conservative social reform...in the last ninety years."[53]

In sum, the two Fox programs on which we focus, Limbaugh's radio show and the editorial content of the *Journal*, attract large audiences in very different media. By cross-promotion, they help build each other's audiences. Each is ready to protect the other from what they see as an ideologically grounded attack. They draw their talent largely from Republican circles. Each is willing to magnify the others' message.

In the next chapter, we argue that the conservative opinion media's embrace of Reagan conservatism and their vigilant protection of the legacy they ascribe to it give their message coherence, serve as a touchstone for evaluating Republicans, and create a powerful rhetorical vehicle for minimizing the cleavages in the Republican voting coalition.

The Conservative Opinion Media as Opponents
of Liberalism and Custodians of the Reagan Narrative

Throughout the summer and early fall of 2007, prochoice Republican presidential contender Rudy Giuliani led the Republican field in the national polls. On television and radio talk shows, speculation abounded about the electability of a candidate whose prospects were launched in the aftermath of 9/11. Fueling Giuliani's run was the public perception that as New York's mayor on September 11 he had dealt resolutely with the terrorist attack on his city and, by implication, the nation. At the same time, his social liberalism and two divorces raised questions about his capacity to appeal to "family values" voters. If faced with a choice between a prochoice Democrat and the socially liberal former New York mayor, would social conservatives stay home on Election Day 2008?

In the fall of 2007, a group of Christian conservative leaders, including Focus on the Family leader Dr. James C. Dobson, raised an alternative: field a third-party candidate. "Winning the presidential election is vitally important," wrote Dobson in an op-ed, "but not at the expense of what we hold most dear."[1] Cautioning these troubled conservatives to carefully consider their actions was Gary L. Bauer, the candidate backed by the Christian right in primaries of 2000. For Bauer, Democratic front-runner Hillary Clinton was an enemy who spelled catastrophe for conservatives. "I can't think of a bigger disaster for social conservatives, defense conservatives and economic conservatives than Hillary Clinton in the White House," he noted.[2]

Our contention in this chapter is that one way the conservative media preserve their party's winning coalition in the face of such discontent is by focusing on enemies so threatening that the need to thwart them becomes a transcendent goal. From this frame of reference, socially conservative Republicans are invited to ask not: Does the former New York mayor stand with us on such issues as abortion?, but rather: Is Giuliani the best candidate to defeat the terrorists and Hillary Clinton?

Winning elections is the central task of the two major political parties. Doing so requires configuring a majority in two-way elections, a plurality in three-way contests. Majorities are made up of individuals whose shared interests transcend their ideological differences. The majority forged by President Ronald Reagan in 1980 was maintained in the 1988 election of George H. W. Bush and reassembled in the two victories of George W. Bush. Included in its embrace were "libertarians and traditionalists," "religious conservatives and the business community," free marketers and those who embrace "heartland values."[3] Unless a candidate can draw in a new voting block, ensuring that the Republican umbrella shelters these groups is critical to that party's ability to hold power.

If the social conservatives part ways with the party over moral objections to fiscal conservatism or vice versa, Republican electoral prospects plummet. The reverse is true as well. There is no inherent reason that someone championing tax cuts and deregulation should oppose abortion rights, favor the Defense of Marriage Act, or support prayer in the schools. As political scientists observe, coalitions are fragile. "All party alignments contain the seeds of their own destruction," note political scientists Edward Carmines and James Stimson. "Lurking just below the surface a myriad of potential issues divides the party faithful and can lead to a dissolution of the existing equilibrium."[4] Ensuring that those seeds do not germinate is the task of the political party and, in the case of the Republican Party, of the conservative opinion media.

Unsurprisingly, the conservative media mirror both the consensus and the ideological fault lines within the larger movement. In June 2007, for example, when the ABC/*Washington Post* poll results were entitled "Immigration: Bush Base Erodes on Immigration Debate,"[5] conservative media had done more to precipitate that state of affairs than Bush's usual opponents on the left, who were in this case his allies. On immigration, the *Wall Street Journal* embraces a probusiness position; Limbaugh does not. The *Journal*'s position is long-lived. In 1984, for example, it urged President Reagan to veto a bill and argued that if "Washington still wants to 'do something' about immigration, we propose a five-word constitutional amendment: 'There shall be open borders.'...So long as we keep our economy free, more people means more growth, the more the merrier."[6] In the debate of 2007, the *Journal* contended that its philosophy of "free markets and free people" encompassed a commitment to flexible labor markets. However, it also noted that "no issue more deeply divides American conservatives today than immigration."[7]

Limbaugh[8] and *Journal* opinion page contributor Peggy Noonan were among those condemning the Bush proposal.[9] Calling it an "amnesty bill," Limbaugh inveighed against the Bush proposal on both political and economic grounds.

> If this bill were to be signed tomorrow...John Sweeney and his boys from the unions are going to be in there and they're going to [be] trying to unionize as many of those places and people as possible, start collecting dues from them, get their wages up...which is going to create the need for more illegals. (June 11, 2007)

He also took on the free market argument head on. "I understand cheap labor. I understand it's the greatest single cost business[es] have...[but] the free market in products is not analogous at all to the free market in immigration. There's no such thing as a free market in immigration" (May 25, 2007).

Trumpeting his influence, Limbaugh played a clip of Senator Trent Lott explaining the demise of the immigration bill, in which Lott said:

> We came out and said, "We have a grand compromise."...Republicans and Democrats, moderates, conservatives, liberals. "We got a deal." And then we went home to celebrate, but we didn't bother to say what was in it. Rush Limbaugh said, "This is amnesty." We were dead at that moment because they had a one-word bumper sticker, "amnesty," and we had a six paragraph explanation. We got killed. So talk radio has a real impact. (October 9, 2007)

Other issues divide the conservative media as well.[10] On abortion, for example, Limbaugh's and Hannity's pronouncements on the air are prolife, and both argue their positions on moral grounds. Limbaugh famously "aborted" callers he found offensive in the early days of his nationally syndicated show. From the first years of his radio program, Limbaugh consistently portrayed abortion as a "sacrament" to liberals. "It's a sacrament to their religion," he said in 2007 (March 14). "Normally people go for communion. Liberals go to the abortion clinic." "To those of us on the right, of course, it is a moral issue. It's a life issue," he stated (April 18, 2007). The difference between Limbaugh's position and the *Journal*'s is fundamental. "We do not happen to accept the pro-life belief that conception is a magic moment in defining 'life,'" a *Journal* editorial noted, and declared that "in scientific terms, life includes sperm, eggs, frogs, plants, amoebas and maybe viruses."[11]

Although the *Journal* editorially supported *Roe v. Wade* as "social policy," in a move consistent with Limbaugh's view, it argued that it is "poor law, a judicial intrusion into the legislative arena."[12] Both the *Journal* and Limbaugh agree with the position taken by Justice Antonin Scalia that the decision was made in the wrong venue. "It's a shame," says Limbaugh, "that nine people wearing black robes in 1973 decided to usurp all kinds of democratic power from the American people and proclaim this" (April 18, 2007). The *Journal* invokes the same conservative principle by arguing that the fight over abortion belongs "not in Washington but in the state capitals."[13] Importantly, even while the *Journal* editorial disagrees with the social conservatives intellectually, it acknowledges the sincerity and respectability of their view and sides with their distress at the intrusions of an "unelected elite."

The Enemy as Unifying Force

Despite their occasional differences, the conservative media feature a common rogues' gallery of enemies. These include "liberalism" and its outward expressions: big government (with its high taxes, entitlements, and intrusive antimarket regulations) and judges who read new rights into the Constitution. "Many people have suggested that with our victory over communism and the demise of the Soviet Union, Republicans no longer have an enemy around which they can rally," noted Limbaugh in the early 1990s. "I disagree. We have plenty of enemies."[14]

One way the conservative opinion media consolidate the Republican base is by summoning their readers, watchers, and listeners to fend off these adversaries. Accordingly, they champion a version of the past that asserts conservatism as David against the Goliath of liberalism. In this parable, the slingshot that fells Goliath is Reagan conservatism. Several premises ground the defense of Reaganism. Specifically, Reagan conservatism succeeded where the liberalism of President Franklin D. Roosevelt failed. In this view, Reagan's growth-producing military and economic policies saved the economy from destructive "liberal" taxation and sent the communist enemy into a death spiral. Conservatives are at war with the "liberal media," in part, because they believe that this elite transmission belt perverts the public's understanding of conservatism's successes and transmutes liberalism's failures into successes.

THE "LIBERAL" AS ENEMY

The commonplace "My enemy's enemy is my friend" holds true in politics. In 1960, William F. Buckley observed: "At the political level, conservatives are bound together for the most part by negative response to liberalism.... Negative action is not necessarily of negative value. Political freedom's principal value is negative in character. The people are politically stirred principally by the necessity for negative affirmations."[15] Limbaugh was among those who argued that Republicans had to abandon that reactive mode. "We are not a party of people cemented together by bonds of negativity," he argued in his book *See, I Told You So*. "We are a party of ideas—positive ideas." So, for example, he tells his audience:

We must perceive and sell ourselves

Not as the party that opposes government, but that which champions individual freedoms!;

Not as the party that opposes higher taxes, but that which champions entrepreneurship!;

Not as the party that opposes abortion, but that which champions every form of human life as the most sacred of God's creations!;

Not as the party that opposes the expansion of the welfare state, but that which champions rugged individualism![16]

Although Reagan conservatism and the conservative media embrace this agenda, the binding force of attacks on "liberalism" remains powerful. By voting against "liberals," this message says, conservatives can increase the likelihood that the enemy abroad will be defeated by a strong military and the nation led by a president with the resolve to use it. A principled conservative president will be tough on crime, favor small government and local control, be fiscally prudent, and staunchly oppose the "culture of death." By contrast, "liberals" jeopardize economic growth and the country's safety. As important, under a conservative president, the country will be led by a person who believes in its greatness. "There isn't a conviction I hold that makes liberals livid more quickly than this one," writes Limbaugh; "America is the greatest country on Earth and in history, still abounding with untapped opportunity for ordinary citizens."[17]

On the domestic front, social and fiscal conservatives share an aversion to "Big Government" with what they see as its lethal combination of high taxes, out-of-control spending, and intrusions into the market and people's lives. The conservative assault on the New Deal's concept of government is encapsulated in such words as "big government," "federal bureaucracy," "entitlements," "unelected elite," and "welfare state" and a pejoratively tagged concept of liberalism. By contrast, American conservatism is said to stand for moving "power away from large and bureaucratic entities and toward individuals and the country's many local governing institutions."[18]

Evidence that "big government" and "government bureaucracy" can be cast as devil-terms to social conservatives appeared in 1995, when fiscal and social conservatives joined forces to lobby Congress to pass a balanced budget amendment. Conservative leader Ralph Reed characterized such coordinated action as the liberals' "worst nightmare." Government intrusion, explained Reed, is antithetical to social conservatives' values. "The values we advocate are learned, not mandated.... These values suffer when weighed down by the heavy hand of government. Therefore, anything that reduces the role of the Washington bureaucracy in the lives of families is a step in the right direction."[19]

The conservative coalition is most likely to crumble, of course, when the Democratic nominee is a southern centrist and, as such, harder to excoriate as a "liberal." To salvage the "liberal" enemy, conservative opinion media paint centrist Democratic candidates as either liberals-in-disguise or as centrists potentially in thrall to the Left. Democrats used the "in thrall" argument in 1952 when they asserted that once in office, the centrist Eisenhower would embrace the more conservative agenda of the Taft faction of the Republican Party; the former had a Democratic incarnation in 1996, when in Democratic attack ads, the name of the Republican nominee became Dole-Gingrich.

In the Limbaugh lexicon, "centrists" are defined as "liberal Democrats."[20] Consistent with this view, on the eve of the 1992 election, the *Journal* implied that Democratic presidential nominee Bill Clinton's centrism was a ruse and portrayed the "young" prospective Democratic president as ready prey for the sinister "liberals" in his party. "The Clinton campaign, if you choose to believe, has driven a stake through the heart of American liberalism." But the impaled "liberal" might nonetheless rise at dawn. "Like Bela Lugosi, the liberals possess great, destructive strength. They have the power of hypnosis[.] (Has anyone checked the necks recently of Justices Souter and Kennedy?)" Were Bill Clinton to take the White House, the *Journal* surmised, "the liberal undead would produce a great many fitful pre-dawn hours for a young President Clinton." And it told its readers, "if Bill Clinton wins, don't bother to fax your congratulations to the White House. Send cloves of garlic."[21] "I tried to warn you, folks," Limbaugh reminded his audience as the Clinton health care reform initiative was unfolding. "Day after day, I told millions of Americans that Clinton was pulling a scam of monumental proportions."[22]

The Clinton administration's "bureaucratic" "big government" "redesign of one-seventh of the nation's economy" made it easier for the conservative media to suture the "liberal" label to the Clinton administration. "Mr. Clinton's deceitfulness in campaigning as a moderate has been more than equaled by his unabashed arrogance in governing as a full-fledged liberal," Limbaugh said in 1994.[23] With the Clinton health care reform plan on life support, the *Journal* editorialized, "Despite a clever and *ambitious liberal president* and overwhelming majorities in Congress, Democrats couldn't persuade Americans or even all of their own Members to turn over the health-care system to the government. We may be watching the demise of entitlement politics" (emphasis added).[24]

Not all Democrats and Democratic policies are rejected, however. Conservative support for tax cuts means that John Kennedy's statement that "a rising tide lifts all boats" is a mantra, and the tax cuts of 1962, 1981, and 1986 a vindication of supply-side economics. "If Mr. Kerry wants to follow President Kennedy as a tax-cutting Democrat," the *Journal* said, "he'd skip the corporate welfare and use all the revenue from repatriated profits to fund a bigger cut in corporate tax rates. JFK understood that the best way to promote new jobs without creating perverse incentives is to lower marginal rates."[25]

When their audiences grant them the power to define conservatism and contrast it to "liberalism," Limbaugh and the editorial page of the *Journal* serve the function usually performed by reference groups such as unions and churches. Psychological attachment to a reference group provides "cues for structuring attitudes and behavior on matters relevant to the group."[26]

Party and ideological labels such as "conservative" and "liberal" also can serve as an heuristic, a cognitive judgmental shortcut.[27] We tend to take heuristic cues from groups we see as trustworthy and credible.[28] If a voter knows that conservatives are usually prolife, oppose gun control, and favor tax cuts, in the absence of conflicting information, that person can reasonably infer that an unknown candidate running as a conservative and supported by conservatives such as a Limbaugh holds those positions.

Consistent with these notions, "when parties and elites attach brand names (e.g., 'Democratic' and 'Republican') to issues...[they send] signals that help citizens respond coherently to an array of questions."[29] "Conservative" and "liberal" are such brand names. This signaling function is particularly likely in an environment in which, as is generally the case, the two parties and two ideologies within those parties offer discernibly different agendas.[30] When presented with clear alternatives, voters are better able to make the ideological connections between different issues.[31]

COMMUNISM AS ENEMY

The power of external threat to suppress tensions in the base was explained by *Journal* columnist Peggy Noonan in February 2002.

> President Bush the elder backed a lot of big government spending; he didn't make the government smaller; the deficit grew; he was open to adding on new spending. And by 1992 his Republican base turned on him, and he was finished. Now Bush the younger comes along and

promises more government spending, a government getting bigger, the return of deficits. And yet after the speech on Tuesday his base is more rock solid than ever. How come?

Her first answer:

> The president's base shares with him the conviction that nothing— nothing—is more important than the war on terrorism. Conservatives always think the first job of government is to look to our national security, keep defenses strong, ensure public safety. So Mr. Bush's base is willing to give him a lot of room to maneuver to get what he needs on security and safety.[32]

On the international scene, communism was the demonic threat in the Reagan era; "IslamoFascist terrorism" serves the same role after 9/11.

For social conservatives, communism was a godless force; for business conservatives, the antithesis of free market capitalism. In Reagan's rhetoric, what protected both the nation's spiritual values and economic freedom from the threat of communism was the United States's military strength and a willingness to deploy it. Unsurprisingly, the 1984 Reagan campaign's slogan equated preparedness and peace.

In the televised speech that launched him onto the national stage in the closing days of the Goldwater campaign of 1964, Reagan tied the fiscal and social conservatives together in the anticommunist cause. Nikita Khrushchev "has told them [his people] that we are retreating under the pressure of the Cold War, and someday when the time comes to deliver the ultimatum, our surrender will be voluntary because by that time we will have weakened from within spiritually, morally, and economically," Reagan told the audience. Adopting the language of religious conservatives, Reagan tied the nation's spiritual and national identity together with a cascade of rhetorical questions. "Should Moses have told the children of Israel to live in slavery under the pharaohs? Should Christ have refused the cross?" "Should the patriots at Concord Bridge have thrown down their guns and refused to fire the shot heard 'round the world'?"[33]

THE CULTURAL "LIBERAL" ELITE AS ENEMY

To gain and hold power, conservatives must also frustrate the possibility that one pillar of the base will see another as a threat to its fundamental values. The base melts down if the traditional Democratic attack—that the Republican Party is the party of the few—resonates sufficiently with social conservatives to turn them against the policies that disproportionately benefit wealthy business conservatives. Seeking that wedge, Democratic presidential nominee Al Gore argued in 2000 that the tax policies of his opponent, Governor George W. Bush, favored the upper 1% of income earners. Democrats also position their party as the party of the middle class, and by implication not the party of the poor, by promising "middle-class tax cuts" and assuring audiences that they will only raise taxes on the rich. In this Democratic configuration of the world, social conservatives who do not share the values or the wealth of the Wall Street business conservatives are invited to see conservatism as an ideology of wealthy, amoral elites. "So 'middle-class' tax cuts, even phony ones, are offered as a 'wedge' to divide middle-income earners from the greedy 'rich,'" observed the *Journal* of the Clinton campaign of 1992. "The theme of resentment—encapsulated in the word 'fairness'—is designed to break voters away from the opportunity based coalition of Ronald Reagan and, at least in 1988, of George Bush."[34]

In a skillful act of redefinition, conservatives sidestep that alternative by substituting a more threatening "cultural elite"—one that is godless, patronizing, and a threat to every value social conservatives cherish. Doing so requires disassociating the notion of "elite" from that of "the wealthy" and attaching it instead to those who embrace "liberal" social values. The displacement of one elite by another gains traction if at the same time the beneficiaries of Republican tax policies are cast as residing on Main Street, not Wall Street, and defined as the owners of "small businesses" and "family farms," not "giant corporations" and "agribusiness." Accordingly, the conservatives argue that increases in the minimum wage hurt small businesses and the estate tax denies family farmers and owners of small businesses the ability to hand down their means of livelihood to their children. If "small businesses" are the beneficiary, then social conservatives should embrace the conservative economic policy for a second reason, argued the then director of the Christian Coalition, Ralph Reed, in the *Journal* in 1995: "43% of all small-business owners are evangelical Christians."[35]

Facilitating the frame shift from wealthy elites to cultural elites is the contention that wealth is an earned reward and the wealthy are those who create the jobs that sustain the economy. Instead of the "liberal" view that conservative tax policies reward the wealthy materialistic elites, this reframing offers social conservatives a benign construction of those who are advantaged and a threatening adversary—the elitist cultural "liberal."

Distaste for anything tied to the cultural "liberal" elite is cultivated by the *Journal*'s dispassionate assertion that "American liberalism has traditionally derived much of its energy from a volatile mixture of emotion and moral superiority"[36] and Limbaugh's more visceral claim that this amoral class holds social conservatives in contempt. The cultural elite's disdain is evidence that they share none of the values the social conservatives treasure. In the world Limbaugh describes for his listeners and readers, "liberals" "survive and thrive on a fundamental belief that the average American is an idiot—stupid, ignorant, uninformed, unintelligent, incapable of knowing what is good for him, what's good for society, what's right and what's wrong."[37] Consistent with that argument, the conservative media portray "liberal" elites as an enemy that despises Christian conservatives and southerners. Those who hate Christians try "to portray Christians as a bunch of hayseed southern hicks. The real reason is that they're afraid of them" (February 20, 2004). "These [the discussion includes Democratic contenders] are the people that run around ridiculing conservative Christians, make fun of them," notes Limbaugh. "You people drive the pick up trucks. You live in Mississippi, wear the plaid shirts. You got a bottle of Old Crow sitting next to you. You're going to go bomb an abortion clinic in a couple of days. You watch NASCAR. You don't have your two front teeth. That's what they think of you, and you know it" (June 5, 2007). Inclusion of the word "southern" in the first passage and "Mississippi" in the second is strategically consistent with the notion that he is addressing an important part of the conservative base.

With a message that casts the "liberal" elite as their enemy, Limbaugh reinforces conservative churchgoers' belief that those committed to "the sanctity of human life, the institution of marriage, and other inviolable pro-family principles"[38] belong in the conservative fold. Limbaugh's response to discussions of the need for gun control after the killings at Virginia Tech in April 2007 illustrates his skill at excoriating the values and policies of the "liberal" enemy. Not only does "liberalism" embrace a "culture of death" and "bar God and faith" but also it opposes gun rights and the war in Iraq, supports activist judges, and is ill disposed to protect the individual against crime. "There is a culture of death with liberalism," says Limbaugh, "from abortion on, embryonic stem cells, you name it, euthanasia? They own that as well as they own defeat in Iraq. Maybe the instant effort to bar God and faith from the public sphere is a problem here. Maybe the coddling of criminals by liberals, including judges, has created this environment" (April 17, 2007).

Since Aristotle's time, students of rhetoric have known that persuasion is most compelling when the audience forges its own conclusions by investing messages with shared meaning. Limbaugh's churchgoing listeners are well positioned to invest his brief telegraphic statement with such enthymematic meaning. The Christian right speaks in a language that includes the concepts "culture of death," "coddling criminals," "barring God from the public sphere," and "euthanasia." There is no need for Limbaugh to tell the audience that he and they oppose abortion and embryonic stem cell research, no need to explain what he means by "euthanasia" and "coddling of criminals," and no need to flesh out the argument that "liberals" (not the Bush administration) "own defeat in Iraq."

The disdain of the elite for Reaganism and its champions is unjustified, according to the conservative media. Past Republican successes vindicate the notion that this patronizing cadre of northerners is ill-informed, if not ignorant. So, for example, a May 10, 2001, *Journal* editorial notes that both Reagan and Bush were derided by the "American and European intelligentsia." The editorial then heralds the successes of policies embraced by Republican presidents in the face of elite opposition:

> Mr. Reagan showed himself a bad global citizen by dumping the Law of the Sea Treaty; with George W. Bush, it's the Kyoto accord on limiting dioxide emissions. Mr. Reagan was accused of fomenting nuclear war for wanting to protect America from it; with Mr. Bush it's the same issue, though the charge now is the vague one of "unilateralism."...Ronald Reagan's steady hand won deployment of the Pershings, and ultimately the Cold War. Mr. Bush should probably consider being damned in the same terms as our most successful foreign-policy President in generations a pretty auspicious start.[39]

This editorial reveals that well before 9/11, the *Journal* was applauding a tendency of the Bush administration that would become a defining feature of it after the attacks on that day—a feature the *Journal* continues to champion.

Although the cultural elite remained a ready menace, with the fall of the Berlin Wall and the demise of the communist threat, the Republican coalition lost its international enemy. In an effort to glue the coalition back together, in 1996 a *Journal* editorial shored up the common ground under "the two biggest voting blocs in the conservative movement."[40] "Most religious conservatives back free-market economics, and most economic conservatives deplore the liberal culture's denigration of traditional values." The reasons for the coalition were pragmatic as well. "If social and economic conservatives cannot unite in this year's Presidential election," noted an editorial in February 1996, "neither will like the result: a new lease on political life for the discredited notions of redistributionist economics, class warfare and a continuation of the rampant secularism and value-neutral attitudes that prevail in our public institutions." This is a rhetoric that invites each audience to see the other as a compatible part of a voting block.

Preserving and Protecting the Conservative Story
of Reagan's Legacy

In his first book, *The Way Things Ought to Be*, Limbaugh predicted, "Liberals are arrogant and condescending and will pursue relentlessly their goal of destroying the legacy and truth of the Reagan Presidency."[41] "Liberals correctly perceive the Reagan record as their most dangerous enemy," his second book explains. "Why? Because what happened during the 1980s—prosperity at home...strength abroad—directly contradicts every liberal shibboleth."[42] The conservative opinion media are custodians of Reagan conservatism and of a specific account of the Reagan legacy that vindicates that philosophy. Their archived memory of the Reagan years provides conservatives with a standard to which to aspire, a touchstone against which to assess Republican leaders, and a way to cast conservatism as a philosophy vindicated in practice. "If the real lesson of the 1980s were allowed to take hold," says Limbaugh, "it would have been the death knell for liberalism."[43]

The conservative opinion media pledge allegiance to Reagan conservatism. True to Limbaugh's embrace of that catechism, the ninth of his Undeniable Truths declares that Ronald Reagan was the greatest president of the twentieth century. "I am never going to compromise on Reaganomics," states Limbaugh.[44] He is not alone in his adherence to Reaganism. "I am a Reagan conservative," says Hannity.[45] So is Brit Hume. Reagan's views on foreign affairs, taxation, regulation, and the Cold War were "right," concludes Hume.[46] "What would this world be like had Ronald Wilson Reagan not served these eight important years in our history? I can't even imagine," says Hannity.[47] "Those of us who lived in and feel we understood the age of Ronald Reagan have a great responsibility: to explain and communicate who [Reagan] was and what he did and how he did it and why," wrote Peggy Noonan in the *Journal*."[48]

For conservatives, the Reagan narrative functions in the same way as the liberals' belief that Roosevelt's policies ended the Great Depression and set the country on course to win World War II. Each account warrants the claim that their ideology has been redeemed in practice and the opposing one discredited. In Roosevelt's case for Democrats and Reagan's for Republicans, decisive electoral victories are a sign that the public at the time ratified the story now being told. Reagan's Electoral College victory over Walter Mondale in 1984 sets the Electoral College record for the last half of the twentieth century, just as FDR's 1936 win over Alf Landon captures it for the first half. Only Minnesota, the home state of the Democratic challenger, failed to fall to the incumbent Republican president in 1984.[49] For their ideological descendants, the fact that each was elected and reelected cements the notion that their philosophies were translated into effective action.

That notion assumes that the actions that produced the outcome were not the product of chance but were instead intentionally grounded in a coherent philosophy of governance. Accordingly, conservatives dismiss the view that Reagan was out of touch or ill informed. Their Republican exemplar was not the "amiable dunce" liberals saw him to be but instead "a disciplined, orderly thinker who, contrary to popular myth, wrote much of his own material—and did so with style and verve," notes John Fund in the *Journal*.[50] Longtime *Journal* editor Robert Bartley agreed: "Because he didn't talk like a policy wonk, his detractors attribute his success to luck and historical inevitability. The secret is that precisely because he refused to get bogged down in detail, he was able to get the big things right."[51]

REAGAN'S POLICIES PRECIPITATED THE END OF THE COLD WAR

The coherence of the conservatives' narrative of the Reagan years is drawn together in a story line that says that his policies and principles accelerated the collapse of the Soviet Union. By identifying the communist regime as an "evil empire," by demanding that Gorbachev tear down the Berlin Wall, by advancing his Strategic Defense Initiative, and by engaging in a military buildup the Soviet economy could not match, the man who had ended his acceptance speech at the Republican Convention in 1980 with a "moment of silent prayer" had helped end the Cold War and with it the threat of godless, anti–free market communism. Challenge the belief that Reagan played a key role in winning the Cold War, as liberals do, and you contest a grounding premise that vindicates conservatism to its two central factions—the fiscal and social conservatives.

"As President for eight years, Mr. Reagan accomplished no few things," noted the *Journal* in a concise summary of the conservative Reagan narrative; "cutting taxes to reinvigorate economic growth, arming the military to win the Cold War and renewing the spirit of America and the world."[52] The Democratic story tells of a different set of forces at play. Writing on the op-ed page of the *Journal* early in the fall 1992 campaign, historian Arthur Schlesinger Jr. observed:

> The Republican campaign is putting forward a couple of propositions of some interest to historians. The first is that, despite foot-dragging

and faint-heartedness by the Democrats, the Republicans finally succeeded in winning the Cold War.... Will historians really give the Republicans primary credit for the defeat of communism? ... What really defeated communism was communism itself—that in practice it proved to be a political, economic and moral disaster.[53]

Embrace the Republican plotline, and Reagan's tax cuts produced the economic growth and his military buildup the defense posture that undercut the Soviet Union's viability. Tax cuts and defense buildups are thus good policy. Adopt the Democratic tale, and Reagan's role was one of bystander.

REAGAN REVIVED THE ECONOMY; ROOSEVELT'S POLICIES DID NOT END THE DEPRESSION

The liberals' story of FDR and the conservatives' account of the presidency of Reagan are incompatible narratives as well. To replace Roosevelt with Reagan in the presidential pantheon, conservatives try to debunk the notion of a tie between New Deal policies and economic resurgence. By contrast, they see Reaganism as the genuine article. Writing in the *Journal* in 1944, Frank R. Kent reprised the Republican version of the New Deal years:

> It is likely ... that history will record that in June and July of 1932 we were on our way out of the depression with employment increasing, but that recovery was halted when business confidence was shaken by the impending election of the New Deal. ... The rest of the world, not having a "New Deal," went straight out of the depression and recovered its employment by 1934 or 1935. ... Governor Dewey told the exact truth when he said it took a war to get us out of it.[54]

"The New Deal did not revive the American economy; World War II did,"[55] declares Limbaugh. "There's so much revision of history going on today," he noted after reiterating the claim about the New Deal in his second book. "It's not just the liberals who are behind this. The media are either willing accomplices or unwitting dupes. And this nonsense has permeated our universities and other institutions. This is at the root of our misunderstanding of problems and solutions."[56]

The foreign and domestic policies of the president who saw the country as "a shining city on a hill" are vindicated in the conservative narrative. Whereas Roosevelt's policies worsened the situation, Reagan's were a success. Reagan "resolved the economic malaise of the 1970s, set off an economic boom, restored the nation's spirit and won the Cold War," wrote the *Journal's*

Robert Bartley.[57] Attempting to inoculate (i.e., arm or defend in advance) its conservative audience against the view that Reagonomics failed, the *Journal* editorialized in 1992 that "in the U.S., of course, the same critics who said the growth of the 1980s could never happen now say it was all illusory. The 18 million new jobs, the creation of such entirely new industries as biotechnology and the vanquishing of inflation and 20% interest rates presumably never happened."[58]

Part of preserving an account of history is controlling the language in which it is expressed. Writing during Clinton's first term, Limbaugh declared: "we've probably got to stop using the term 'trickle-down.' It has been corrupted beyond repair by the Clinton gang and the media." Instead Limbaugh favors "referring to the kind of free-market entrepreneurial capitalism we witnessed in the 1980s as 'Reaganomics' [because]....Once the truth is universally understood, the eighties will have been so effectively vindicated that the term 'Reaganomics' will be used only as a term of endearment and respect."[59]

For the conservative opinion media, it is axiomatic that, in Sean Hannity's words, "cutting taxes increases revenue to the government." Raising taxes spells disaster. During the last two years of the presidency of George H. W. Bush, the top tax rate, set at 28% in the Reagan years, was upped to 31%, with the addition of a third bracket. Having fought that change, both Limbaugh and the *Journal*'s editorial page cautioned other would-be apostates that in the first year after the institution of the new bracket, tax receipts from those making over $200,000 had fallen, the first time such a reduction had occurred in eight years. Limbaugh explains: "The total income-tax receipts in 1991, the first year after the 1990 budget deal was signed, fell—the first decline since 1983, because the wealth[y] found tax shelters, stopped investing, decided not to put their money at risk, and curtailed other activities that would increase their tax burden."

The conservative story line about Reagan's governorship and presidency features some facets of his record, particularly reductions in marginal income tax rates, and downplays or ignores others, such as increased deficits and spending. Reduced to parenthetical status, when it is mentioned at all, is the fact that Reagan not only raised taxes as governor but also presided over a state whose budget deficit was greater when he left office than when he was sworn in. Moreover the welfare reform that occurred on his watch "authorized increased state aid for those most in need of public help."[60]

In the conservative account of history, Reaganomics also revived the economy and vindicated supply-side economics. While it is true that Reagan presided over major tax cuts, it is noteworthy as well that he approved the tax increases in the Tax Equity and Fiscal Responsibility Act and Highway Revenue Act in 1982, approved raising the Social Security tax rate in 1983, and signed off on the taxes in the Deficit Reduction Act of 1984 and the Consolidated Omnibus Budget Reconciliation Act of 1985, the Tax Reform Act of 1986, and the Omnibus Budget Reconciliation Act of 1987.[61] So, for example, Hannity says simply that "Reagan cut taxes and doubled revenue in his eight years."[62]

True to his disposition to inoculate his audience against charges to which conservatives are vulnerable, Limbaugh acknowledges that "even Reagan begrudgingly agreed to sign on to a couple of 'deficit reduction' tax increases, one of which was at the time the largest tax increase in the nation's history." Importantly, Limbaugh then adds that the package Reagan agreed to "included $2 of spending cuts for every $1 in increased tax revenue." Why then were the offsets dropped? "But guess what?" says Limbaugh. " In a foreshadowing of its double-cross of George Bush in 1990, the Congress failed to make the budget cuts it had pledged."[63] So the fault lies with Congress, not with the Republican president.

Here Limbaugh is echoing the argument Reagan himself made. Two years after leaving office, the Gipper admitted that although he accomplished "a lot of what I'd come to Washington to do" with tax cuts, "on the other side of the ledger, cutting federal spending and balancing the budget, I was less successful than I wanted to be. This was one of my biggest disappointments as president. I just didn't deliver as much to the people as I'd promised."[64] After that admission, he shifts blame to Congress. "Presidents can't appropriate a dollar of taxpayers' money; only congressmen can."[65] To address the problem, he recommends more discipline, a constitutional amendment requiring a balanced budget, and a presidential line item veto.[66]

In their telling of the history of the Reagan years, conservatives and liberals marshal different facts to sustain their interpretations. The liberal narrative remembers that Reagan increased the national debt by $1.5 trillion, borrowing one dollar for every five spent. Conservatives feature the data showing that "by the end of the Reagan era, the federal deficit as a share of gross domestic product was falling, and rapidly—from 6 percent in 1985 to 3 percent in 1989."[67] "If you look at 1987, 1988, and 1989, when the real economic growth reached full steam," notes Limbaugh, "the deficit fell to $150 billion, even with the unchecked spending. It fell because of economic growth that created a bigger base of taxpayers and, therefore, more tax revenue."[68] In the conservative narrative, George H. W. Bush's economic policies "compound[ed] a cyclical recession." "Liberals" then misattributed that recession to Reaganomics.[69]

The "Liberal" Media and Cultural "Elite" as Enemy of the Reagan Narrative

"The Republican base considers the media to be part of the enemy that has to be defeated and overcome," observed Limbaugh (October 9, 2007). In his world, the "liberal" media subvert the truth about Reagan's role in ending the Cold War. "The Drive-Bys give him [Gorbachev] credit for ending the Cold War," notes Limbaugh, "and the American left does, but of course it would never have happened were it not for Ronaldus Magnus" (July 27, 2007). Crediting Reagan's Strategic Defense Initiative as a key factor in the collapse of communism, Limbaugh explains, "The Soviets knew that we could do it, we are Americans.... We have the economy to pay for what we want to do in our national defense. The Soviets didn't. They were a Third World country at best with a first-rate military." Lost in conservative accounts of the end of the Cold War is the fact that "by 1986 his [Reagan's] conservative base had taken to calling him the Soviet Union's 'useful idiot' for pursuing arms negotiations with Mikhail Gorbachev."[70]

The supposed liberal cultural elite are portrayed as "scathing" in their rejection of the Reagan legacy. "No one was more persistent, or eloquent, in describing how a dynamic economy joins men and women of ideas to workers than Ronald Reagan," noted the *Journal* in the middle of the 1992 general election. "The economy during his tenure created 18 million new jobs, and it was an era that marked America's complete entry to the world of high-tech, knowledge-driven employment. No one is more scathing in his abhorrence for this period than Bill Clinton and his followers."[71]

In the conservative account of history, the "liberal" media also routinely showcase facts that benefit their cause while ignoring or distorting those advantaging the other side. The Trent Lott case study in chapter 2 provides evidence in point. The speed and effectiveness with which the conservative opinion media rallied opposition to a made-for-television movie about Reagan illustrates an instance in which they bested a "liberal media" attack on the Reagan legacy.

In the fall of 2003, the *New York Times* reported that a forthcoming CBS made-for-television movie about Ronald Reagan contained controversial material, including statements that no one could confirm Reagan had made. In response, Limbaugh, Hannity, Fox, and the *Journal*'s editorial pages joined the charge that ultimately elicited both changes in the content and a move by CBS to shuttle the movie out of prime time and onto premium cable's *Showtime*. "That stupid movie on the Reagans was a bunch of hogwash," said Limbaugh; "the people who hate Reagan knew the essence, and they're nowhere near oriented toward promising that" (November 25, 2003). "Does the whole episode expose the Reagan hating, liberal leaning tendencies of the mainstream press?" asked Hannity on Fox. "CBS has a history of Reagan bashing."[72] "Though the *New York Times* broke the story," noted a *Journal* editorial,

> what caused this particular network wall to come tumbling down was largely the new media: Drudge, cable, talk radio, and so on. Not only did the new media disseminate information about the script to CBS viewers, it also provided these viewers, via the immediacy of e-mail, the means to ensure that [CBS chairman] Mr. Moonves would feel their pain.[73]

By positing a common set of enemies and offering audiences a view of history that vindicates conservative policies, the conservative media help hold together a voting coalition that has produced Republican presidential victories in the past. If, as political scientists Paul Sniderman and Matthew Levendusky argue, "citizens are capable of making coherent choices to the degree that political institutions, and particularly political parties, do the heavy lifting of organizing coherent choice sets,"[74] then the conservative opinion media are heavy lifters who organize the choices they favor under the label "Reagan conservatism." The political function served by a consistent articulation of Reagan conservatism versus the "liberal" enemy creates a discourse of self-identity that tells listeners who they are (conservatives) and who they oppose ("liberals," the "liberal media establishment," communists, cultural elites).

The role of Reagan conservatism is central to understanding the coherent, conservative ideology of the conservative media establishment. These media argue that Reaganism is a principled, simple, coherent political philosophy. That political philosophy provides the core arguments to which the conservative media establishment turns on a consistent basis; their arguments are deployed regularly not only against liberals but also against Republicans who do not toe the line. Importantly, Reagan conservatism is a positive political philosophy and not merely a negative one. It gives its adherents principles to embrace and opponents to fend off. Finally, the criticism the conservative media direct against "liberals" and "liberal media" parallels the isolation of enemies that allowed Reagan conservatism to solidify its base through the identification of an out-group ("liberals") with policies threatening the in-group (conservatives).

By reinforcing a shared identity, the conservative media establish that conservatives and conservatism and liberals and liberalism are antithetical. At the same time, they argue that the divide between the two is consequential. This basic move sets in place the polarities on which two arguments that we will explore in later chapters pivot: that the mainstream or "liberal" media cannot be trusted and that "liberals" and their policies are misguided, extreme, and dangerous.

Effects of an Echo Chamber

ommunication scholars have long wrestled with the complications produced by the fact that meaning exists at the intersection of a text, a context,
and an audience. From the earliest days of theorizing about persuasion, audience
complicity in the act of persuasion has been studied. Aristotle famously argued
that the enthymeme, in which the audience invests a message with presupposed
but unarticulated premises, is the soul of persuasion. Few, if any, citizens come to
a political season as a blank slate on which they invite leaders to write attitudes.

In the complex dance that is the persuasion process, audiences enter the
political arena with existing attitudes and preferences. Once there, they are
more likely than not to seek out information that is compatible with these
beliefs and to shun data that challenge them. When confronted with discomforting information, humans readily find ways to reject it. Among other moves,
they (and we) apply tests of evidence to it that all but ensure its rejection. By
contrast, information that shores up existing attitudes is welcomed uncritically.
In short, selective exposure, selective perception, and selective retention pervade the process by which we make sense of who we are as political creatures.

All of this means that those most likely to be found in the audience of
any partisan persuader probably already share that person's convictions. As
a result, any argument about the effects of such communication is freighted
with evidentiary traps. In this chapter, we explain our efforts to spring the
traps without being bloodied by them.

To capture the ways we understand the relationship between the conservative opinion media and their audiences, we considered a number of metaphors,
finally settling on that of an echo chamber. In brief, this concept captures the
interrelations of text, context, and audience that are of interest to us.

What Do We Mean by "Echo Chamber"?

A person picking up a book with this book's title might reasonably ask:
In what sense do Limbaugh, two programs on Fox News, and the editorial page of the *Wall Street Journal* create an echo chamber of voices from

a conservative media establishment? And why focus on these individuals and outlets and not the many others who also espouse conservatism? In this chapter, we offer our answers and explain how we have studied these sources.

First, consider the definitions. The metaphor of an echo chamber captures the ways messages are amplified and reverberate through the conservative opinion media. We mean to suggest a bounded, enclosed media space that has the potential to both magnify the messages delivered within it and insulate them from rebuttal. As we illustrated in the first two chapters, this "echo chamber" creates a common frame of reference and positive feedback loops for those who listen to, read, and watch these media outlets.

At times, the "echoing" is literal and works through direct citation. For example, Limbaugh increases the *Journal* editorial page's influence when he relays its material onto the air waves and also includes it in the support material he posts on his website. When James Schlesinger, former secretary of defense, published an op-ed in the *Journal* defending the Iraq war on April 22, 2004, Limbaugh read from it on his radio show the same day. "He makes the case," says Limbaugh. "Are we going to strengthen the U.N. or be strong ourself? He is a former secretary of defense and understands this." In this instance, as in others, Limbaugh encourages his audience to read the entire op-ed piece by creating a link to it on his website.

We mean "echo" in a second sense as well: each outlet legitimizes the other. So, for example, the *Journal* features Limbaugh's op-eds. Sometimes the conversation among conservative opinion leaders takes place in public view. On the air, Limbaugh occasionally even advises other conservative hosts on questions to ask. Speaking about former Clinton cabinet member Robert Reich, he reported reminding Sean Hannity to ask Reich, his frequent guest, a specific question about his proposal that Democrats advocate a payroll tax cut (November 27, 2002).

Limbaugh, Hannity, the *Journal*'s opinion pages, and Fox hosts and panelists also safeguard each other's reputations. When Limbaugh was under investigation for doctor shopping for prescription pain pills, Fox featured his attorney Roy Black making Limbaugh's case. When the conservative *American Spectator* pursued an investigation suggesting that the prosecution of Limbaugh was being treated in a discriminatory fashion, *Hannity and Colmes* included an extended, sympathetic interview with the investigation's author (April 30, 2004). Similarly, when journalists (largely on CNN) raised questions about the revelation by Bob Woodward that Fox's Roger Ailes had sent an "important–looking confidential communication" to President Bush after 9/11, the *Journal* editorialized:

Our own policy is to give advice to politicians every day in these columns. But let's be candid and admit that this Ailes kerfuffle has nothing to do with ethics. What's really going on here is that the news executive in question happens to be a conservative and heads the successful Fox News Channel, which built its success on offering an alternative to what everyone understands is the dominant liberal media. We can't recall hearing similar press outrage, for example, when Rick Kaplan, former head of Fox News rival CNN, slept over at the White House.[1]

What the notion of echo chamber misses is the complementarity of the *Journal's* highbrow editorial page, which speaks largely to upper-class fiscal conservatives, and the mass appeal of Fox and Limbaugh's conservatively framed exchanges. The broad reach of Limbaugh's radio show and Fox's network makes it feasible to adapt the message of Reagan conservatism to the social and fiscal conservatives of the middle class and more specifically to the group once called Reagan Democrats. "We've had a little different audience," former *Journal* editorial page editor Robert Bartley told Limbaugh, "but we're basically on the same wavelengths."[2] In chapter 2, we illustrated the ways format, genre, and audience led the conservative media to ideologically consistent, complementary messages about the Trent Lott affair.

Nor is "media establishment" an unproblematic notion. By it we mean that media outlets are firmly in place, support each other, share a coherent ideological identity, and in the cases of Fox and the *Journal*, have the same parent company. We also see a useful similarity between our concept of conservative media establishment and Bartley's notion of a more general conservative establishment. Writing on the *Journal's* editorial page, January 20, 2003, Bartley argued that the Bush administration "could conceivably consolidate a new Establishment, dominating the next half-century as FDR's progeny dominated the last one." Drawing on the *Oxford English Dictionary*, he defined "Establishment" as "a social group exercising power generally, or within a given field or institution, by virtue of its traditional superiority, and by use especially of tacit understandings and often a common mode of speech, and having as a general interest the maintenance of the status quo." Glossing the text, Bartley added, "Politics may ebb and flow, but the Establishment wields moral authority; society tends to defer to its judgments and assumptions despite much arm-flailing by critics."[3]

Bartley's definition of "establishment" is useful in characterizing media as well. The conservative media establishment is a well-financed, commercially successful, mutually reinforcing, influential cluster of outlets that share an ideological disposition toward politics, a set of presuppositions about morality and core values, and a common view of other media. These media also nourish and nurture the establishment on which Bartley focused.[4]

Finally, we use the term "conservative media establishment" to highlight the fact that these individuals provide a deliberate counterpoint to the media they characterize as "the liberal media establishment." The notion of a "liberal" establishment was percolating through conservative writings as early as 1965, when M. Stanton Evans published *The Liberal Establishment: Who Runs America...and How.*[5]

Venues for Study: Why the Journal, Fox, and Limbaugh?

Given the many other conservative voices in the U.S. media, one might reasonably ask why we focus on Limbaugh, two programs on Fox News, and the editorial pages of the *Journal*. Three criteria guided our selection. First, we wanted to study dissimilar media with distinct but overlapping audiences— a talk radio show, a cable network, an editorial page, and their Internet sites. Second, we wanted to examine consequential outlets with audience reach. Limbaugh has the largest political talk radio audience in the nation, Fox the largest cable audience, and the *Journal* the second largest readership of any U.S. newspaper and the most widely read conservative editorial page.

Another selection criterion was wide accessibility. These media are available to anyone with a radio, an online computer, and cable access. There is, of course, a cost to secure Internet and cable access, just as there is to purchasing a television set and hooking it to an electrical supply. But the Internet is now available across the public library system, and cable reaches more than 80% of the nation's households. Although the *Journal* is available by subscription, its editorial page can now be accessed on the Internet without charge at WSJ.com.

Our justification for a focus on specific programs on Fox News was driven by the questions for which we sought answers. Including Fox News's *Special Report with Brit Hume* permitted us to compare its news segments to those in the mainstream broadcast network evening news. Because Fox's brand includes the concept "We report, you decide," we wanted to include a program whose hard news segments embrace the same form as mainstream news, with reporters narrating short, produced, edited segments. The selection of *Special Report with Brit Hume* made it possible in chapter one to compare mainstream accounts of John Kerry's exchange over his supposed "foreign leaders" remark with the news report of the same exchange by Fox's Carl Cameron.

Our justification for focusing on *Hannity and Colmes* rather than Fox's more highly rated *O'Reilly Factor* is more complicated. Because Hannity's talk radio audience approaches the size of Limbaugh's, selecting *Hannity and Colmes* permitted us to concentrate on a host with impact in two of the media of interest to us. While O'Reilly also has a strong radio presence, his numbers in that medium do not match Hannity's. Moreover, Fox's theme, "fair and balanced," seemed to be captured better in a show with liberal and conservative hosts than in a show with a single moderator. Finally, we concluded that the exchanges on *Hannity and Colmes* made it easier for us to determine whether the access provided to the Left and the Right on that show differs or is comparable. We also wanted to ask how this "balanced" format affects framing, as each side argues its point of view and interrogates guests from that angle.

Limbaugh, Fox News's two programs, and the editorial page of the *Journal* differ in style, format, and genre. One contains the classic advocacy of an editorial page with a companion op-ed page filled with regular columnists and occasional guests and freelancers. Another consists of political talk on radio that combines digested news with advocacy and tightly controlled interaction with listeners. Fox's *Hannity and Colmes* pairs a conservative and a liberal host. *Special Report with Brit Hume* is a hybrid of news and opinion that includes a brief multipart broadcast op-ed (Hume's "Political Grapevine"), a panel composed of journalists and pundits, and traditional hard news stories.

In tone, the *Journal*'s editorials are more measured and in substance more argumentatively complex than are the monologues or dialogues offered by Limbaugh or Hannity. Whereas the latter use irony, humor, caricature, hyperbole, and occasional invective to advance their cause and sustain audience interest, the editorials in the *Journal* employ a more detached form of argument that presupposes audience familiarity with the issues. When an opposing view is featured on the op-ed pages, it is given a full say, a difference dictated by the medium and demands of an op-ed page. By contrast, Limbaugh excerpts comments by opponents in order to skewer them. Whereas the *Journal*'s editorial pages often conduct a seminar worthy of an ivory tower setting, Limbaugh regales his buddies with commentary over a beer in a neighborhood bar.

The emotional voltage emanating from the *Journal*'s editorial pages is lower than that on Limbaugh's talk show. So, for example, whereas the *Journal* writes: "this theme of resentment—encapsulated in the word 'fairness'—is designed to break voters away from the opportunity-based coalition of Ronald Reagan,"[6] Limbaugh writes: "Bill Clinton may be the most effective practitioner of class warfare since Lenin."[7] The *Journal*'s parallel to the cutting thrust-and-parry of Limbaugh and Hannity is James Taranto's postings on WSJ.com, as our extensive references to them in our case studies would suggest.

The differences in style and tone between the *Journal*'s editorials and the comedic polemics of Limbaugh reprise a long-lived pattern in American politics in which some are the keepers of the high church book of prayer and others employ the rhetoric that moves the people in the commons. Political parties of the nineteenth century, writes historian Robert Wiebe, "also tried to bridge the distance between proper styles and rough-and-ready ones. On the one hand, party orators spoke a rhetoric of respectability; on the other, partisan bands bawled their political preferences and cursed their opposition in public."[8]

The boundaries of discourse differ in the two genres. The tactics we will discuss in chapter 11, including ridicule and impugning motives, have been part of mass mobilization from the earliest days of recorded politics. Stylistic and tonal differences aside, if the areas of ideological agreement among these players do not exceed the differences, the premise on which we have built this book collapses. Our first two chapters were designed to showcase Limbaugh, the *Journal*, and Fox's common assumptions and frames as well as the synergy among them. As our study of the conservative media's management of the Trent Lott affair suggests, the *Journal* often provides intellectual content consistent with that which Limbaugh and Hannity translate into everyday meaning and Fox interjects into panel discussions and news frames.

Limbaugh, Hannity, and the editorial page of the *Journal* share an interest in economic matters, particularly taxing, spending, and regulating. From calls for tax cuts and reduced government spending to assaults on intrusive big government and appeals to free market capitalism and federalism, the agreement among the players we study on the role of government (particularly in economic matters) is high.

Making Inferences about an Echo Chamber

In the remainder of this chapter, we will discuss how we have gone about studying the conservative media establishment through Limbaugh's radio programs, the editorial pages of the *Journal*, and the two programs on Fox News. Our studies have several different purposes, but one of the more important is identifying what effects, if any, these three sources of political information and perspective have on their audiences. Several problems arise when trying to make inferences about the effects of any medium, especially a partisan one, on its audiences. We take time to point these difficulties out here because we want to be clear throughout the book about when our claims about the effects of the conservative media establishment are strong and when they are merely suggestive. Many of the problems we confront are common in studies of media effects.

SELECTIVE EXPOSURE

As we will show in subsequent chapters, the audiences of the conservative media establishment are disposed to hold attitudes, opinions, and ideology that agree with these media sources. The conservative media establishment is "preaching to the choir."

Several questions pervade studies of what is commonly called selective exposure.[9] How homogeneous is the audience of the conservative media establishment? Is it possible to influence an audience's attitudes, opinions, knowledge, and beliefs if that audience comes to the media with predispositions consistent with those of the source? If the audience agrees or is predisposed to agree with the voices of the conservative media establishment, is it even possible to separate effects on opinions that are created as a result of exposure to the conservative media's messages from those created by the audience's tendency to selectively choose, selectively attend, and selectively perceive the information because of its dispositions?

SPILLOVER

The audiences of the conservative media establishment have many choices within and beyond these outlets for obtaining their political information and developing their perspectives. In the chapters ahead, we will examine our own and other data that describe how individuals select sources congenial with their ideologies and how they approach uncongenial sources. No one would be surprised to find that audiences consume (and are increasingly able to consume) a variety of ideological news sources, even if they exhibit preferences for one or another perspective. One difficulty is that it is impossible to know the full variety of political information to which a person is exposed. This means that inferences about the effects of the conservative media establishment's influence will always be embedded in the messy composite of all the political information to which a person attends.

EFFECTS OTHER THAN OPINION CHANGE

In the environment we are studying, most studies fail to find direct media effects on attitudes, opinions, beliefs, and behaviors. Our research agenda was predicated on the assumption that we would be more likely to detect effects if we did not focus solely on direct consequences on attitudes, beliefs, opinions, and behaviors. Accordingly, we were on the lookout for direct effects on beliefs and behaviors as well as other kinds of consequences.

An audience with opinions, attitudes, beliefs, and behaviors that are already in line with those of the host will not be readily changed or will have little room to change as a result of the source's political rhetoric. Instead, effects might occur in other arenas, including the menu of media selections a person chooses from, polarization of opinion across different media audiences, confirmation—rather than alteration—of existing opinion, priming or framing effects, specialized rather than generalized political knowledge, emotionally based judgments of candidates, and increased exposure to congenial media in times of threat or uncertainty.

For example, consider priming effects.[10] "Priming" refers to a media source's ability to make one criterion for a decision assume greater importance in the audience's collective consciousness than another. If the conservative media establishment focuses heavily on party considerations, then the expected importance of party will be intensified in the political judgments made by regular members of the audience.

Each of these possible outcomes of exposure to the conservative media establishment will be explored in subsequent chapters. However, the general point is that when an audience self-selects its media content to be like-minded, the typical media effects—changing attitudes, opinions, beliefs, and behaviors—will not be readily detected. Instead, effects may manifest themselves in more subtle processes.

Theories of Media Effects Tailored to the Echo Chamber

The problem of inferring media effects predates the rise of opinionated and partisan media and is present any time an audience self-selects some media content to the exclusion of other material. More than 50 years ago, sociologists Bernard Berelson, Paul F. Lazarsfeld, and William McPhee found that explaining opinion formation in a presidential campaign required taking into account both the process of selecting media content as well as the effects of the media themselves, given an audience's predispositions toward the content it purposefully selected.[11]

Recently, building on the work of Vincent Price and Scott Allen, Michael Slater formalized what had been implicit in previous research about media, namely the mutual reinforcement that can occur between media selectivity and media effects when trying to account for effects on beliefs, behavior, and identity.[12] Slater proposes the "reinforcing spirals framework" for understanding mutual influence between two different processes—media effects and media exposure. The approach aims to explain the ways media exposure and media effects mutually reinforce one another and to account for socialization and the "maintenance of political, religious, lifestyle subcultures in contemporary societies."[13]

The basic theory is elaborated in a series of research-driven propositions. The first posits that media exposure is itself an object of explanation and not simply a causal factor in accounting for people's attitudes, opinions, and social identities. The proposition moves the study of media effects from exposure as a force accounting for outcomes to exposure as an object of explanation. Within this framework, one asks not just what the effects of exposure to the conservative media establishment are but what leads to exposure in the first place.

The second proposition suggests that typical media outcomes, such as opinions and attitudes and other factors related to personal and social identity, themselves influence media exposure. This of course is the classic claim about selective exposure, which confounds most media effect studies. This proposition is captured by the notion of the echo chamber—suggesting that a large percentage of people who listen to conservative political talk radio come to this medium already disposed toward content that is consistent with their previously held opinions and attitudes.

The third proposition links the first two and raises the possibility of "spirals" of effects. If prior opinion leads to exposure to media content consistent with that opinion, and this exposure at a minimum confirms the prior opinion or even makes it more extreme, then the spiral is positive and the sounds heard in the chamber are indeed echoes of initial opinion. The only conditions under which the mutual causal relationship between media exposure and media effects might not be mutually reinforcing is when the effects of media messages boomerang, as occurred for example in 1996 in some of Limbaugh's attempts to undermine the candidacy of Pat Buchanan, a political figure much admired by Limbaugh's audience (see chapter 7). Otherwise, most of the processes we describe in this book are mutually reinforcing spirals of effect and exposure.

The fourth proposition has two parts and is focused primarily on how closed or open a person's media exposure is to alternative sources of information. In a perfectly closed system, in which a person is exposed only to ideologically pure media content, spirals of media selectivity and effects would have their maximum consequences. Environmental influences and other social influences that produce more open systems will limit the mutual reinforcement spirals described by the theory. A central question in our assessment of the audiences of conservative media is the extent to which they are open to alternative, ideologically uncongenial media sources. We ask: Is the chamber increasingly open or closed in the face of more media outlets with more varied political content?

Because social and personal identities are also at play in this process, they are the subject of Slater's fifth, sixth, and seventh propositions. "Personal identity" refers to the way individuals differ in their preference for, say, more complex material or for violent material; differences in self-identity also may be reflected in differences in individual opinions, attitudes, and beliefs that are characteristic of political environments. "Social identity" refers more to identification with social groups—whether religious, polit- ical, or ideological—or interest groups. The fifth proposition states that individuals with a particular social identity—for example, conservatives or liberals—would be expected to prefer media outlets whose content is consis- tent with their ideological presuppositions. We will explore this basic claim in the next chapter in our discussion of demographic differences in exposure to different media.

The sixth proposition refers to the other side of the causal sequence: a person's use of a particular media source consistent with his or her social identity will make that identity more salient and accessible to that person. In turn, specific aspects of social identity could very well be influenced by the content one selects. This proposition is of special importance in the Echo Chamber, because it hypothesizes an effect on those in the chamber that pro- duces self-affirmation and confirmation of their prior views, a consequence seldom identified in media effects research.

The seventh proposition suggests that interpersonal communication with others in general can reinforce the dynamic patterns of media exposure and effects by reinforcing them in turn.

The final propositions of Slater's theory focus on the consequences of more closed communication systems. Closed systems, Slater argues, are ones that are more univocal and homogeneous in their content. In contrast to more open systems, which are characterized by diversity of opinion and heteroge- neity of content, audiences in closed systems—that is, audiences that close themselves off to alternative perspectives—will exhibit strong social identi- fication with the target group and increase their tendency to view out-group members from an antagonistic frame. In later chapters, we explore the use of sarcasm, irony, specialized codes, emotional labels, and so on among talk radio hosts as techniques to reinforce identification and increase cohesion for those who are a part of the conservative in-group.

Implications of Slater's Theory for Studying the Echo Chamber

The propositions in Slater's theory about media effects and media selectivity will help us focus on exposure to media and effects that are less obvious than direct changes in opinions, attitudes, beliefs, and behaviors. In addition, Slater argues that media exposure and media effects are both causes and effects themselves. This simultaneity means that to ask how to untangle which is cause and which is effect is to pose the wrong questions.

So in the complexities of the media environment in which effects and exposure intertwine, it is necessary to (1) recognize the limits of causal claims; (2) recognize that exposure is an outcome as much as a cause; (3) seek and use dynamic data to untangle causal priority where feasible; and (4) employ experimental data to establish causal priority where possible.

Data Sources

In the chapters that follow, we employ a wide variety of data to build our circumstantial case about the effects of the conservative media establishment on its audiences and on the public more broadly. Five core sources of data are employed: (1) the 1996 Political Talk Radio (PTR) Survey, done over five periods from February through November; (2) the 1996 PTR Experiment; (3) the 2000 National Annenberg Election Study (NAES 2000); (4) the 2004 National Annenberg Election Study (NAES 2004); and (5) the 2008 National Annenberg Election Study (NAES 2008). Since we will refer to these data several times in different chapters, we will describe each briefly here to give a sense of the kinds of data we generated and employed. (We will refer to the five sets as PTR Survey 1996, PTR Experiment 1996, NAES 2000, NAES 2004, and NAES 2008. When data from sources other than these five are employed, they will be described briefly in the text.)

PTR SURVEY 1996

During the presidential election year of 1996, a five-wave survey of regular and nonregular listeners of PTR was conducted. All surveys were conducted on the telephone by Princeton Survey Research Associates. Survey respondents were divided into four groups: (1) nonlisteners; (2) regular listeners to Limbaugh only; (3) regular listeners to conservative shows but not to Limbaugh; (4) regular listeners to moderate or liberal shows (and not to Limbaugh). A fifth group of regular listeners—those listening to Limbaugh and a second show regularly—was excluded from study. Regular listeners were those who listened to PTR at least twice a week. In the initial survey, 1,203 respondents were sampled; an oversample of regular listeners pushed the final sample to 1,666. Unlike our other studies and most other studies of PTR, this one focused on regular listeners; in other words, it did not mix heavy with occasional ones. Differences between PTR consumers and others in this study reflect differences between heavy consumers and occasional and nonlisteners. The initial sample was reinterviewed twice more during the election year's primary period.

Care was taken to define to respondents what we meant by "political talk radio"—"where the host talks mostly about politics, government, and public affairs. Sometimes listeners are invited to call in to discuss these issues on the air." Some of the early studies of talk radio did not distinguish political talk from other forms of talk radio that can be about health, car maintenance, personal psychology, relationships, and sports, among other topics.

Previous research on PTR identified those listening to Limbaugh and those listening to PTR in general. Our procedures indicate that many regular listeners to Limbaugh are also regular listeners of other PTR. Of the 18% of the initial sample who listen to at least one show regularly, roughly 1 in 6 is listening to two or more shows. These findings mean that previous surveys of "Limbaugh listeners" are really surveys of a mix of Limbaugh and other listeners. And previous surveys of "PTR Listeners" are surveys of Limbaugh listeners and listeners to other hosts. In the PTR Survey 1996, when we refer to Limbaugh listeners, they are regular listeners to Limbaugh who are not regular listeners to other hosts.

Those listening to other PTR hosts were further divided into two sub-groups: regular consumers of *conservative PTR* and regular consumers of *liberal/moderate PTR*.[14] The reason that moderate and liberal program listeners were combined to form a single group designated liberal/moderate throughout our discussions is that the number listening to liberal and moderate hosts was too small to permit separate analysis of each. Four groups were studied: three groups of regular listeners—Limbaugh only (N = 213), conservative PTR (N = 139), and liberal/moderate PTR (N = 283)—and a group of non-listeners (N = 988). Distributions of respondents by listening group in the first three waves are summarized in the appendix to this chapter (located on our website).

We followed the first three panels of talk radio listeners and their nonlistening counterparts during the primary period of 1996 as well as during the fall presidential election. The fourth wave took place October 17–27, 1996, immediately following the second presidential debate between Bill Clinton and Robert Dole. The fifth wave was carried out in the period November 12–18, 1996, in the week following the presidential election.

The fourth wave surveyed 1,376 people, and the fifth included 973. Those agreeing to be surveyed received a $10 phone card.

The goal was to follow people from the primaries through the conclusion of the election. In order to ensure that there was a sufficiently large sample to carry out analysis of the election period alone, those sampled during the primary season were supplemented by additional participants. The appendix to this chapter describes how many persons continued from the initial sample and how many were new (see the website for sampling details).

Overall, a total of 2,402 respondents participated in the study. Statistical comparisons were made to examine differences in the character of the sample across waves as people dropped out or were added. Few statistically significant differences emerged, and the samples remained comparable on demographic attributes (age, gender, education, income, and race), thus reducing concerns about the comparability of the sample across waves.

PTR EXPERIMENT 1996

During the week of May 12–18, 1996, in a research project carried out in the Philadelphia metropolitan area, participants were required to listen to five hours of PTR taken off the air and provided to them on audiotapes. People were randomly assigned to listen to one or another type of talk radio, ranging from nonpolitical talk (NPR's *Car Talk*) to the highly partisan Limbaugh. They were surveyed before and after on a variety of issues related to social attitudes, perceptions of the programs and hosts, participation in political matters, and knowledge of politics and social issues.

In the experiment, people listened to five hours of audiotapes—one each day—that we gave them. The tapes had been prerecorded with various types of PTR content spanning the spectrum from liberal to conservative. Our intent was to simulate exposure to PTR of different types for people who had had experience with PTR and for people who had not. We were especially interested in the effects of different types of PTR on people of different political stripes and with differential experience with the format. One of the problems with survey studies of PTR is that the audience that listens to a particular host self-selects the program on the basis of content, whether the bent of the content is sampled by the listener or presumed. One cannot easily know if the audience is affected by the content or is already disposed toward the host's views and chooses to become a regular member of the listening audience. In an experiment, people agree to participate in a study of radio formats and are assigned content randomly so the forces of selective exposure are minimized—although selective attention and perception can certainly operate.

People were recruited to participate for pay ($70) in a study purportedly about the evaluation of radio formats. More than 400 people agreed to be in our study (N = 442), and after initial dropouts, our sample was reduced by 19. Their average age was 41 years; 41.4% were male; 46.8% had never been married; modal income was $30,000 to 50,000 per year for the household; 3.8% were Hispanic or Latino, 11.3% African American, 83.2% Caucasian, and 5.2% Asian and other. The group was predominantly Democrats (43%), with 20.6% Republicans and 34% Independents. Those identifying themselves as ideologically moderate dominated the group (44.9%), with liberals next (37.8%) and conservatives fewest (15.9%). The sample was highly educated, with 41.8% having at least a college degree and 28.8% some college; 19.2% had a high school degree or less. Both heavy and light consumers of PTR were represented, with 46.8% listening at least three times per week and 42.7% participating two or fewer days per week.

The design of the experiment was simple. Participants were randomly assigned to one of six conditions. Each person received five one-hour tapes and an initial questionnaire. Anyone needing a tape player was given one to keep, and their payment was reduced by $20.

Six conditions were created on the basis of the kind of PTR that people received. The six groups were:

Group 1: Control (talk radio that was not political)
Group 2: Conservative PTR (not including Limbaugh)
Group 3: Liberal PTR
Group 4: Limbaugh
Group 5: Conservative and liberal mix (taken from groups 2, 3, and 4)
Group 6: NPR's PTR show *Talk of the Nation*

Participants were randomly assigned to their conditions, except that we tried to ensure an equal distribution across conditions of regular and infrequent listeners and conservatives and liberals. We checked whether people listened to the tapes, how they listened, and whether they followed instructions. (For the details about how well participants followed our instructions during the week see the website www.annenbergpublicpolicycenter.org).

The content of the programming in each condition was selected from PTR shows appearing in the period January 15, 1996, to April 30, 1996.

We attempted to control content across conditions by choosing topics that had been treated across the ideological spectrum. Five topics were found: affirmative action (more generally, the role of government in assisting minorities because of past discrimination); assisted suicide; problems in the educational system; the proposal for a flat income tax; the Muslim religion (specifically Minister Louis Farrakhan and the Muslim National Basketball Association player Mahmoud Abdul-Rauf). Each of these had been discussed in the period by liberal and conservative hosts, by Limbaugh, and on *Talk of the Nation*. The liberal and conservative points of view were represented through the programming of several different hosts, including G. Gordon Liddy, Ken Hamblin, Mario Cuomo, and Tom Leykis. The Annenberg Public Policy Center website for the book describes in detail the hosts, the content, and the days of the week each were consumed.

NAES 2000, NAES 2004, AND NAES 2008

These three surveys were conducted during the presidential campaign cycles in the years 2000, 2004, and 2008. The surveys sampled adults and interviewed them by telephone on a wide variety of topics pertinent to the elections. These topics include an extensive battery of questions about the media, including exposure and opinions, political participation, opinions about candidates, groups, and issues, political knowledge, voting behavior and attitudes, participant demographic, and other topics. These surveys are the largest academic studies of the American electorate ever conducted within a campaign cycle.[15] The 2004 survey included more than 79,000 respondents and 2004 more than 86,000. The data we report from the NAES 2008 survey were drawn from interviews conducted during the early primaries of 2008. When multiple interviews with the same person are included, the number of interviews in 2000 and 2004 is in the vicinity of 100,000 each year. These surveys have unique design characteristics (called a "rolling cross-section") that are not the focus in this book. However, these surveys do ask questions about specific PTR hosts, specific newspapers, and specific news networks that allow us to take advantage of some of these data for our study of the conservative media establishment. However, the surveys focused primarily on the presidential campaigns of 2000 and 2004 and not on the conservative media establishment. The data from the 2000 and 2004 surveys are already available to the public, along with extensive discussion and analysis of the results. We will not describe the samples, designs, or questions posed in them but invite readers to consult other sources for additional details.[16]

Conclusions

In the chapters that follow, we will build our case for the effects produced by the conservative media establishment. The complex interplay of media selectivity and media effects will produce a case that is circumstantial, an outcome that Richard Miller argues characterizes scientific claims throughout the natural and social sciences.[17] In the context of a particular claim, we will do our best to help the reader understand the kinds of data we have marshaled and the strength of the causal claim we are able to make.

Speaking to the Republican Base:
An Analysis of Conservative Media's Audience

In an op-ed in the *Wall Street Journal,* Limbaugh has proclaimed that conservatives believe in "individual liberty, limited government, capitalism, the rule of law, faith, a color-blind society and national security."[1] The *Journal*'s editorial page has said that it stands for "free people and free markets."[2] Embedded in any communication is an image of the speaker and of the intended audience.[3] As the telegraphy in this language suggests, the audience implied by and drawn to Limbaugh, the Fox News shows on which we focus, and the editorial pages of the *Journal* is a combination of groups whose loyalty to the Republican Party increases its chances for electoral success.

The Republican base is more conservative, and more likely to be male, white, upper-class, churchgoing, and southern than the Democratic coalition. In 2004, incumbent president George W. Bush carried the majority of voters in all of these categories. With some segments, the win was substantial. More than 8 in 10 of the self-identified conservatives supported Bush, as did a solid majority of those who attended church weekly or more often. Exit polls also found that 55% of all men and 62% of the white male voters did the same—as did 6 of 10 white voters and 54% of those over 60, as well as a majority of individuals with incomes of $50,000 or higher.[4]

This does not mean that any one of these media draws large numbers from across the entire Republican base. Like the Republican Party base, the audience for Fox and Limbaugh tends to be disproportionately white, of above average income, older, churchgoing, and southern. Like the core Republican voter, those tuning to Limbaugh or reaching for the *Journal* are more likely male than female. Whereas those drawn to Fox and Limbaugh are more likely to be upper middle class, the *Journal*'s readers are on average securely in the upper class. Conservatives are more likely to be found reading, watching, and listening to these outlets than liberals.

In this chapter, we focus on the ways the issue positions of *Limbaugh* and the *Journal* resonate with the groups that make up the Republican

TABLE 6.1. Demographic differences in 2004 among audiences for Fox News,
Limbaugh, and WSJ (2004 NAES. Unweighted data)

	Fox **	Limbaugh***	WSJ****
	n=17,548	n=1,640	n=1,020
Age (median)	49	53	48
Gender	50.1% male	66.6% male	68.2% male
Race (white)	85%	92.9%	85.9%
Income	–		
$100–150,000	11.3%	13.9%	22.4%
150,000+	7.7%	10.7%	30.4%
Churchgoing			
Once a wk or more	46.6%	53.4%	37.8%
Geographic loc*.	38.6% South	37.5% South	27% South
% Republican	55.2%	78.0%	51.0%
% Conservative	59.2%	85%	46.4%

(*States defined as Southern: Florida, Georgia, North and South Carolina, Virginia, West
Virginia, Alabama, Kentucky, Mississippi, Tennessee, Arkansas, Louisiana, Oklahoma,
and Texas.
**Which of the cable news networks would you say you watch most often—Fox News
Channel, CNN or MSNBC?
***Which talk radio hosts or radio programs did you listen to most often (those listing
Limbaugh first)?
****What newspaper did you read most in the past week?)

base and illustrate at the same time the different style and tone that characterize these two media sources.[5] Our focus is largely on the *Journal* and
Limbaugh and only to a lesser extent on *Hannity and Colmes* and *Special
Report with Brit Hume* because some of our analysis addresses periods in
which Fox News was either not yet available or in the process of building
its audience.

In the past two decades, conservatives have developed media, including
talk radio shows, newsletters, books, and websites, that address and attract
audiences that are more likely than not to include the older white male
with higher than average income who is conservative and politically active.
This is a desirable audience for advertisers because the skew of its income
means that it has money to spend on advertised products. It is an attractive

audience for Republicans because the typical listener is more likely to cast a Republican than a Democratic ballot.

Creating an Audience

The content and tone of the *Journal*'s editorial pages and Limbaugh's message on his radio show, in his books, on his website, and in his newsletter, combine what rhetorical critic Edwin Black called the first persona—that of the speaker, Limbaugh—and the second, the implied audience, in a fashion that invites attention from the audience indispensable to Republican political victory: an audience of fiscal and social conservatives. Limbaugh's various channels of communication articulate a rhetoric designed to shore up the Republican base. At the same time, as we showed in chapter 2, he is careful to invite Hispanics and African Americans into the Republican fold. The same is true of the nation's most read conservative editorial pages. In this chapter, we show the *Journal* and Limbaugh's consistent appeal to the Republican base and examine the alignment between the target constituency of the Republican Party and the audience of the conservative opinion media.

Primarily Republican and Conservative

The audiences for Fox, Limbaugh, and the *Journal* are more conservative than liberal, with the highest percent of moderates and liberals in the *Journal*'s audience and the largest percent of conservatives in Limbaugh's. With its higher income and educational level, the *Journal*'s audience members are more upscale and hence more financially secure. This profile means that the *Journal*'s readership is more likely to contain groups traditionally called "business conservatives" or "country club conservatives."

Importantly, the audience for the nation's most widely read financial pages is less Republican and more socially liberal than that of Fox and Limbaugh. The NAES 2004 data indicate that the *Journal*'s readership is more socially liberal than the audiences for Fox or Limbaugh, while Limbaugh's listenership is more economically conservative than the audiences for the other two. For example, the median respondent in Limbaugh's audience "somewhat favors" making abortion more difficult to obtain; the same is true of the median attitude among Fox viewers. By contrast, the median reader of the *Journal* "somewhat opposes" making abortion more difficult to obtain. But whereas the median position among *Journal* readers and Fox watchers "somewhat opposes" repeal of the Bush tax cuts, the median Limbaugh listener strongly opposes repeal. While *Journal* readers in 2004 held that the Iraq war was worth it, the percent holding that view was lower (60.9%) than the comparable figures in the audiences of Fox (73.1%) and Limbaugh (91.3%). At the time of the survey, 48.7% of the public at large held the same position. As our examples will demonstrate, where Limbaugh and the *Journal* differ on issues, the *Journal* generally holds the more moderate social position.

We start with a reminder that the *Journal* and Limbaugh both attract numbers at the top of the rankings for those in their medium. Despite slightly different definitions of what constitutes a Limbaugh listener, our surveys reliably suggest that about 6–8% of the U.S. adult population listens to his show in a given week.[6] Surveys done by the Annenberg School in 1996, 2000, and 2004 confirm that that audience is overwhelmingly Republican and ideologically conservative.[7]

Figure 6.1 compares the percentage of Democrats, Republicans, and Independents who listen to Limbaugh, listen to other talk radio hosts, or do not listen at all to PTR.[8]

As the chart indicates, those listening to Limbaugh in each of the past three general election presidential periods are overwhelmingly Republican (about 63%), with some identifying as Independents (about 23%), and a scattering of Democrats (about 12%). Over the period from 1996 to 2004, Limbaugh's audience has become increasingly Republican and less Independent

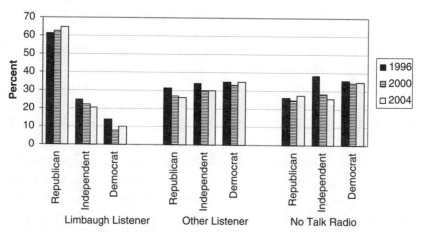

FIGURE 6.1. Percentage of audience made up of Democrats, Republicans, or Independents by PTR host (Limbaugh, other, and none) and presidential election year.

and Democrat. By contrast, those listening to other hosts are more evenly distributed among the political parties, despite the fact that conservative talk radio shows substantially outnumber liberal ones.

An Annenberg Foundation Trust at Sunnylands' survey in 2003 confirmed that talk radio continues to be more popular among Republicans and Independents than Democrats.[9] A majority of Republicans (60%) and Independents (60%) listen to talk radio at least monthly, compared to fewer than half of Democrats (46%). More than a third of Republicans (39%) and Independents (36%) listen to talk radio every week.

Limbaugh attracts a remarkably high number of those who consider themselves Republicans. In 2003, nearly a quarter of those who so self-identified (22%) listened to Limbaugh every week, and more than a third (37%) at least once a month. Self-identified Independents weren't far behind; 2 in 10 (20%) also listened to Limbaugh at least once a month. However, fewer than 1 in 10 Democrats (9%) reported ever listening to Limbaugh's show.

By contrast, in 2003 the audience for NPR was ideologically balanced, with Independents (34%) more disposed to listen to NPR weekly than either Democrats (25%) or Republicans (22%). Four in 10 Republicans (40%) and Democrats (41%) and nearly half of Independents (47%) listened to NPR at least once a month.[10] A year later, the much larger NAES 2004 painted a different picture. Of those (N = 469) who reported that NPR was the radio program to which they listened most often, 21.7% self-identified as conservatives, 38.6% as moderates, and 38.6% as liberals. The percent saying that they were Democrats held at the level we found in 2003, 40.7%, but the percent identifying as Republicans dropped to 25.5%.

Those identifying themselves as Limbaugh listeners were even more conservative than they were Republican, suggesting that Limbaugh listeners self–identifying as Independents and Democrats are more likely to be on the conservative side of their ideological groups. Figure 6.2 reports these percentages.

The ideological distribution of Limbaugh listeners remained roughly the same between 1996 and 2004, with approximately 70% of listeners reporting being conservative in 1996, 2000, and 2004. (In 2004, 85% of those who listened to Limbaugh "most often," i.e., more often than other radio hosts or programs, self-identified as conservative.) The listeners who called themselves liberal ranged in percent between 1996 and 2004, from 8.6% to 6.2%. The ideological makeup of listeners to other kinds of talk radio was also relatively stable, with conservatives remaining approximately the same and liberals shifting almost imperceptibly between 1996 and 2004 (33.5% to 33.8% and 23.8% to 26.7%, respectively). The proportion of moderates

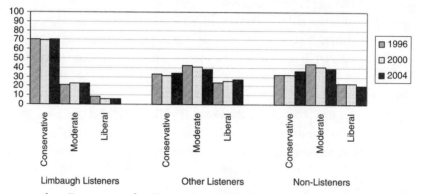

Ideology by Type of Listeners

FIGURE 6.2. Percentage of audience who are Liberal, Moderate, or Conservative by PTR host (Limbaugh, other, and none) and presidential election year.

listening to other kinds of talk radio decreased slightly during the same time period (42.6% to 38.1%).

The 2004 (NAES 2004) audience for Fox (FNC) is also more conservative than liberal, with 59.2% of Fox viewers identifying as conservative, 30.4% as moderate, and 10.4% as liberal. So, too, although less so, for the *Journal,* where 46.4% of readers identify as conservatives, 39.3% as moderates, and 14.3% as liberal. (We do recognize that the profile of the person who reads the news pages of the *Journal* may differ from the person who reads both the news section and opinion pages or the opinion pages alone. We have no reliable way to isolate those in the second two categories.) In the remainder of this chapter, we examine the issue alignment between four central Republican groups: middle- and upper-class earners, churchgoers, men, and southerners and the kind of conservatism championed by Limbaugh and the *Journal*; we also illustrate the similar and dissimilar ways each medium's conservative exemplar speaks to the economic, gender, religious, and regional interests of its audiences.

Middle- and Upper-Class Earners

At any moment, every person has multiple possible social identities. Rhetoric invites us to feature some of those self-concepts over others: child or parent, northerner or southerner, believer or atheist, liberal or conservative. The conservative media's focus on economic issues invites their audience to see themselves in the role of taxpayer, and to see the economic system in terms of entrepreneurial capitalism, individual initiative, and free markets.

ISSUE POSITIONS

With the exception of the tax increases during the presidency of George H. W. Bush, which the *Journal* and Limbaugh opposed, conservatives can cite the fact that in general Republicans have stood for lowering the marginal tax rate on income. Under Reagan's leadership, the top marginal tax rate on income was reduced from 70% in 1980 to 38.5% in 1987.

The conservative opinion media share the conviction that, in Limbaugh's words, "cuts in marginal tax rates spur economic growth by providing entrepreneurs an incentive to invest their marginal tax dollars, causing many of them to earn more money and pay more taxes on their earnings, albeit at a lower marginal rate, and create new jobs."[11] Promises that fiscal conservatism will spell both more jobs and growth for business appeal directly to both the upper middle class and the upper class. "Tax cuts spur economic growth by improving incentives to work and invest and by making more money available for new ventures and small business, where the real job growth occurs in our economy,"[12] says the *Journal*. Both the *Journal* and Limbaugh favor making the tax cuts put in place under President George W. Bush permanent.

The message the conservative opinion media offer speaks directly both to the worries of the middle-class older male and the self-interest of the upper-class reader: You are overtaxed and overregulated by a government that gives unfair breaks to others, Limbaugh tells his listeners. You deserve your wealth and invest it for socially productive ends, the *Journal* tells its readers. Both suggest that conservative leaders have and will continue to cut taxes and burdensome regulation. The same views are found on Fox. "I believe in the [Reagan] economic theory," notes Sean Hannity. "Economically, we're cutting taxes and we're reaping the rewards."[13] Fox's Brit Hume is a Reagan fan as well. Reagan, he has noted, "believed that...our system of economy in particular was the right one....We were not free enough economically. The taxes were too high. Regulations were too stiff, and so on....He was right."[14]

Limbaugh's listeners' average income places them securely in the middle class. Unsurprisingly, his political discussion focuses on the economic interests not of the poor or lower middle class but of this target audience. The rhetoric constitutes an extended argument that this group's interests align with the Republican and not the Democratic Party. The idea of tax cuts is appealing to this group because, unlike those in the lower income brackets, these listeners are likely to pay both payroll and income taxes. Democrats will argue that this appeal to the middle class is a ruse that tricks gullible citizens into votes that benefit not them but the rich and large corporations. Republicans respond that the middle class benefits from income tax cuts both directly and indirectly.

ECONOMIC ANXIETY

When Limbaugh's show was nationally syndicated in 1988, his ideas played to the economic anxiety of the time. Buying power was down and joblessness up. In the 1980s, the purchasing power of the middle class dropped. In 1988, the unemployment rate was 5.5%. By 1992, it had reached 7.5%. It was not until after 1996 that it dropped below 5%.[15]

Nor were those in the labor market working in conditions conducive to feelings of economic security. A comparison of two groups of young men, the first entering the labor force in 1966, the second in 1979, demonstrated that in their first 15 years in the labor market the 1979 entrants had lower real wages than those who drew their first paycheck in the mid-sixties. [16] Increases in gross family income were likely to reflect not a real increase in the wages of one member of the family but rather entry of a second family member into the labor market.[17] Despite the prosperity of the 1990s, "the top 20 percent of earners were the only group to increase its share of the nation's income."[18]

Liberals translated these data into concerns about income inequality, conservatives to reminders that those in the highest income bracket paid the largest numbers of dollars in taxes. In the late eighties, with a Republican in the White House and the Congress in Democrats' control, Limbaugh directed the economic anxieties of his audience toward taking back Congress from the "tax and spend" "liberals." Once Clinton was elected, that appeal changed to attacking the incumbent president and his policies and arguing for turnover in Congress. As noted, influential Republicans credit Limbaugh with an important role in the Gingrich revolution that ended 40 years of Democratic control of the House in the middle of Clinton's first term. With a Republican president in the White House and Congress in Republican hands, Limbaugh kept up his attacks on Democratic tax and regulatory policies and, as we will show in the next chapter, worked to ensure that the Republicans seeking the presidency stayed true to Reaganesque conservatism.

Because Limbaugh's is a middle-class audience and the *Journal*'s an upper-middle- to upper-class one, neither is likely to be personally affected by such central Democratic agenda items as raising the minimum wage and universal

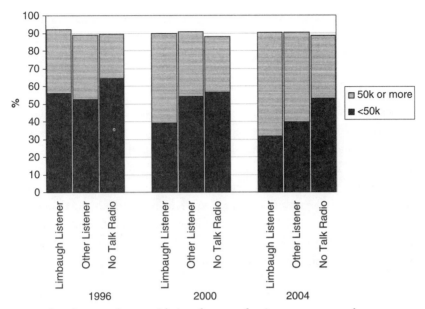

Income by Type of Listener (1996, 2000, and 2004)

FIGURE 6.3. Income above and below $50,000 for three groups: 1996, 2000, 2004.

health insurance. These listeners and readers are receptive, as a result, to the conservative claim that what raising the minimum wage does is cut the number of jobs. Because it is not wealthy, Limbaugh's audience has cause to worry about the cost and availability of health care and is thus susceptible to the conservative claim in 1993–94 that under the proposed Clinton health care reform plan, care would be rationed and government would obstruct the access that those with insurance currently have to quality care.

There is a difference on average in the income of those who listen to Limbaugh and those who do not. In the year 2004, about 67% of Limbaugh's audience members reported incomes above $50,000 per year; in 2000, the percentage was about 55%; in 1996, about 40%. By contrast, the majority of the audience that does not report listening to PTR has incomes under $50,000 per year.

One of the reasons conservatives are better than liberals at attracting the sponsorship needed to attract a large audience for political rhetoric in the form of radio, newsletters, and books is that the conservative audience Limbaugh and the *Journal* attract is a desirable target for advertisers. With the exception of NPR and paid satellite services, talk radio in the United States is funded by those who are selling products and services. Overall, of course, Republicans tend to have higher incomes than Democrats.

With higher income also comes access to the alternative technology that increases access to talk radio. Even in the early days of our study, Limbaugh listeners were more likely than nonlisteners to have access to the internet and to spend time online looking at information about the presidential campaign.[19] Limbaugh streams the audio of his show on his website. The editorial pages of the *Journal* are available online at no charge as well.

Throughout our study but especially in the early years, both those of higher income and men have been more likely to own a computer than others—hence have access to Limbaugh's website. They are more likely to own multiple cell phones, hence to be able to call in. They are more likely to hold the sorts of jobs that permit listening to talk radio. And men are more likely than women to use the Internet. The NAES 2000 survey found that Limbaugh listeners also were more likely to have cable or satellite access at home. They watched more cable news and read newspapers more than other people.

Churchgoers

Limbaugh listeners are more likely than nonlisteners and more likely than *Journal* readers to be churchgoers. In our 2000 survey, 62% of his audience claimed to attend church services at least one to two times per month. In contrast, fewer listeners to other hosts (54%) and nonlisteners (56%) attended at that rate. More of his listeners identify themselves as born-again Christians (39%, 38%, and 42% in three surveys from 1996 to 2004) than do listeners to other talk radio (23%, 36%, and 32%) and nonlisteners (30%, 36%, and 37%). As figure 6.1 indicates, in NAES 2004, Limbaugh's listeners were the most frequent churchgoers of those in the conservative media's audience, and the *Journal*'s readers were the least.

Still, the *Journal* creates editorials hospitable to churchgoers when it champions adoption,[20] argues that "short of unimaginable police tactics" one cannot reasonably suppose that "teaching about religion can be divorced from the American education with which it is inextricably bound up as a central fact of our heritage,"[21] and suggests that "the school prayer decision is a symbol of what's wrong with the activist judiciary" while proposing a text for a school prayer amendment to the Constitution.[22] These are positions Limbaugh shares.

For religious conservatives, politics and religion mesh to create a world-view opposed to moral relativism. "The umbrella under which all of the other things like abortion would come," says Limbaugh, "is moral absolutes. These are people who have a definite idea of what's right and wrong, what is sinful and virtuous and they're not afraid of saying so, and at the same time they are viewed to be people who condemn others for their moral failures." Attacks on moral relativism tap a core value that is then tied to issue positions on such issues as abortion and stem cell research.

The focus on concerns relevant to churchgoers characterizes Fox's treatment of what its regular hosts portray as an attack on Christmas.

> For much of the day, FNC grinds out news that looks a lot like what everyone else offers but with snappier graphics and faster pacing. You have to pay attention to understand stories they do, like the current obsession with anything perceived as anti-Christmas (such as a ban on public displays of Christian celebration), to understand there is always an agenda.[23]

As Limbaugh's defense of the Mel Gibson's movie *The Passion* suggests, conservative media defend the concerns of the churchgoing audience. "So now what does the left attack the President for?" Limbaugh asked in his April 2004 newsletter.

> His belief in God! . . . Well, I'm going to predict something. If enough voters hear Bob Woodward berate Bush for relying on God, get ready for it. "The Passion of the Christ II" at the polls. . . . Let them impugn the President of the United States for his belief in the Almighty, let them impugn the President of the United States for his admitting that he prays for the safety of troops and the American people, let them make fun of him for that. They're going to pay the price.

Using the contrastive rhetoric we examined in chapter 1, Limbaugh characterized Kerry's base by saying, "They hate God; they hate people of religion. They're afraid of them."[24]

Older, Educated White Males with Higher-Than-Average Incomes

On issues, the conservative message appeals to men more than women. Few issues are as directly focused on gender as the questions whether the Constitution should be amended to enshrine equal rights for women, and whether *Roe v. Wade* should be modified or overturned. Answers to these questions divide on gender lines. The 1980 platform of the Republican Party opposed the Equal Rights Amendment (ERA) and pledged to appoint federal judges who respected "the sanctity of innocent life." Consistent with the notion that its audience is more socially liberal, as we note elsewhere, the *Journal* did not take a strong stand against the decision in *Roe v. Wade* or against the ERA. The battle over the ERA had ended long before Limbaugh was nationally syndicated. Limbaugh and the Republican Party are in lockstep, however, on many of the issues that divide men and women voters. More women than men favor family medical leave. Republican men are more likely than Republican women to be prolife. More men than women oppose gun control, including the assault weapons ban.

Limbaugh and the Republican Party are also in tune with the circumstances in which men are more likely to find themselves than women. More women than men make the minimum wage; Limbaugh and the *Journal* oppose increases in it. Women are the beneficiaries of public affirmative action; Limbaugh and the *Journal* oppose it as "quotas." And, importantly, men are more likely to be economically well-off than women, a status that means that on average they are more likely than women to be advantaged by Republican tax policies. Specifically, "with the increase in single females from 1960 to 2000, females have become a notably larger share of the lowest [income] quintile respondents and a smaller share of the top quintile."[25]

Because the audiences for the *Journal*, Fox, and Limbaugh's show are predominantly white, championing "equal opportunity" and opposing "quotas" has special relevance to them. The *Journal* argues that "the application of racial and gender quotas has become a corrupting and divisive process that violates our Constitutional heritage of equal rights and fairness."[26] "I made the point in the early eighties, mid eighties when this all started," Limbaugh recalled in April 2007. "Affirmative action is about making sure that the race wars never end" (April 12, 2007).

The Limbaugh audience remained disproportionately male between 1996 and 2004, with 61% of listeners on that half of the gender divide in 1996 and 64.2% in 2004. Limbaugh attracts a higher percentage of male listeners (above 60%) than do other hosts overall. This difference remained relatively stable from 1996 to 2004.[27] Both the *Journal* and Limbaugh attract significantly more men than women. Whereas most cable networks attract more women than men, Fox attracts each in about equal numbers.

Nowhere are the stylistic differences clearer between Limbaugh's barroom approach to issues and the *Journal*'s seminar-like discussions than on feminism. Whereas Limbaugh paints with a broad brush, dismissing all feminists on some shows, the *Journal* marks off those who hold what its sees as extreme views. "For years, I've been telling you that the feminist leadership is basically anti-male," noted Limbaugh in the early 1990s.[28] Limbaugh has consistently treated feminism as a nemesis. "I blast feminists because they're liberal," he reports in 2007. "Feminism is liberal. It screwed women up as I was coming of age in my early twenties.... It changed naturally designed roles and behaviors and basically, they're trying to change human nature which they can't do" (May 21, 2007). Limbaugh famously coined the term "femi-Nazi" as a derogatory term for "a very small, hard-core group of militants" that he says in his second book he distinguishes "from well-intentioned but misguided people who call themselves 'feminists.'"[29] Limbaugh's Life Truth Number 24, posted on his website, is that "feminism was established so as to allow unattractive women easier access to the mainstream of society." There is apparently no comparable movement to facilitate the social integration of unattractive men.

The more measured tone of the *Journal* was on display in its editorial "Equality and the Equal Rights Amendment," in which it acknowledged that women were discriminated "against in several vital ways (unequal pay for equal work) and many lesser but still important ways (denial of credit, laws regulating their occupations and hours of work, giving brothers preference over sisters in administering estates)" but added that it had some doubts about whether these concerns rose to the level needed to justify amending the Constitution. At the same time, the *Journal* castigated "the ultra liberal feminists who blur distinctions and appear bent on creating animosities where none existed" and the "ideological frenzy that seeks to portray motherhood and marriage as somehow morally corrupt and intellectually debilitating."[30] The audience envisioned by the *Journal* editorial is the business community. So the piece suggests that "private employers who treat women as merely a fractional equivalent of males deserve all the wrath and censure their discriminatory policy brings down upon them."

Southerners

The solid Republican South has been the foundation on which Republican presidential candidates since Richard Nixon have built electoral majorities. As table 6.1 shows, both Fox and Limbaugh draw more than 1 in 3 of their audience members from that region. Since in the next chapter we argue that Limbaugh builds his attack on cultural elites on the premise that they despise southerners, we will reserve discussion of the ways the conservative media speak to this segment of the country for that chapter.

In sum, Limbaugh and the *Journal* justify the policies of conservative Reagan Republicanism to a target audience that is disproportionately male, upper-middle-class and upper-class, churchgoing, and southern. This audience constitutes both the Republican base and, if it remains loyal, the electorate required to ensure election of a Republican president. In the next chapter, we begin our examination of the functions performed by the conservative opinion media by showing how the *Journal* and Limbaugh vetted Republican candidates in presidential primaries in 1992–2008 and have held those elected accountable to their brand of Reagan conservatism.

Vetting Candidates for Office

In days gone by, party power brokers safeguarded their constituencies' interests by selecting candidates who delivered the promised agenda once in office. Dependent on their party for resources and workers, candidates and officeholders toed the party line. Those toying with ideological defection knew that doing so risked the loss of the resources required to be nominated or elected. In the candidate-party relationship, the party had the upper hand. One result was a political arena brimming with party-reliant, party-representing officeholders.

Direct state-run primaries and the ability of candidates to appeal to voters through the mass media turned that world on its head. No longer could parties control the selection of candidates. Now the party was as likely to reflect the nominee as the nominee the party. Into that world stepped the conservative opinion media.

Through his nationally syndicated radio program, Limbaugh, for example, helps his audience choose from among those contending in the Republican presidential primaries.[1] He is able to do so because, as we argued earlier, his audience contains a large number of conservatives who are likely voters. When his views and those of some in his audience diverge, he enters this arena with only a slight risk, confident that he controls the ability of callers to express their dissent. Although the *Wall Street Journal* does not endorse candidates, its editorials and op-ed pieces offer similar opinions on the merits of candidates' proposals and on their standing as conservatives. We focus on Limbaugh's messages because our survey data permit us to assess their possible effects.

In presidential primaries as well as in the California recall race of 2003, Limbaugh used the sorts of Reaganesque conservative criteria we examined in chapter 4 to vet candidates. He allies his favorites with Ronald Reagan and his nemeses with "liberals." In 1992 and 1996, Texas Independent Ross Perot was on Limbaugh's list of undesirables. Whereas in the New Hampshire primary of 1992 Limbaugh endorsed conservative presidential aspirant Pat Buchanan, a former Nixon speechwriter, for his no-new-taxes attacks on incumbent President George W. Bush, in 1996, Limbaugh blacklisted Buchanan for his protectionist stands. In 2000, Limbaugh hammered the candidacy of Arizona senator John McCain. Confronted with Arnold Schwarzenegger, a social liberal but fiscal conservative, in the 2003 California gubernatorial recall, Limbaugh hedged his bets, trying to keep the candidacy of conservative Tom McClintock alive while urging Schwarzenegger to adopt anti-tax-and-spend messages. In the primaries of 2008, Limbaugh actively opposed the candidacies of Governor Mike Huckabee and Senator John McCain and suggested that former Massachusetts governor Mitt Romney came closer than they to Limbaugh's expectations. When we have been able to study this process, as we were in the presidential primaries of 1996, 2000, and 2008, we have found suggestive evidence that Limbaugh's message matters.

1992: Bill Clinton

Clinton's centrist Democratic appeal to the middle class co-opted three central premises of the Reagan revolution. His was a campaign constructed on the realization that middle-class voters "have not trusted us in national elections to defend our national interests abroad, to put their values into social policies at home, or to take their tax money and spend it with discipline."[2] With the Cold War over and voters perceiving the economy as a liability, not an asset, for the Republican incumbent, as we argued in chapter 4, Limbaugh and the *Journal* focused on casting Clinton and his policies as potentially dangerous, extreme, and "liberal."

The 1990–91 recession, coupled with the Bush tax increase, multiplied the chances that the alliance Reagan forged in 1984 would fracture in the 1992 general election. In the primaries, the incumbent Republican president confronted a challenge from the Right as Patrick Buchanan took on George H. W. Bush over his tax increase. The forty-first president also faced a third-party challenge from Texas billionaire businessman H. Ross Perot, who had little good to say about Bush's time in office. In the primaries Limbaugh backed Buchanan against Bush and attacked Perot for dividing the vote and jeopardizing Republicans' hold on the Oval Office. Buchanan "made it clear that the heart and soul of the Republican Party is conservatism,"[3] noted Limbaugh.

In the runup to the general election of 1992, Limbaugh and the editorial page of the *Journal* shared the view that by reneging on his 1988 pledge "Read My Lips, No New Taxes," the incumbent president had betrayed conservatives and made a political mistake. "It's now established," editorialized the *Journal* in early March 1992, "that the budget deal...will stand as one of the great political mistakes. Before the deal, Mr. Bush stood for something; after the deal, many of his constituents concluded he stood for nothing."[4] "The Reagan legacy has suffered most...at the hands of the man whom Ronald Reagan did so much to elect, George Bush,"[5] noted the *Journal* in August 1992. Among the factors contributing "to the anti-incumbent mood prevalent in America today," Limbaugh wrote in 1992, was "George Bush's abandonment of the Ronald Reagan legacy."[6]

1992: Ross Perot

Limbaugh recognized the extent to which the candidacy of Ross Perot threatened Republicans' ability to hold the White House. Employing strategies usually reserved for Democrats, he labeled Perot, who at one point bested both incumbent George H. W. Bush and Democratic challenger Bill Clinton in the polls, "the little hand grenade with a bad haircut." Limbaugh was not alone in seeing the Perot candidacy as a problem. A *Journal* editorial noted, "We now get Candidate Perot threatening to wreck a U.S. presidential election, merely so he can run out his $40 million of ads."[7]

Part of Limbaugh's audience saw Perot as a better choice than George H. W. Bush. In 2003, Limbaugh recalled the first half of 1992, when he "was warning you people that you were making a mistake, and you were telling me I was wrong, and it got to the point that the hero worship of Ross Perot was such that it didn't matter what he stood for. I had people calling me on the phone." At the time, he reported, his syndication partners worried that his opposition to Perot would drive away his audience. Chuckling, Limbaugh recalled that the ratings books proved them wrong. Perot "made promise after promise, then broke them all," noted Limbaugh in 1992. "I shouted till I was without voice that his entire campaign was based on the profound deceit of manipulating people into thinking they had created his candidacy, when in fact it was he who had orchestrated the whole thing."[8]

The conservative media's concerns about Perot were justified by the election results. He lured from the Reagan coalition many who were unhappy with what they saw as big government's profligate ways and disregard for the deficit under the Republican president. In 1992, "Perot's voters were, in general, the middle- to lower-middle-income portion of the Reagan-Bush coalition, who saw their livelihoods recede during the Bush presidency."[9] As the *Journal* noted after the election, Perot's total vote "approached a remarkable 30% in such GOP bastions as Kansas, Utah and Nevada."[10]

The 1992 election splintered the Reagan coalition. Indeed, as Democratic pollster Stan Greenberg notes, that election "brought historic collapse for the Republicans. The Republican presidential vote sank 16 percentage points from George Bush's performance in 1988 and 21 points from Ronald Reagan's in 1984, the high point of Republican ascendancy."[11] The conservative opinion media, which had opposed the Bush tax increase, drew one overarching lesson from the 1992 election: betray Reagan conservatism and lose elections.

As Republican contenders argued over the North American Free Trade Agreement (NAFTA), abortion rights, the flat tax, and each other's records during the 1996 primaries, Republican Party leaders remained on the sidelines. Not so Limbaugh. In 1996, when the Republican Party was functionally leaderless, Limbaugh continued to provide a coherent, consistent ideological frame through which his Republican followers could see their party and its opponent, the "liberals"—including the incumbent Democratic president.

During the 1996 primaries, the *Journal* and Limbaugh boosted Forbes and bashed Buchanan. A *Journal* editorial called Forbes "the party's most Reaganite candidate."[12] The *Journal* placed distance between itself and Buchanan's views on trade as well by describing his mission as "chasing the fool's gold of protectionism and nativism."[13] Consistent with the view that the conservative media offer Republicans advice on how to hew to conservatism and win, a *Journal* editorial cautioned Republican contender and eventual nominee Bob Dole: "instead of imitating Mr. Buchanan, Mr. Dole would do better to start emulating Mr. Forbes."[14]

At the same time, Limbaugh refurbished the anti-Perot line of attack he had devised in 1992. The *Journal* took Perot on as well. An editorial proclaimed "his candidacy is the best thing going for the Washington status quo."[15]

1996: Steve Forbes

Limbaugh did more publicly to thwart the candidacy of Pat Buchanan and advance the cause of Steve Forbes than any spokesperson for the Republican Party. On February 28, 1996, Limbaugh indicated: "There's somebody who's closer [to my views], but he's not all the way there—this is not an endorsement—it's Forbes." To his listeners Limbaugh argued that "virtually everything" Forbes proposed and his opponents ridiculed was going to be part of the platform—tax reform, Social Security reform, and "policies oriented toward economic growth" (February 20, 1996). Limbaugh responded to news that Forbes was dropping out by leaving the studio, to show "in my own way to all of you Buchanan ballers and all of you Perotistas [that] I consider Steve

Forbes's message as important as anything else in America today.... Unlike you... I will not demand 'my way' or 'no way'" (March 14, 1996). Consistent with Limbaugh's views, his regular listeners were more likely to support a flat tax, the centerpiece of the Forbes candidacy, than were listeners to other political talk. (See the appendix to this chapter on our website). Limbaugh's support of a flat tax continued in 2002. "The whole root of the progressive tax system is, in essence, unfair and based on some people setting arbitrary judgments," Limbaugh noted (December 3, 2002).

The *Journal,* too, praised Forbes's basic philosophy. Although the flat tax had been popularized on the editorial pages of the *Journal* by economists Robert Hall and Alvin Rabushka and the *Journal* had noted in 1992 that it was "favorably inclined toward the flat tax,[16]" in 1996 the *Journal* was not ready for wholesale commitment to it. "We've deferred judgment on the flat tax itself," it editorialized, "while noting that it clearly pushes tax policy in the proper direction—to ultimately lower marginal rates for all." But it was the second prong of the Reagan legacy that the *Journal* found most appealing about Forbes. "Indeed, the Forbes proposal we like most of all is his intention to build strategic defenses against missiles."[17]

1996: Ross Perot

Not only did Limbaugh implicitly advocate Forbes in 1996 but also he maintained a steady drumbeat of opposition to Perot and his "Perotistas." From Limbaugh's perspective, Perot's followers belonged in the Republican fold. Limbaugh told Perot's followers: you're going to waste your chance to take the country back by voting for Ross Perot. "You're going to end up third in a three- or four-person race, and your vote is going to do nothing but further the advances of those who stand in the way of what you want" (March 29, 1996).[18]

1996: Pat Buchanan

Attracted by Buchanan's opposition to taxes, Limbaugh supported his run against incumbent George H. W. Bush in the 1992 New Hampshire primary. But on the issue that had taken center stage in 1996 for Buchanan, a populist protectionist, he had strayed from Limbaugh's free trade, free market conservatism by championing taxes in the form of tariffs on imports and protectionism.[19] In Limbaugh's view, both meant an increased role for big government. His doubts about Buchanan put Limbaugh at odds with part of his core audience. "You've got Clinton sounding like Buchanan," he said on March 5, 1996. "You've got Buchanan sounding like Clinton. And Rush sounds like Rush."

Because talk radio callers are more conservative than either non-call-making listeners or the population at large, it is unsurprising that Buchanan's supporters frequently called talk radio shows in 1996. Indeed, *Talk Daily*'s analysis of 60 hours of shows in February 19–23 found that they had seven times as many pro-Buchanan callers as pro-Dole ones (63 to 9) and that Buchanan fans outnumbered those of Dole, Lamar Alexander, and Forbes combined by almost 3 to 1.[20] This raised the prospect that talk radio would mobilize Buchanan voters and sympathizers whose reluctance to embrace his candidacy was based in the conviction that he could not win. But that didn't happen.

Determining whether Limbaugh played a role in that outcome is complicated. Limbaugh took on Buchanan head-on, arguing that he was not a conservative (February 21, 1996) at all but a progovernment, Washington-establishment protectionist whose views coincided with those of labor unions. "If anybody's part of the Beltway establishment, it's Pat Buchanan" (February 26, 1996).

"You think . . . you are the leaders of the antigovernment movement," said Limbaugh to the Buchananites, "but you are not. You are asking government to come in and protect your job—just as . . . any of the liberals asking the government to protect something in their life. . . . Liberalism is designed to help you feel better and I think that's what Buchanan's 'conservatism of the heart' really means." "One of the things that worries me about this redefinition of conservatism [by Buchanan]," noted Limbaugh in early March, "is that now there's going to be a sect of the conservative movement which wants government action on its behalf" (March 3, 1996).

Limbaugh's attacks on Buchanan capitalized on the fact that "liberal" and "Democrat" are pejoratives in Limbaugh's lexicon and specific "liberal Democrats" are routinely vilified. For example, Limbaugh likened Buchanan's positions to those of Edward Kennedy (D. Mass.), David Bonior (D. Mich.), and Dick Gephardt (D. Mo.) on trade and to Hillary Clinton's proposed "big government" "health care takeover" (February 12, February 21).

Limbaugh's position on Buchanan pitted him against Ronald Reagan's son, talk show host Michael Reagan, who noted, "Rush Limbaugh may run around with a letter from my dad, but Pat Buchanan's running around with delegates for a convention, which is a heck of a lot more important at this point in time" (February 25, 1996).

In response to Limbaugh's refusal to champion the candidate they saw as the true conservative in the race, insurrection broke out among callers who argued that it was unfair of Limbaugh to say that Buchanan sounded like Clinton. A self-identified former Limbaugh fan went so far as to claim to despise Limbaugh for trying to destroy Buchanan. Dolores accused Limbaugh of injecting an "underhanded zing" into his discussion of Buchanan. Christina wanted Limbaugh to apologize for being unfair to Buchanan. Indeed, in an apparent attempt to channel the information into mainstream news, Limbaugh expressed surprise that Vladimir Zhirinovsky's "endorsement" of Buchanan had received scant news coverage, which Limbaugh said pleased him, because Zhirinovsky was a "nut." Zhirinovsky led an opposition party during Gorbachev's time in the 1990s.

In mid-March 1996, Limbaugh altered his screening policy. Justifying the resulting drop in pro-Buchanan calls, he said he didn't want to listen to "campaign speeches." "If you don't like the rules, call some other show where they're interested in that.... We have conversations here. We don't open this program up to people who make speeches" (March 12, 1996).

However, throughout the exchanges about Buchanan, Limbaugh worked hard not to drive Buchanan's supporters from the party, a move in keeping with both those we will describe shortly in the 2003 California gubernatorial race and with a party's traditional function of assembling winning coalitions. "If the Buchanan brigades out there are mocked and impugned, laughed at and made fun of," intoned Limbaugh, "you can kiss [the presidency] goodbye" (February 21, 1996). If the party wanted to retake the White House and hold the House, it should not marginalize either Buchanan or his supporters, said Limbaugh, because it "is going to need those votes" (February 21).

Our three-wave 1996 national survey suggested that Limbaugh did in fact affect his listeners' impression of Buchanan but that his anti-Buchanan posture also took a toll on his popularity with his regular listeners. Figures 7.1 and 7.2 show that in the Limbaugh listening group, attitudes toward Buchanan became less favorable over time but so, too, did attitudes toward Limbaugh himself. Especially telling is the finding that those who had not listened to Limbaugh's show at all in the previous week became more favorable toward Buchanan (an increase of .22) while those listening for at least one to two days became less favorable (−.28). Changes in attitudes toward Limbaugh himself also depended on listening in the prior week, with those listening most becoming less positive and those listening less changing not at all.

An interesting pattern emerged when we separated regular Limbaugh listeners into those who had not listened at all during the period of the survey, those who listened sometimes, and those who tuned in almost daily. The

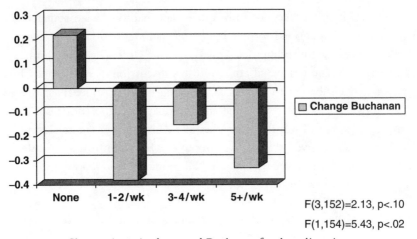

FIGURE 7.1. Changes in attitude toward Buchanan for those listening to Limbaugh versus not

differences among the groups are displayed in figures 7.1 and 7.2. Among Limbaugh regulars, those listening more frequently changed most toward both Buchanan and Limbaugh. This group accepted his attacks against Buchanan but penalized him for making them. Those Limbaugh regulars not listening during the studied period changed favorably toward Buchanan and not at all toward Limbaugh. Although other possible causes cannot be ruled out, Limbaugh's attacks on Buchanan provide one possible explanation for changes in attitudes both toward Buchanan and toward Limbaugh himself.

The drop in listener affection for Limbaugh during the same period may be the audience's way of responding to cognitively inconsistent information. A valued source speaking negatively about a highly regarded person could well produce change in evaluations of the source. Such a process could explain the shift in Limbaugh's listeners' attitudes toward him and is consistent with the absence of change in attitudes among listeners to other conservative talk radio during the same period.

Whether these changes can be attributed to the content of Limbaugh's commentary or to other outside forces or to both is not completely certain. However, there is a good circumstantial case for Limbaugh's impact from the survey evidence and from the content of Limbaugh's rhetoric toward Buchanan in the time period. (For technical details see the appendix to this chapter on our website.)

Some analysts credit Limbaugh's consistent defense of free trade and attacks on protectionism with guiding the Republican Party away from the path advocated by Buchanan in the 1990s. In an interview with Limbaugh, Michael Barone, author of *The Almanac of American Politics*, noted that "one

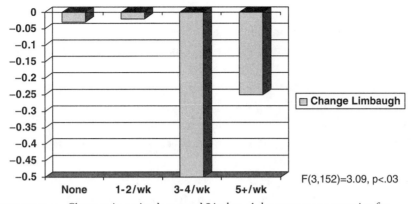

FIGURE 7.2. Changes in attitude toward Limbaugh become more negative for those listening more than 1–2 times per week

avenue the Republican Party might have taken [when Clinton was in office] is the Patrick Buchanan avenue: isolationism, negativism, dislike of other people who are different from you, protectionism." But, he told Limbaugh, "You spoke out consistently against those things to the core audience that Buchanan was aiming at, and he failed completely, and you...played a great role in shaping opinion in the 1990s" (November 12, 2004). Although our 1996 survey was not large enough to isolate *Journal* readers, it is important to note here that Limbaugh and the *Journal* embraced mutually consistent positions on trade in the 1996 campaign.

2000: *John McCain*

Whereas Forbes and Buchanan were Limbaugh's targets in 1992 and 1996, in 2000 Arizona senator John McCain received the Limbaugh treatment. In the primaries of that year, Limbaugh argued that McCain was a Rockefeller Republican trying to pry the party out of the hands of the Christian conservatives. Followers of John McCain were labeled "McCainiacs."

After McCain's victory in the New Hampshire primary, Limbaugh began an aggressive attack reminiscent of the one he launched against Buchanan in 1996. Just as he had done with Buchanan, he likened McCain to Clinton. "Limbaugh's just beating the hell out of McCain," said Michael Harrison, the editor of a publication focused on talk radio.[21] "He's found McCain to be a temporary replacement for Bill Clinton." The media was "orgasmic" over McCain, concluded Limbaugh. The "love 'em and leave 'em liberals" were responsible for his success at the ballot box. In a parody on the show, a woman sang of McCain: "He's the candidate that I adore / He can keep my tax cut and I'll be poor / and I'll smile and send him more." Just as Limbaugh may have moved his listeners against Buchanan in 1996, so, too, he may have shifted attitudes against McCain in 2000.

Data from NAES 2000 indicate that listening to Limbaugh negatively affected New Hampshirites' *postprimary* favorability ratings of McCain, even after taking into account how favorable they were to him before the New Hampshire primary. (See the appendix to this chapter at our website.) Although their self-reported votes for McCain were not significantly affected by listening to Limbaugh,[22] the direction of the effect is the same as for favorability to McCain. This suggests that Limbaugh's attacks on McCain reduced his audience's favorable response to McCain and were tending to reduce the likelihood of their voting for him as well. However, where the effects on favorability are significant, the results on vote intention are not. This lack of significance may be a function of the strong preprimary intention to vote on postprimary intention, which takes up most of the variation in intention allowing little room for change.

In other words, after the New Hampshire primary, Limbaugh listeners became much less favorable toward McCain, even controlling for their preprimary favorability. The data also indicate a negative influence from listening to Limbaugh prior to Super Tuesday. Specifically, before Super Tuesday, those in Super Tuesday states who listened to Limbaugh were less favorable toward McCain[23] and had less strong intentions of voting for him. Being part of Limbaugh's audience was associated with lower favorability toward candidate McCain and this audience had a lower intention to vote for him in Super Tuesday states.

There was no additional change after the Super Tuesday primary. Those in Super Tuesday states who listened to Limbaugh were not less likely to approve of McCain or less likely to report having voted for him *after* the primary. We surmise that Limbaugh's influence on perceptions of McCain was felt early in the primary season (New Hampshire was February 1) rather than later (Super Tuesday was March 7). (For results summarizing these effects see the tables on our website.)[24]

Just as Limbaugh's attacks on Buchanan in 1996 angered some in his audience, so did the 2000 attacks on McCain. "'Rush really has gone overboard in his bashing of McCain, but I guess it's understandable since Rush represents the status quo, and Senator McCain is attacking the status quo," said Tom Abbott, a conservative from Oklahoma who reports having listened to Limbaugh for years.[25]

The assault on McCain persisted after Bush's election. Both on his radio show and elsewhere, Limbaugh dismissed McCain as a Democrat. In an interview with Tim Russert, Limbaugh listed McCain as a prospective Democratic candidate in 2004. "Wait," Russert said. "He's a Republican." "So they say," responded Limbaugh (November 23, 2002). In a parody by Paul Shanklin, played on the radio show and available for purchase on the website, "McCain" sings "Just call me maverick John McCain / My only straight talk is my name. With the Left I often vote / It's just to get old Trent Lott's goat."

Limbaugh disapproved of a key piece of legislation McCain championed—a campaign finance reform bill McCain sponsored with Senator Russ Feingold (D. Wis.). Moreover, in the spring of 2007 the two were at odds over immigration reform. Limbaugh also regards McCain as self-important. "Senator McCain says President Bush must consult allies and him before any action in Iraq," said Limbaugh. "Well, McCain said 'Congress' but he is Congress in his own mind" (August 23, 2002). McCain characterized Limbaugh in turn as a "circus clown" and then apologized saying, "I regret that statement because my office was flooded with angry phone calls from circus clowns all over America. They resent that comparison, and so I would like to extend my apologies to Bozo, Chuckles and Krusty."[26]

2003: Arnold Schwarzenegger

Quoting snippets of Limbaugh's commentary on candidates diminishes one's sense of both the coherence of his rhetoric and the adaptive nuances that refresh his arguments as events emerge and circumstances change. To convey a sense of his pragmatic dexterity as an opinion and party leader, we identified an instance in which the Republican most likely to win the party's nomination and the election was not the one most closely aligned with Limbaugh: the 2003 gubernatorial recall election in California. This race also permitted us to observe Limbaugh facing a situation analogous to the revolt of Buchanan-supporting callers in 1996. Finally, the recall election revealed how Limbaugh responded to the candidacy of a popular actor whose ideological identity was largely unknown as the contest began.

The California election pitted Limbaugh's desire to hold Republicans to a conservative standard against his desire to see this influential state in the hands of a Republican governor. The true conservative in the race and Limbaugh's favorite was the long-shot state senator Tom McClintock. Before polls confirmed that McClintock had little chance, in mid-August it looked as though Limbaugh would oppose actor and businessman Arnold Schwarzenegger's bid. However, he cautioned, "I've not come out against Schwarzenegger yet, but I guess my lack of support is being interpreted as the same as being against him. But don't make that mistake. It's too soon, folks" (August 13, 2003).

One of Limbaugh's challenges as a talk show host is holding the attention of listeners. That task is eased when the audience confronts a difficult choice, in this case, between supporting a solid social and fiscal conservative and ensuring that a social liberal but presumably fiscally conservative Republican wins the race. The California case also raised questions for which there was not a ready conservative answer. For instance, did Schwarzenegger's pragmatism, personal style, and tax-cutting disposition qualify the former Mr. Universe and current box office draw as an heir of the revered Ronald Reagan? What troubled conservatives was the fact that the person in question was married to the niece of liberal icon Edward Kennedy, had advocated a California ballot initiative increasing funding for after-school programs, opposed the impeachment of Bill Clinton, and was on record supporting gun control, gay rights, and abortion rights.[27]

Some self-identified conservatives in Limbaugh's audience saw Schwarzenegger as one of their own and viewed Limbaugh's ambivalence as problematic. A caller reported, "I'm furious at you. I can't even say mega dittos. I am a conservative, California Republican, and I am so angry at you right now that my anger exceeds my fear of talking with you. I am so angry that you are not backing Arnold Schwarzenegger for governor." Limbaugh responds, "I never said I opposed or supported Arnold or anyone else in this race."

On the following program (August 15), Limbaugh certified Schwarzenegger's authenticity, noting that he had "long said that Arnold has made no secret of his liberalism, so it's not like he's pretending he's something he's not just to win votes." Early in the recall process (August 12, 2003), Limbaugh indicated "Arnold Schwarzenegger is not a conservative. He may be conservative on certain issues....But it is important that we be intellectually honest....Schwarzenegger is not Reaganesque. The similarity is they're both actors. That's where it ends. There's no policy similarity."

To those who said it would be good to have a governor with the Republican "R" behind his name, Limbaugh cautioned, "issues matter," and instructed listeners to vote on candidates' stands on issues. He added, "California has no money. Its debt is stretched to the limit; Schwarzenegger's campaigning on a theme of government doing even more than it is now. The two don't go together....Liberal Republicans never do establish a movement that will help the Republican Party build a foundation for future victories."

Schwarzenegger's past statements made it impossible to argue that he is a social conservative. But his business background could be cast as evidence that on economic matters he was a true believer. That is the frame that Limbaugh-the-pragmatic-party-leader adopted on August 20, when he noted, "We've got a golden opportunity out here in California if Schwarzenegger would simply be who he is."

> I think Schwarzenegger is a conservative. . . . Not based on anything he said. I think Schwarzenegger's natural inclinations, when he arrived in this country and who he is (I know there's the Kennedy thing there) I think that's who he is. . . . If Schwarzenegger would simply run on a conservative fiscal agenda, he would win. He doesn't need to do all of this stuff to go to "the middle." He doesn't need Warren Buffett there. He doesn't need to talk about raising taxes.

If Schwarzenegger would run as a fiscal conservative, he seemed to have Limbaugh's blessing.

Limbaugh appears to be instructing Schwarzenegger on how to appeal to conservatives while at the same time featuring a facet of conservatism not at odds with Schwarzenegger's past statements. Limbaugh easily could have cast Schwarzenegger as a liberal by featuring his marriage to a Kennedy and his social policy positions. Instead Limbaugh portrayed him as a person who had succeeded in business and invested wisely—the biography of a conservative in the making. How did Limbaugh know that Schwarzenegger might be a conservative after all? "I can tell you [by] the way Arnold Schwarzenegger invests and lives his life and runs his own businesses, there's nothing liberal about it. There just isn't."

The same program showed the extent to which Limbaugh felt conflicted. He said,

> You have [Democratic Lt. Governor] Bustamante offering nothing different than [incumbent Governor] Gray Davis, and you have Arnold saying he wants to bring businesses back so he can tax them, and continue the social programs that are in place out there. Both of them are basically advocating things that have led to the state's problems.

Within five days (August 25), Limbaugh was publicly advising Schwarzenegger that he would "win big" if he talked

> about revitalizing the Silicon Valley by creating enterprise zones where investment, creativity and opportunity will be encouraged via reduced regulations and taxes. I have no doubt that he'll win big if he talks about building more power plants and removing the burdens on businesses. This is what we won on in the eighties, and this is what led to the prosperity we enjoyed throughout the nineties.

If the candidate will embrace the proposed agenda, then he will be incorporated into the "we" that won in the 1980s, a tacit assertion that adopting the conservative economic agenda would be sufficient to ally Schwarzenegger and the person who won in the 1980s, Ronald Reagan.

After the gubernatorial debate on September 25, 2003, Limbaugh confirmed that he saw McClintock as the true conservative in the race: "Tom McClintock chose to stay above the fray, which he credited with gaining him $20,000 in campaign pledges and 4,000 new members on his website. He was totally unlike any of the others who appeared in this debate last night: clear, concise, detailed, and conservative from beginning to end." In other words, unlike Schwarzenegger, McClintock is both a fiscal and a social conservative.

When the votes were counted, Schwarzenegger had captured 48% of the total cast and McClintock only 13%. Limbaugh framed the victory as a function of the actor's conservative fiscal policies. The day after Californians elected Schwarzenegger, Limbaugh cautioned the White House not to misread the lesson of California: "For instance, the lesson is not that being liberal on social issues and good on tax cuts is the right combination.... Arnold didn't run on his liberal social views. They were known, yeah, but that's not even what this election was about." "Instead," he said, "the fact is what we've had out there [in California with Davis] is pure liberalism and they [the people of California] just threw it out!"

Limbaugh now had it both ways. If Schwarzenegger was successful, it was because he followed Limbaugh's advice about fiscal conservatism. If Schwarzenegger failed, Limbaugh could argue that he never contended that he was a pure conservative and never endorsed him. After Schwarzenegger won, Limbaugh noted: "Schwarzenegger repeatedly emphasized he would repeal and cut taxes. We cannot allow the message on his campaign to be distorted in an effort to diminish the power of the conservative ideas that won the day."[28] At the same time, Limbaugh had preserved his status as the voice of conservatism by championing McClintock.

As the Schwarzenegger and Buchanan cases attest, Limbaugh is ultimately interested in electing Republicans rather than Democrats. He is pragmatic about ensuring the election of those of as like mind as the electoral process permits. At the same time, he works diligently to hold potential defecting voters within the fold.

Consistent with the model he employs when addressing national politics, in an op-ed in the *Journal*, Limbaugh praised Governor Schwarzenegger when he hewed to Republican principles, for example when he lauded "liberty and capitalism" and invoked Ronald Reagan in his speech to the Republican Convention in 2004.[29] By contrast, Limbaugh took Governor

Schwarzenegger on when he began talking about raising taxes (January 19, 2007) and supported an increase in California's minimum wage and extending health care coverage for children (March 21, 2007; March 26, 2007). In the latter instances, Limbaugh's position was unequivocal but his memory somewhat selective.

> I have said he's not a conservative—and, by the way, I want to remind all of you people in California, from the get-go I have told you he was not a conservative. He's a good guy, but he's not a conservative. He's a Republican.... Governor Schwarzenegger ran for office as a conservative.... Now, here's the truth of the matter. Arnold Schwarzenegger has done the typical sellout move. (March 20, 2007)

On his website, Limbaugh posted what could be either a book cover or a movie poster featuring a menacing photo of Schwarzenegger. On the image is overlaid "Schwarzenegger. Get ready for the RINO ride of your life. TOTAL SELLOUT." Whereas on the program Limbaugh credited Schwarzenegger with being a Republican albeit not a conservative, here he was labeled Republican In Name Only (RINO).

Limbaugh was not alone in his objections to Schwarzenegger's shift to the left. In the *Journal*, John Fund observed:

> Arnold Schwarzenegger used to claim he admired Ronald Reagan most "because he stuck by his principles when others wouldn't." But with his Rube Goldberg health plan Mr. Schwarzenegger has demonstrated that at his core he prefers roles more suited to Tricky Dick than the Gipper. Should he succeed, the long term dream of nationalized health care held by Ted Kennedy, and Hillary Clinton, will be closer to reality than ever.[30]

Four days later, Fund echoed Limbaugh, noting that "the over-the-top absurdity of the Schwarzenegger statement ["It is not a tax, just a loan, because it does not go for general (expenditures)"] led Rush Limbaugh into fits of laughter last Friday. 'Bill Clinton calling [tax increases] 'investments' was bad enough,' Mr. Limbaugh says."[31]

Driving Schwarzenegger from the Republican Party would not serve Limbaugh's interests, however. Nor did Schwarzenegger want Limbaugh as a regular antagonist. When Schwarzenegger asked to come on the show, Limbaugh welcomed him. In a tough exchange, each defended his position. The encounter closed with Limbaugh noting, "Governor, look, I've always liked you, and I've always admired you.... We've all got so much hope for you. Everybody wants you to be who you are. I know there are lots of Republicans…hoping you wake up one day and become a conservative again" (March 21, 2007). The next day, Limbaugh featured the fact that he is holding a cigar he received from Schwarzenegger. The cigar, he reported, arrived "via overnight courier" and "is one of his own personal cigars, complete with his own band." The humidor in which it came "has the Seal of the Governor of the State of California." Schwarzenegger had autographed the box. So, said Limbaugh, "truce" (March 22, 2007).

During the course of the 2003 California recall campaign, Limbaugh assumed that his national audience was interested in the political implications of the California contest and in an outcome favorable to the Republican Party. He assumed as well that it would be better for conservatives if McClintock were to win. But a charismatic Republican committed to fiscal conservatism was preferable to a Democrat. So while helping McClintock, Limbaugh did nothing to cause his California listeners to turn from Schwarzenegger to the Democratic candidates. In other words, in this state-level election, as in the presidential primaries of 1992, 1996, and 2000, Limbaugh served as a pragmatic conservative opinion leader. Once Schwarzenegger was elected, Limbaugh treated him as he does other Republicans in power. The test in California politics, as on the national stage, is fidelity to Reagan's principles.

Limbaugh is not alone among conservative opinion hosts in performing a candidate-selecting function. Using data from the political insiders' guide the *Hotline*, in August 2007, the *New York Times* crafted a chart entitled "Tracking Face Time" that focused on "news programs on six major cable and network channels this year through July 15." During that period, former New York mayor and Republican presidential hopeful Rudy Giuliani garnered 115 minutes on Fox, the highest total of any candidate. In an accompanying article, the *Times* noted that "more than half of those minutes, 78, were spent with Mr. Hannity, co-host of the 'Hannity and Colmes' talk show."[32] Later that month, Hannity appeared at a fundraiser for the Republican hopeful.[33]

2008: McCain, Huckabee, and Romney

With the 2008 primary season in the offing, Limbaugh reiterated the criteria he would apply in choosing a Republican candidate. "People ask me all the time," he said on March 20, 2007,

> "Have you chosen a Republican presidential candidate?" I answer, "Not yet," and one of the things I'm concerned about is there's not

one Reagan conservative in the bunch.... Don't tell me that candidate A—be it Giuliani or Mitt Romney or McCain or whoever else—is the new Reagan. There isn't a Reagan out there.... Conservatism is not subject to redefinition on the basis of presidential candidates who are 30% conservative, 40%, 50%.... That's not the new conservatism, at least it won't be for me.

As we noted in chapter 1, when social conservative and former Arkansas Governor Mike Huckabee emerged as a serious contender in the weeks before the 2008 Iowa caucuses, Limbaugh, writers on the *Journal*'s editorial pages, and some Fox commentators found his conservative credentials wanting. Another presidential contender remained in Limbaugh's sights as well. On the eve of the Iowa vote, Limbaugh asked his audience:

> If somebody told you that a conservative was someone who supported amnesty for illegal aliens, who supported limiting free political speech [this is a reference to McCain–Feingold], who embraced the ACLU's brief for terrorist detainees getting U.S. constitutional rights, if someone told you that a conservative is someone who opposed tax cuts during the Bush administration, and has recently confirmed he would do it again, what would you say?

He answered his own question in a way longtime listeners could have anticipated: "I just described to you several of Senator McCain's positions over the years. Now the idea that he's a great conservative in this race is an affront to conservatives" (January 2, 2008). The day after a debate following the New Hampshire Republican primary in January 2008, Limbaugh launched into an extended attack on McCain, who had won that contest. Limbaugh then concisely explained his rationale for the move. "I know people are asking, 'Rush, why are you doing this?' I'll tell you why I'm doing it because no Republican in the debate last night did it. Somebody has to do it." On the day before the Republican South Carolina primary, which McCain had lost to Governor George W. Bush in 2000, Limbaugh asked listeners, "If you Republicans don't mind McCain's positions, then what is it about Hillary's positions you dislike? They're the same." The next day, McCain won South Carolina. Limbaugh's other nemesis, Mike Huckabee, came in second.

The conservative talk show host escalated his attacks on the Republican contender from Arizona in the days before and after McCain's January 8 victory in the New Hampshire primary. "McCain has stabbed his own party in the back," Limbaugh stated on February 4, "I can't tell you how many times." Consistent with our 1996 and 2000 findings, after Rush Limbaugh began strongly attacking John McCain's conservative credentials in 2008, NAES data show that people who listened to the talk show host were more likely than the nonlistening population—including those who described themselves as conservatives—to believe that Senator McCain was a moderate. Before the New Hampshire primary about half of Limbaugh's listeners said McCain was a conservative. That number dropped almost 12 percentage points (11.8%) after McCain won in New Hampshire. After January 8, the number of Limbaugh listeners who said McCain was a liberal jumped nine percentage points (9.1%). During this period, the political perceptions of McCain among non-Limbaugh listeners remained stable. Immediately after the New Hampshire primary, Limbaugh listeners begin to shift away from their view that McCain is a conservative. These results hold after controlling for gender, race, education, party identification, and respondents' own ideology.

Limbaugh's listeners were more likely than conservatives not in his audience to know that Senator McCain was the Republican endorsed by the *New York Times* (a frequent object of the host's attack on the "liberal media") and that he had opposed some of the Bush tax cuts. Controlling for gender, race, education, party identification, and ideology, Limbaugh listeners were 3.94 times more likely than nonlisteners to know that the *New York Times* endorsed Senator McCain and 3.75 times more likely than nonlisteners to know that Senator McCain had opposed some of President Bush's tax cuts. In addition to altering his listeners' ideological placement of McCain and increasing their information about the *New York Times*'s endorsement and McCain's tax record, listening to Limbaugh reduced his listeners' sense of the senator's trustworthiness.

Consistent with Limbaugh's message during the period from the New Hampshire primary to Super Tuesday 2008, his listenership also increasingly came to share the view that former Arkansas governor Mike Huckabee was less conservative and former Massachusetts governor Mitt Romney more so than Limbaugh listeners previously had thought. (On February 4, Limbaugh informed his audience that "there probably is a candidate on our side who does embody all three legs of the conservative stool, and that's Romney.") The shift in listeners' assessments of Governors Huckabee and Romney also paralleled Limbaugh's views of those candidacies (for support data see our website).

Assumed in Limbaugh's discourses on the merits of some candidates over others is that this is not an academic exercise. His listeners are ultimately voters. Limbaugh reinforces the notion that his listeners can make a difference—in their own lives through individual initiative and in their community by fearlessly espousing their point of view. He also reminds them to vote.[34]

On the eve of the November 2002 elections (November 4), his call to action was clear: "Folks, this is it. It is on us now. We all meet at dawn tomorrow. They say turnout is going to be a record low. Make sure they're not talking about us." He added, "Do you remember how I signed off the program the day before the election in 1994? . . . So, again, this year, the posse shows up. We all meet at dawn tomorrow." On Sean Hannity's radio show, Senator Orrin Hatch (R. Utah) remarked, "I thank my father in heaven every day for people like you, Rush Limbaugh and others." In Hatch's view, "talk radio gave Republicans the winning edge" in the 2002 election.[35]

The question "Does Limbaugh increase the number of votes cast for Republicans in general elections?" is often asked and difficult to answer. Because his audience is upper-income, educated, and politically interested, it is likely to vote to begin with. With more than 80% of it identified as conservative, it is likely to vote Republican. So whereas his influence in the primary selection process is plausible, it is unlikely that in a general election he increases vote totals for Republicans by directly influencing his listeners. Limbaugh is more likely to exert influence when the choice involves multiple Republicans, as it does in primaries or general election recalls.

But it is possible that Limbaugh influences general elections in other ways—for example, by increasing the disposition of his listeners to argue the conservative case with those who are undecided or not initially disposed to vote at all. Although the data we have been able to marshal are insufficient to permit us to make that case, we do regard it as a plausible supposition.

In addition to vetting candidates and holding those in office accountable, the conservative media perform a third party–like function by reinforcing ideological identity. If the conservative media serve this protective function for their listeners, watchers, and readers, then we would expect these audience members to be more firmly attached to the Republican Party and hence less likely to defect from it than those who are otherwise similar but not in the conservative media establishment's audience.[36]

Some researchers have suggested that the way citizens process political information is through simple tallies of positive and negative information about candidates and parties—more like summaries of positive and negative feeling than detailed knowledge and information.[37] If so, then regular exposure to the conservative media establishment should ensure that the tally for conservative candidates is positive and the tally for Democratic Party positions and candidates is negative. In short, one would predict from the rhetoric of the conservative opinion media that exposure would anchor the audience's vote.

Since George Belknap and Angus Campbell tied the concept of party identification to political behavior in 1952, party affiliation has played a central role in explanations of individuals' political behavior in the United States.[38] Indeed, as Norman Nie, Sidney Verba, and John Petrocik noted in 1979, in the 1950s and 1960s, party identification "was the central thread running through interpretations of American politics"; it was considered "a stable characteristic of the individual: it was likely to be inherited, it was likely to remain steady throughout the citizen's political life, and it was likely to grow in strength during that lifetime."[39]

If one holds that party identification is a given, then the role of the conservative media establishment would be to reinforce an existing identification. But if party identification can be shifted by persuasion and events within a campaign, then the outlets on which we focus could serve a second function: ensuring that those vulnerable to such shifts remain identified with the Republican Party. Both NAES 2000 and NAES 2004 data reveal shifts in party identification across the campaign season.[40]

The question our survey employed for party identification was "Generally speaking, do you usually think of yourself as a Republican, a Democrat, an Independent or something else?" Interviewers recorded verbatim responses from those who said "something else."

The variation figure 7.3 shows in party allegiance during the campaign indicates that it is not a constant but ebbs and flows as the impact of events and campaigns is felt. The existence of such changes suggests that whether directly though contact with their own audiences or indirectly as those audience members interact with others, Limbaugh and his colleagues have the

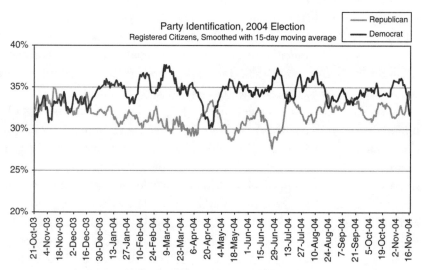

FIGURE 7.3. Overtime Analysis of Party ID, 2004 Election

opportunity not simply to reinforce party loyalty but to protect audiences from defection.

The NAES provides some evidence that Fox and Limbaugh may in fact perform this function. Consistent with the notion that listening to Limbaugh or watching Fox may protect audiences from forces that might push them to defect from the Republican Party, we found in the NAES 2004 data that Limbaugh and Fox's audiences were less likely than others to defect. Evidence for this conclusion comes from a preelection to postelection panel (preelection panel July 15–November 1, 2004; postelection panel November 1–December 28, 2004). In both panels, respondents were asked to provide both party identification, if any, and ideological leanings. Those in the Fox and those in the Limbaugh audiences were less likely to report any changes in ideology or party than those not in the Fox or Limbaugh audiences. There was no evidence that Limbaugh listening or Fox viewing was linked to conversions from the left to the right or from the middle to the right (details available at our website).

———

In sum, we have illustrated the ways Limbaugh advances the candidacies of some and undercuts those of others, and we have suggested that Limbaugh listening and Fox viewing help anchor conservatives to identification with the Republican Party. In chapter 4, we argued that, as with Hannity on Fox and the *Journal*'s editorial page, the template that creates Limbaugh's screening criteria and standard of accountability is Reagan conservatism, a philosophy the *Journal* argues was its own long before it became known as the Gipper's.

Stirring Emotion to Mobilize Engagement

On January 20, 1981, in the opening section of his first Inaugural Address, newly installed President Ronald Reagan declared: "Government is not the solution to our problem; government is the problem." "It is my intention to curb the size and influence of the Federal establishment and to demand recognition of the distinction between the powers granted to the Federal Government and those reserved to the States or to the people," he noted later in that speech. "All of us need to be reminded that the Federal Government did not create the States; the States created the Federal Government."[1]

Since the president and the party in control of the House and Senate are in charge of much of what we consider government, conservative attacks on government are attacks on Democrats when a Democrat is in the Oval Office and the Democratic party is running the Congress. When two of the three branches of government are in Republican hands, as they were in 2005, the conservative distrust of government takes a different form. Under these circumstances, Limbaugh attacked big government while in general supporting the Republicans who were superintending it. He did this by arguing that government would be even bigger and more intrusive were the Democrats in power while at the same time criticizing the Republican president and congressional leadership when they supported an expansion in government's role, as they did in championing the addition of a large and expensive prescription drug benefit to Medicare. The conservative message faces a second challenge, insofar as it attempts to engender mistrust of the problem-solving capacity of government without converting that mistrust into a cynicism that might dampen political involvement.

Attacking Democratic leaders while touting the value of engagement appears to work for Limbaugh's audience, which is both politically involved and confident that being politically engaged has value. Here we explore the rhetorical and psychological means Limbaugh uses to produce these effects. We do so in order to argue that he invites political engagement, not detachment, from his audience by mobilizing emotion in service of a "we/they" contrast between Democrats and the conservatives and conservatism he champions. In short, Limbaugh reinforces his audience's disposition to participate in the political process.

Do Limbaugh's Attacks Lead Listeners to Mistrust the Political Process?

It would be easy to assume that attacks launched by political commentators such as Limbaugh magnify their audience's political mistrust and in the process breed cynicism about politics, elections, and public policy discussion.[2] Were that the case, our claim that Limbaugh functions as a surrogate leader of the Republican Party would be undermined, because he would demobilize rather than energize his listeners.

TRUST IN GOVERNMENT 1996

At first glance, some of our evidence might suggest that Limbaugh engenders mistrust. But that inference does not withstand scrutiny. During the primaries and the fall presidential campaign of 1996, we asked a series of questions about the public's trust of government, political campaigns, and politicians (PTR Survey 1996). In response to the question "How much of the time do you think you can trust the government in Washington to do what is right?" Limbaugh listeners were more likely to give the less trusting response than other listening groups and than nonlisteners. Figure 8.1 shows these results for the average response across listening groups after adjustment for factors that could also account for differences (e.g., party affiliation, education, and other factors). (For details on trust in government see the appendix to this chapter at our website.) However, this finding does not warrant the conclusion either that Limbaugh listeners are mistrustful of political processes in general or that they are disconnected from politics.

Instead, the kind of mistrust they express is ideological. Conservatives and Republicans tend to mistrust what they see as the big government that the federal government in Washington exemplifies. It is not surprising, then, that given the overwhelmingly conservative leanings of Limbaugh's listeners, they would be more mistrustful of the government in Washington, especially when the Democrats are in charge of the executive branch, as they were in 1996. As we noted at the beginning of this chapter, a central tenet of Reagan

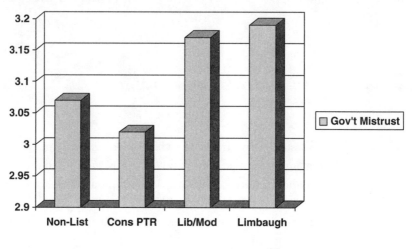

FIGURE 8.1. Adjusted means for mistrust of the government in Washington: Four listening groups, 1996.

conservatism is that the government in Washington is too big, too bloated, too inefficient to conduct the people's business well.

When people were asked, in our 1996 survey, whether they agreed or disagreed with statements about politicians' honesty ("Politicians won't talk honestly about the hard issues . . . because that would lose them support") and money buying votes ("Money buys the votes that determine the laws that are passed"), Limbaugh listeners were no different from other groups on mistrust of politicians during the primary period. Limbaugh listeners distrusted big government in Washington but did not find statements about the honesty of politicians or the role of money in legislative processes any more true than nonlisteners did. The fact that their mistrust did not extend to these domains supports the view that their mistrust of Washington is ideological and as such is attributable to Washington and government when the Democrats are in power but not when the Republicans are.

Neither does their mistrust of Washington extend to the presidential campaign, the candidates involved in the campaign, or the way political campaigns are run. No differences among listening groups were found in 1996 when respondents were asked to choose between more and less cynical alternatives. ("Candidates tell voters what they believe is best for the country" versus "Candidates tell voters what they think voters want to hear.")[3] When the focus shifted to the major party candidates for president rather than political candidates in general, we found the same result. Even after the election was over and the Republican candidate, Bob Dole, had been soundly defeated, Limbaugh listeners were no more or less likely than other groups to agree that political campaigns have to change so that the country can choose good leaders. Despite their disdain for Bill Clinton as a president, Limbaugh listeners were not more likely than others to accept the idea that the political process required reform.

MISTRUST, NOT INDIFFERENCE

Instead, Limbaugh listeners were politically active and anything but indifferent about politics. We measured political indifference in 1996 by asking respondents if they agreed or disagreed with the statement "I really don't care who wins the presidential election this fall" and "There aren't any important differences between Republicans and Democrats in what they stand for these days." Limbaugh listeners were less indifferent when compared to nonlisteners and listeners to liberal/moderate talk radio. (See fig. 8.2 and the technical details in the appendix to this chapter at our website.)

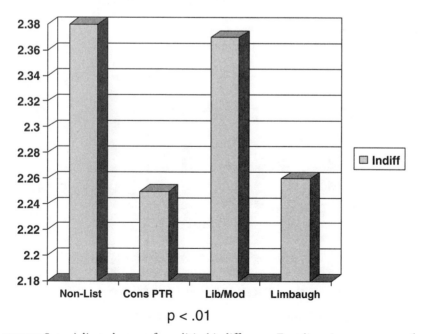

FIGURE 8.2. Adjusted means for political indifference: Four listening groups, 1996.

We found similar results when we compared answers about political inefficacy across groups. For our purposes, "lack of political efficacy" was defined as agreement with three statements: "People like me don't have any say"; "Public officials don't care about what people like me think"; and "Sometimes politics is so complicated that a person like me can't really understand what's going on." Here the pattern of results is similar but not identical to the one we just reported. Limbaugh listeners report higher feelings of efficacy than do nonlisteners.

The reports of elevated efficacy and less indifference are evident in reported behavior as well. Participants in our 1996 surveys answered a series of questions about their political activities during the election so far (the second to third week of October 1996). They were asked to report if they had given money to a candidate, watched one or both of the nominating conventions, watched the first debate, watched the second debate, volunteered to work on the campaign, personally heard a speech live, or contacted a newspaper or television station to comment on the campaign. Overall, Limbaugh listeners reported higher levels of participation across the list of activities than other listening groups. Figure 8.3 shows that reported political participation of those listening regularly to Limbaugh is higher than that of all three other groups—listeners to other sources and nonlisteners as well. (For details see the appendix to this chapter at our website.)[4]

The results charted in figure 8.3 are consistent with the claim that those listening to Limbaugh regularly also are politically involved. Other

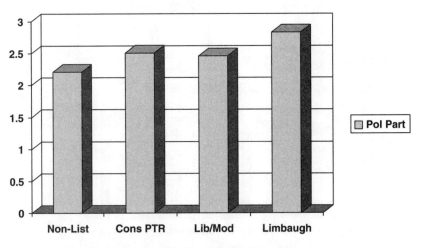

Political Participation: Fall 1996

p < .001; Limbaugh > NL, Con & Lib/Mod, p < .05

FIGURE 8.3. Adjusted means for political participation: Four listening groups.

researchers have made similar claims (see note 4). However, these findings cannot demonstrate that listening to Limbaugh is a causal factor in activating political involvement. It is perfectly plausible that those with a strong propensity for political involvement may find their way to Limbaugh's show. Of course, both can occur as well.

DOES PTR IN GENERAL CAUSE LISTENERS TO BE MORE POLITICALLY INVOLVED?

Our PTR Experiment 1996 gives some indication of the causal effects of PTR in general on listeners' political involvement. After a week's exposure to one of several kinds of PTR, people were asked how they thought they would respond in four different scenarios where their responses would consist of some form of political involvement. The scenarios involved the flat tax, doctor-assisted suicide, Louis Farrakhan, and educational vouchers. For example, people were asked how likely they would be to attend a speech by Farrakhan if their neighbors asked them to attend with them.

Only the questions on educational vouchers produced clear-cut effects. On educational vouchers, the scenario was attendance at a neighborhood forum on the issue. The conservatives who heard Limbaugh reported a greater willingness to attend than did either those in the control or conservatives hearing liberal programming or NPR's *Talk of the Nation.* Liberals in turn were energized by listening to liberal programs on the vouchers and became more willing to go to a forum with their neighbors than liberals in the control group. In sum, in at least some scenarios, there is evidence that PTR can activate the intention to act even after very brief exposures.

———

Overall, Limbaugh listeners were more politically involved during the 1996 election than the other groups we studied. They were more politically efficacious and less indifferent than those in the comparison groups. They exhibited no more or less mistrust of politicians, candidates, or political campaigns than any other group during the primary and election periods. Their only expression of mistrust was about the federal government in Washington getting it right. This mistrust can be described as toothless, in that it has little impact on behavior or civic engagement. Mistrust of the government in Washington is associated with political participation, but the association is positive—specifically, people who report greater mistrust are more likely, not less likely, to also report political activities in the election period. In fact, this relationship is strongest for the Limbaugh group and virtually absent for the nonlisteners. (For analytical details, see the appendix to this chapter at our website.)

Our data show what may appear to be a different pattern when the Republicans are in power in Washington. The 2003 Annenberg survey of attitudes toward government and the executive branch suggests that those who listened to Limbaugh at least "twice a month" were more likely to trust the government to operate in the public's "best interests."[5] This seems to be at odds with the findings in 1996 that Limbaugh listeners were more mistrustful of government to do what is right—data gathered while Democrat Bill Clinton was in the White House. The praise for government offered by Limbaugh fans in this 2003 study is presumably for the uses the Bush administration has made of government. However, other data from this survey suggest that the ideological mistrust of big government is still present. Respondents who listened to Limbaugh were more likely to believe that the federal government should be cut back, even while believing that under President Bush the federal government was well-run and hard-working and that the president could be trusted to act in their best interests. (For details on the analysis, including controls, see the appendix to this chapter at our website.) Of course, long before Fox or Limbaugh were on the scene, political scientists had observed that conservatives report higher trust in government when conservatives are in charge; similarly, Democrats trust government more when their party is in charge.[6]

Limbaugh's Content Differs from Mainstream Media

To determine whether Limbaugh's rhetoric differs systematically from that of other PTR hosts and the other media, we conducted a two-part content analysis. The topics treated on the *Rush Limbaugh Show* for the weeks from February 3 through March 29, 1996, were coded.[7] During the same period, the front-page news stories of three major newspapers—the *New York Times*, *Washington Post*, and *Wall Street Journal*—were coded. Similarly, the number of minutes of coverage from the nightly television news programs (ABC, NBC, and CBS) was obtained from a news analysis service.

Across the eight weeks studied, Limbaugh gave scant attention to foreign affairs and military matters, in contrast to the mainstream media, which devoted fully one-fourth of their coverage to these topics. (See the appendix to this chapter at our website.)[8] Limbaugh gave greater attention to the Clinton administration and its scandals, to the Congress, to third parties and the religious right, and to the general topic of personal efficacy, responsibility, and public cynicism and optimism. For example, Limbaugh devoted a scant 2.2% of his program to "foreign and military affairs" during this period, in contrast to the 24% that broadcast news programs devoted and 27% that print news did. Public optimism and cynicism occupied almost 9% of Limbaugh and was virtually absent from the mainstream. These differences suggest that during this period Limbaugh focused more on domestic politics than did the mainstream media. At the same time, Limbaugh promoted personal responsibility and worked to reinforce personal efficacy in support of political involvement in rejecting big government and affirmative action.[9]

Using computerized word search techniques from transcripts of the show provided at first by a Limbaugh audience member at an online site and later by our own group from audiotapes, we also carried out content analysis over a longer period. For the approximately 11 months from early January to the end of November 1996, Limbaugh mentioned President Clinton every day at least once and often many times more. Bob Dole was mentioned in 92% of the shows, Hillary Clinton in 88%. The Republican and Democratic parties were mentioned in 94% of the shows and contrasted in 96% of them. Other prominent political leaders Limbaugh concentrated on were Newt Gingrich (52%), Ross Perot (55%), Al Gore (47%), and Jack Kemp (36%).

The content analysis revealed two of Limbaugh's important and unique foci. The first, personal responsibility and individual efficacy, were not themes in the mainstream media. While the mainstream was focused on the Clinton scandals, Limbaugh's emphasis was more pronounced in its critique of both Democrats and Clinton and not just Clinton. The daily focus on political parties and on political personalities from each party reflected the rhetorical structure of identity building and enemy creation (described in other chapters).

The analysis revealed the way Limbaugh evoked moral outrage at "liberals," "liberal media," Democrats, and the Democratic Party by means of the "double standard" argument that has been a focus of this book from its opening chapters. For example, as we discussed in detail in chapter 1, when Lott was accused of praising a segregationist, Limbaugh attacked the Democrats for failing to criticize Byrd for his alleged relationship with the Klan, criticized Al Gore because his father failed to support the Civil Rights Act of 1964, and castigated the mainstream media for its "double standard" in focusing on Lott and not these other instances. This strategy takes advantage of what psychologists call a *core theme associated with the production of anger*—namely, a transgression, often moral, against the self or someone close to the self.[10]

As noted, Limbaugh's focus on the inadequacies of opposition party leaders does not seem to drive his listeners from the political process. On the contrary, this move invites involvement in activities, including discussion with those of like and dissimilar mind. But why? Why does a more partisan, one-sided, conflict-oriented treatment of political battle as entertainment lead to political involvement when a more balanced, dispassionate, compassionate, and consensus-oriented style does not?

Limbaugh Invites Moral Outrage at Behavior of Democrats

The answer lies in what some critics of Limbaugh find most disturbing about him—he rouses passion through various types of emotional appeal, especially employing a form of moral outrage activated by examples of the "double standard" employed by mainstream mass media and by "liberals" (and Democrats) in criticizing conservatives.

We reject the assumption that use of emotion is either illegitimate or fundamentally nonrational. Recent research and theory in emotion and persuasion argues that one's emotional reactions to a persuasive message are a kind of information one can use to gauge one's response to the message.[11] We believe that the conservative opinion media use emotion to heighten attention to politics and spur political engagement. Our conclusion is based in research suggesting that emotions can serve as powerful detectors that signal the importance or relevance of stimuli to basic goals and as a result reveal the extent to which an environment is beneficial or harmful to us.[12] At the same time, emotions can enhance our readiness to respond or act.[13] In addition, anxiety can heighten interest among those with a high level of internal political efficacy,[14] a tie consistently forged by Limbaugh in particular. Emotion can increase the efficiency with which we process needed information as well.[15]

Later, we discuss the ways the conservative opinion media semantically prime or heighten the cognitive salience of key words and concepts. What is called affective priming uses emotion to make affective information more salient. Like semantic primes, affective ones can shape judgments and choice.[16] Emotional associations can be readily accessed from memory by the mere presentation of the relevant stimulus.[17] As we argue in this chapter, Limbaugh in particular successfully attaches strong negative affect to the people and policies he opposes and strong positive affect to those he favors. The cognitive and affective link he forges increases his persuasive capacity to produce two effects we describe in later chapters—balkanizing and polarizing.[18]

In the final thread of our 1996 survey, we asked a number of questions about emotional reactions to Bob Dole and Bill Clinton. These included: "Has Bill Clinton because of... something he has done, ever made you feel..." followed by the words "angry," "hopeful," "afraid," and "proud." The same question was asked about Bob Dole. The response alternatives were simply yes and no. The responses were combined into negative emotions toward Bill Clinton (angry and afraid) and positive emotions toward Bill Clinton (hopeful and proud). Similar combinations were calculated for Bob Dole.

When the total emotional response was summed (Dole and Clinton, positive and negative), the three PTR groups—Limbaugh regulars, regular listeners to conservative hosts, and regular listeners to liberal and moderate hosts—were similar in their total emotional reactions to the candidates and were different from nonlisteners who had less strong emotional reactions. However, Limbaugh listeners did differ from other PTR groups in the kinds of emotional reactions— positive and negative—they had to the candidates (see fig. 8.4). The Limbaugh listeners expressed more positive emotion toward Bob Dole and more negative emotion toward Bill Clinton than any other group; they had less positive emotion toward Bill Clinton than all the other groups and less negative emotion toward Bob Dole than nonlisteners and listeners to liberal/moderate PTR.

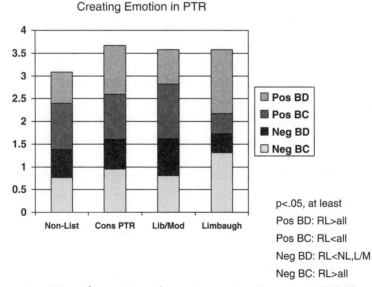

FIGURE 8.4. Means for positive and negative emotional reaction to Bill Clinton and Bob Dole: Four listening groups. (BD is Bob Dole; BC is Bill Clinton. Pos is positive emotions and Neg is negative emotions. RL is Rush Limbaugh listening group; NL is non-listeners; L/M is listeners to liberal/moderate talk radio.)

These data do not show that Limbaugh listeners report more total emotional reaction to the presidential candidates in 1996 but instead that the emotion generated is directed toward Limbaugh's political ends.[19] The emotional reaction of PTR listeners compared to nonlisteners might be interpreted as antithetical to the rational, deliberative outcomes favored by political theorists.[20] However, affect can be a mobilizing force for politically important behaviors. In our listening and nonlistening groups, the relationships between political participation and emotional reaction to candidates were positive. As the election approached, those who reported more emotion about the political candidates also were more likely to participate in political activities near the election.[21] The association between emotion and participation is consistent with the link between emotion and feelings of political efficacy (for example, about government and public officials) and indifference (for example, not caring who wins the election, seeing no important differences between Democrats and Republicans). Those with more emotional reaction to the candidates are less indifferent to who wins and feel more personally efficacious about their role in influencing government.[22]

Emotional response also is associated with projected vote, strength of intention to vote for Dole versus Clinton, and favorability toward the candidate. Our data for 1996 show these relationships consistently, as do data from the 1996 National Election Study.[23] However, if PTR listeners with their stronger emotional responses to the candidates were to weigh emotional factors more than, say, issue or character factors in their political judgments, then PTR audiences in general and Limbaugh listeners in particular might be said to be hijacked by their emotional considerations.[24] Political theorists tend to view emotional responses as undesirable, as antithetical to rational decision making. Are Limbaugh listeners' attitudes toward political candidates, compared to those of nonlisteners, based more on emotional reactions and less on "rational" considerations such as those tied to issue stands and character?

To test this possibility, respondents were asked, in October 1996, "For whom do you intend to vote?" Those choosing Perot were dropped from further analysis. The strength of each respondent's support was coded as strong, moderate, and weak (i.e. leaning toward one candidate). To create a single index of support where +3 indicated strongest support for Clinton and −3 strongest support for Dole, the strength of Dole support was subtracted from that for Clinton.

Three important factors were assessed as predictors of strength of support: emotion, character judgments,[25] and perceived similarity on the issues.[26] If Limbaugh listeners (or any PTR group) were using emotional factors as the basis for their judgments, then the salience of emotion in accounting for candidate support would be greater for this group than for others. Emotion, character, and issue similarity were all strong and consistent predictors of the strength of people's support for the candidates. However, there was no evidence that either listening to Limbaugh or other PTR correlated with stronger emotional considerations in candidate preference. (For a summary of these results see the appendix to this chapter at our website.) The variance explained in strength of vote intention was substantial (in the vicinity of 80%), indicating that the factors of party identification, character, issue similarity, and emotion are sufficient to explain vote intention. But the emotion factor does not systematically have stronger or weaker effects by listening group.

A second analysis of negative emotions about Clinton and Dole indicates no impact of negative emotion on strength of vote for Dole either in any of the studied groups or in the sample as a whole. Negative emotion toward Bill Clinton was about the same in all groups (overall the effect is $-.36$, $p < .001$) but is least predictable in the Limbaugh listening group ($-.26$, $p < .05$).

Although Limbaugh listeners had strong negative emotional reactions to Bill Clinton and more positive ones to Bob Dole than any other listening (or nonlistening) group, this emotional response does not undermine what have been the ordinary criteria for good citizenship—political participation, a sense of efficacy, and informed voting decisions. The contrary is the case—more emotional respondents in general are more likely to participate in campaign events and to feel efficacious. The negative emotions about Bill Clinton and positive emotions about Dole among Limbaugh listeners do not translate into more emotionally based voting intentions; all groups seem to employ character, issues, and emotional response to similar degrees.

Finally, the attacking, inoculative character of Limbaugh's rhetoric does not seem to undermine his audience's trust of others or its willingness to engage in conversation with other citizens, whether those of like mind or not. When asked questions about trust, 60% of Limbaugh listeners responded that most people can be trusted (versus the option "You can't be too careful in dealing with other people"), in comparison to 48% of nonlisteners and 62% of listeners to other PTR; 66% of Limbaugh listeners said that most of the time other people try to be helpful (as opposed to looking out for themselves). In contrast, 57% of nonlisteners and 60% of liberal/moderate PTR listeners chose the more trusting alternative.

Limbaugh listeners talked to people in their neighborhoods regularly at about the same rates as other groups. Thirty eight percent of Limbaugh and conservative PTR listeners talk to at least four people in their neighborhoods regularly; 34% of nonlisteners said they do as well. After the second presidential debate in 1996, 64% of Limbaugh listeners who watched the debate talked to family, friends, or coworkers about it, while 60% of other PTR listeners and 51% of nonlisteners did. Of those who had conversations, 38% of Limbaugh listeners had five or more of them, compared to 31% of other PTR listeners and 26% of nonlisteners. In an experimental test of exposure to various types of PTR, certain subgroups of the sample showed increased levels of interpersonal trust after exposure to one-sided political talk, in contrast to those who listened to two-sided political radio for a week.[27] At a minimum, these findings suggest that the emotionally evocative rhetoric of the one-sided programming of some forms of PTR does not undermine the interpersonal trust that is the basis for political interaction with others.

In short, there is no evidence in our data that the emotionally evocative character of PTR's rhetoric about political candidates undermines other socially desirable outcomes such as social trust and increased political conversation. We found no evidence that political emotion undermines participation or a sense of efficacy or hijacks political judgment by diminishing the role of issues and character.

Conclusion

What all of this means is that when Democrats are in power, Limbaugh listeners are more likely to distrust the government in Washington to do what is right. This mistrust does not extend to campaigns, political candidates in general, or the way elections are run. On the contrary, Limbaugh listeners are more likely to participate in politics, have feelings of greater efficacy, and have a stronger sense of the importance of political decisions and differences between the stands of the political parties. The mistrust of the government in Washington that we found in 1996 seems to be an ideological statement about big government run by Democrats that invites efforts to minimize government's reach. Those feeling greater mistrust of the government also tend to report greater participation in the election. The bottom line, then, is this: this kind of mistrust is not corrosive; instead it represents an ideological stance toward what is seen as ineffective big government in Washington.

The emotional intensity of Limbaugh's rhetoric may account for the stronger negative and positive emotional reactions his listeners reported in 1996 to Bill Clinton and to Bob Dole, respectively, but these reactions do not alter the way Limbaugh listeners weigh factors in their voting decisions. While different from those of other more liberal citizens, their responses to Clinton and Dole do not suggest that in voting they give greater or lesser weight to emotion over character and issue factors.

Contrary to the views of those who decried the effects of PTR on the body politic in its early days,[28] those who listen to political talk, in general, and Limbaugh in particular, are not an ignorant, disengaged public but, instead, an audience that is engaged, outraged, and with strong opinions. We see these consequences as the byproduct of Limbaugh's success in creating a virtual community of like interests and like minds—a virtual political party.

In sum, Limbaugh's combined message attacking Democratic leaders while touting the value of engagement appears to work for his politically involved and engaged audience. In the next chapter, we explore the rhetorical and psychological means Limbaugh uses to produce these effects.

Framing and Reframing the Mainstream Media

In the closing weeks of the hotly contested and closely watched Senate race in Minnesota in 2002, incumbent Democrat Paul Wellstone and some members of his family and staff were killed in the crash of a small plane in icy weather. After his memorial service became the subject of controversy, the person named to run in his stead, Walter Mondale, former Minnesota senator, vice president, and Democratic presidential nominee, narrowly lost the seat to Republican Norm Coleman.

Among the theories proffered by the pundits to explain Mondale's loss was public rejection of the behavior of Wellstone's presumed supporters at his memorial service. How did the public come to learn that at that service, speakers urged that a Democrat fill his seat and some in attendance booed both Independent governor Jesse Ventura and U.S. Senate minority leader Trent Lott? During an interview with Rush Limbaugh on *Meet the Press,* Tim Russert reported that a Democratic pollster found that 69% of the Minnesota electorate had heard about the memorial before voting in the 2002 elections. Limbaugh explained, "It was only broadcast on C-SPAN. How did they hear about it, Tim? CBS, ABC, Washington—there wasn't a whole lot of coverage of that in the mainstream press the next day." "Talk radio?" Russert asked. "I think so," says Limbaugh. "That's my point."[1] Russert did not contest the answer. If talk radio created the effect, that fact had now been broadcast more widely. Whether it did or not, that presumption had now been legitimized in an elite mainstream venue.

The relationship between the conservative opinion media and the mainstream is complex. Probing those complexities and understanding how the conservative media use framing to insulate their audiences from outside media influence are our goals in this chapter. The notion of an insulating function is central to our argument, because even as they gravitate toward conservative media sources, these audiences continue to view, read, and listen to mainstream media and are at the same time drawn to candidate communications in forms such as debates and, in the example from the Wellstone memorial service, C-SPAN. If the conservatives in these audiences carry conservative frames into mainstream exposure, then the conservative opinion media will have provided ready alternatives to insulate their audiences from counterattitudinal forces, as well as from the power of competing frames presented by mainstream media.

Framing and Priming

As already discussed, we argue that the conservative media perform an insulating role through a process that the scholarly literature calls framing. Frames pervade politics. Is welfare a helping hand or a government handout?[2] Is affirmative action a way of remedying the injustice of past discrimination or reverse discrimination?[3] These alternative frames carry with them very different assumptions, lines of argument, bodies of evidence, and policy preferences. In the process of finding that framing can shift audience opinions,[4] scholars have shown the effect of conservative and liberal frames. So for example, political science scholar Laura Stoker found that Americans were more likely to accept affirmative action when it was framed as a way to make up for past discrimination.[5] Scholars summarize this process by saying that "a framing effect is one in which salient attributes of a message (its organization, selection of content, or thematic structure) render particular thoughts applicable, resulting in their activation and use in evaluations.[6]

Media frames are organizing structures that tell audiences "what the issue is through the use of selection, emphasis, exclusion and elaboration."[7] Frames "affect the likelihood that particular options will be selected" by audiences.[8] In the process, frames increase the importance of some arguments over others, some evidence over other.[9] Frames are ways of seeing the world.

The literature on framing provides strong support for the notion that when a one-sided frame is offered to audiences, they are likely to adopt the perspective within it. However, even in an insulated political world in which partisans are disposed to seek out supportive media and like-minded friends and associates, they are exposed to framing from other ideological perspectives. The influence of that kind of exposure can be countermanded, however, for as Paul Sniderman and Sean Theriault's experiments have persuasively shown,

> when citizens are exposed to a complete rather than an edited version of political debate, they do not succumb to ambivalence or fall into confusion. On the contrary, even though as part of the process of debate they are exposed to an argument at odds with their general orientation, they tend "to go home," to pick out the side of the issue that fits their deeper-lying political principles.[10]

The implications of this finding for understanding the different formats we focus on are important. If Sean Hannity and Alan Colmes present alternative frames with equal dexterity, their conservative audience will default to the frame consistent with its conservative principles, hence to Hannity's frame. When the *Journal* publishes an alternative point of view on its conservative op-ed pages, its audience, too, which is mainly conservative, can be expected to default to the frame of the editorials. And Limbaugh's use of inoculation—the presenting of the opposing frame in order to rebut it—can be expected to increase adherence to the conservatively framed argument because inoculation minimizes the likelihood of counterpersuasion, because Limbaugh's is the dominant frame on his show, and because any strong counterframing that might seep through if a liberal caller is persuasive will produce default to conservative principles in the audience.

Importantly, framing can effectively attribute responsibility to political leaders or deflect responsibility from them.[11] So, for example, the conservative opinion media credit conservative leaders and blame "liberal" ones; they also attribute problems that occur when conservatives are in power to forces beyond their control.

In a world in which the public sphere is full of competing frames,[12] the consistent redundant framing the conservative opinion media use gives their audiences a way to navigate politics, but also should increase the likelihood that these frames will become for them cognitive structures that invite consistent ways of seeing politics,[13] even when the conservative opinion media are silent or distracted. Framing is a powerful means of focusing attention on some facets of an argument or situation and excluding others. The frames the conservative opinion media offer are consistent and repeated, features that heighten their power.

Framing can be done by means of priming. People don't make decisions on the basis of all of the available evidence, nor do they feature all the issues at play in an election when they decide how to vote. The priming hypothesis, which many scholars find credible, assumes that individuals embrace criteria for assessment on the basis of their accessibility—how quickly and automatically they come to mind. If a criterion has been the subject of a lot of attention, it will be accessible. For example, if discussions of the economy dominate news commentary and other issues receive less attention, then the economy will become more salient to news consumers than issues that are featured less. By focusing on some issues and ignoring others, the media prime the criteria by which we evaluate leaders and policies.[14] The conservative opinion media prime evaluative criteria that bolster the prospects of their chosen conservative contenders and undercut those of their opponents.

At the same time, Limbaugh, the conservatives on Fox, and the opinion pages of the *Journal* make some criteria (such as conservative positions and the traits identified with the Republican and Democratic candidates) more salient and create positive affective associations to conservative topics and language and negative affective associations to Democratic ones.

Semantic priming (i.e. specific word choices) can increase the salience of words and their associated concepts, topics, or issues. By employing a common vocabulary that expresses conservative views in appealing ways (e.g., "liberal media," "double standard," "death tax," "partial birth abortion") the conservatives prime and reinforce these words as the language with which the audience should think politics. To these, Limbaugh adds labels for positions and people he opposes that tie pejorative concepts and negative emotion to them simultaneously.

———

All things being equal, the advantage in framing goes to the side of an exchange whose message receives more exposure. A study of the relative amount of exposure achieved by the group that called itself Swift Boat Veterans for Truth (SBVT) in the summer of 2004 suggests that they received substantial free airtime on all three cable networks. However, in this mix the conservative shows played the SBVT ads more often than did the more liberal ones. Annenberg researcher Jeffrey Gottfried led our effort to track the controversy in 2004 that pitted the Kerry campaign against the SBVT. To do so, he analyzed the amount of free airtime devoted to ads sponsored by the "SwiftVets" and to rebuttal ads for John Kerry on Fox's *Hannity and Colmes,* MSNBC's *Scarborough Country,* and *Hardball with Chris Matthews* during the same period in August 2004.

The number of seconds of SBVT ads aired on *Hannity and Colmes* from August 4 to 27, compared to the Kerry rebuttal ads, was about 5.5 to 1 (about 374 seconds to about 68 seconds). More important, however, is the fact that the ratio of Kerry ads to SwiftVet ads was far more favorable to the anti-Kerry case on MSNBC's conservative *Scarborough Country*—where the ratio was about 6.28 to 1 (785 seconds to 125 seconds). On MSNBC's *Hardball with Chris Matthews*, the ratio still favored the SBVT ads at about 1.19 to 1 (207 to 174 seconds). The fact that on all three programs the SwiftVets' ads received substantially more time is a tribute to their visually evocative nature and to the absence of an equally evocative pro-Kerry rebuttal ad. Nevertheless, *Hannity and Colmes* on Fox and the conservative *Scarborough Country* on MSNBC provided much more access to the SBVT ads than did the program hosted by former Democratic operative Chris Matthews on MSNBC. (For a more detailed summary of the findings, see the appendix to this chapter on our website.)

This analysis raises a caution about treating networks rather than their programs as the unit of analysis and justifies our focus on two Fox programs rather than on the entire network. It also suggests the extent to which Fox— like MSNBC and CNN—is subject to forces under the control of campaigns. Kerry's inept response to the SBVT attacks produced an imbalance in access to his ad content even on Matthews's show. This notion is consistent with the one advanced by Lance Bennett and his colleagues that "even as the much-discussed Fox News may bend the uniformity principle of mainstream journalism a bit to the right, it does so not by sampling outside official versions of events, but by sampling even more narrowly within them."[15]

Although studying the content of the mainstream media is beyond the scope of this book, we think it important to note that one recent study finds that MSNBC and CNN provided more interview time to Democrats than Republicans. Consistent with our analyses, Fox gave Republican contenders for the presidency more talking time than it gave Democrats.[16] It is important to note of course that just as they refused to participate in a debate hosted by that network, Democrats may be just saying no to Fox.

Conservative Media as Opinion Leaders

Although widely misremembered as a claim about television, the notion of "opinion leader" was developed to explain the way information and influence flowed in the age of radio—in two steps, from elites to nonelites and from opinion leaders to opinion followers. Suggested by Paul Lazarsfeld, Bernard Berelson, and Hazel Gaudet in *The People's Choice*,[17] published in the mid-1940s, and developed by Elihu Katz and Lazersfeld in *Personal Influence*,[18] the concept envisioned a first step in which information was transmitted from the media to opinion leaders and a second in which it was carried by these leaders to opinion followers. Whether or not one sides with those who believe Katz and Lazersfeld's evidence for the phenomenon was weak,[19] the concept of two-step flow underscored the limited effects of mass media. Specifically, people influenced others in ways media did not.

The opinion leaders identified by Katz and Lazersfeld were respected individuals (or groups) living in the communities studied; they were media consumers, not media stars. Followers listened to the information they conveyed about politics and in the process accepted the information and the leaders' take on it. The mode of influence was face-to-face interaction.[20]

Except for the fact that he is part of the media, Limbaugh meets the definition of opinion leader. Information passes to him from a wide array of media sources from which he selectively draws. Indeed, his website contains a daily list of the stories he has perused in preparing for his show. Subscribers to the site can link to those articles themselves from the site. As we argue in this chapter and as we illustrated with case studies in chapters 1 and 2, a central mission of his talk show is to provide a sustained critique of the "liberal" bias of the mainstream media. His mode of influence is an extended conversation in which he talks to listeners, engages in exchanges with callers, and responds to emails.

The conservative opinion media see their role as balancing the mainstream outlets, consisting of both major newspapers such as the *New York Times* and the *Washington Post* and major broadcast and cable networks, including NBC, CBS, ABC, PBS, MSNBC, and CNN and their counterparts on radio and the internet. These are, in conservative eyes, the "liberal media," or in Limbaugh's lingo, C-BS, NBC-BS and ABC-BS, PMS-NBC, or, more recently, the "Drive-Bys." Turning the tables on those who consider the conservative media biased, Limbaugh calls NBC, ABC, and CBS the "partisan media."

Not only does Limbaugh vigilantly monitor the mainstream media for bias but also, as we demonstrate throughout this book, he reframes those channels as purveyors of a double standard that disadvantages conservatives and their ideology. In this view, the mainstream distorts, makes serious uncorrected mistakes, and omits key information. Here, to our argument about the centrality of the double standard argument, we add the notion that the conservative opinion media displace mainstream interpretations of events by offering alternative frames. We will argue, for example, that when in the California recall race of the fall of 2003 the *Los Angeles Times* featured allegations that Republican gubernatorial challenger Schwarzenegger had sexually harassed and assaulted women, the conservative opinion media charged instead that incumbent governor Gray Davis was a batterer. The notion that the *Los Angeles Times* was not focusing on the allegations against Davis was used as evidence of the double standard, and the allegation that Davis was a batterer served as the displacing frame. Later we will offer evidence that Limbaugh's alternative frames may affect those of his audience.

Vigilantly Monitoring the Mainstream for Bias

Before examining the notion that the conservative opinion media displace mainstream news frames with frames of their own, we will explore the larger argument that the conservative media have a different focus, concentrating on information ignored or misrepresented by the mainstream.

A DIFFERENT FOCUS

When Fox News was a mere glimmer in Rupert Murdoch's eye, the conservative opinion media were preoccupied with the scandal known as Whitewater. The *Journal*'s editorial page and Limbaugh were among the voices who took the mainstream media's comparative lack of interest in it as a sign of media bias and a double standard.

"To critics of our Whitewater coverage, I have a simple reply: It's news, stupid," wrote Robert Bartley in the *Journal*; and

> Here we have the president of the United States under investigation by a specially appointed prosecutor. We have the death of one close associate of the president and first lady, and the jailing of another.... We have revelations about the first lady's implausible commodities profits.... The question, that is, is not why we're covering it on the editorial pages of the *Journal*. The real question is why the mainstream press isn't covering it far more extensively than it has.[21]

In a 1996 op-ed in the *Journal* entitled "And the Networks' Whitewater Whitewash," conservative media critic Brent Bozell III noted that Limbaugh and the other radio talk show hosts were discussing the Clinton scandals "virtually every day."[22]

As we found in the content analysis of Limbaugh's show in 1996 and reported in chapter 8, Limbaugh was dogged in his attention to three major topics: Bill Clinton, Bob Dole, and the mainstream media. Over the spring, summer, and fall of that year, all three consistently ranked in the top 10 issues treated.

Limbaugh's discussion of the mainstream media during the summer and fall included newspapers (98% of the shows) and to a lesser extent television news (85.2%). He tended to focus on presumed "liberal" newspapers such as the *New York Times* (83.3%) and the *Washington Post* (65.7%). Those with conservative editorial pages such as the *Wall Street Journal* (48.1%) and the *Washington Times* (32.4%) received substantially less attention from him. And whereas the former were often singled out for critique, the latter were usually included to magnify a message.

To illustrate Limbaugh's treatment of these media, let us briefly examine his attacks on the *New York Times*. Limbaugh's interpretation of the influence of the *New York Times* credits it with the same power we ascribe to him in an earlier chapter—a party building, party advising role. So, for example, in objecting to the paper's editorializing in favor of admitting women to the Augusta National Golf Club and in critiquing the paper for its initial decision not to publish columnists critical of its view, Limbaugh says, "This paper has become a coordinated leftist house organ—just as newspapers run by Horace Greeley and others were for their parties in the nineteenth century.... The *Times* carries the liberal line.... I see the editorial pages advising Democrat leaders like Nancy Pelosi and others on how to behave" (December 5, 2002). "The *New York Times* bent over so far into bias that they laughably reported Kerry's medal controversy with a front-page headline on an old, closed story: 'Kerry Questions Bush Attendance in Guard in '70s,'" reported Limbaugh (April 27, 2004).

Occasionally Limbaugh's critique misfires. On November 4, 2002, for example, he reported that *New York Times* reporter Adam Clymer's article saying that the Republicans were poised to make gains in the House had not appeared in the *New York Times*. "I found it in [a local paper] in Vermont," says Limbaugh, "It's an Adam Clymer story, but it's not in the *Times*. It's so good for the Republicans, they must have left it out of the paper, but it went on the *New York Times* wire service" (November 4, 2002). However, he had simply missed its publication in the *Times*; as the liberal media monitor FAIR (Fairness & Accuracy in Reporting) noted in a media advisory entitled "Limbaugh's Liberal Media Proof: Too Good to Be True": "It appeared in the top right-hand column of the paper—the spot the paper reserves for what it considers its most important stories."

The Limbaugh lexicon vilifies prominent players at the *New York Times*. Columnist Paul Krugman becomes "Ferret" Krugman, his head attached to a weasel-like body on Limbaugh's website. Editor (at the time) Howell Raines becomes "Mullah" Raines (November 6, 2002) and is shown on Limbaugh's website wearing a superimposed turban. In honor of reporter Adam Clymer, who was tagged "a Major League asshole" by Republican vice presidential nominee Dick Cheney in 2000, Limbaugh coins the notion that one can "rip" someone a "new Clymer."

Among the networks, CNN (57.4%) received the greatest attention daily during the summer and fall from Limbaugh in 1996, followed by CBS (38.9%) and NBC (38.9%).[23] The high rate of discussion of CNN is not surprising, since at the time Limbaugh's nickname for CNN was the "Clinton News Network," underscoring his perception of its bias. When all the other media are counted, we can say that Limbaugh discussed the news media on every one of his shows in the period in 1996 during which we closely monitored his content.

According to Limbaugh, the "liberal" and conservative media swing to opposite ends of the ideological pendulum. When he oriented the 1994 freshman class of congressional Republicans, Limbaugh recalls telling them "the liberal media is not happy they're there. I told them they [the "liberal" media] were the enemy" (January 9, 2003). "There's no question the left will do whatever they can to find fault in Bush," noted Limbaugh in April 2003. "Let them. They only make fools of themselves. The EIB Network, Fox News Channel, the *Washington Times* and a dozen other fair media sources will report the other side of the issue rather than toeing the party line" (April 10, 2003).

In the conservative critique, the media's liberalism is evident in what they fail to cover. Since they ignore some significant stories and slant others, one must turn to Limbaugh, Fox, the *Journal,* or other conservative outlets for accurate information. Bias is evident as well in what is seen as the fact that the mainstream covers politics in ways that distort and demonize Republicans and the Republican agenda and support the Democratic "liberal" agenda and its advocates.

FEATURING ERRORS IN THE MAINSTREAM TO SHOW "LIBERAL" BIAS

The vigilance with which the conservative media monitor the mainstream is evident in the following cases. On October 6, 2003, the *Journal* published an editorial entitled "The WMD Evidence."[24] At issue were interpretations of the closed-door report by weapons inspector David Kay on the findings of the U.S. investigation to date. The *Journal* noted:

> West Virginia Democrat Jay Rockefeller walked out of the Kay briefing to assert his dismay that nothing he'd heard proved Saddam's threat was "imminent" and thus preemption is wrong in all cases. In fact, the Bush Administration never subscribed to the "imminence" test when making its case for deposing Saddam. Mr. Bush flatly rejected it in this year's State of the Union address as too risky. The argument was that Saddam was continuing to hide the WMD capabilities he was known to possess in the 1990s and had used against Iran and his own Kurdish population—with the clear intention of resuming these programs once the political heat was off. The Kay report proves this is precisely what Saddam intended.[25]

The same day on Fox, Brit Hume observed in his "Political Grapevine":

> The *Associated Press* says it. *Reuters* says it. The *New York Times* says it repeatedly. Senator Levin says it. So does Senator Rockefeller. What they say is that the Bush administration claimed as a justification for going to war in Iraq that Saddam Hussein posed an "imminent threat."

In fact, President Bush has publicly said just the opposite, most conspicuously in his State of the Union address last January.[26]

PRESENTING REPORTERS' PRAISE OF DEMOCRATS
AS PROOF OF BIAS

To document the supposed pro-Democratic bent of mainstream news reporters, Limbaugh recounted an instance of a columnist praising Democratic president Bill Clinton. The UPI reporter-turned-columnist Helen Thomas introduced former president Clinton in October 2002 by saying, "He brought unprecedented prosperity to our nation, and because of that, President Bush can use the surplus Mr. Clinton left behind to pay for many of the nation's needs in this time of crisis....He's the man from Hope, and that's what he's given us, hope. We miss him." Limbaugh quoted the statement and added, "That's Helen Thomas, the objective journalist from UPI, now a columnist.... Thank you, Ms. Thomas, for finally being honest about your persuasions. All we've ever asked from the liberal media was for you to just be honest" (January 3, 2003).

When the perception that the media are liberal seems borne out in survey data, the conservative opinion media both tout the fact and use evidence that nonconservative outlets are ignoring the finding to indict their bias. On October 8, 2003, for instance, Limbaugh noted, "We have a great Gallup poll, folks. Sixty percent of conservatives, 40% of moderates, 18% of liberals say the media is too liberal." Limbaugh then creates an interpretive frame for the information. "We all know that the moderates are liberals, anyway, so that would be 58% of liberals and 60% of conservatives, that's over 100% of the people who think that the media is liberal." Meanwhile, on *Fox News Sunday,* October 12, Tony Snow reported the findings of the same Gallup poll and suggested that underreporting of its findings was attributable to liberal bias in the media.

REFRAMING MAINSTREAM MEDIA AS "LIBERAL"
AND AS IGNORING IMPORTANT DATA

Sins of omission. According to the conservative media establishment, the mainstream or "liberal" media, by omission and by slanting what they report, distort the public's perception of events in order to discredit conservatives and conservatism both. For example, when only Fox covered a speech on Iraq by President Bush in early October 2002, Limbaugh interpreted it as the final confirmation of "liberal bias." "If there was any remaining doubt about the networks' editorial bias and ideological preferences," he said, "there shouldn't be any longer" (October 9, 2002).

Sins of Commission: Taking Conservative Statements out of Context. "Trust in the press has plummeted to a pathetic 36 percent, barely higher than the all-time low of 32 percent during the 2000 election recount," noted Tony Snow on *Fox News Sunday*, June 1, 2003.

> The next story offers a case study of why. *Vanity Fair* has published, to great fanfare, the [Sam] Tanenhaus piece about the White House and its foreign policy. The normally thorough Tanenhaus [now editor of the *New York Times Book Review*] generated nationwide headlines with a quote that turns out to have been distorted. It cites Deputy Defense Secretary Paul Wolfowitz on the topic of the president's case against Saddam. Here's the quote in the piece: "For bureaucratic reasons we settled on one issue, weapons of mass destruction, because it was the one reason everyone could agree on." Left out was the remainder of the quote, which we will now supply: "But there have always been three fundamental concerns: One is weapons of mass destruction, the second is support for terrorism. The third is the criminal treatment of the Iraqi people. Actually, I guess you could say there's a fourth over-riding one, which is the connection between the first two."

On the same program, *Weekly Standard* editor Bill Kristol reiterated that the quotation "was actually misquoted, taken out of context."[27] The next day on Fox's *Special Report with Brit Hume*, Mort Kondracke reiterated that Wolfowitz in his next sentence said that "weapons of mass destruction and their link to terrorism were very important reasons."[28]

On June 2, 2003, an editorial in the *Journal* joined the attack, claiming that a *Vanity Fair* press release promoting the Wolfowitz interview in its May issue "distorted" the same Wolfowitz quotation. The press release, said the editorial,

> spun as news the fact that Mr. Wolfowitz has said the following during an interview in early May: "The truth is that for reasons that have a lot to do with the U.S. government bureaucracy, we settled on the one issue that everyone could agree on which was weapons of mass destruction as the core reason." In Europe this has been seized on by the anti-war left as a source of vindication. . . . Mr. Wolfowitz's words were no contradiction of anything the U.S. said before the war. The allies had always given multiple reasons for ridding the world of Saddam. . . . The

Vanity *Fair* press release also failed to include that immediately after his WMD remarks, Mr. Wolfowitz had added [further statements] in the interview.[29]

The editorial then quoted Wolfowitz's additional sentences.

Encouraged to do so by Limbaugh, his listeners scrutinize the mainstream media for bias and worry about its effect on others more gullible than they. On his radio show in mid-April 2003, for example, a friend emailed Limbaugh with the worry that if weapons of mass destruction were not found in Iraq, the "liberal media" would make George Bush "toast." Limbaugh responded:

> This is a new era, these people in the elite media. They do not exist in a vacuum. They are not a monopoly. I'm getting email that is scrutinizing the tiniest detail. These networks aren't going to get away with it. Their days of getting away with it en masse are over. They have been unmasked. People know that their agenda is.... They put what they get from these networks in context.... It's going to be the elite media and the Democrats and the Frances [*sic*] and Germany who will have a lot of explaining to do. (April 10, 2003)

A year later, on April 22, 2004, Limbaugh featured a Harris poll showing that a majority of those surveyed believed that Saddam Hussein had weapons of mass destruction when the Iraq war started. Limbaugh used the survey to remind listeners that they should not listen to the "liberal" media.

Part of Limbaugh's unmasking of the mainstream involves decoding its language. Notice, he said, that "trial lawyers are never, ever called 'special interests' by the mainstream press" (November 19, 2002). "For Democrats, a tax cut is not [any] longer a tax cut; it's a tax 'holiday,' and a tax increase is now a 'no new tax cut.'... Tort reform is not tort reform. Tort reform has become a battle over the 'right to sue'" (December 6, 2002). "We're onto them, now, friends," said Limbaugh. "They're not going to get away with all of this." They don't call their plan a "tax cut," he reminded listeners in early January 2003, they call it a "tax rebate" (January 8, 2003).

Creating Alternative Frames

Media of all sorts frame their audiences' views of events. Conservative media are no exception. But in this process of framing, the conservative opinion media add a dimension missing in other media by regularly engaging in metacommunication about the frames of the mainstream. In short, conservative media not only frame the political world but reframe the content and identity of nonconservative media. One way in which they do this is by attaching the labels "liberal" and "bias" to them and then by arguing that they employ a "double standard," as we mentioned in our earlier analysis of the Trent Lott case. To show the impact of this sort of reframing, we will report survey evidence of the Limbaugh listeners' acceptance of Limbaugh's framing of both the Unabomber and the Oklahoma City bomber.

Before doing so, we will illustrate this process through an analysis of conservative media's treatment of the charge in the California gubernatorial race of 2003 that the Republican frontrunner, Arnold Schwarzenegger, had sexually harassed women.

REFRAMING SCHWARZENEGGER AS GROPER VERSUS DAVIS AS BATTERER: THE DOUBLE STANDARD OVERLOOKS DEMOCRATS' CRIMES

On the Thursday before the California gubernatorial recall of Tuesday, October 7, 2003, the *Los Angeles Times* carried an investigative report under the headline "Women Say Schwarzenegger Groped, Humiliated Them," which included interviews with six women who reported that they had been fondled by Schwarzenegger. The story reported: "Six women who came into contact with Arnold Schwarzenegger on movie sets, in studio offices and in other settings over the last three decades say he touched them in a sexual manner without their consent."[30]

The Republican contender's spokesperson, Sean Walsh, initially denied the charges. Soon afterward, Schwarzenegger labeled the accusations "trash politics." At the same time, however, he acknowledged that he had "behaved badly sometimes" and "done things that were not right, which I thought [were] playful [on movie sets]. But I now recognize that I have offended people. And to those people that I have offended I want to say to them I am deeply sorry about that, and I apologize."

Schwarzenegger's supporters engaged in a complex strategy to minimize the effect of the allegations. The response included testimonials from the candidate's wife, newscaster and Kennedy family member Maria Shriver, that Schwarzenegger was a good father and husband and an "A-plus human being." Shriver also claimed that many of the stories had been fabricated and attacked the *Los Angeles Times* for the investigation and for publishing the story so close to the election.

The conservative media outlets responded by suggesting that whereas the *Los Angeles Times* had investigated Schwarzenegger for abusing women, it had not awarded comparable treatment to charges that Gray Davis had battered his female staff; hence the *Times* was employing a double standard. If successful, this move would both undercut the credibility of the source newspaper and associate Davis with actions more offensive than groping. The conservative claim was a standard one: the "liberal media" were eager to undercut conservatives and protect "liberals." And voters were encouraged to reject the Schwarzenegger groping allegations but trust those about Davis's supposed staff abuse.

Noteworthy is the fact that the columnist who alleged that the *Los Angeles Times* was "sitting on" the Davis story was featured in the conservative but not the mainstream media. Among those embracing the story were Fox and Limbaugh, though not the *Journal*. In a *Los Angeles Daily* column published October 4, 2003, the Saturday before the election, columnist Jill Stewart stated: "Since at least 1997, the *Times* has been sitting on information that Gov. Gray Davis is an 'office batterer' who has attacked female members of his staff, thrown objects at subservients and launched into red-faced fits, screaming the f-word until staffers cower."[31] The day before the election, Stewart's column was synthesized approvingly by Bill Whalen in the *Daily Standard*, on Fox's *Hannity and Colmes*,[32] *The Big Story with John Gibson*,[33] and *Special Report with Brit Hume*,[34] and—consistent with our notion that conservative media exist and carry conservative frames, albeit to much smaller audiences—on other cable stations, as well as on MSNBC's *Scarborough Country*. Stewart also appeared not only on Fox but also on MSNBC's short-lived *Buchanan and Press*.

In the *Daily Standard*, Whalen made a connection to the Stewart piece, noting: "Something else the *Times* has to explain: why it took a pass on allegations of Gray Davis mistreating women. Davis-is-an-ogre stories are the stuff of Sacramento lore, going back to the '70s when he was Jerry Brown's chief of staff."[35] On *Scarborough Country*, Stewart noted:

> I think it is journalistic malpractice, because the *L.A. Times* assigned, as you know, two hard-hitting teams seven weeks ago to get Arnold Schwarzenegger on his steroid use. They published that a week ago Monday. And on his sexual harassment charges, they even went to foreign countries to track it down. Did they assign a team to look into the Gray Davis violence charges? No, they did not. And it is just a horrible, horrible bias on the part of the paper.[36]

As Californians were balloting to determine whether Davis would be recalled, Limbaugh drew his listeners' attention to the story, both by reading extensive passages from the Stewart column and by linking to it on his website.

His argument was consistent with the one advanced in the other conservative shows.

> The *Los Angeles Times* has become a casualty of their naked bias against Arnold Schwarzenegger, with a thousand people canceling their subscriptions to the paper after these last-minute stories from women. The paper barely seems to have checked its sources before running to press. The latest allegation was proven totally false in about 30 minutes. But the double standard becomes even more clear and infuriating when you read Jill Stewart's *Los Angeles Daily News* story asking why the *Times* did not reveal Gray Davis's serial abuse of women staffers.

(Limbaugh was a day behind the other conservative outlets because on October 6 he devoted the first portion of his show to addressing revelations that he was under investigation for abuse of prescription painkillers.)

What interests us about Stewart's column and its afterlife is the fact that her charges were all but ignored by the media not in the conservative ambit. At the same time, the conservative media reframed the Schwarzenegger charges to argue that Davis was worse than Schwarzenegger and the mainstream media were complicit in suppressing that fact.

On Sunday, October 12, 2003, *Los Angeles Times* Editor John Carroll defended the process by which the Schwarzenegger story and been researched and written and noted: "It was written that the paper failed to follow up on reports that Davis had mistreated women in his office. Fact: Virginia Ellis, a recent Pulitzer Prize finalist, and other *Times* reporters investigated this twice. Their finding both times: The discernible facts didn't support a story."[37]

After Schwarzenegger was elected governor of California in the recall of 2003, Limbaugh reminded his listeners that there was a lesson to be learned from the *Los Angeles Times's* report that the actor had groped women.

> As you think back to what the *LA Times* did in this gubernatorial race, remember that's not even the half of it. The next time the *LA Times* or any other mainstream liberal institution starts talking to you about the aftermath in Iraq or the war on terrorism, I want you to remember this business of what they did with Schwarzenegger, and I want you to tell yourself "Schwarzenegger is not an isolated episode." If they're doing it there, where else are they acting as Democrat house organs? (October 10, 2003)

In 1996, we were able to find out whether reframing has an effect on the target audience because during our election study that year Limbaugh argued that the media were treating Timothy McVeigh, the alleged Oklahoma bomber, and Ted Kaczynski, the alleged Unabomber, differently.

For Limbaugh, the Kaczynski case was an object lesson in media bias. On his April 8, 1996, broadcast, Limbaugh read what he called a "great" letter to the editor of *USA Today* in which the writer blasted the paper and the media in general for its differential treatment of the Unabomber and the Oklahoma City bombing. The letter asserted that the media would not likely make any strong connections between the Unabomber and the radical environmental group Earth First! although it drew the connection between the Oklahoma City bombing suspects and militia groups. Limbaugh said: "That's exactly right. I mentioned last week, if they had found one nine millimeter pistol in this guy's shack, they would have portrayed him as a right wing, anti-government zealot, [with] links to the militia movement." On his April 9, 1996, broadcast, Limbaugh added:

> Now there's the February 2, 1994, edition of the publication called
> *Earth First!* And I love the way the *Washington Post* refers to *Earth
> First!* "an outspoken environmentalist group." When is the last time
> you have ever read in the *Washington Post* about me being outspo-
> ken? Rush Limbaugh . . . it's the radical right wing, controversial, talk
> show host.

After reading the article in the *Washington Post* about Earth First!'s negative comments about a public relations firm executive who had Exxon as a client, Limbaugh related how this executive was killed by one of Kaczynski's bombs.

> Kaczynski read all this and sent a Burston-Marsteller PR executive,
> Thomas Moser . . . a pipe bomb, because of this *Earth First!* journal. . . .
> Now even in this [the *Washington Post*] story nobody gets on *Earth
> First!*'s case. But if this were a conservative, right-wing publication that
> had inspired this guy, the headline and cover story would be about the
> group and the Unabomber would be simply a mindless twit little tool of
> the extremist right-wing group. There'd be no talk about genius gone
> awry. . . . And the *Weekly Standard* apparently asks this question . . . "If
> it's OK to blame Rush Limbaugh for Timothy McVeigh, can't we agree
> that Al Gore is responsible for the Unabomber?"

Limbaugh's commentary on Kaczynski and McVeigh attempted to balance what he saw as an ideological bias in the mainstream media's treatment of extremists. With this event, as with others, Limbaugh tried to teach his audience to interpret the mainstream news media by pointing to what he perceived as their inconsistencies and ideological slant. In the case of Ted Kaczynski, he may have succeeded.

When asked in our 1996 survey, "Do you think that news stories about Kaczynski have been more favorable than ones about McVeigh, less favorable, or have they been about the same?" Limbaugh listeners were more likely than nonlisteners to say the media favored Kaczynski. Other PTR listeners' views were more like those of PTR nonlisteners than Limbaugh listeners. Although all groups reported that Kaczynski got more favorable coverage, Limbaugh listeners were strongest in this view. As we mentioned earlier in regard to using survey data, it is possible that those holding this view were simply more likely to be in Limbaugh's audience. If that is the case, his exposition was a reinforcement rather than a cause of their inference about the relative treatment of the two terrorists. We think it improbable, however, that Limbaugh's listeners would be more likely than conservative nonlisteners to hold a view that is not tied to usual Republican Party heuristics.

How the Mainstream Media Present Limbaugh

When he is featured on mainstream media, Limbaugh underscores his own importance (he was after all invited) and helps those shows build ratings by urging his listeners to turn to the mainstream to catch his appearance. After being asked to deliver election night comments on NBC in 2002, he told his listeners, "So I'll be on between 10 to 11 PM ET and then again at 1 AM.... So be sure to tune in Tuesday night on your local NBC broadcast affiliate" (November 4, 2002).

LEGITIMIZATION

When Democrats respond to Limbaugh, they enhance his prominence by increasing his access to the mainstream media. Occasionally influential players in the mainstream even rise to his defense. A set of exchanges with Senate Majority leader Tom Daschle is illustrative.

For Limbaugh, Daschle was "El Diablo" (December 9, 2002), "Puff," or "the Puffster" ("The Puffster is all excited about running for president," January 3, 2003). Limbaugh also impugned Daschle's patriotism by calling him "Hanoi Tom" (November 15, 2002). His attacks on Daschle challenged his motives, in effect accusing him of being a traitor and allying him with "Hanoi Jane" Fonda and Tokyo Rose. "What more do you want to do to destroy this country than what you've already done?" he said of Daschle.

> It is unconscionable what this man has done! This stuff gets broadcast around the world, Senator. What do you want your nickname to be? Hanoi Tom? Tokyo Tom? . . . You sit there and pontificate on the fact that we're not winning the war on terrorism when you and your party have done nothing but try to sabotage it.[38]

Limbaugh's callers picked up the theme. "He [Daschle] should be ashamed of himself," said a female caller. "They gave aid and comfort to the enemy. He's not interested in the safety of this country" (November 20, 2002).

On November 20, 2002, Daschle responded: "Rush Limbaugh and all of the Rush Limbaugh wannabees have a very shrill edge. And that's entertainment. Even they—we were told that even people who don't agree with them listen because they're entertaining." He continued:

> And you know, but what happens when Rush Limbaugh attacks those of us in public life is that people aren't satisfied just to listen. They want to act because they get emotionally invested. And so, you know, the threats to those of us in public life go up dramatically, and on our families and on us in a way that's very disconcerting. You know, we see it in foreign countries. And we think, well my God, how can this religious fundamentalism become so violent? Well, it's the same shrill rhetoric. It's that same shrill power that motivates. They—you know, they—that somebody says something, and then it becomes a little more shrill the next time, and then more shrill the next time.

Do these encounters damage Limbaugh with his listeners? G. Gordon Liddy said that when he was attacked by Clinton, it was "a feather in my cap."[39]

Some mainstream media critics, including the *Washington Post*'s Howard Kurtz, dismissed the notion that Limbaugh's words could elicit threats and violence against those he attacks. Kurtz noted:

> Limbaugh is an entertainer with sharp claws, but he is more policy-oriented than many of the people who shout on cable night after night. He doesn't give out phone numbers or urge his listeners to call anyone. . . . But to try to link the actions of a few crazies to a prominent commentator—one so "extreme" that he sat next to Tom Brokaw on election night—only elevates Limbaugh in the eyes of his fans.[40]

The hardest hitting interviewer on national television did not challenge Limbaugh in their *Meet the Press* encounter (November 23, 2002). The questions were instead designed to elicit expository answers. When Limbaugh alleged "there are mainstream liberals" who believed that "Bush had some role in Wellstone's death," Tim Russert did not ask Limbaugh to name them, for example.

When Russert said, "Democrats said when you compared him [Daschle] to Yasir Arafat that that was over the line," Limbaugh asked, "When did I do this? You know, we—th—this—I—I don't—that—that was—that was said on *Crossfire* earlier this week, and then whoever said it apologized for it because they couldn't find evidence of it in the s—in the place they thought they had seen it. I don't recall that. I have no clue what that's about." Instead of turning to other examples, such as Limbaugh's question about whether Daschle wanted his nickname to be Hanoi Tom or Tokyo Tom, Russert changes topic.[41]

LIMBAUGH ATTRACTS SUBSTANTIAL MEDIA ATTENTION

Prominent treatment of Limbaugh in the mainstream media is not a new phenomenon. To analyze Limbaugh's presence in mainstream media, our colleague Joseph Turow created an index. He examined how often 28 daily newspapers mentioned talk radio and a number of prominent individuals, including talk radio hosts, from November 1989 to November 1995. The papers were the only top-50-circulation newspapers in the Lexis Nexis or Dialog databases that go back before 1989. Figure 9.1 shows that from 1989 to 1995, the yearly appearance of the phrases "talk radio" and "radio talk" in these daily newspapers rose from about 2,700 to almost 7,000.

The number of items in the mainstream press that mentioned Limbaugh compared favorably to the number that have mentioned key U.S. government and media figures. About 225,000 items mentioned President Clinton between November 1993 and November 1995. About 67,000 mentioned Vice President Gore, 15,000 mentioned then senator George Mitchell, almost 28,000 mentioned David Letterman, and about 4,200 mentioned Ted Koppel. Talk radio and Limbaugh fell into the middle of these rankings (20,799), with fewer articles than Gore but substantially more than Mitchell, House leader Richard Armey (R. Tex.), and the host of ABC's *Nightline*, Ted Koppel. A Lexis Nexis search reveals that from fall 2001 through fall 2003, Limbaugh was mentioned in 7,511 articles. (We did not carry this analysis from late fall 2003 through the end of 2004 because allegations of Limbaugh's doctor-shopping to obtain narcotics would have required that

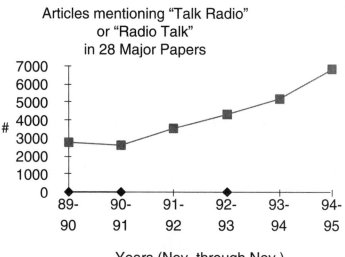

Articles mentioning "Talk Radio"
or "Radio Talk"
in 28 Major Papers

FIGURE 9.1. Articles mentioning Talk Radio

we analyze each article to determine whether it was about his show or about that scandal.)

THE MAINSTREAM CRITIQUES LIMBAUGH

The complexity of the relationship among the conservative media, the Republican-controlled White House, the mainstream media, and liberal commentators was on display in the period between April 30 and May 17, 2004. On May 4, 2004, Limbaugh analogized the humiliation of Iraqi prisoners by U.S. forces in an Iraqi prison to a Skull and Bones initiation. "This is no different than what happens at the Skull and Bones initiation," he observed, and went on to comment:

> and we're going to ruin people's lives over it, and we're going to hamper our military effort, and then we're going to really hammer 'em because they had a good time. You know, these people are being fired at everyday—I'm talking about the people having a good time. You ever hear of emotional release? You ever hear of need to blow some steam off? These people are the enemy.

On May 6, White House press representative Scott McClennan was challenged by a reporter on the Limbaugh comment. "If you stand out strongly trying to let the Arab world know that this is wrong and then you have the proverbial spokesperson for the conservative party saying this, doesn't that send a mixed message?" asked the correspondent. Whereas in the Trent Lott case, Limbaugh had helped guide the White House to a politically desirable outcome, in this case he was off the White House message. The liberal media-monitoring website MediaMatters.org responded to Limbaugh's comments with a 30-second ad featured on its website and aired for four days in Washington, D.C., on CNBC, CNN, ESPN, FOX News, and MSNBC. The ad said:

NARRATOR (*voice-over*): Secretary Rumsfeld called the torture of Iraqis sadistic...cruel...
RUMSFELD: *Fundamentally un-American.*
NARRATOR (*voice-over*): But here's what Rush Limbaugh said:
LIMBAUGH: *This is no different than what happens at the Skull and Bones initiation.... I'm talking about people having a good time. These people—you ever heard of emotional release? You ever heard of needing to blow some steam off?*
NARRATOR (*voice-over*): This is the most listened-to political commentator in America?

In the mainstream media, others chimed in to express their consternation at Limbaugh's statements. "In desperation," wrote Frank Rich,

some torture apologists are trying to concoct the fictions the administration used to ply so well. Limbaugh has been especially creative. The photos of the abuses at Abu Ghraib "look like standard good old American pornography," he said as the story spread, as if he might grandfather wartime atrocities into an entertainment industry that, however deplorable to Islam, has more fans in our Christian country than Major League Baseball. In Mr. Limbaugh's view, the guards humiliating the Iraqis were just "having a good time" and their pictures look "just like anything you'd see Madonna or Britney Spears do onstage.... I mean, this is something that you can see onstage at Lincoln Center from an N.E.A. grant, maybe on *Sex and the City*."[42]

"Of course, some people didn't even mind the pictures," noted Jonathan Alter in *Newsweek*. "Rush Limbaugh told his audience last week that the whole thing reminded him of a 'Skull and Bones initiation.' He argued that the torturers should be cut a little slack."[43] Responses such as these to Limbaugh's content are part of a mutual monitoring system in which the mainstream monitors the conservative media and vice versa.

This form of media accountability has a number of advantages for the democratic system. Among others, it ensures that there is an ongoing critique of media conduct from both the left (where Media Matters.org, MSNBC's *Countdown with Keith Olbermann*, and *Air America* provide regular commentary) and the right. This monitoring process should increase the sense among reporters and commentators that theirs is not the final word. Unseemly or inaccurate comments will be flagged and critiqued. This should produce a self-policing that dampens down bizarre or indefensible comments. One might surmise, for example, that Limbaugh abandoned his practice of "aborting" callers and largely discontinued his use of the term "femi-Nazi" after both were (mistakenly we believe) offered up by the mainstream as typical of his commentary.

The process of mutual critique is politically significant as well. The conservative and mainstream media's castigation of both Republican Trent Lott and Democrat Chris Dodd for their statements about Strom Thurmond and Robert Byrd, respectively, strongly signaled crossparty disapproval of the country's segregationist past.

Conclusion

Taken together, these analyses suggest that not only does Limbaugh vigilantly monitor the mainstream media for bias but he also reframes those channels as purveyors of a "double standard" that disadvantages conservatives and their ideology. In this view, a perspective shared by the Fox hosts on whom we focus and by the *Journal*'s editorial pages, the mainstream distorts, makes serious uncorrected mistakes, and omits key information. The material we have presented in this chapter strengthens our claim that the double standard argument is central to the conservative opinion media's strategy: they displace mainstream interpretations of events by engaging in a special form of reframing. They accomplish this by offering alternative frames. In the Kaczynski-McVeigh example, we found some evidence that such framing by Limbaugh affects his listeners.

This rhetoric about "liberal media bias" also gives conservatives a common set of lines of arguments and a shared vocabulary for dismissing mainstream interpretations of news. When a listener notices an instance in which the bias identified by Limbaugh is exemplified by a Democratic speaker or a reporter, that person can feel in-the-know, clever in his or her capacity to unmask the maneuver, and superior in his invulnerability to it. The unnoticed becomes noticed at the same time the observation tags it as evidence of a larger claim. The tropes are simple: Democrats have a playbook. The media are liberal, are biased, and employ a double standard that disadvantages conservatives. You will be influenced by the media-reinforced playbook unless you come to see the media as Limbaugh does. Limbaugh positions himself as the one who reveals what the "liberal media" would otherwise conceal about their biases. In the process of becoming part of this community of interpreters of mainstream bias, the conservative opinion media set the stage for creating what we will call in a later chapter a knowledge and opinion enclave.

Engendering and Reinforcing Distrust
of Mainstream Media

Complaints from the Right about the bias of the mainstream media are not new. Speaking in Des Moines, Iowa, on November 13, 1969, for example, Vice President Spiro Agnew stated:

> The people can let the networks know that they want their news straight and objective. The people can register their complaints on bias through mail to the networks and phone calls to local stations. This is one case where the people must defend themselves, where the citizen, not the Government, must be the reformer; where the consumer can be the most effective crusader.[1]

Long before Limbaugh embraced it, the *Wall Street Journal* and organizations such as Accuracy in Media, founded in 1969 by Reed Irvine, had made "liberal bias" a conservative catchphrase. The argument gained traction from and may have contributed to public dissatisfaction with the press. As communication professor Yariv Tsfati[2] found in his examination of trends in confidence in the media tracked on the General Social Survey from 1973 through 1996, those who responded that they "have hardly any confidence in the press" increased from 15% in 1973 to 41% in 1996. The 1990s show an almost 10% increase alone. Forty percent having "hardly any confidence" is hardly a vote of confidence.

In this chapter, we show that the rhetoric Limbaugh employs in his daily attacks on the mainstream news media goes hand in hand with his audience's mistrust of these outlets. Through the mid-1990s, he made these attacks while at the same time his audience continued to consume large amounts of mainstream news. His attacks have continued unabated whether the Republican Party has been in power in Washington or not. In 1996, when our surveys began, the impact of generally increasing mistrust of the mainstream news media seemed to have had little effect on his audiences' use of them; however, this initially (i.e., in 1996) higher level of consumption of mainstream broadcast news had declined by 2004, in part because of the emergence of Fox as a serious alternative to mainstream broadcast and cable.[3]

In what follows we will argue that (1) listeners to Limbaugh have greater mistrust of the mainstream news media than other groups; (2) through the mid-1990s, Limbaugh's rhetoric portrayed the mainstream media in ways likely to engender mistrust; (3) through the same period, this activation of mistrust in the mainstream media did not substantially diminish his audience's consumption of mainstream news sources, though it did coincide with increased consumption of nonmainstream sources. However, we also show that by 2004 Limbaugh's audience was turning away from mainstream broadcast news and, as noted, becoming more reliant on conservative outlets such as Fox.

Mainstream News Media Activate Mistrust

Our previous research showed that certain forms of news coverage activate public cynicism about political campaigns and policy debates.[4] That research did not include talk radio.

As we reported earlier, in 1996 we conducted a survey (PTR Survey 1996) of regular and nonregular listeners of PTR as a part of a large-scale national study of PTR, including Limbaugh, during the presidential election year. The study deployed a five-wave national survey, an experiment, and content analyses. (For discussion of some of the study's procedural details, see the appendix to chapter 5 at our website.)

To understand the reaction of the audience of PTR to mainstream sources of news, we both asked a series of questions over the course of the 1996 presidential election year and conducted an experimental test of the impact of PTR on audience attitudes (PTR Experiment 1996). Our survey included an oversample of talk radio listeners. In addition, as we noted earlier, we scrutinized the content of Limbaugh's programing over the 11-month period from January until just after the presidential election in November 1996.

We assessed trust in the mainstream news media four times during the 1996 election season. Early in the primary, respondents were asked a general question about the major news media, including television news, the newspaper with which they were most familiar, and news magazines. Our question asked whether these media "help society solve its problems or get in the way."

Figure 10.1 shows that Limbaugh listeners compared to other groups were more disposed to accept the claim that the major news media were standing

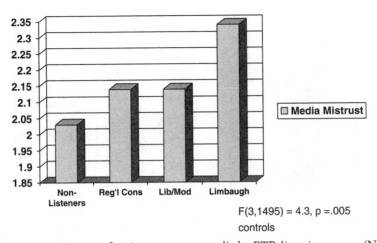

FIGURE 10.1. Mistrust of mainstream news media by PTR listening group. (Note: MSMM is mainstream mass media; size of F statistic indicates differences between listening groups are significant)

in the way of rather than helping solve society's problems. Regular Limbaugh listeners were not only more likely than nonlisteners to choose this option but also more mistrustful of the mainstream news media than were listeners to either liberal/moderate or conservative political talk programming.[5]

Later in the primary period, we asked respondents how fair and balanced they considered each of several news sources.[6] These included newspapers with which they were familiar, television evening news, and PTR. We registered their responses in numbers from 1 to 7, with 1 being least fair and balanced and 7 being most fair and balanced. The findings summarized in figure 10.2 show that listeners to Limbaugh rated television and newspapers as least fair and balanced while they rated PTR as most fair and balanced, even after controlling for a variety of other factors. (For analytical details see the appendix to this chapter at our website.) As before, nonlisteners are most trusting of the mainstream news sources and least trusting of PTR, with other PTR listening groups in between.

During the heat of the 1996 presidential election, we asked respondents whether the mainstream news media were doing a good job with the campaign. Our question was one we had used in earlier studies of mistrust. It asked respondents to choose between two options: "Network TV evening news tells people what they need to know about the presidential candidates' stands on issues" OR "Network TV evening news spend too much

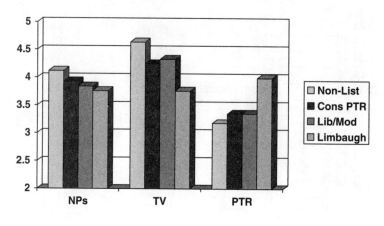

Fair & Balanced: 3 Media

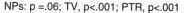

NPs: p =.06; TV, p<.001; PTR, p<.001

FIGURE 10.2. Judgments of fairness and balance for three media by PTR listening group. (Note: Non-List = nonlisteners; Cons = listeners to conservative PTR; Lib/Mod = listeners to liberal and moderate PTR; Limbaugh = regular listeners to Limbaugh; NPs = newspapers)

time reporting on campaign strategies to tell people what they need to know about issues." Responses were scored 3 for focusing on strategy rather than issue, 1 for issues, and 2 for a voluntary response of "both" or "it depends." Figure 10.3 presents a familiar pattern, with Limbaugh listeners responding that the established media are most likely to focus on the strategic aspects of the campaign rather than campaign issues.

After Bill Clinton defeated Bob Dole to win his second term in office, we recontacted our respondents to ask about the election's outcome and, in particular, their perceptions about the media's role in it. We wondered whether the respondents felt that major news media helped citizens make good decisions about the candidates or got in the way. We also asked whether television news and newspaper coverage of the political campaigns were fair and balanced. The responses to these two were similar enough to combine them in an index.[7]

The overall pattern remains about the same across four periods and across somewhat differently worded questions. Limbaugh listeners were more mistrustful of mainstream (print and television) news sources. Specifically, they considered them more likely to (1) get in the way of society solving its problems, (2) not be helpful to citizens' decision making, and (3) be unfair and imbalanced. There were sharp differences between Limbaugh listeners and

Mistrusting Campaign News

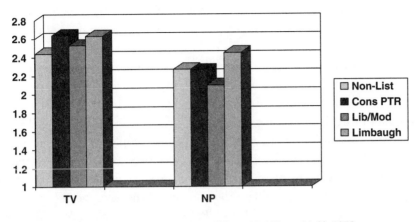

TV: p<.02; NP: p<.01; N=1279

FIGURE 10.3. Adjusted means for issue-oriented judgments about news media by PTR group. (Note: TV = mainstream TV news; NP= mainstream newspapers; Non-List = nonlisteners of PTR; Cons = listeners of conservative PTR; Lib/Mod = listeners of liberal and moderate PTR; Limbaugh = listeners to Limbaugh).

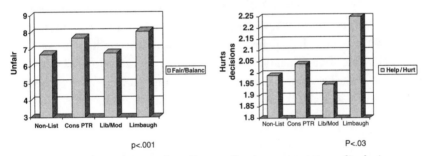

FIGURE 10.4. Adjusted means for mistrust of mainstream mass media during election: Unfair and imbalanced and hurts decisions rather than helps.

nonlisteners and even some differences between Limbaugh's audience and those who listen to other conservative programs.

What our results cannot show is whether the effect was produced by listening to Limbaugh's rhetoric about the news media. As the model we outlined in chapter 5 suggests, it is plausible that mistrust of the mainstream news media drives people to PTR in the first place, where their prior dispositions are reinforced.

To see if exposure to PTR could affect people's perceptions of the news media's biases, we conducted an experiment in which people of all ideologies were exposed to various types of talk radio for a week. (For details of this experiment see the appendix to chapter 5 at our website.) Six listening groups were created, and each listened, each day for a week, to one hour of the following on tape: (1) *Talk of the Nation* on NPR; (2) Limbaugh; (3) conservative hosts other than Limbaugh; (4) liberal hosts; (5) a combination of liberal and conservative hosts; and (6) nonpolitical talk including relationships, movies, health, cars, and so on. Each day focused on a different topic. On a given day, each host focused on the same topic.

At the conclusion of the week, participants completed a questionnaire about the programs as well as political and social issues. One question sought their evaluations of the mainstream news media, including specifically the degree to which they agreed with the statement "The news media get in the way of society solving its problems." Participants were grouped into those who were politically liberal, moderate, and conservative. These three groups were mostly similar and were nearly neutral in their agreement with the claim that news media get in the way. However, conservatives exposed to conservative PTR, including Limbaugh, tended to agree more with the claim than did liberals exposed to the same PTR. Interestingly, the same pattern existed when liberals and conservatives listened to NPR's *Talk of the Nation* for the week. Apparently, ideological conservatives were primed to think of their disdain for the news media's role in society both by the conservative hosts and the more liberal hosts of PTR, while liberals had the opposite reaction.[8] These experimental data suggest that exposure to PTR can affect attitudes toward the media, even after exposures as brief as five one-hour segments of political talk about events and about the media.

Limbaugh's Rhetoric about Mainstream News Media

During the 1996 presidential campaign, our research group conducted detailed content analyses of various news media, including PTR and especially the programs of Limbaugh. For most of the year, transcripts of Limbaugh's shows were made available to us from one of Limbaugh's audience members. Comparisons of his transcripts and audiotapes showed that the transcripts were a faithful rendering of what Limbaugh had said. After a while, Limbaugh's unpaid transcriber decided it was time to get a life outside of the world of Limbaugh's programming, so for the remainder of the study, we recorded Limbaugh's shows and transcribed them. The transcripts made it possible to conduct computerized word searches as well as more subtle forms of content analysis.

As noted, two topics were discussed every day on Limbaugh's program from January through November 1996. They were President Bill Clinton and the mainstream mass media. The next four topics not related to the news media were Democrats (96% of shows), Republicans or the GOP (94%), Bob Dole (91%), and Hillary Clinton (88%). Not only was Limbaugh preoccupied with the mainstream print and broadcast press but also he was specific about the outlets. Mentions of the *New York Times* occurred on 83% of his shows; the *Washington Post* was mentioned 66% of the time, CNN 57%, and the three major networks (ABC, CBS, NBC) at least 39%. Limbaugh also drew in content from and invited attention to content in two conservative outlets, the *Journal* (48%) and the *Washington Times* (32.4%).

From just after Labor Day (September 3) until just after Election Day (November 11), we evaluated Limbaugh's comments about the mainstream news media. The comments were not always negative. We divided them into three broad categories: attacks, positive citations, and reframings. On these 47 dates, we found clear examples of 58 reframings, 52 attacks on the media for their actions and commentary, and 76 positive citations of news with which Limbaugh agreed.

Limbaugh also attacked the mainstream media for their failings, inaccurate reporting, and biases against his friends, including his former television producer Roger Ailes, whom Murdoch had named head of Fox News. On October 21, 1996, for example, Limbaugh criticized the mainstream news media for their concerns about Murdoch's takeover of Fox News Network. He argued that the mainstream claimed Fox News would become a home for conservative points of view. Limbaugh said:

> Fox News Channel is being portrayed by other mainstream media organizations. You cannot read a story or listen to a report about the new Fox News Channel without hearing some jerk throw in the fact that Rupert Murdoch is going to have a conservative slant on the news. It's going to be a conservative network.
>
> Now that is not what Murdoch has said and that's not what Roger Ailes has said. All they said is they want to have people who can report the news and get things factually correct and they tried to hire people who do not have a bias against conservatives.

In the context of this event and its reporting by the mainstream news media, Limbaugh takes the opportunity to reframe the issue as one of double standards, one for liberals and Democrats and one for conservatives and Republicans. At issue is the hiring of former Clinton aide George Stephanopoulos as a reporter and commentator.

Now, would you describe George Stephanopoulos as unbiased? Would you describe George Stephanopoulos as nonpartisan? Would you describe George Stephanopoulos as objective? No, George Stephanopoulos is a Democrat. George Stephanopoulos is a liberal. George Stephanopoulos is an advisor to Bill Clinton. George Stephanopoulos's job the past four years has been doing everything he can to make Bill Clinton look as good as he can and CBS has no compunction about having a guy like Stephanopoulos as a reporter but you let the Fox News Channel go out and say they're just going to try to hire some people to do the news accurately.

Limbaugh then proposes a hypothetical to his audience to show the media's double standard.

I tell you something folks, this is akin to any network wanting to hire me to be a reporter. Of course, if that happened—if word of that leaked out I'll guarantee you that whoever was responsible for it at whatever network would be summarily dismissed and fired and maybe sent to the gallows for daring to have a guy like Limbaugh. You want to have such a partisan person as Limbaugh on your news?

Limbaugh's comments about the mainstream news outlets were not invariably unfavorable. When a news report gave him ammunition to skewer Bill or Hillary Clinton or to attack the Democrats in Congress, he did not hesitate to formally cite the article or broadcast, sometimes including its author, always noting the network or newspaper. For example, on his show of October 10, 1996, he said:

My friends I read a little story here in the *New York Times* today that is troubling. There is a bunch of cables back and forth from the State Department. And the White House is doing what it can now to bury this cable, but I have to give credit to the *New York Times* because the *New York Times* is the one that reports this in their editions today.

After blasting the *New York Times* for endorsing Bill Clinton for a second term, Limbaugh uses the paper's coverage to bring up what he casts as an unfolding scandal:

Now let's go back to the front page of THE *New York Times*. Keep all this in mind as you hear this. A few days after leaving the employment of an Indonesian billionaire to become a trade official in the Clinton Administration, John Wong attended at least two meetings at which important Indonesian trade issues were discussed. Well finally, what

I told you about last week in our list of our undisputed facts...have now made to the front page of the *New York Times*.

Mistrust and Consumption of Mainstream News in 1996

The picture that emerged was that Limbaugh listeners mistrusted the news media more than did any other group. Keep in mind that Fox News was not yet a serious alternative for these listeners. Our claim in 1996 found support at several points in time and with several different questions assessing the trustworthiness of the news media. The finding invited the questions: Does this mistrust translate into behavior? Do Limbaugh listeners consume lower quantities of news from mainstream sources than other listeners to PTR and the general public of nonlisteners? The short answer to the second question is that in 1996, they did not consume less. In fact, Limbaugh listeners were heavy consumers of mainstream news, despite their elevated mistrust of these sources. However, as we will argue in a moment, by 2004, that had changed.

THE PRIMARIES OF 1996

When asked during the primaries of 1996 about their consumption of news and editorials from a daily newspaper, 53% of Limbaugh listeners reported they were regular readers (i.e., they read a daily newspaper two or more times a week). Of other PTR listeners 51% said the same, and 38% of nonlisteners. When asked about "national TV evening news," 63% of Limbaugh listeners claimed to be regular consumers, 64% of other PTR listeners, and 58% of non-listeners. (During the 2004 primaries, 50.1% of Limbaugh listeners reported watching network broadcast evening news two or more times a week.)

In 1996, Limbaugh listeners were big fans of C-SPAN, with 50% reporting watching regularly or sometimes, in contrast to 44% for other PTR listeners and 32% of nonlisteners. These comparisons indicate that despite their mistrust, in 1996 Limbaugh listeners were heavy consumers of mainstream news. However, they were not likely consumers of NPR or *News Hour with Jim Lehrer,* whereas listeners to other forms of PTR were.

THE ELECTION

During the heat of the election in October 1996, participants were asked how many days in the past seven they had watched national television news or read a newspaper for national news. Of Limbaugh listeners, 44% said five

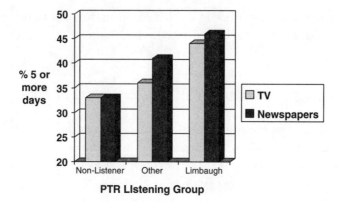

FIGURE 10.5. Percentage reporting 5 or more days of TV news or newspaper reading during 1996 presidential campaign.

or more days for television and 46% said five or more days for newspapers. By contrast, listeners to other PTR said 36% for television and 41% for newspapers. Nonlisteners reported 33% for television news and 33% for newspapers. So during both the primary and election periods, Limbaugh listeners were as ready consumers of mainstream national news sources as other groups. The fact that they consumed more than nonlisteners is unsurprising, given their strong political interests. In 1996, Limbaugh listeners' mistrust of mainstream news media did not undermine their interest in or consumption of news from these sources. Nor did it create a substitution effect whereby exposure to Limbaugh replaced exposure to the mainstream.

In order to make sure that these simple percentages warranted our inferences from them, several other analyses were carried out. (We report some of them in the appendix to this chapter at our website.) These included creation of an index of exposure and attention to the two most important mainstream sources developed from our questionnaire. This index was elevated when people report high levels of exposure and attention to news sources. Even after controlling for other possible explanatory factors, Limbaugh listeners were the strongest on this index in comparison to the three other groups and significantly different from nonlisteners and listeners to liberal/moderate PTR. Moreover, if Limbaugh listeners' mistrust of mainstream news sources affected consumption of news from those sources, then we would expect that those with greater mistrust would be more likely to use the mainstream news less. We assessed this possibility during both the primary period (late February to early March 1996) and the runup to the election (October 1996). Those who were more mistrusting were neither more nor less likely to consume mainstream news media, either in general or for individual groups of listeners.[9]

THE POSTELECTION PERIOD

In the period just following the election, November 12–18, 1996, respondents were contacted again about their reactions to the election. When we evaluated their trust of the news media at this crucial postelection juncture, we found that Limbaugh listeners were even more mistrusting of the news media. They saw them as more biased, more likely to get in the way of citizens' making good decisions in the election, less fair and balanced, and biased toward "liberals." (For details, see the appendix to this chapter at our website.)

The fact that the Limbaugh listening group and the conservative PTR group were significantly different from every other group[10] suggests very strong skepticism about the media in the postelection period by those whose candidate lost. While this result is a convenient explanation for the election results, it is consistent with other findings about Limbaugh listeners throughout the primary and election period.

However, this strong measure of mistrust of the mainstream media did not affect exposure to sources of news from the mainstream in 1996. Exposure to mainstream print and television news was unaffected by mistrust of mainstream sources, with no significant differences among the four listening groups and no effect of mistrust on exposure to print and television news. (For the regression results for PTR exposure on listening groups, controls, and mistrust of mainstream media, see the appendix to this chapter at our website.) In this case, Limbaugh listeners used PTR more than any other group and significantly more than nonlisteners and liberal/moderate PTR listeners.

Even though Limbaugh listeners were mistrustful of mainstream news media in 1996, that mistrust did not drive down their levels of consumption of these sources. Instead, they consumed more, sometimes significantly more, especially during the election period itself. The fact that those with elevated mistrust of mainstream media still consumed mainstream media seems counterintuitive. Why continue to pay attention to untrustworthy media sources of information? Some other research on mistrust and consumption of mainstream and nonmainstream media has reported that those with greater mistrust tend to consume more nonmainstream sources, such as PTR and internet news, and also tend to consume less of mainstream sources.[11] However, the magnitude of decrease in consumption of mainstream news is very modest—estimated by the authors at 1.6 days of reported news per week separating the most and least mistrustful audiences. The consistent result across studies finds mistrust of the mainstream associated with more exposure to PTR and internet sources. Yariv Tsfati and Joseph Cappella[12] also show that some people who mistrust media still consume it and that these mistrusting consumers of mainstream media are people high in need for cognition.[13] People who need cognitive stimulation and puzzle solving are most likely to still follow mainstream media even when they have elevated levels of mistrust of the very sources they consume.

A simple explanation for the heavier broadcast consumption in 1996 is the absence of conservative television or cable outlets. That changed with the advent of Fox News. Recall that in 2004, Limbaugh listeners were frequently viewers of Fox. Unsurprisingly, Fox viewership coincided with reduced viewership of mainstream broadcast, specifically viewership of network news on ABC, NBC, CBS, and PBS.

When comparing Limbaugh listeners both to those who did not listen to talk radio at all and to those who listened to talk radio other than Limbaugh's show, we found evidence in the NAES 2004 data that a significantly higher percent of Limbaugh listeners did not watch mainstream network news. In the NAES 2004 sample of more than 80,000 respondents, 47.4% of Limbaugh listeners did *not* watch television news from the mainstream news networks, while 37.6% of those not listening to any talk radio *failed to* watch mainstream television news. Of other talk radio listeners, 33% avoided mainstream television news. (For details see the appendix to this chapter at our website.)

This conclusion holds when adding the usual controls, for example education and income, among others. This does not mean, of course, that Limbaugh listeners are unexposed to mainstream news. In fact, they tend to consume more print news than nonlisteners—a consistent finding in data from 1996, 2000, and 2004, despite differences across samples and procedures. These differences survive a wide variety of controls, including controlling for Fox News viewership in the 2004 data. In that survey we had, for the first time, specific questions about Fox News.

Protecting the Conservative Disposition of the Audience

Our argument for the insulating function of conservative media does not presuppose exclusive or even predominant exposure to conservative media but rather argues that the framing and related persuasion effects of existing exposure protect the conservative dispositions of the conservative media's audience from persuasion when their members encounter or select mainstream sources of information and opinion. However, we do believe that the rise of the conservative media has increased the likelihood that individuals will be exposed to information and opinion they find congenial. We find evidence for that conclusion in the survey data across time that we just reported. Others have found evidence of this phenomenon as well.

Relying on Nielsen's people meter data across 62 prominent television networks in the first week of February 2003, media scholar James Webster found modest evidence of polarization, defined as "the tendency of channel audiences to be composed of devotees and nonviewers." Importantly, Webster's analysis of Fox viewers concluded that "even the audience for FOX News...spends 92.5% of its time watching something else on television. The rest of their time is widely distributed across the channels they have available." "Of course," he adds, "it may be that even a little exposure to certain materials has big social effects, but if these viewers live in cloistered communities, they evidently spend a good deal of time out and about."[14] The limitation of analysis by cable network for our purposes is, of course, that where we posit a pattern of reinforcement in exposure to news and opinion talk, these data include both entertainment and nonentertainment programming.

Drawing on Webster's analysis of Nielsen data, political scientist Marcus Prior narrows the field to focus simply on cable content on networks that program news and opinion talk and notes that "those who watched at least some Fox News spent 7.5% of their overall viewing time with the Fox News Channel, but another 6% with the other four cable networks (CNN, CNN Headline News, CNBC, MSNBC). After analyzing these patterns, he concludes the data "offer little support for claims that the fragmentation of the cable news environment fosters political polarization by encouraging selective exposure to only one side of an issue."[15] Prior's analysis differs from ours, in that he makes the assumption that what is on Fox is one-sided, a view that fails to account for cohosted programs featuring ideologically opposed individuals such as *Hannity and Colmes,* and assumes as well that each cable network offers an ideologically consistent set of programs, when, as we have noted, there are programs hosted by conservatives on CNN, CNN Headline News, and MSNBC.[16]

Of central interest to us are the sources to which conservatives turn for information and opinion about politics. Relying on data from the Pew Research Center's 1998 to 2004 Biennial Media Consumption Survey to identify factors predicting exposure to cable and nightly news, Jonathan Morris finds that the audiences for Fox and CNN are becoming increasingly polarized, with Fox watchers less likely than CNN viewers to watch accounts critical of the Bush administration and more likely than nonwatchers to underestimate the number of Americans killed in the Iraq war.[17] The study found that "the Fox News audience prefers news that shares their own point of view on politics and issues, while CNN and network news watchers do not."[18] The conclusion about causalities is consistent with the one we will offer later when we advance the claim that Fox viewers are more likely than non-Fox-viewing conservatives to reside in a world whose factual presuppositions coincide with their ideology.

As we argued earlier, Limbaugh relays mainstream examples to his listeners, often playing them on the air before or after critiquing their "liberal bias." Yet despite the fact that his listeners are more likely to avoid mainstream broadcast news, many are still part of the mainstream media audience. But the shift from higher consumption of mainstream network news in 1996 to lower in 2004 is important, because it suggests both the important role Fox News may have played in giving conservatives an option and that Limbaugh's audience is now somewhat more likely to be insulated within a media environment filled with reinforcing cues. The options for conservatives are multiplied as MSNBC and CNN move to attract conservatives with the sorts of programing that were once Fox's unique selling proposition.

Conclusion

Overall mistrust of mainstream news media has increased steadily over three decades. The conservative media's rhetoric about the mainstream is complex. They critique mainstream news sources for bias and inaccuracy, use the same sources to advance their arguments when they provide support, and reframe their content to make the case that it adopts a double standard on issues relevant to ideology and party. When Limbaugh's audience was absorbing a great deal of mainstream broadcast news, he risked the possibility that they would be swayed by it; now that his audience is somewhat more averse to it, at least in broadcast and cable form, his capacity to reinforce its conservative ideology is enhanced. For those who attend to other conservative media, that effect should be magnified. And when the conservative audience swims in the mainstream, the frames reinforced in the echo chamber should increase the likelihood that they remain loyal to their conservative principles.

Defining and Defending an Insular Interpretive Community

A passage in the April 2005 *Limbaugh Letter* illustrates the theme of this chapter. In this missive to subscribers, Limbaugh fuses pejorative names, Republican frames, emotionally evocative claims, and categorical language to distinguish the Democrats and their positions from those of conservatives:

> Dingy Harry Reid and those absolute wimps have nothing positive to offer anybody in this country. They're doing nothing but trying to instill fear and loathing, forming coalitions (i.e., their new bosom buddies MoveOn.org) built on seething hatred and rage.
>
> That is why it was no real surprise when CafePress.com began selling a yellow T-shirt with a red gash and the slogan, in big words, "KILL BUSH." The whole message was, "FOR GODS [*sic*] SAKE, KILL BUSH SAVE THE UNITED STATES AND THE REST OF THE WORLD." This was the same website that earlier posted a T-shirt for sale with the message, "DEAR TOM DELAY, PLEASE COMMIT SUICIDE, SINCERELY, EVERYONE."
>
> The same left-wing inhumanity was on display last year when Hillary Clinton spoke at the pro-abortion "March for Women's Lives." According to the *American Spectator*, placards held by the marchers read: "If Only Barbara Bush Had Choice"; "Barbara Bush Chose Poorly"; and "The Pope's Mother Had No Choice."
>
> As I say, no shocker. This is the mainstream of the Democratic Party and their wacko voters and supporters.[1]

This is an in-group rhetoric seeking to reinforce the views of a like-minded audience eager to draw extreme conclusions about Democrats. The strategy capitalizes on tendencies scholars of in- and out-groups have repeatedly observed: that members of a group exaggerate their differences with out-groups,[2] believing out-group members to be rather homogeneous and in-group members less so,[3] and believing members of out-groups to be less human than those in the in-group.[4] Studies also show that people in one group think that the attitudes of an opposed group are more extreme than they actually are, a finding consistent with the one we will report in the next chapters.[5]

As Limbaugh reinforces in-group language, his use of naming imbues the mix with visceral emotion. Flooded by the evocative cascade, the reader is likely to grant the implications in the ambiguously referenced (Is Senator Clinton the object of the same left-wing inhumanity or the sentiments expressed in the placards at the rally?) bridging inference ("the same left-wing inhumanity") and conclude that Hillary Clinton abetted, if she did not outright endorse, the notion that the incumbent president and the pope should have been aborted and the incumbent president killed. At the same time, the audience is unlikely to challenge the conclusion that the T-shirt statements reflect the view of the Democratic mainstream ("This is the mainstream of the Democratic Party"). If these are the sentiments of the Democratic mainstream, then, of course, the Democratic Party is the home of "wacko voters and supporters."

To this point, we have argued that Limbaugh and conservative hosts on Fox and the opinion pages of the *Wall Street Journal* share a common repertoire of enemies and a shared commitment to defend the narrative of Reagan's supposed success in reviving the economy and ending the Cold War. We have also shown that these outlets attract a key Republican audience and reinforce its conservative dispositions. We have suggested as well that the conservative opinion media provide this audience with a consistent way of seeing nonconservative media and engender mistrust of these outlets.

In this and the following chapter, we argue that Limbaugh, Hannity and others on Fox, the *Journal* editorial page, and Taranto of the WSJ.com use standard rhetorical devices to create an in-group, composed of the like-minded, and an out-group, consisting primarily of "liberals," Democrats, and those portrayed as trying to sabotage the Reagan legacy. The conservative opinion media speak to and reinforce the identity of an in-group—that is, an insulated interpretive community protected from attitudinal assault by those of opposing view. They do so through definitions and arguments that encapsulate conservative positions while attacking the other side in evocative emotional language, balkanizing knowledge by featuring information and interpretations of it that advantage their side, and, particularly in Limbaugh's case, polarizing perceptions of their opponents through disparaging labels and ridicule.[6] In chapter 12, we will argue that the in-group shares specific knowledge, interpretations, and attitudes that are dissimilar from those of nonlisteners. In the process, they take on some of the characteristics of a balkanized knowledge enclave. In chapter 13, we show that the attitudes of both Limbaugh listeners and Fox viewers cast the out-group as significantly dissimilar from themselves, a result that reinforces their in-group status, minimizes defection to the out-group, and reinforces their disposition to defend their ideology and attack that of "liberals" and Democrats.

The Presupposed Definition

From elimination of the "death tax" to a ban on "partial birth abortion," Limbaugh and the conservative opinion media offer a consistent emotionally charged vocabulary advancing the policies conservatives favor and undercutting the positions of the Democrats. The process by which these labels come to embody lines of argument that drive public policy is well illustrated in the linguistic contrast between "partial birth abortion" and "intact dilation and extraction."

Any terminology is, as literary critic Kenneth Burke noted, "a *selection* of reality; and to this extent it must function as a *deflection* of reality."[7] The most powerful forms of definition occur when the audience is unaware of the selection or deflection. In these cases, the assumption that the word reflects a reality is simply accepted. In such cases, naming functions in a fashion that rhetorical critic David Zarefsy calls "argument by definition."[8] Citing such terms as "the death tax" and "partial birth abortion" as examples, Zarefsky notes that the

> definition is stipulated, offered as if [it] were natural and uncontroversial rather than chosen and contested.... The definition of the situation affects what counts as data for or against a proposal, highlights certain elements of the situation for use in arguments and obscures others, influences whether people will notice the situation and how they will handle it, describes causes and identifies remedies, and invites moral judgments about circumstances or individuals.[9]

Ultimately, such specification can alter "the rhetorical landscape by changing the terms in which people think about an issue."[10] These sorts of definitional moves are powerful means of framing and reframing issues.

Creating an In-Group and an Out-Group through Shared Definitions

Communities create a collective identity and the bonds that sustain it. They do so, in part, by employing a distinctive common vocabulary that carries with it a way of seeing the community and its adversaries. The notion that group identity is built through adoption of a common language is important because, as Burke noted, language does our thinking for us.[11] Indeed, political theorist Murray Edelman argues that "political language is political reality."[12] If a person sees and expresses the world through a conservative language, that individual is for all intents and purposes a conservative. Use of the language of the in-group is a signal of identification with a certain form of conservatism, as well as an expression of its assumptions. A person who talks about the anticonservative "double standard" and "liberal bias" in media is talking and thinking within conservative assumptions that Limbaugh, prominent Fox News hosts, and the editorial pages of the *Journal* reinforce.

Creating a common enemy is, as Edelman argued persuasively, a central means of establishing and sustaining a group identity.[13] As earlier chapters argue, for the conservative opinion media, the enemy consists of the "liberal media," Democrats, and, for Limbaugh in particular, turncoats such as Republican senator John McCain. Here we will explore how the conservative media name the enemy while infusing their ideological case with vivid detail, unique language, and disparaging labels and ridicule. The disdainful language elicits emotion that creates bonds within the community and reinforces the notion that the Democrats and their policy positions are the enemy. These moves help shape both what we will later explore as knowledge enclaves or balkanization and a polarized rejection of Democrats.

Emotionally Evocative Language in Service of Conservative Frames

Conservatives don't have a unique claim on use of emotion-laden rhetoric. Partisans of all stripes employ vivid evocative language for their own purposes. Our interest here is in the way the conservative opinion media harness emotion to create in-group bonds and distance their audiences from the enemy: Democrats and their ideology. These strategies are powerful because vivid, concrete, image-oriented language tends to evoke emotional reaction, and be retained in memory longer than more abstract material.[14] Anecdotes expressed in concrete language are more persuasive and memorable than those without it.[15] Emotion can also short-circuit analytic assessment of the claims bring offered.[16]

In the news accounts we are about to discuss, the conservative definition embodied in the name "partial birth abortion" has been adopted by the mainstream media. The naturalized use of this label constitutes a rhetorical victory for those opposing the method this term so graphically represents. Despite this similarity, the conservative and mainstream accounts we feature illustrate that they select and deflect reality in dissimilar ways. The bias in Fox's selections favors the ban on so-called partial birth abortion; by contrast, although they document the impact of conservative framing of the issue, the mainstream accounts tip against the ban. In addition, the Fox and the mainstream accounts differ in the level of detail they use to describe "partial birth abortion" and in the nature and extent of evocative language they attach to the procedure.

By the time the legislation banning the procedure was signed, the mainstream media had adopted the conservative characterization "partial birth abortion." For example, Charles Osgood noted on CBS: "Doctors call it dilation and extraction, more commonly known as partial birth abortion" (October 22, 2003).[17] In extemporaneous exchanges, reporters and pundits dropped the qualifier. On the *Today Show*, for instance, Katie Couric noted: "The same day the Senate passes a bill banning partial birth abortions" (October 22, 2003).[18] After earlier tagging the phrase with "as they say partial birth," on the same show, Tim Russert noted: "Of all of the debates the Republicans could have on this issue of abortion this is the one they want to have because most Americans agree that they should—they should ban late term or partial birth abortions."[19]

Fox and the mainstream differed in the evocative detail they used in describing the procedure and in the language carrying the description. The Fox segment was introduced by host Brit Hume, who said, "The Senate voted overwhelmingly today for a bill that would outlaw that abortion procedure in which the fetus is partially delivered before a doctor punctures its skull." Fox News correspondent Major Garrett then reported: "The outcome was certain, the Senate voted twice before to ban partial birth abortions, but President Clinton vetoed both bills" (Fox, *Special Report with Brit Hume*, October 21, 2003). Then, unlike the nonconservative media, Garrett described the process in detail: "Partial birth abortion . . . occurs in the second or third trimester. A physician pulls a fetus from the womb by its feet, punctures the base of the skull and inserts a tube into the wound. The brains are then sucked out and the skull collapses."

Note the differences in the use of vivid detail in this account and that in the AP: "The 281–142 vote culminated an eight-year drive by the Republican House to end the procedure that abortion opponents call partial birth abortion. . . . The legislation bans a procedure, generally in the second or third trimester, in which a fetus is partially delivered before a doctor punctures the skull" (October 3, 2003).[20] Whereas both use the words "punctures" and "skull," the news account on Fox personalizes with the words "womb" "wound," "feet," and "brains," which more descriptively convey method. The Fox reporter indicates how the fetus is extracted (pulled by the feet), where the skull is punctured (the base), how the brain is removed (sucked out), and what happens (the skull collapses). In the AP account, the process is more passive (a fetus is partially delivered, a doctor punctures); in the Fox account more active and more tied to the actions of a doctor (a physician pulls from the womb, punctures, inserts a tube). In the ABC description by reporter Linda Douglas (October 21, 2003) there is no agent in the sentence. "The laws would ban a procedure used after the third month of pregnancy that involves partially delivering a fetus and puncturing its skull."[21]

Of interest as well is the fact that in the Fox account, the reporter and not a quoted partisan offered the evocative details. In the mainstream, the quoted content is not as graphic as that voiced by the Fox correspondent. Whereas the Fox reporter's news account contained a high level of descriptive detail, the news accounts of CBS's *Evening News, NBC Evening News,* and the *Today Show* employed a partisan characterizing the process. For example, Senator John Ensign (R. Nev.) was shown saying "This procedure is so grotesque that when it is described, it makes people shudder" (October 22, 2003). And CBS made a similar decision showing Senator Bill Frist (Republican majority leader) saying "It's an egregious, outlandish, ghoulish procedure."

Even the mainstream network with the most graphic content did not include the amount of detail offered by Fox's reporter. And, interestingly, and consistent with the notion that the networks tilt to the left, in the battle over which side's sound bite was the most graphic, on NBC the advantage went to the Democrats. In other words, on *NBC Nightly News* the most graphic language on each side gave an edge to the opponents of the ban. A fragment was included of a statement by Republican senator Rick Santorum: "They place a vacuum hose." By contrast, Senator Barbara Boxer was shown indicting the absence in the bill of an exemption for the health of the mother. "She could have blood clots, an embolism, a stroke, damage to nearby organs, or paralysis if this particular procedure is not available to her."[22]

Central to the conservative media's rhetoric on the "partial birth abortion ban" legislation was the emotionally charged term "infanticide" offered by President George W. Bush. In the *Journal,* an editorial argued, "Even *Roe v. Wade* recognized the right of the government to draw some lines around abortion. That's just what Congress and the President have now done, by outlawing a practice the overwhelming majority of Americans find repellent and hard to distinguish from infanticide."[23]

The editorial position of the *Journal* differed substantially from that of the *New York Times,* which wrote:

The new Congressional law lacks an exception to protect a woman's health. Even worse, the imprecise...wording inserted into the bill to describe the medical procedures it purports to regulate in the third trimester would in fact outlaw common methods of abortion that are used after the first trimester of pregnancy, but well before fetal viability. With this legislation, Mr. Bush and his Republican allies in Congress are clearly mounting an assault on women's reproductive rights that aims to undercut the basis on which *Roe v. Wade* has guaranteed those rights for 30 years.[24]

Whereas the language of the *New York Times* is clinical and features "fetal viability," the *Journal* raises the specter of infanticide. The assault in the *New York Times* is on the rights of women, in the *Journal* on the infant. In this example, all of the networks are making linguistic choices freighted with ideological assumptions. Whereas the mainstream advantages the "prochoice" side, Fox and the *Journal*'s editorial align with those who take a prolife position.

Polarizing with Disparaging Labels and Ridicule

In the example we just developed, the definitions and evocative language were tied to a procedure and a policy position. Those favoring the opposing position were not vilified. The audience was invited by the language used in the Fox news story to disassociate itself from this method of abortion; the audience for the mainstream was encouraged instead to see its use as a medical decision.

Ridicule is an effective means of polarizing perceptions of the disparaged person or activity. For a moment, we will concentrate on the ways in which Limbaugh creates dismissive labels for prominent Democrats and their ideology. We focus on Limbaugh because the sorts of labeling he employs are not as likely to characterize Fox segments or to appear at all on the *Journal*'s opinion pages. Importantly, Limbaugh's strongest use of ridicule is more readily found in his most highly targeted medium, the subscription-based newsletter, and less frequently on the radio. In his mainstream television appearances, it all but disappears. Neither the hosts on Fox News nor the *Journal* have a ready venue that is as targeted to believers as Limbaugh's subscription-based newsletter.

We are interested in his labels because they ridicule Democrats in a way we believe contributes to the sorts of polarization and balkanization we will examine in the next chapter. The labels suggest that those of opposite ideology hold illegitimate views and are themselves menacing.

An Insider Language of Identification

Limbaugh invites his callers to employ an insider language that both embeds definitional assumptions hospitable to his conservative philosophy and makes it difficult for those who embrace the language to speak about Democrats and the presumed Democratic ideology without attacking them. The June 2005 issue of the *Limbaugh Letter*, for example, contains the statements "Democrats are the enemy;"[25] "When she first ran for her Senate seat, Hillary Rodham Clinton told citizens of the Empire State that she had been endorsed by environmental-wacko groups because ... in her words: 'I've stood for clean air' "; and after Harvard president Lawrence Summers's comments on intrinsic differences between the sexes, Limbaugh noted: "Led by foaming-at-the-mouth feminists, the liberal elite experienced a mass politically correct tantrum."

Identifying terms such as "foaming–at-the-mouth feminists," "liberal elite," "enemy," and "environmental-wacko groups" both create an insider language and distance those who adopt the labels from those labeled. One of the ways Limbaugh's supporters telegraph their identification with him is by adopting his language. "There's not a femi-Nazi among us," reported House freshman congresswoman Barbara Cubin (R. Wyo.).[26] Listeners say "Ditto" or "megadittoes" to telegraph their enthusiasm for Limbaugh, his latest argument, or his show in general. "It's an honor to speak to my hero," a caller said (April 29, 2004).

On Limbaugh's radio program, denigrating nicknames become shortcuts signaling a common understanding of the "liberal" adversary. In the process of investing language with unstated understanding, the audience participates in the creation of meaning. The first-time listener must pay additional attention to determine the referent for Clintonistas, Sheets, the Swimmer, Puffster, the Forehead, the Breck Girl, Ashley Wilkes, and Gray-Out Davis. Once a regular has adopted these terms for such Democrats as Edward Kennedy (the Swimmer), John Edwards (the Breck Girl), and Wesley Clark (Ashley Wilkes), he has embraced terms enwrapped in negative associations. The Swimmer stands for "murderer," swimming away from the dying Mary Jo Kopechne at Chappaquiddick; the Breck Girl stands for vain, empty-headed, and feminine; Ashley Wilkes stands for feckless poseur.

Periodically Limbaugh freshens the references to aid understanding by those uninitiated in their intended meaning. "Mr. Sheets Goes to Washington" notes a headline in the *Limbaugh Letter*.[27]

> You'd think Sen. Robert Byrd (D. WV), the former Ku Klux Klan Kleagle who cut his Senate teeth by filibustering the Civil Rights Act

of 1964, would stay away from the whole issue of filibustering. And you'd think Democrats would keep "Sheets" (so nicknamed by the late Democratic Speaker of the House, Tip O'Neill) under wraps.

Limbaugh's indictment of Byrd closes: "So if you wonder, 'When will the Democratic Party retire this duplicitous, pompous, doddering old KKK-er?' The answer is: Never. Hallelujah." Some of Limbaugh's labels are alliterative spin-offs on people's names. The same article tags "Sen. Patrick "Leaky" Leahy, aka Senator Depends." Claiming the right to name assumes a posture of both familiarity and superiority. The names telegraph political meaning as well. On the Limbaugh website, these labels are reinforced by concocted visuals. Edward Kennedy is shown wearing a superimposed snorkel.

By early January 2003, Limbaugh had coined names and identities for many of the Democratic presidential aspirants, "Plagiarist Joe Biden" among them. Senator John Kerry becomes John F. Kerry-Heinz (December 4, 2002), " 'Lurch' Kerry-Heinz" or "Mr. Big Ketchup" (December 2, 2002) and is repeatedly identified as "the richest man in the Senate" (December 6, 2002). The identification as "Lurch" emerges with Kerry's appearance on *Meet the Press*. "He was so bad," says Limbaugh, "that I inaugurated a new update theme for him: the song from the *Addams Family* because this guy looks like a clone of Lurch" (December 2, 2002). By spring 2004, Kerry is John F-ing Kerry, an insider reference to Kerry's use of the "f-word" in an interview. This combination of labels rhetorically emasculates Kerry by suggesting that he is dominated by his wife, Heinz Ketchup heir Teresa Heinz. At the same time it implies that Kerry became wealthy not by accomplishment but by marriage and that he is ineffectual, intellectually weak, robotic (Lurch), and vulgar.

The phrases linked to the labels form the basis of lines of argument as well as ad hominem attacks. Bill Clinton becomes Der Schlick Meister (January 3, 2003) or Der Schlick (October 18, 2000). Al Gore becomes Algore and Dr. Frankengore (November 27, 2002). Having tagged them with nicknames, Limbaugh then builds up a store of negative opinion about each. "Algore," for instance, "has the IQ of a pencil eraser" (September 24, 2002). The "pencil eraser" has his moments of insight, however. In the same show, Limbaugh noted that it was Gore who, in his debate over NAFTA with Perot in 1993, called Limbaugh a distinguished American. Limbaugh uses that observation by Gore to imply a second indictment. Gore is an opportunist, praising Limbaugh only when it suits his purposes.

Underlying the demeaning names applied to Democrats past and present is the assumption that they are panderers, appeasers, and liberal. Jimmy Carter becomes "Jimmuh" (November 14, 2002) or "the Nobel Appeases Prize—winning Jimmy Carter." Carter is also tagged a "Numbskull screwball" (January 3, 2003). The NAACP becomes the National Association for the Advancement of Liberal Colored People (NAALCP)" (November 27, 2002).

The nicknames also affix responsibility for bad policy to prominent Democrats. "Gray-Out Davis" indicts of Davis's manner, gray hair, and name and tags him with blame for the 2002 California energy crisis (September 23, 2002). As Limbaugh's language becomes their own, his listeners pass it on to nonlisteners in conversation. In California in the fall of 2003, for instance, Jamieson was at dinner with an acquaintance who referred to "Gray-Out Davis." The person was not a Limbaugh listener. Where did he pick up the term? "It's what my father calls him," said the acquaintance. And the father's favorite talk radio show? "Limbaugh."

Republican candidates would verbalize labels like Limbaugh's only at very high risk. To suggest that Frank Lautenberg is too old to run to fill a Senate seat, Limbaugh identifies the New Jersey Democratic contender as "Frank Lautencadaver," for example (October 3, 2002), and as "1881-vintage Lautenberg" (November 5, 2002), as well as "War of 1812 veteran Lautenberg—who has spent the last several years in the grave anyway" (November 4, 2002). If listeners recall these associations, they can read them into the more subtle references the Republican candidate makes to the age of the Democrat aspirant. When this occurs, the Republican benefits from the associations without risking a backlash from those who find them offensive.

Many of Limbaugh's labels play on the name of the labeled person to attack his or her manner. North Carolina Democratic senatorial aspirant Erskine Bowles becomes "Irksome Bowels" (November 7, 2002). When former vice president Walter Mondale, for example, ran for Democrat Paul Wellstone's seat in Minnesota, Limbaugh called him "Mondull" (October 30, 2002).

Those who differ with Limbaugh are not portrayed as offering reasoned alternatives. They are instead operating from a playbook with not many pages. At worst they are deranged, suffering from mental illness (e.g., Gore), nuts, or wacko. "We are witnessing a collision between our civilization and the Earth," Limbaugh quotes Al Gore saying. "Actually," responds Limbaugh, "it's a collision between you and lunacy" (*Limbaugh Letter*, June 2005).

The labels push perceptions of ideological opponents to the extreme. Environmental activists are "dunderhead alarmists and prophets of doom"; individual environmentalists are "long-haired maggot-infested FM-type environmental wackos"; "if humans worked at it, they could not destroy the Earth"; "There's no reason the communists shouldn't have a couple days every year, and this is one of them, Earth Day" (April 22, 2005).

Prochoice feminists are "pro-aborts," "femi-Nazis" (a term Limbaugh uses less often since its use was critiqued in the mainstream); they burn bras, dominate television shows, charge into men's locker rooms, and despise Ronald Reagan; Democrats are elected by "beggar-based constituencies."

Limbaugh's gender-based attacks are as polarizing as any of those that are tied to specific issues. Put simply, Democratic women are either sexualized manipulators or unattractive man haters. He implied that accomplished Democratic women were unattractive when he recast the Clintons' tribute to women as "Biddies Night Out" (Limbaugh's TV show, February 11, 1994). By contrast, "babes" is used to sexualize women (e.g., "Congressbabe Jane Harman," October 18, 2002). House Democratic leader Nancy Pelosi is a "babe" whose head is affixed to Miss America's body on the website. Neither label invites the audience to take these leaders seriously.

In the battle between Limbaugh and women who do not share his ideology, Limbaugh claims that those on the other side remind him of the wives he supposedly cast off. He describes Arianna Huffington's performance in a California gubernatorial debate as "screeching," for example, and reports that his staff considers her "wifey." After playing a tape of Senator Hillary Clinton loudly delivering her message to a prochoice rally, Limbaugh notes that listening to her "hurts," and reminds him of his first wife (April 15, 2004).

Women whose political views Limbaugh abhors are cast as "broads," "lesbians," or occasionally "femi-Nazis." During the Clinton presidency, Hillary Clinton and Janet Reno are tagged as closeted lesbians. When the National Organization for Women endorsed the presidential candidacy of Carol Moseley Braun in September 2003, Limbaugh responded:

> When they assert that the NAGS have 500,000 members, don't you believe it. They have nowhere near that many members. Have you ever seen the number of people that show up at a NAG convention? There are more German shepherd guard dogs being escorted around by some of the lesbians than there are actual members in there. Don't ask me for any delineation on this. I'm just telling you. (September 18, 2003)

At the same time, the innuendo in Limbaugh's labeling impugns the masculinity of "liberal" men. Those he disapproves of are "two inchers." Richard Gephardt is "Little Dick Gephardt" (December 10, 2002). (In the subscription-based section of the Limbaugh website, the punctuation occasionally changes to "Little Dick" Gephardt.) Comparing Daschle and Bush, Limbaugh noted: "Bush: stands six feet tall. Daschle: Five foot six inches in heels. Bush: Big feet, big hands. Daschle: Small feet, small hands" ("You do the math," January 7, 2002). (Limbaugh did not compare the heights of President George W. Bush, 5'11", and Senator John Kerry, 6'4".) "Leadership to Tom Daschle is apparently making those little limp-wristed linguini-spined Europeans happy with us," Limbaugh noted (October 21, 2002). He called Democratic contender General Wesley Clark "Ashley Wilkes," after "that wimpy, pathetic *Gone with the Wind* character," he said, and compared "Bill Clinton to Rhett Butler. Clark is just sitting around waiting for some Scarlett to tell him what he believes" (October 10, 2003). In the early primaries of 2004, Limbaugh shifted to identifying Clark as "Jack D. Ripper," a reference to the mad general in *Dr. Strangelove*. Descriptors traditionally tied to women rather than men are affixed to male Democrats. Instead of "complaining," "objecting," or "attacking," Democrats "whine." Joe Lieberman was "Moaner" Lieberman. The Democrats' leader in the Senate was tagged "Whiner Tom Daschle" (January 3, 2003).

Whereas most Democratic objects of his attention are tagged as deficient males, Gary Hart and Bill Clinton are exceptions. Of Clinton, Limbaugh noted, "I've said literally hundreds of times that Mr. Clinton looks like a fun guy to catch a ballgame or chase women with" (December 18, 2002). Gary Hart was described as "oversexed." Potential Democratic 2004 contender Christopher Dodd was identified as "the other half of the infamous Ted Kennedy waitress sandwich who has followed the Swimmer's lead and got hitched" (January 3, 2003). Democrats' sexual escapades are of interest and worthy of repeated recall but not those of Republicans such as former Republican Speaker of the House Newt Gingrich, who divorced his second wife so he could marry a member of his staff, or Gingrich's heir apparent, Bob Livingston, who stepped aside during the Clinton impeachment trial after evidence of marital infidelity surfaced.

Limbaugh, who disapproved of President George W. Bush's reliance on UN inspections to ascertain whether Saddam Hussein was building weapons of mass destruction, sexualized his disapproval and indicted Clinton in the process by saying "The United Nations is sending intern inspectors to the Clinton compound in Chappaqua, New York, where they're searching for weapons of mass penetration. The lead inspector is a man by the name of Hans Dix" (December 3, 2003). The UN inspector was, of course, Hans Blix.

Limbaugh's attempts at gender-based "humor" are of the locker room variety. As the California gubernatorial recall was heating up, Limbaugh informed his followers that Lieutenant Governor Cruz Bustamante—"whose name loosely translates into Spanish for 'large breasts'—leads the Terminator by a few points" (August 18, 2003). A photomontage on the Limbaugh website shows a photograph of Schwarzenegger's head and shoulders from his Pumping Iron days as a body builder. A naked woman has been transposed onto his shoulders. Over her breasts is a sign reading BUSTAMANTE. When Madonna endorsed General Wesley Clark, Limbaugh reported that she had "opened herself" to him. Why the vulgarity in this message does not alienate the churchgoing conservatives in his audience is a question for which we have no ready answer.

Limbaugh advises conservatives to beware the sexual but not the intellectual wiles of "liberal" female reporters. Even though that congressional class included women, notably newly elected Florida representative Kathryn Harris, he seemed to assume that all the first-year members in Congress to whom he gave his advice were either lesbians or men. Limbaugh reported that when he addressed the Republican freshman class in November 2002, he warned them that "they shouldn't fall for the tricks of any reporterette who claims to want to befriend them" (November 13, 2002). One might surmise that conservative women are not advised to beware the sexual wiles of "liberal" male reporters because they are invulnerable to the advances of emasculated "liberal" men. Alternatively, any implication that conservative women might be able to be seduced might risk offending the audience with the possible assumption that women with the good sense to be conservatives have values that are suspect or virtue able to be compromised. In Limbaugh's radio world, it is "liberal" women who control weak-willed Democratic men. As noted, John Kerry is tagged "John Kerry-Heinz" and "Mr. Ketchup"; Limbaugh quoted a caller saying "Kerry does his fundraising every night when he goes to bed" (December 4, 2002).

Reading these labels on the printed page here could lead one to conclude that Limbaugh's tone is routinely angry or vitriolic. Were that the case, it is unlikely that he would hold the attention of his listeners. Rather, his commentary ranges from the acerbic to the wry. As befits "the MahaRushie," with "talent on loan from God," he treats much of this as hyperbole that invites a chuckle and knowing nod from parts of his audience and eye-rolling tolerance from others. Those who find it offensive are unlikely to remain in the listening audience. Importantly, regardless of the tone in which they are delivered, these labels attach a dismissive, demeaning vocabulary to "liberals" and at the same time reinforce polarized perceptions of them and the "liberal media."

Conclusion

In this chapter we have explored the ways Limbaugh and the conservative opinion media wrap their audiences in a conversation built on words and phrases that embody conservatism's ideological assumptions. Our analysis is built on a series of examples. News accounts about so-called partial birth abortion suggest that the messages of the conservative opinion media create an insulating language backed by a repertoire of supportive descriptions to protect audiences from assault by those with opposing views. This is in-group language enwrapped in arguments that inoculate the audience against opponents' positions.

Limbaugh, in particular, deploys naming and ridicule to marginalize those named as part of an out-group. Specifically, he indicts presumed liber-als in coherent, emotion-evoking, dismissive language and marshals lines of arguments consistent with those labels. Because language does our thinking for us, this process constructs not only a vocabulary but also a knowledge base for the audience. That language and the view of the world carried by it are presumed by loyal conservatives and alien to the nonconservative audi-ences. These interpretations of people and events also reinforce Limbaugh's defense of conservatism and its proponents. The evidence we offer in this chapter for these conclusions is qualitative and text based. In the following chapter, we add audience-based data suggesting that the rhetorical strategies we have described are linked to two effects: they balkanize and polarize the knowledge and attitudes of the audience of the conservative opinion media.

Balkanization of Knowledge and Interpretation

In his book *Republic.com*, Cass Sunstein argues that the highly segmented and partisan content of internet sites can lead to polarization of public opinion and the balkanization of knowledge and understanding.[1] This argument resonates with Elihu Katz's concern that fragmentation in media consumption will undercut social integration and our sense of shared national identity,[2] and with Joseph Turow's notion that the "creation of customized media materials...will allow, even encourage, individuals to live in their own personally constructed worlds, separated from people and issues that they don't care about or don't want to be bothered with."[3]

Sunstein believes that polarization and balkanization undermine public deliberation, social consensus, and united action within societies. Although his argument is directed at the internet with its proliferation of partisan sites, the notions are relevant as well to other partisan sources of information such as those provided by Limbaugh, the Fox News programs on which we focus, and the online and print editorial pages of the *Wall Street Journal*.

In this chapter, we argue that Limbaugh's listeners and, by implication, the audiences to other partisan sites, whether liberal or conservative, can come to hold specific knowledge largely unshared by those unexposed to these or similar outlets. The audience can at the same time come to hold common frames of interpretation different from those deployed by audiences reliant on other media outlets. And if the cues from the host of the program persuasively invite hostility to other sources, such as, in Limbaugh's case, the mainstream media, exposure can over time reduce the attention given to those alternative sources and in the process minimize susceptibility to points of view persuasively argued from alternative ideological vantage points.

One byproduct created by these insulating, knowledge-building phenomena is what we call balkanization—a metaphor drawn from the way the Balkan countries degenerated into separate, individual, self-contained political units after World War I. Specifically, we will show that Limbaugh's audience differs in the kind of knowledge it holds and in its interpretation and distortion of political information. In the following chapter, we add to this argument the notion that distortion of political information in a way that is both systematic and consistent with a source's rhetoric can create a polarized view of political phenomena. Whereas in this chapter we focus on the possibility that Limbaugh helps turn his audience into a balkanized cohort in a sometimes distorted knowledge enclave,[4] in the next we argue that exposure to his message and to that on Fox News polarizes these audiences' attitudes toward Democrats and the mainstream media.

To advance our argument, we first look at the nature of the content. At the core of our analysis is the phenomenon of selective exposure.[5] We show as well that Limbaugh's content—isolated in analyses of transcripts of his show and compared to that of other PTR and mainstream news sources—is distinctive.

After considering content, we will present evidence that exposure to Limbaugh creates balkanization in three arenas: knowledge, interpretations of current events, and rationalizations about election outcomes. We extend these claims to include the effects of exposure to Fox News. In sum, we show here that Limbaugh's audience differs systematically from those not in his audience in its views of politics and social affairs and its interpretations of events. To make this argument, we compare those who are exposed to Limbaugh to other citizens exposed to more general forms of mainstream mass media who are just as motivated and just as able as Limbaugh's audience when it comes to politics. Our analysis begins with Limbaugh's rhetoric.

What Limbaugh's Audience Hears

Throughout this book, Limbaugh's rhetoric has been examined in a variety of specific cases. Here we report more systematic investigations of the content of his program over an extended period, during the presidential campaign in 1996. We asked whether Limbaugh's discussion each day differed from that of the mainstream news and from ideologically similar and dissimilar PTR.

To assess such differences, as noted, we conducted a content analysis of Limbaugh and the mainstream mass media during the primary election period in 1996. The topics treated on the Limbaugh show for the weeks from February 3 through March 29, 1996, were evaluated. Limbaugh had guest hosts during one of these weeks. Even though the results were virtually identical, topics from the guests' shows were excluded from the Limbaugh summary. During the same period, the front-page news stories from three major newspapers—the *New York Times*, the *Washington Post*, and the *Wall Street*

Journal—were coded. Similarly, the number of minutes of coverage from the nightly television news programs (ABC, NBC, and CBS) was obtained from a news analysis service.

CONTENT DIFFERENT FROM MAINSTREAM NEWS
AND SOME OTHER PTR SOURCES

As we noted in earlier chapters, the *Rush Limbaugh Show* gave scant attention to foreign affairs and military matters, in contrast to the mainstream media, which devoted fully one-fourth of its coverage to these topics. Limbaugh redistributed this agenda[6] by giving greater attention to the Clinton administration and its scandals, to the Congress, to third parties and the religious right, and to the general topic of personal efficacy, responsibility, and public cynicism and optimism. These differences suggest that at that time, his program was more focused on domestic politics than were the mainstream media. His talk show also promoted a fundamental value of personal responsibility and efficacy in support of political involvement and as a basis for rejecting big government and affirmative action. The priority given topics by Limbaugh's show is also at odds with the mainstream news.[7]

The *Rush Limbaugh Show* was different from news coverage not only in the mainstream media but also in other PTR outlets.[8] Conservative PTR shows are too diverse to permit extensive content analysis of them. However, we did compare Limbaugh's topics to those of other PTR shows in a limited time frame during the 1996 primary. In the two-week period from March 4 to 18, we calculated the proportion of coverage on 13 topics by Limbaugh, conservative, liberal, and moderate PTRs, and the mainstream print and broadcast media.

Large differences emerged in the category of foreign affairs and military, with conservative shows (other than Limbaugh's) devoting a great deal of time to this topic area, while Limbaugh all but ignores it. In fact, Limbaugh gives less time to this topic than any other outlet, including liberal shows. Instead Limbaugh allocates this time to discussion of Congress and the president, third parties and the religious right, and especially business and technology and personal responsibility and political efficacy. In contrast to Limbaugh's show, conservative talk radio in that 1996 period gave its attention to crime, punishment, and the justice system, as well as family, education, and ethics.

In 1996, Limbaugh's content differed from that in liberal and moderate talk radio as well. Business and commerce, Congress, and personal efficacy were more prominent in Limbaugh's show and lower in the other three ideological groups; foreign affairs, crime, and family and education were elevated in the other three talk radio groupings. The pattern, put broadly, is that Limbaugh's show focused on domestic politics, personal (and political) efficacy, and business. Conservative, moderate, and liberal PTR tended to concentrate more centrally on family and education (especially the liberal shows), foreign affairs (especially conservative and moderate shows), and crime and justice.

Limbaugh's agenda did not agree with that of the mainstream media during this two-week period, nor did it coincide with that of other typical PTR sources regardless of their ideological stance. Other PTR and network television news and print news gave fairly similar priorities to topics, while Limbaugh's show assigned different priorities. We would expect these differences in focus to show up in differences in knowledge, interpretation, and opinion.

We cannot be sure that these weeks are representative of Limbaugh or of conservative PTR, but if they are, significant differences do emerge. These differences distinguish Limbaugh's agenda from that of other PTR, even differentiating it from its closest ideological ally, conservative PTR. In fact, Limbaugh's priorities of coverage are just as different from those of other PTR shows (conservative, moderate, or liberal) as they are from the mainstream media's priorities. It is important to note that this content analysis was conducted in 1996, before the advent of Fox News, and did not include a comparison to the editorial page of the *Journal*.

In 1996, Limbaugh's agenda concentrated on domestic politics, personal and political efficacy, and business and free enterprise. We will explore whether these themes are linked to differences in the audiences' knowledge about interpretations of political events and actors.

Differences in Knowledge and Interpretation

CREATING APPROPRIATE COMPARISON GROUPS

In order to compare regular Limbaugh listeners to other audiences, we segmented our 1996 survey respondents by media consumption. Three of the groups were the usual regular listeners to PTR: Limbaugh only, conservative PTR, moderate/liberal PTR. Two other groups were created from those reporting that they were not regular listeners of PTR (i.e., listening fewer than two times per week). This nonlistening group was divided into those consuming mainstream mass media (MSMM; television or print) news heavily and those not. This yielded five groups, three of which listened to PTR regularly and two which did not. (For details about these groups and how they were created, see the appendix to this chapter at our website.)

Those consuming MSMM news less were quite different from the heavy users and from the PTR groups, particularly in terms of exposure and attention to and interest in politics.

Those in the heavy media consumption groups were similar to the three PTR groups in education and political involvement. Party affiliation and ideology were as expected. This means that the most liberal and democratic groups were those listening to liberal and moderate PTR. The audience becomes increasingly Republican and conservative in the conservative PTR group. Limbaugh's group is the most conservative and Republican.

The isolation of these groups makes it possible for us to make some simple comparisons among them. The minimal news consumption group is lower in education and political involvement than the other four. As a result, any differences in knowledge or in interpretation we find between the low-news group and the others will not be particularly informative, while differences between Limbaugh and other more heavily exposed groups will be. Differences among groups in knowledge or opinion will be informative when the groups being compared are similar in education and news exposure. In short, the interesting comparisons are among the three PTR groups and the heavy MSMM group, with the light MSMM group serving as a baseline group likely to be different from all the other groups.

KNOWLEDGE

If the balkanization hypothesis is correct, those who attend to partisan PTR will have different levels of knowledge about campaign topics, with these differences reflecting discussion of those issues by the host, and not simply mirroring educational and involvement difference across audiences. Similarly, when there are differences in coverage of campaign issues by PTR and the MSMM, we can expect differences in knowledge between PTR listeners and those exposed only to MSMM. Because the groups have similar levels of education and similar levels of political interest, differences in knowledge should reflect different levels of discussion and reinforcement across sources. When differences in knowledge emerge across our exposure groups, this can imply the creation of more well-informed and less well-informed subgroups in the larger society on specific issues. These differences are not across-the-board but are issue specific and reflect the biases in coverage across sources.

Our surveys in 1996 focused on a wide variety of topics and events. Here we present ones raised in the campaign by the candidates and receiving some coverage in one or more media outlets, whether mainstream sources or PTR. (For summary of the questions employed, which are detailed in our survey instruments, see the appendix to this chapter at our website.)

During the primary, participants responded to nine questions assessing their knowledge of issues discussed in the campaign. (For a list of these questions, see the appendix to this chapter at our website). Of the answers, four exhibited patterns relevant to and supportive of the balkanization hypothesis (see figs. 12.1a–12.1d).[9] These queries focused on U.S. troops in Bosnia, Republican contender Bob Dole's involvement in the Trilateral Commission, whether exports were increasing or decreasing, and an issue surrounding the Unabomber, Ted Kaczynski.

In cases B and C in figure 12.1 (Bob Dole's association with various international groups and knowledge about exports), the PTR groups are significantly different from both the light and heavy MSMM users. Since light news users are less interested and involved in politics, their limited knowledge is unsurprising. Since heavy users consume a great deal of political information from MSMM, we would expect them to be as well-informed as PTR

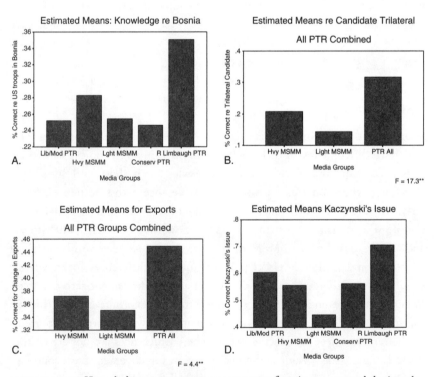

FIGURE 12.1. Knowledge as a percentage correct on four issues covered during the primary campaign: Differences among PTR and mainstream news groups.

consumers; in many cases, they are. However, in these two cases, PTR groups have significantly greater knowledge than either MSMM group. In cases A (U.S. troops in Bosnia) and D (issue involving Kaczynski), Limbaugh listeners not only were more accurate than heavy MSMM users, they were also more knowledgeable than other PTR groups, conservative and liberal.

These four cases show enhanced knowledge both for those who consume Limbaugh and for the broader group of PTR listeners including Limbaugh listeners. When our focus shifts from the primary period—where the vast majority of the content on PTR (and in the MSMM) is about the primary candidates and hence Republican issues—to the fall election campaign, some instructive differences emerge.

During October 1996, we asked respondents about eight different knowledge items that were discussed heavily by the campaigns and, therefore, covered by PTR hosts and the MSMM. Three were about issues central to the Clinton campaign—funding for job training, permitting late-term abortions under some circumstances, and banning cigarette ads targeted to children. Two were addressed by both candidates—a reduction of spending on Medicare and not legalizing same-sex marriages. Overall on these issues, Limbaugh listeners were *less* accurate than those listening to liberal/moderate PTR and than heavy consumers of MSMM while being more accurate than light consumers of MSMM. They were no different from listeners to conservative PTR.

So just as there was a kind of balkanization of knowledge favoring Limbaugh listeners with regard to Republican issues during the primary, there was a comparable differentiation favoring listeners to liberal/moderate PTR (and heavy MSMM), indicating balkanization as well, but of a qualitatively different kind. (For details of these findings, see the appendix to this chapter at our website.)

The basic message here is that knowledge of campaign-related issues is balkanized across media consumption and ideological divides. While Limbaugh may see an advantage to being certain that his conservative listeners are well-informed about Bob Dole's, Pat Buchanan's, and Steve Forbes's views, there is less value to Limbaugh's listeners knowing that Clinton favors a ban on cigarette advertising that targets children or, even more, does not favor legalizing same-sex marriages. These differences in the accuracy of political knowledge can impair informed political decision making, leading audiences to make false inferences about candidates and about their supporters. If citizens wish to choose their candidates on the basis of self-interest (or not for that matter), then it is crucial that they be informed about how candidates will serve that self-interest. To the extent that they are minimally or incorrectly informed, then sources that provide such information—while serving their own political vested interests—are not serving the needs of the common good.

What about views of the presidential candidates' positions during the fall election period when attention to these issues is intense in a variety of outlets?

CERTAIN LIMBAUGH LISTENERS HAD DISTORTED PERCEPTIONS OF BILL CLINTON'S VIEWS

In the 1996 presidential election, we explored people's judgments about the positions of candidates. To do so, we asked eight questions about "proposals that have been discussed during this year's election." Respondents indicated whether Bob Dole, Bill Clinton, both, or neither favored the proposal. Three were Dole proposals, three Clinton, one was both, and one neither. The questions focused on which candidate(s) favored the following:

"Reducing spending on Medicare" (both)
"Developing an anti-missile system" (Dole)
"Increased federal funding for job training" (Clinton)
"A 15% across-the-board tax cut" (Dole)
"A ban on cigarette advertising that might reach children" (Clinton)
"Eliminating the U.S. Department of Education" (Dole)
"Permitting late term abortions" (Clinton)
"Legalizing same-sex marriages" (neither)

Later in the interview, the same set of questions was asked of the interviewee using the format "Now I'd like your own views."

Four measures of distortion were created, two for Dole and two for Clinton. Total distortion is distortion due to what is called assimilation[10] (thinking a politician's position is more like your own than it is) and to contrast (thinking a position is more different from your own than it is); our scale ranged from 0 to 8. Directional distortion indicates how much contrast and how much assimilation there is; our scale ranged from –8 to +8. When the value is negative, people think their positions are more different from the candidate's than they actually are—a distortion toward contrast. (For a more detailed description of these measures, see the appendix to this chapter at our website.)

What the directional and total distortion measures provide is a way of assessing the extent to which campaign information is getting through to various groups. We were interested in ideological groups and specific PTR audiences and sought to determine whether there was an association between the PTR environment and direction and the amount of accuracy audiences had about candidates' positions.

RESPONDENTS' MEDIA NEWS CONSUMPTION AND
DISTORTION OF CANDIDATES' POSITIONS

To investigate the possible role of media consumption in people's judgments of candidates' positions, we first divided those who were not regular listeners to PTR into two subgroups: those who were not attentive or regular consumers of news through mainstream news sources (print and/or broadcast) and those who were. (For the details about how this was done, see the appendix to this chapter at our website.) The regular PTR listeners were grouped into those listening to Limbaugh and those consuming other forms of PTR (liberal, moderate, or conservative, but not Limbaugh).[11] Thus, we compared four groups, two PTR and two non-PTR, with one of the latter groups being attentive consumers of mainstream news.

We compare the distortion of candidates' stands in figure 12.2 for the four groups of news consumers. The graphs invite the following four conclusions (for the statistical details, see the appendix to this chapter at our website).[12] (1) There is more distortion of Clinton's positions than Dole's. (2) No group shows evidence of thinking that a candidate's views overall are more similar to their own positions than is actually the case; the opposite is true. (3) The low-consumption nonlisteners exhibit more distortion than the other groups, which is not surprising, since they tend to be less interested and to consume less information about the campaigns and candidates. (4) Limbaugh regulars tend to have more distorted views of candidates' positions, especially thinking that Bill Clinton's views are more different from their own views than they actually are.

We then explored the distortion of Clinton's positions among Limbaugh listeners to see what group among his listeners were most susceptible to this effect. Here we built on the work of researchers who have carefully studied differences in the public's ability to absorb information from the media about politics. John Zaller and Vincent Price have shown that people with high levels of "civics knowledge" are likely to be more disposed toward successful and habitual reception of information from news.[13] By "civics knowledge" we mean correctly answering simple questions about which party currently has the majority in the House of Representatives, the number of successive terms of office a president can serve, and so on.

Consistent with past research, we used civics knowledge as an indicator of "habitual news reception." We wanted to separate, even within our high exposure, high-attention news groups, those more likely to store the information they received from those less likely to do so. So, as other researchers have, we assumed that those with elevated civics knowledge would be more capable of obtaining and storing accurate information about political candidates and

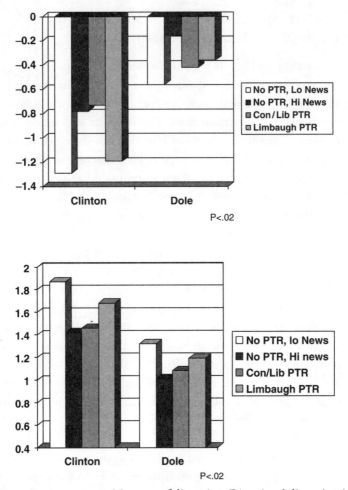

P<.02

P<.02

FIGURES 12.2A AND 12.2B. Measures of distortion: Directional distortion (2a) and total distortion (2b) of Clinton's and Dole's positions for four media groups. (Note: in 12.2a the more negative the more distortion away from one's own position; in 12.2b the larger the score the more distortion regardless of direction.)

their campaigns and, therefore, less likely to make erroneous inferences. For simplicity, we focus here only on distortions about Bill Clinton.

The comparisons between those with better capacity to digest news (high civics knowledge) and those with lower ability are presented in figure 12.3a and b. They show that people who are knowledgeable about politics distort less in every media group: they show less overall distortion and less contrast.

Most important, though, is the comparison between four media groups for high and low in civics knowledge. The figures show that distortion by

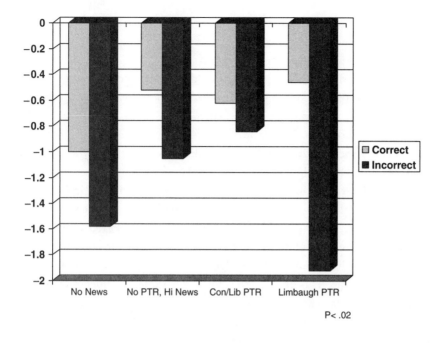

P< .02

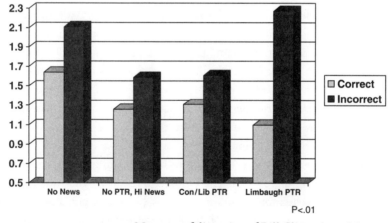

P<.01

FIGURES 12.3A AND 12.3B. Measures of distortion of Bill Clinton's positions: Directional distortion (3a) and total distortion (3b) for four news groups. (Note: No news = low news consumption, no PTR; Con/Lib PTR = listeners to conservative, moderate and liberal PTR)

Limbaugh listeners is greater for those with low civics knowledge. In fact, Limbaugh listeners who are more adept at learning from the media do not distort much at all in comparison to other groups.

Limbaugh's rhetoric about Clinton could have affected his low ability listeners' perceptions of Clinton's policies, leading them to think that Clinton's positions were more different from their own than they actually were. This distorted view occurs with those least capable of making sense of information from sources such as the mainstream media—that is, those who have low levels of civics knowledge.

One likely explanation of the distortion differences among Limbaugh listeners is the balancing effect of other news media. Regular consumers of Limbaugh's attacks on President Clinton carry away distorted views if they ignore other coverage of news. In fact, regardless of their consumption of PTR, those with low civics knowledge do consume less and attend less to mainstream media. This group is the most susceptible to influence by sources they deem credible, such as Limbaugh.

When Limbaugh presents distorted or ambiguously framed descriptions of Clinton's views, for those with low civics knowledge the absence of more complete knowledge from other media sources is associated with acceptance of Limbaugh's presentations of Clinton's views. The Limbaugh regulars with high civics knowledge show less distortion, because they use other news media for their information. Those without such additional, balanced information distort Clinton's position more and think his views are less like their own than they actually are. This finding in 1996 anticipated the possibility that when Fox emerged as an alternative source of news for conservatives, and Limbaugh listeners responded by displacing some of their mainstream broadcast exposure to news with exposure to Fox News, their distortion of Democratic positions would increase.

In sum, in our 1996 study, exposure to mainstream media seemed to be effective in reducing distortions. The Limbaugh listeners who were consuming these sources were more accurate than those who were not. Regular Limbaugh listeners who were less able to integrate alternative news sources into their thinking exhibited more distortion of Clinton's positions than other groups.

Limbaugh's representation of Clinton's campaign and presidency paid off with this segment of his audience. These listeners thought Clinton's positions were more different from their own than they actually were; at the same time, Limbaugh's audience did not show the same distortion in judging Dole's positions. In fact, the high and low civics knowledge groups were equally accurate about Dole. Those who were hearing conservative and liberal/

moderate PTR and were low in civics knowledge exhibited more distortion of Dole's positions than did the comparable Limbaugh group.

The least informed groups were those avoiding other news sources and with little readiness to receive other available information. At the same time, exposure to Limbaugh's show misdirected the judgments of his least politically aware listeners regarding Clinton but correspondingly informed their judgments of Dole.

We next ask whether these differences in the informational base reflect distortions in interpretation of political events.

INTERPRETATION OF EVENTS

We would expect those exposed to partisan PTR to have different kinds of interpretations of the same political events occurring during the campaign. We separate "events" from knowledge and policy proposals because events have a physical reality to them. They are anchored in action. Although events are often filtered through broadcast news or other news sources, they have a presence that is less ephemeral than knowledge gained only vicariously or through policy proposals that are hypothetical. This would certainly be true of presidential debates, which provide viewers with direct experience of the event, even though postdebate commentary is all too often a mad dash toward spin control. Nevertheless, perceptions of real-world "events" may be less susceptible than abstract considerations to exhortation and ideological framings by media personalities.

In most contexts, we would expect liberals to embrace a liberal interpretation and conservatives a conservative one. However, after controlling for these factors, differences across PTR groups and between PTR and MSMM should reflect the effects of information on the creation of homogeneous interpretive communities consistent with partisan, one-sided discussion. These interpretive differences, when they materialize, reflect differences in how the groups understand social and political events. In effect, highly interested, informed, and motivated groups seek to produce interpretations of specific events in ways that support their a priori ideologies, and these interpretive biases may be exacerbated—or at least reinforced—by the rhetoric of partisan media sources.

Respondents were asked for their interpretations of several specific events occurring during the primary period. The interpretive options often reflected more and less cynical, more and less self-interested perceptions. For example, during the primary campaign, Los Angeles police were videotaped beating illegal immigrants in a fashion reminiscent of the Rodney King incident.

Respondents were asked both if they thought these tapes showed only one side of the event and if they thought they represented police brutality. Interpretive questions are not to be confused with opinions about general issues not tied to specific events. A survey choice such as "Government regulation of business (1) is necessary to protect the public interest, or (2) usually does more harm than good," for instance, is an opinion about regulation of business in general, not an interpretation of an event occurring in the public's ken.

Late in the primary period, we asked about respondents' interpretations of six specific events: the Los Angeles police beating captured on video; the death of Clinton cabinet member Ron Brown; Republicans in Congress favoring an increase in the minimum wage (then pending before Congress); President Clinton's veto of the late-term abortion ban; the Republicans' movement for a constitutional amendment on government spending; and the media's coverage of Ted Kaczynski and Timothy McVeigh. For example, regarding changed Republican views on the minimum wage, we asked the respondent which of these reasons he or she thought was closer to the Republicans' motives: compromise on an important political issue or abandoning their principles for political gain. (For the wording of each question listed, see the appendix to this chapter at our website.)

Although answers to these questions certainly have an attitudinal base, they are concerned with interpretations of specific events in the news and not abiding issues. They can be understood as interpretations by the audiences derived from a complex of a priori dispositions, as well as frames for these issues provided by media sources.

Of the six interpretive questions, four exhibit results that are consistent with our hypothesis, and the other two (on minimum wage and police beatings) exhibit the same pattern but not significantly so.[14] Two of the issues are represented in figures 12.4a and 12.4b. In panel A, Limbaugh listeners were more likely to say that President Clinton's words of admiration about Ron Brown after his death in a plane accident were uttered for political advantage rather than because Clinton really admired Brown. No other group leaned toward that reaction. In panel B, a similar result is apparent on the opposite end of the ideological continuum. Limbaugh listeners were more likely to infer that Republicans' purpose in discussing a constitutional amendment to require a two-thirds majority in Congress for tax increases was to hold down deficits (less cynical) rather than to contrast themselves to Democrats (more cynical). These results show that it is not just being conservative or liberal that determines the interpretation of the event but how different sources cast the event. Limbaugh's advocacy could be part of the reason his listeners share his views.

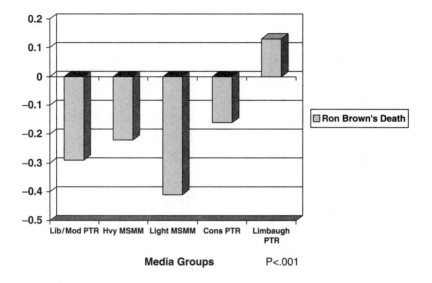

Interpretation of Reactions to Ron Brown's Death (+1 = cynical)

Media Groups: Lib/Mod PTR, Hvy MSMM, Light MSMM, Cons PTR, Limbaugh PTR

P<.001

Ron Brown's Death

Constitutional Amendment Required to Raise Taxes (1= less cynical)

Media Groups: Lib/Mod PTR, Hvy MSMM, Light MSMM, Cons PTR, Limbaugh PTR

P<.02

Consti Amend

FIGURES 12.4A AND 12.4B. Differences in interpretation of events by five media exposure groups. (Note: In panel A, higher score indicates "political advantage for President Clinton versus heartfelt admiration"; in panel B, a higher score indicates "Republicans argue for a constitutional amendment for tax increases to hold down deficits versus contrasting with Democrats.")

The Second 1996 Presidential Debate

We next consider the effect on Limbaugh listeners of exposure to the second presidential debate. Of interest to us was the question whether Limbaugh's listeners' views of Clinton's and Dole's performances differed from those of other PTR listeners and nonlisteners. People's assessments of a candidate's debate performance are based on a more direct experience of the debate (for watchers anyway) than is the case for a candidate's policy positions. The details of candidates' policies are found in lengthy and often complex position papers. The details of performance in a debate are directly experienced using the tools people feel comfortable with—their own eyes and ears and lifelong experience judging the competence and trustworthiness of others.

Distortion of Clinton's policy positions by Limbaugh listeners is perhaps more likely than distortions that arise from a directly experienced event such as a presidential debate. The stands that the Clinton and Dole campaigns took on various issues were generally available through the media outlets covering the campaigns. In 1996, before widespread use of the internet to communicate candidates' positions, misrepresentations of Clinton's positions by Limbaugh were not as easily corrected by locating statements and briefs from the campaigns themselves. By contrast, the presidential debates were directly experienced events, which may be more difficult to distort through media interpretation and framing from ideological spokespeople such as Limbaugh.

The fourth wave of our 1996 PTR survey was timed to be in the field during the week following the second presidential debate. Some of the questions asked about whether interviewees watched the debate or not, which candidate they thought did a better job, their reasons for this judgment, and other aspects of their perceptions and knowledge.

The PTR listeners were more likely to report watching the debate than were the nonlisteners. Limbaugh listeners watched at a higher rate (70%) than nonlisteners (53%) and at somewhat higher rates than listeners to conservative (62%) and to liberal/moderate PTR. That PTR listeners would be more likely to watch the debate is consistent with previous research on their higher levels of political involvement and following of politics.[15]

To evaluate the audience's judgments about who did a better job, we asked: "Regardless of which candidate you personally support, who do you think did a better job in the debate—Bill Clinton or Bob Dole?" The audiences were scaled from +1 for Dole to –1 for Clinton, with those who either volunteered "both" or were unsure scored at 0.

No one would be surprised to find partisans saying that they thought that their candidate did a better job. Indeed, Republicans and Democrats said precisely this about who they thought won the debate. However, in comparing how strong the differences are between Republicans and Democrats across PTR audiences, the disparity is sharpest for those listening to Limbaugh. For this group, the Republicans were more likely to say that Dole won than Republicans in any other media group.

Perceptions of Debate Styles

In addition to perceptions of which candidate did a better job in the debate, we were also interested in people's perceptions of the debaters' performances. Accordingly, those who watched the debate were offered a series of terms to choose from. We asked: "Thinking about what you saw while watching the debate, please tell me if each one [word] does or does not apply to Bob Dole." The words were: "mean," "weak," "warm," "dishonest," "leader-like," and "angry." The list was repeated for Clinton. How people perceive the debaters' styles is certainly not the only criterion they use to judge who does a better job, but it is an important one. [16]

In figures 12.5a and b, we compare perceptions of how much Clinton showed leadership and weakness during the presidential debates for each of three groups—Limbaugh listeners, listeners to other PTR, and those who are not regular listeners. The key comparison is between Limbaugh's moderates and Republicans and the same types of persons in the other groups. To find that Democrats saw Clinton's performance as leader-like and not exhibiting weakness is to define what it means to be a Democrat. But Limbaugh's moderates and Republicans see Clinton as considerably weaker and less leader-like than do other moderates and Republicans.[17]

Bill Clinton was also evaluated differently by some Limbaugh listeners on meanness and anger—two characteristics that could have been applied to either Dole or Clinton. Republicans who were Limbaugh listeners were more likely to say Clinton was mean and angry than Republicans who did not listen to PTR. Combined with the perceptions of leadership and weakness portrayed in figure 12.5, we have more negative judgments of Clinton's style among Republicans listening to Limbaugh than those not listening to PTR at all. In short, Limbaugh's attacks on Clinton may have paid off even among his most partisan listeners.

Perceptions of candidates' performance in the second debate were associated with the styles viewers attributed to the candidates, specifically the

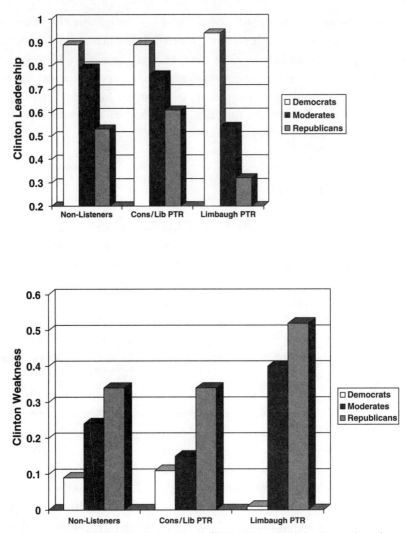

FIGURES 12.5A AND 12.5B. Perceptions of Bill Clinton's leadership and weakness during the second presidential debate: Media groups by party identification.

qualities of meanness, weakness, warmth, and leadership. Perceptions of Clinton's weakness and leadership during the debate were more negative for Republicans who were regular listeners of Limbaugh than for other Republicans. In effect, Limbaugh activated Republicans' negative evaluations more than did being in other listening and nonlistening groups.

Limbaugh's listeners tended to use political party heuristics to judge the candidate who did the best job in the debate more than any other listening or nonlistening group. While party is an important factor in accounting for judgments of debate performance for any partisan, Limbaugh listeners relied on this more than others. These data suggest that he is successful in activating party as a criterion for judgment.

No one was surprised to find Republicans who watched the debate saying that Dole did a better job. However, Republicans who were Limbaugh regulars did so more often than Republicans who were regular listeners of other talk shows and than Republicans who did not listen to PTR regularly at all. In effect, Limbaugh listeners used their party identification as Republicans as a judgmental criterion for debate performance more than other groups did. They were primed to think in terms of their party affiliation, and so party became a more salient basis for judgment among Limbaugh regulars.[18]

Attributions about 1996 Presidential Election Outcomes

At the conclusion of the 1996 presidential campaign, we tested a specific class of perceptions, namely, the reasons that election turned out in favor of Clinton rather than Dole. Through both open- and closed-ended questions, we elicited specific explanations—sometimes called attributions—from respondents as to why they thought the election turned out as it did. Our interest in postelection attributions was motivated by two factors. First, all available evidence anticipated a Clinton win. We wondered how Limbaugh would maintain the spirit and commitment of the party faithful in light of the win by his arch-nemesis. Second, events discomforting to Limbaugh's listeners provided an opportunity to investigate their attributions, or reasons, explaining these outcomes.[19]

To ensure that we wouldn't influence the kind of attributions offered, open-ended questions were posed first. Participants were asked what they thought was "the main reason Bill Clinton was elected over Bob Dole and the other candidates." Later in the interview, respondents were presented with a series of 15 one-sentence explanations for the election results and were asked to indicate whether they thought each was a "major reason," a "minor reason," or "not a reason."

Included were both substantive explanations (e.g., "Clinton has a good record as President during his first term") and justifications dealing with the strategies of the campaigns or characteristics of the voting public. For example, one of the strategy-based explanations posited that "Dole did not stress family values as strongly as he should have"; another suggested: "Dole doesn't come across as well on television as Clinton." Responses ranged from high to low. The most accepted explanation had to do with Dole's lack of presence on television; the least accepted was public rebellion against the treatment Clinton was receiving from some talk radio hosts. (For a complete list of these items and their weighted means, see the appendix to this chapter at our website.)[20]

The topics volunteered in the open-ended responses were compared to the closed-ended ones. By and large, the explanations that were highly ranked in the closed-ended questions were common in the open-ended ones; similarly, the election explanations that were ranked as unimportant tended to be relatively rare in the open-ended responses.

As in the earlier comparisons among those who did and did not listen to PTR, we divided those not listening to PTR during the fall election campaign into heavy and light consumers of mainstream media.[21] As before, five groups were compared on a summary index that included the following explanations: (a) "Bill Clinton stole good ideas from the Republicans"; (b) "The public wasn't interested enough in getting the truth about the candidates"; (c) "Bill Clinton lied about his record"; (d) "Newspapers were biased in favor of liberals"; (e) "Bob Dole didn't make an issue of Bill Clinton's character as strongly as he should have"; (f) "Bill Clinton has a good record as President during his first term"; (g) "The public was easily fooled by Clinton's slick ads and campaign." These were grouped together because people tended to respond to them in similar ways.

Those accepting statements such as these as explanations for the election's outcome were subscribing to accounts that blamed President Clinton, the media's "liberal" attitudes, and the public. Or they were attributing the election's result to strategic factors, such as Dole failing to attack Clinton on the issue of character. The only substantive account in the list was the one stipulating that Clinton had a good record during his first term—a kind of begrudging admiration.

Limbaugh listeners differed significantly from all other media groups in the degree to which they attributed the election's outcome to these types of reasons. Although they differed least from those listening to conservative talk radio, there were differences between the two groups; the non-Limbaugh groups were about the same as one another in their attributions.

Limbaugh's pre- and postelection rhetoric helps to account for these differences in attribution. Limbaugh criticized President Clinton in every coded broadcast from May until Election Day in 1996. The scandals associated with Clinton's administration were often revisited by Limbaugh. They ranked third, behind the Democratic president himself and the mainstream media, in analyses of Limbaugh's subject matter. His ongoing emphasis on character flaws and on the pro-Clinton, anti-Dole bias of the media may have served to prepare listeners for attributions that sidestepped substantive differences between Clinton and Dole and activated other explanations.

For example, both during the campaign and in the voting booth, in the 1996 election women voters preferred Clinton over Dole. The media were aware of and extensively reported this preference. Limbaugh responded by making a significant issue of female voting dispositions in 1996. He characterized these women's judgments as silly and emotion-driven, implying an association between women and untrustworthiness or irrationality. His disdain for mainstream media coverage may have helped his audience to conclude or reinforced its disposition to believe that the mainstream media were manipulative and underhanded. These implications, in turn, could have contributed to his audience's account of the election results as the product of misguided or misled voters or the triumph of style and guile.

The attributions Limbaugh listeners made about the election reinforced their belief in the legitimacy and effectiveness of their conservative beliefs. In their minds, their candidate did not lose because of his proposed programs or because of Clinton's defense of the Democratic agenda. Rather, Dole lost because of an easily duped public, a slick and media-savvy opponent, and biased news media. Such sense-making enables this audience to retain its ideological worldview.

Much of the research into the effects of strongly partisan media such as PTR has focused on the direct effects of exposure on audiences' attitudes and beliefs about the candidates or the issues.[22] Alternatively, we suggest that one way that media frame and thereby affect audience perceptions is by shaping their interpretations of the causes of political events. These interpretations, in turn, can have implications for audience members' feelings and attitudes not only about the issues confronting the nation but also about those seeking and holding elective office.

The "Swift Boat Veterans for Truth" SBVT and Mainstream News (2004)

We had another opportunity to study balkanization in August 2004, when the SBVT aired ads challenging Kerry's patriotism on the basis of statements the SBVT alleged he had made when he testified against the war to a Senate committee. The group also challenged the legitimacy of the medals he had been awarded during that war. The Kerry campaign denied these charges, claiming that the group was misconstruing his statements and impugning his integrity without evidence. Kerry representatives clashed with the SBVT spokesman largely on Fox, MSNBC, and CNN throughout August 2004 as the mainstream media held back. When mainstream print and broadcast news media, including Ted Koppel's *Nightline*, finally weighed in, it was with evidence that largely corroborated Kerry's accounts. Here, in other words, was a classic test case in which facts were contested and the mainstream media largely vindicated one side.

In an Annenberg postelection survey in 2004, we asked whether our respondents had seen or heard about ads by a group called Swift Boat Veterans for Truth (for details about the survey, see our website). Those who indicated that they had were asked, "In general how accurate do you think those ads were?" Listening to Limbaugh and watching Fox each independently predicted an increased likelihood that those surveyed had seen or heard about the SBVT ads and believed the group's claims were accurate, despite extensive controls to account for other explanations. (For details, see the appendix to this chapter at our website.) This finding would suggest that these two outlets magnified their audience's exposure to the attack on Kerry and at the same time insulated that audience from corrective information advanced in the mainstream media.[23]

Conclusion

Balkanization is the byproduct of a process of creating differences among segments of the public in knowledge, interpretation, and opinion. Here we attribute this phenomenon to exposure to specific sources. Balkanization differentiates one group of citizens from another in what they know about, and in how they interpret social and political events. Although differences among members of the public in ideology, knowledge, and opinion are the hallmark of human interest and variability, new media—and specifically partisan PTR—use rhetoric that capitalizes on human needs and motivations to create, in some cases, and reinforce, in others, special knowledge enclaves. In this chapter, we have suggested some ways balkanization might be expressed among the listeners to PTR, especially Limbaugh's programs. His rhetorical style and content distinguish him and, therefore, his listeners not only from those unexposed to his program but also from those attentive to other PTR hosts. In 1996, mainstream audiences were largely unexposed to his daily doses of intense anti-Clinton rhetoric, his lessons about the "liberal biases" of the mainstream media, and his calls for ideological integrity and political and social involvement.

Limbaugh's audience comes away from its daily encounters with the conservator of Reaganism knowing what is necessary to be a good conservative and a good conservative Republican. Listeners experience the minor and major events of political and social life through the lenses Limbaugh offers. When Ron Brown was killed in a plane crash and President Clinton eulogized his close friend and cabinet member, Limbaugh seized the opportunity to criticize Clinton as an opportunist ready to take political advantage of even the death of his friend. When Republican nominee Bob Dole lost the 1996 presidential election to the man Limbaugh had criticized every day for the past year, his listeners emerged from exposure to his program seeing this outcome as evidence that the media were biased in favor of "liberals"; the public, too easily fooled; and Clinton, slicker than their party's nominee.

The concept of balkanization describes in a summary way the kind of influences Limbaugh can have on his audience. The phenomenon may always have existed. But we see it as a harbinger, in 1996, of the effects of newer forms of partisan media as well, including Fox News and partisan blogs.

Distortion and Polarization

Distortion and polarization are processes that emerge on our radar screen because they reinforce and on occasion exacerbate the insular, balkanizing tendencies we focused on in the last chapter. Our definitions are those one would expect. Distortion has to do with one's perception of another person's or group's view compared to their actual view. If I believe that a political candidate supports gay civil unions when in fact the candidate does not, my perception is incorrect, certainly, but also is distorted in a certain direction. I see the candidate as holding more liberal views on this issue than is the case. If you and I hold opposed views of gay civil unions, with me vocally supportive and you fundamentally opposed, our views are polar opposites. Distortion is about inaccuracy, polarization about difference (whether accurate or not).

Polarization refers to sharp differences in the views of groups or persons about some other person or group. If my views about gay civil unions become more extreme and yours don't change, then our views are more different than before; they have become more polarized.

One of the core ideas helping to explain distortion and perceived polarization is the human tendency to process information in a biased way, altering perceived positions to become more extreme than they otherwise would be. Driving polarization is the inclination to seek out or selectively expose oneself to one-sided information compatible with one's existing beliefs. Although distortion and polarization are separable in principle, they often coexist in the real world. An audience prompted by its ideological dispositions to seek out one-sided, like-minded information may become more extreme in its views (i.e., polar) as a result of biased exposure. The result is greater polarization and greater distortion (and perceived difference with the other group). The increasingly partisan nature of news media coupled with the human tendency to seek out ideologically comfortable information could have the effect of increasing polarization and distortion.

Distortion: Assimilation and Contrast Effects in Judgment

The views we consider here are grounded in the social psychological notions of contrast and assimilation[1]—two aspects of what social psychologists call *biased processing*. This term refers to the ways people recast information that is either congenial or uncongenial to their views.[2] When people care about an issue, they are more likely to scrutinize information that seems to challenge their views. Their reactions are not likely to be dispassionate. Instead, their own predispositions for or against the issue can bias how they perceive what information is strong and what weak.[3]

Two kinds of biases operate. Contrast effects distort perception to increase the difference between the audience member's view of a candidate's stand and the candidate's actual position. Assimilation does the opposite, reducing the perceived difference. These two effects can be byproducts of the audience's psychological dispositions—often the extremity of their prior opinions—or the effect of rhetorical manipulation or both. Regardless of how the perceptual distortions are created, the results are the same—a greater distance between one's position and what one thinks an opposing candidate's position is, in the case of contrast, and a greater sense of similarity between one's own and the candidate's position, in the case of a similarity. If Limbaugh's discourse, or simple exposure to Limbaugh's rhetorical style, creates identification with conservatives and alienation from Democrats, then Limbaugh will have served an important political function for the Republican Party.

Polarization of Opinion

Polarization intensifies opinions and attitudes so that they are held more strongly (for or against a given issue) in one group than in another. For example, in the early years of the Vietnam War, public opinion was more supportive of the war than opposed to it, but some Republicans and Democrats held sharply divergent—polarized—views. Over the course of the war, as news coverage began to feature both pro- and antiwar voices and prominent individuals spoke out against the war, public opinion became less polarized.[4] In effect, strong prowar positions weakened in intensity and shifted toward a more neutral or in some cases antiwar position. Public opinion became more homogeneous, that is, less polarized.

POLARIZATION THROUGH EXPOSURE
TO DIFFERENT SOURCES

Polarization can occur through selective exposure to, attention to, and retention of different types of information, and is particularly likely to occur when a like-minded chorus promotes opinion in a given direction. In circumstances in which an audience is exposed regularly to a single, coherent, and consistent point of view and the voices championing that in-group view identify alternative points of view as suspect, the audience's dispositions would be expected to be reinforced or made more extreme (polarization) and its perception of out-groups rendered more extreme (distortion), as well. We are all, of course, disposed to embrace information and opinion consistent with our existing beliefs, a disposition that inclines us toward ideologically consistent sources.[5]

In a moment, we will present results from a field experiment in which ideologically diverse audiences were exposed to one-sided information, in some cases supportive of and other cases opposed to their a priori viewpoints. By exposing these subjects to uncongenial sources, we created a scenario that is increasingly uncommon in our media-rich news environment. The proliferation of media outlets and rise of alternative partisan voices in media means that it is much easier than it once was to select media consistent with one's ideology and to avoid a source whose message is opposed.

POLARIZATION THROUGH BIASED PROCESSING

Biased processing refers to the appeal certain arguments have for those whose attitudes, values, or even ideologies dispose them to accept them. For example, an argument that the flat tax will reduce the overall size of a government bureaucracy such as the Internal Revenue Service should appeal to conservatives, increasing the likelihood they will favor the flat tax. When arguments appeal to the conservative ideology, they will be evaluated favorably by those of that ideological bent. Liberals are less likely to be moved by these arguments. Faced with a strong argument for the flat tax, liberals are more likely than conservatives to counterargue. Indeed, one would expect quite a bit of counterargument by liberals, depending on their own previous knowledge about the plausibility and novelty of the original argument. The result would be increased support, or at least reinforcement, of the attitudes of conservatives who attend to and accept this argument, and no change or a possible boomerang effect among liberals. In short, biased processing refers to differences in mental responses to the same message by groups differing in their a priori support of (or opposition to) the message. The result can be polarization of opinion between the liberal and conservative groups.

Polarization among social groups can be produced either when different groups choose to limit their exposure to sources that are one-sided or through biased processing of a single source. Polarization is a process that increases social separation from those of opposed ideology while increasing cohesion and solidarity within one's own group. Consequently, polarization is a vehicle driving both between-group conflict and within-group cooperation. As partisan sources proliferate and like-minded audiences limit exposure to multiple points of view, it becomes important to understand more fully the circumstances in which attitude change, polarization, and distortion occur.

In the remainder of this chapter, we will craft a circumstantial case for the polarizing effects of exposure both to Limbaugh's rhetoric and to other sources in the conservative media establishment. The evidence will be largely consistent across studies, a precondition for building confidence in a claim. However, given the a priori dispositions of the audiences drawn to Fox and Limbaugh, the causal arrow could run from the viewers and listeners' prior political biases to exposure to the conservative media rather than the other way around. To help untangle the effects, we report results from our week-long experiment with PTR in 1996, PTR Experiment 1996. This move makes it possible for us to examine the persuasive power of various talk radio hosts and formats and also the conditions conducive to the production of polarized opinion.

We explored polarization in 1996 by comparing Limbaugh's audience to other groups in the context of Bill Clinton's policy proposals during the 1996 presidential campaign. These studies were extended in the 2000 and 2004 elections. The observational studies of the 1996, 2000, and 2004 elections were ones in which polarization could come about through the combined effects of selective exposure and biased processing. Our PTR Experiment 1996 controlled selective exposure—since everyone in the same exposure condition receives the same content—while also observing the effects of persuasion and biased processing.

First, we consider some field experimental evidence of polarization from PTR Experiment 1996. This study exposed subjects to the rhetoric of different PTR voices, including Limbaugh.

Polarization from Exposure to PTR

Details of the field experiment were presented in chapter 5 and its appendices. Nonetheless, some basic information follows. Participants were randomly assigned to listen to one of the following six types of PTR: (1) *Talk of the Nation* (NPR); (2) conservative and liberal mix (taken from the content of PTR groups 3, 4, and 5); (3) liberal PTR; (4) conservative PTR (not including Limbaugh); (5) Limbaugh; and (6) talk radio that was not political (the control group). In order to ensure comparability across programs, each focused on the same topic for each of the five one-hour tapes that participants consumed. Thus there were five topics for each type of talk radio, one for each of five days of the study.

The liberal and conservative points of view were represented by the programing of several different hosts, including conservatives G. Gordon Liddy and Ken Hamblin and liberals Mario Cuomo and Tom Leykis. The stimulus tapes were not altered in any way that would misrepresent the host's position. They faithfully represented the hosts' and callers' comments.

To assess polarization, people were asked about their opinions on issues discussed by the radio hosts to whom they had listened during the five-day experiment. Responses were obtained both before and after exposure (a separation of six to eight days). The topics included racial matters, assisted suicide, education, the flat tax, and the Muslim religion and the nation of Islam—topics drawing attention in the media and social environment at the time of the study.

Listeners assigned to each type of talk radio included both liberals and conservatives. Our analyses show that four topics exhibited clear-cut polarization effects, with liberal and conservative groups moving in opposite directions in response to one-sided conservative or liberal rhetoric. These topics were black leaders and institutions, President Clinton's Goals 2000 education initiative, Dr. Kevorkian's assisted suicides of terminally ill patients, and flattening the taxes on capital gains. Since each of these had received considerable attention in the media prior to our study, politically involved audiences already had some prior knowledge of them. Despite the attitudinal inertia that prior exposure can create, we observed different responses—polarized ones—between liberals and conservatives listening to Limbaugh, in contrast to similar liberal and conservative groups not listening to Limbaugh but to those in the control group listening to nonpolitical talk.

In the interests of space, we will only present the results for the racial and flat tax issues.

RACIAL ATTITUDES

Four measures of racial attitudes were employed to assess any direct effects of the hosts' messages about affirmative action and any indirect effects of those messages on related issues. Only the measures assessing attitudes toward black leaders and related groups will be discussed here. None of the other measures on racial matters reflected polarization. The measures evaluating Black leaders and African-American-related groups included attitudes toward Jesse

Jackson; Abdul Mahmoud Rauf; Louis Farrakhan; the NAACP; the Muslim religion (in the context of Black Muslims); and the Nation of Islam.[6]

In response to Limbaugh's show, liberals and conservatives become more separated in their views in comparison to the control group. This can be seen in figure 13.1 in the spread between the attitudes of liberals and conservatives in comparison to the control. By contrast, the liberals and conservatives who heard *Talk of the Nation* showed a narrowing of difference in racial attitudes. Limbaugh made prior differences among groups larger, while *Talk of the Nation* made them smaller. This may reflect a polarization phenomenon for the Limbaugh show and an accommodation effect for *Talk of the Nation*.[7]

Note that the liberal group that listened to Limbaugh actually exhibited more positive attitudes toward Black leaders than might be expected if no message had been received (control), while the conservative group had more negative attitudes. This polarization can be seen as a boomerang effect for the liberal listeners and a persuasion or intensification effect for the conservative ones. These results show that Limbaugh not only exhibited no power to convert liberal listeners on this issue but actually may have had the opposite effect on those who opposed his views, at least in this case. Shows such as *Talk of the Nation,* however, may reduce polarization under some conditions, ameliorating the a priori differences in racial attitudes.

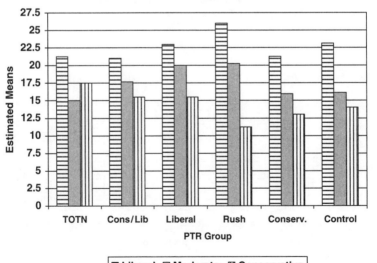

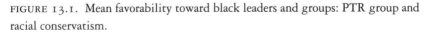

FIGURE 13.1. Mean favorability toward black leaders and groups: PTR group and racial conservatism.

ATTITUDES TOWARD THE FLAT TAX

The issue of a flatter income tax was a hot topic in the presidential primaries of January through April 1996—the time of our experiment. Steve Forbes made it the central—indeed the only—major issue in his bid for the nomination. Those listening to Limbaugh tended to have stronger ideological responses to the capital gains question than did the control group and the liberal group.[8] Figure 13.2 shows how these groups responded. The spread within the Limbaugh listening group was the polarization effect, with liberals taking the least favorable stance on this issue of any of the liberal groups and the conservatives taking the most favorable one. Although the PTR groups did not differ on average on the question of capital gains, they did differ within ideological subgroups. The liberals boomeranged away from the Limbaugh message, while the conservatives most strongly embraced it. However, contrary to the trends exhibited by conservatives in other groups, conservatives listening to liberal PTR group did not reject the arguments of liberal hosts but instead moved toward them. This acceptance by conservatives may reflect the comparatively greater credibility they attributed to liberal PTR in 1996, in contrast to the more negative credibility liberals assigned to Limbaugh's program in general. Indeed, almost all our participants in the experiment had heard of Limbaugh in advance of their participation.

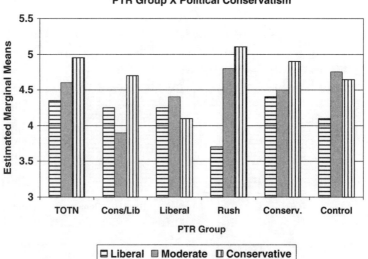

FIGURE 13.2. Favorability toward capital gains: PTR group by political conservatism.

An Experimental Test of Interpretive Differences

In our experiment, participants came together after a week's exposure to the assigned talk radio content. At that time, they filled out questionnaires about their perceptions and attitudes, some of which we have just reported. In the PTR programs we selected for use—as in much of PTR—the interpretation of events invited by the host is not subtle. Instead, it is stark and distinctly partisan and ideological. This fact permitted us to investigate whether hosts' interpretations would invite listeners to similar interpretive dispositions.

After a week's exposure to conservatively oriented messages, for example, one might very well be primed to think in conservative terms, perhaps employing arguments from the conservatives' repertoire, even if one's natural inclination was liberal in orientation. We investigated this question at the end of our experiment, when participants attended a final session to complete a questionnaire and see a videotaped political debate.

Increasing the minimum wage was a significant issue in congressional debates at the time. The Republicans in Congress were considering an alternative: giving taxpayers an earned income tax credit (EITC) instead of upping the minimum wage.[9] Begun under a Republican administration in 1975 to aid low-income workers, the earned income tax credit is a refundable tax credit. (A refundable tax credit reduces the dollar amount paid in taxes. As a result, a $1 tax credit has the same dollar value to a person in a lower tax bracket as it has to a person in a higher bracket. The Republican proposal in 1996 would have extended the EITC's reach.) Participants were shown a debate between a Democrat advocating an increased minimum wage and Republican member of Congress arguing the advantages of the EITC. After viewing the videotaped debate, participants were asked: "Is the EITC (a) more unnecessary interference by the government in solving our country's economic problems or (b) the kind of government assistance for the less fortunate that our country needs?"

Of interest to us was not whether people with different political party identification would choose in a way consistent with their party. We expected that they would. However, after a week's exposure to partisan PTR—ideologically congenial for some but not for others—we wondered whether choices within ideological groups would be primed by the ideological slants of the media hosts to which they were exposed.

What was unique about the debate our participants watched was that the Democrats were arguing "unnecessary interference by the government"—typically a conservative frame—and the Republicans were championing "government assistance for the less fortunate," typically a liberal frame. The alternatives were phrased so that if one were opposed to government interference, one had to choose the first alternative—typically the conservative choice. But if a conservative made this selection maintaining ideological purity, he or she was going against legislation proposed by the Republicans. To stay with one's political party requires being ideologically inconsistent in the basis for the choice.

The EITC question produced a differential reaction from liberals, depending on what kind of PTR they had heard in the prior week.[10] Figure 13.3 illustrates the nature of the interaction between the PTR group and political ideology. There are significant differences between the group assigned to listen to Limbaugh and the control group, and between the group assigned to the conservative non-Limbaugh condition and the control group.[11] But the differences are due primarily to the presence of liberals in these two groups.

The liberals who heard conservative programing interpreted the EITC more as "unnecessary interference" than liberals hearing control (non-PTR) or other PTR programs. In effect, they rejected the EITC program advocated by Republicans, even though it would help the less fortunate and even though such an interpretation would be consistent with a liberal ideological disposition. Importantly, only the liberals who listened to the Limbaugh and conservative PTR behaved in this way. Liberals were not simply rejecting a Republican program, but rather, liberals exposed to counterideological programs were boomeranging away from the host's partisan position and becoming more entrenched in their own positions—more entrenched in fact than other liberals. In this case, PTR polarized the interpretations of liberals when, during their week of exposure to Limbaugh and to conservative hosts, these hosts invited them to hold the point of view that "big government" was too interfering. Liberals exposed to balanced programing (conservative and liberal hosts) did not show the same effect.

The apparent differences between conservatives listening to liberal PTR and those listening to conservative and control PTR are not reliable ones. Liberals ended up rejecting the ideological and partisan tones of Limbaugh and of the other conservative hosts even if it meant taking an ideologically inconsistent position on government intervention.

After a week's exposure to PTR from the left, center, or right, liberals who heard conservative talk (Limbaugh or others) judged a Republican proposal, the EITC, to be "unnecessary government interference," while other liberals tended to interpret the EITC as "help for those less fortunate." This was the case even though there was no specific discussion of the EITC during the week's programming and even though it was ideologically inconsistent for the liberals to adopt this interpretation. In short, they rebelled against the Republican and conservative rhetoric of the prior week, becoming more entrenched in an interpretation they would otherwise be reluctant to offer.

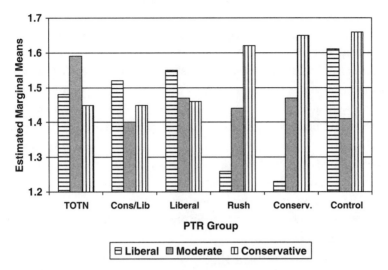

Mean Evaluation of ETIC

Higher score = favors government program

FIGURE 13.3. Favorability toward EITC for PTR groups and three levels of political ideology.

Political party operated as an interpretive filter, but in this case one that directed oppositional judgments, polarizing liberals and conservatives. Equally important, this polarization took place in the context of a political dispute between Democrats and Republicans. It's possible that PTR primed listeners to think and evaluate using political party schemas rather than substantive criteria consistent with their values. After all, the EITC involves no greater governmental interference than does setting the minimum wage. And liberals hearing nonconservative programs felt that the EITC would benefit disadvantaged taxpayers. It was only those liberals who heard a week of conservative programing who rebelled.

Polarization Created by Differential Exposure

A second type of polarization can occur as a result of exposure to different messages on the same topic. Some participants in our experiment heard only Limbaugh for a week, others heard liberal sources only, and still others received two-sided messages such as those from NPR's *Talk of the Nation* or from a mix of sources on the left and on the right.

Consider two of the issues that produced postexposure polarization: attitudes toward adopting a flat tax policy for income taxes in the United States and attitudes concerning voting for or against a law allowing doctor-assisted suicide. Figure 13.4 (and the tables in the appendix to this chapter at our website) presents the results for these cases. Those who listened to Limbaugh's program for the week of our experiment had the most favorable attitudes toward the flat tax, while those listening to *Talk of the Nation* and liberal shows had the least favorable attitudes. By contrast, those listening to Limbaugh were least likely to vote for a law permitting assisted suicide while those listening to liberal PTR and *Talk of the Nation* were most likely to do so. Remember that these patterns are not significantly different for liberals and conservatives in our sample. Instead, the effects are attributable to the rhetoric of the week's hosts and the assigned exposure to their arguments.

The PTR experiment suggests that polarization can occur under conditions in which certain issues—for example, "hot button" ones such as those concerning racial groups and taxing policies that favor richer Americans—lead one group to move against and one to move toward the rhetorical stances of a host such as Limbaugh.[12] Polarization can also occur across ideological groups when issues that are relatively new to listeners—for example, assisted

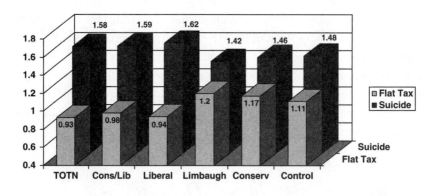

Attitudes toward two issues: Six PTR experimental groups

Suicide: p < .001, SE=+/–.03
Flat Tax: p < .0001, SE=+/–.04

FIGURE 13.4. Favorability toward voting for assisted suicide and flat tax for six PTR listening groups. (Note: TOTN = Talk of the Nation; Cons/Lib = mix of conservative and liberal shows; Liberal = liberal PTR shows; Conserv = conservative PTR shows; Control = nonpolitical talk shows)

suicide and flat tax policies—come into the ken of opinionated sources such as Limbaugh. The latter effects would only lead to polarization under conditions in which the audiences selectively chose to attend to sources that framed presentations from one side's perspective. The sources in our experiment were one-sided in some conditions, and selective exposure was created through random assignment to condition. The polarization that resulted was not because of liberals and conservatives listening to a one-sided presentation but rather because of selective exposure to two different one-sided sources.

We now consider some differences in opinion across groups that arise naturally from the combination of selective exposure and persuasive effects in our observational studies of 1996, 2000, and 2004.

Polarization of Attitudes about Issues

ATTITUDES ABOUT PROPOSED POLICIES

During the primary and election of 1996, numerous issues and proposals were raised by the candidates and discussed in the media. At each wave of our 1996 PTR survey, respondents evaluated policies that were under public scrutiny. Because they were both specific and in active contention, the proposed policies we studied were different from general attitudes toward groups (e.g. the Christian Coalition) and from broad, ongoing social issues (e.g. affirmative action for minorities and women). For example, while his candidacy was active, Steve Forbes's flat tax proposal elicited a great deal of commentary, especially on Limbaugh's radio show.

Over the three waves of the 1996 PTR surveys, we studied reactions to 11 proposed policies. Because some were measured two or more times, we could test for changes in polarization. The issues assessed at multiple points were Forbes's flat tax (waves 1, 2, and 3); legalizing same-sex marriages (waves 2 and 3); reducing welfare payments to mothers (waves 1 and 2); vouchers (waves 1 and 2); NAFTA (waves 1 and 2); and eliminating affirmative action (waves 2 and 3).

It is important to distinguish polarization at a point in time from polarization over time for the various exposure groups. Many of the listeners' attitudes toward the 11 issues reflected polarization across media exposure groups. Consider Forbes's proposal for a flat tax. Figure 13.5 presents how favorable the five media groups were toward the flat tax proposal early in the primary. (For similar results later in the primary and after Dole had essentially won the nomination, see the appendix to this chapter at our website.)

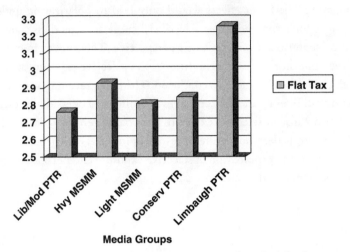

FIGURE 13.5. Favorability toward the flat tax (5 = very favorable) for five groups during the early period of the primary of 1996. (Note: MSMM = mainstream mass media)

In the early period, the Limbaugh group was more favorably disposed to the flat tax than any of the four other groups, and the other listening groups were similar to one another. However, with time and exposure, approval for the proposal increased among those in the conservative PTR group; in other words, they caught up in their favor for the flat tax proposal. By contrast, those in the liberal exposure group and the audiences of the mainstream programs remained opposed.[13] These data suggest that Limbaugh listeners initially held or were influenced to hold favorable attitudes toward the flat tax, while other media groups were less favorable (even negative, since 3.0 was the midpoint of the favorability measure). Listeners to conservative PTR moved in the direction already held by Limbaugh listeners.

The pattern in figure 13.5 was replicated for several issues, including reduced welfare payments, school vouchers, same-sex marriages, and elimination of affirmative action.[14] However, causal order is problematic. We did not find support for increasing polarization on policy issues over the course of the election period. Certainly, Limbaugh listeners a priori have attitudes and political affiliations that dispose them to favor Republican positions. Consequently, they may have favored the flat tax proposal before any discussion by Limbaugh. Alternatively, a new proposal such as the flat tax receiving the approval and extensive rhetorical support of a trusted host (as Limbaugh's listeners view him) could yield quick favorable reaction by the audience through a process we were unable to detect.

ATTITUDES ABOUT THE IDEOLOGICAL ORIENTATIONS OF POLITICAL CANDIDATES

In the previous chapter, we saw that certain groups of Limbaugh listeners attributed more ideologically liberal positions to Clinton in 1996 than were justified by his actual stands. This outcome should minimize defections to Clinton. In the 2000 and 2004 campaigns, we found that similar kinds of distortion of the ideological stances of candidates occurred among Limbaugh listeners (2000, 2004) and Fox News viewers (2004) during those years as well.

POLARIZING PERCEPTIONS OF CANDIDATES

During the primary campaign in 2000 and in 2004, Limbaugh made a concerted effort to ensure that his listeners would see sharp differences between the ideologies of the Republican and Democratic candidates for president. If listeners saw the Republican candidate as a true conservative and the Democratic candidate as an unregenerate "liberal" (indeed, more liberal than other groups see the candidate to be), the stark perceived differences between the candidates would reinforce listeners' commitments to Limbaugh's chosen candidate. In both the general elections of 2000 and 2004, that candidate was George W. Bush.

To evaluate the impact of listening to Limbaugh on respondents' perceptions of the liberal and conservative nature of the candidates, we examined data from NAES 2000 and NAES 2004. The procedures for these surveys were described briefly in chapter 5. In both surveys, respondents were queried about their radio listening habits. In NAES 2000, those who said they listened to PTR were asked to identify the host they listened to. Those identifying Limbaugh by name were treated as Limbaugh listeners, while those who identified another host or who said they listened but could not identify the host were treated as separate types of listeners. Nonlisteners were identified as well. These distinctions produced four groups: Limbaugh listeners, listeners who identified another host, listeners who did not, and nonlisteners.[15]

In both surveys, we tapped the perceived ideological positions of various candidates by asking: "Which of the following do you think best describes the views of George W. Bush? Very conservative (1), conservative (2), moderate (3), liberal (4), or very liberal (5)?" In NAES 2000, our focus was on the perceived ideologies of George W. Bush and Albert Gore. In the early primary period in NAES 2004, we obtained respondents' views of various candidates, including the incumbent, George W. Bush, John Kerry, John Edwards, Howard Dean, and Joseph Lieberman.

We expect perceptions of candidates' ideologies to be filtered through the lens of personal ideology and partisanship. In order to control for the distorting effects of these dispositions on respondents' judgments of candidates' ideologies, we will focus only on the perceptions expressed by strong Republicans. Since Limbaugh listeners are overwhelmingly Republican, they can be compared to other PTR listeners and to nonlisteners.

In figures 13.6a and 13.6b, Limbaugh listeners' judgments of how candidates' liberalness are compared to those of others in the sample. The charts indicate that in 2000, Limbaugh listeners perceived Gore as more liberal than did those not listening to Limbaugh (which included both PTR listeners and nonlisteners). They same was true in 2004 for perceptions of Kerry and other Democrats during the 2004 primaries. These differences are highly significant,[16] in part because the sample sizes are so large.

We do not present the data here, but we have found that if four groups of listeners are compared (no PTR, PTR Limbaugh, PTR no Limbaugh, and PTR host unnamed), the significance of the effect remains, as does the difference between Limbaugh listeners and those listening to PTR other than Limbaugh. It is important to keep in mind that the comparisons presented in these charts are for strong Republicans only who already think Gore, Kerry, and the other Democrats are very liberal. That judgment is even more extreme for those strong Republicans who are consumers of Limbaugh.[17]

The data from the presidential campaigns of 2000 and 2004 suggest a clear effect. Strong Republicans listening to Limbaugh have more extreme perceptions of how liberal Democratic candidates are than do other groups of strong Republicans. This effect mirrors Limbaugh's message. He employs intense language, disparaging information, and negative framing to distance perceptions of the Democratic candidate from those of the anointed Republican candidate.

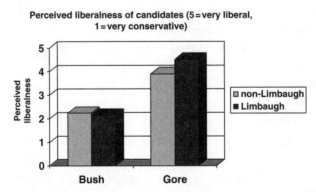

FIGURE 13.6A. Perceived liberalness of Bush and Gore by strong Republicans 2000: Limbaugh listeners and non-Limbaugh listeners.

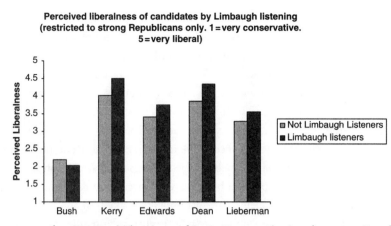

Perceived liberalness of candidates by Limbaugh listening
(restricted to strong Republicans only. 1 = very conservative.
5 = very liberal)

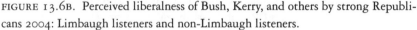

FIGURE 13.6B. Perceived liberalness of Bush, Kerry, and others by strong Republicans 2004: Limbaugh listeners and non-Limbaugh listeners.

A second finding from the entire NAES 2004 data set supports our thesis that regular Fox viewing produces effects similar to those produced by regular listening to Limbaugh.[18] Both Fox viewing and Limbaugh listening significantly increased the perception that Kerry was liberal, while exposure to network news (ABC, CBS, NBC, PBS) and to local broadcast news predicted, though less strongly, that Kerry would be seen as less liberal. (For a description of the method used to reach these conclusions, see the appendix to this chapter at our website.)

Creating an Informational Enclave: The 2004 Campaign

The political world the public encounters presents itself in large, complex bundles of competing information and contested data. To begin to understand the forces that shape individuals' grasp of these information complexes and to test the idea that the conservative opinion media create an informational and attitudinal enclave around their like-minded listeners and viewers, we created a map of the competing claims in the 2004 presidential general election offered by the camps of the two major candidates.[19]

Our goal was to see what effect, if any, being part of the audience for Fox or Limbaugh has on receptivity to both the Republican and Democratic campaign claims in the context of the presidential election of 2004. A battery of questions that reflected the claims offered by and on behalf of the Democratic and Republican presidential campaigns of 2004 was crafted. The battery included a total of 38 questions; 27 were contested facts and opinions generated by the Republican and Democratic campaigns, and 11 were facts uncontested by either side. In the weeks immediately following the election of 2004, we quizzed a national random sample of 3,400 U.S. citizens about their knowledge and beliefs about Kerry and Bush. That group was large enough to study the responses of Limbaugh listeners and Fox viewers.

Twenty-seven questions (which we will present shortly) gave us the opportunity to determine whether (controlling for gender, party identification, education, and ideology) these audiences were more likely than those not exposed to our conservative opinion channels to reject Democratic attacks on Bush and embrace Republican promotion of his cause while accepting Republican attacks about Kerry and rejecting Democratic attempts to make him and his positions palatable. The questions were written to reflect central claims and counterclaims made by the Democrats and Republicans in the 2004 presidential campaign. One political side contested the premise embedded in each question.

In all of our analyses, we were trying to determine whether the Fox or Limbaugh audience differed from those of similar education and ideology. Of course, we expected Republicans to be more likely to reject the Kerry claims and adopt the Bush ones. We wanted to know whether the audiences for Limbaugh and Fox were significantly more likely than comparable nonlisteners and nonviewers to make those moves. We also wanted to know whether an embrace of the partisan view of the contested facts and opinions would extend to distortion of uncontested fact. We examine the evidence for polarization on the contested facts and opinions and differences in knowledge of uncontested fact for Limbaugh and Fox's audience compared to those who are nonlisteners and nonviewers.

CONTESTED FACTS AND OPINIONS

The list of contested facts and opinions is long; it is presented here. A summary of these items was created to reflect pro-Republican and anti-Democratic positions. Respondents answered each statement in terms of its truthfulness—"very," "somewhat," "not too," or "not at all." Whether the issue was objectively true or false is not of concern to us here; differences in subjective perception across audiences are our focus. These items represent beliefs about the candidates' positions and character that some theories link to attitudes, intentions, and behaviors.[20] Those with a high score were more likely to accept the Republican view of the offered claims. They believe, for example, that Kerry never told the truth about Bush's record but Bush always told the truth about Kerry's. They also accepted as fact Republican assertions that Kerry would increase taxes on all small business owners, and specifically that he would raise taxes on 900,000 small business owners. Those with a high score were also more inclined to regard as true the claim that Kerry's health care plan would take medical decisions out of the hands of doctors and patients and put them under the control of government bureaucrats. Their world of presumed fact also increased the chances that they would reject as untrue Democratic attacks on the Republican incumbent, including the following claims:

President Bush's Social Security plan would cut benefits 30–45%
Bush wants to privatize Social Security
Bush favors outsourcing American jobs
Vice President Cheney profited from Halliburton's contracts in Iraq

Accordingly, in the debate over job loss during the first Bush term, they accepted the conclusion that under the Bush Administration, the United States had gained more jobs than it lost. At the same time, they were more likely to embrace the following claims of the SBVT:

John Kerry did not deserve his Vietnam medals
Because of John Kerry's statements against the Vietnam War in 1971, U.S. prisoners of war were tortured
John Kerry said that every American soldier who served in Vietnam was a war criminal

And they adopted the anti-Kerry beliefs that he had said the following:

He would not use military force until after he had been able to justify it to the world
He would only use military force after the U.S. was attacked
He wanted to repeal the use of wiretaps in the Patriot Act

At the same time, they accepted claims about Kerry's past actions that included the assertion that he had voted in the Senate against body armor for the troops in Iraq and had done the following:

Repeatedly supported an increase in the gasoline tax
Voted for cuts in intelligence after 9/11
Voted against major weapons systems after 9/11

In these respondents' world of "facts," Democratic claims were likely to be rejected out of hand and Republican ones accepted. So, for example, they were more likely to reject the following Democratic claims:

Bush failed to fully fund the No Child Left Behind education program
Bush said he was not concerned about Osama Bin Laden
Bush sent some soldiers to Iraq without the latest body armor

Other presumed facts favorable to the Bush administration that rounded out their view of the claims of the campaign included a disposition to believe the following:

World opinion favored U.S. intervention in Iraq

Bush's plan to limit damages in medical malpractice cases would reduce the cost of medical care a great deal

Bush proposed creating the new Homeland Security Department right after 9/11

The Bush tax cuts favored the middle class and not the wealthy

And finally, their belief structure ascribed benign motives to Republicans and malignant motives to Democrats. Among other things this meant that they accepted the belief that when President Bush said the United States would find weapons of mass destruction in Iraq, he believed what he was saying.

Fox viewing and Limbaugh listening each predicted a greater likelihood that respondents in our survey would answer this total group of questions in the way our theory forecast. We found independent effects for Fox and Limbaugh, even after extensive controls for the effects of party and ideology and other factors. Unsurprisingly, both party identification and ideology were strongly linked to responses on this summary index. But the effects of Limbaugh listening and Fox news viewing were substantial. Even though self-identified conservatives or self-identified Republicans drew inferences consistent with their partisan views, Fox viewers and Limbaugh listeners were even more likely to do so. These analyses indicate an opposite pattern for Democrats and those who listen to NPR and watch CNN; no significant associations were observed for those watching network broadcast television news sources, including specifically PBS or MSNBC. The relative strength of association between media sources and inferences about the claims and counterclaims of the Bush and Kerry campaigns suggests that audiences for Fox and Limbaugh are more likely to accept Republican claims and reject Democratic ones than the audiences of other media news sources. This result occurs in part because these audiences consume political information in an interpretive community that we would characterize as an echo chamber or one-sided enclave, an in-group clear about its views about the out-group. On the other side of the ideological divide, audiences for CNN and NPR seem to behave in the same way. (For the analytical details supporting this effect, see the appendix to this chapter at our website.)

The opinion enclave in which Limbaugh listeners and Fox viewers reside protects their attitudes about Bush from assault by Kerry and increases the likelihood that Republican attacks on Kerry will be accepted.

There is factual content underlying the questions in the 27-question battery, but the facts are contested ones. In the campaign, in other words, the Democratic and Republican views of the facts at issue differed. For example, the Bush campaign argued that his tax cuts favored the middle class because the proportionate reduction in their taxes was higher than that for the wealthy. The Democrats contended that the dollar amount of benefit for the wealthy was higher than that for the middle class. The two parties also calculated the tax cuts differently, with the Democrats focusing on the cuts in the estate tax and the income tax and the Republicans excluding the effects of the estate tax cut.

Did world opinion support U.S. intervention in Iraq? The Republicans cited the number of nations that provided support. The Democrats cited public opinion against the war in some of the same countries.

Did Kerry support an increase in the gasoline tax? Republicans pointed to a statement he made in support; Democrats pointed out he had not actually cast any votes on an increase.

Did the Bush administration gain more jobs than it lost? The Democrats cited the payroll survey to say no; the Republicans cited the household survey to say yes.

We would, of course, argue that outside the contest over a fact, there is often a basis for saying that one side is making a problematic statement or that one interpretation is more accurate than the other. But for our purposes here, that is not the relevant distinction. Regardless of whether they are true or false, accurate or inaccurate, in or out of context, we are separating those claims that are disputed from those that are not.

UNCONTESTED FACTS

To this point, we have examined the perceptions of the Fox and Limbaugh audiences about contested facts. By moving to a second category, uncontested fact, we were able to assess the audience's grasp of the background data that neither side disputed. On 11 additional questions (not included in the 27) for which an uncontested factual answer existed, listening to Limbaugh and watching Fox functioned in the same way as reading newspapers, watching national broadcast news (viewing the nightly network newscasts of ABC, NBC, CBS, or PBS's *Newshour with Jim Lehrer*), watching only *Newshour with Jim Lehrer*, watching CNN or MSNBC, and listening to NPR.[21] Each form of media exposure predicted accurate responses to the questions assessing knowledge of uncontested fact.

The fact questions included: How many troops, including the National Guard, does the United States have in Iraq (140,000)? How many nations are providing troops in Iraq (30)? What percent of the coalition casualties are American (90%)? Other items were claims that respondents evaluated as either true or false. Among these were some that had been advanced by the Bush camp to hurt Kerry, some advanced by the Bush camp to help Bush, some advanced by the Kerry camp to hurt Bush, and some advanced by the Kerry camp to help Kerry. Other items were ones whose salience neither side visibly advanced, taken simply from background information at play in the campaign or from news accounts of the campaign.

Claims Advanced by the Kerry Camp to Hurt Bush or Help Kerry

Kerry was onc.e a prosecutor (True)

John Kerry wanted to pay for the $87 billion allocated to the Iraq war by eliminating part of the Bush tax cut for those paying the highest income tax rate (True)

When in Congress, current CIA head Porter Goss supported cuts in spending for intelligence (True)

Claims Advanced by the Bush Camp to Hurt Kerry or Help Bush

The Bush administration discovered that flu vaccines were contaminated and decided to stop their distribution (False)

The United States has found weapons of mass destruction in Iraq (False)

AARP (formerly the American Association of Retired Persons) supported the Bush prescription drug plan (True)

The unemployment rate is now about where it was in 1996 when Bill Clinton ran for a second term (True)

George Bush was honorably discharged from the National Guard (True)

On both the pro-Bush and pro-Kerry uncontested facts, Limbaugh listeners and Fox viewers are as accurate as those reliant on other forms of media (controlling for ideology and education). This effect is consistent with a similar one on knowledge of uncontested facts that we reported in an early report on PTR.[22]

There has been an ongoing controversy about the accuracy of Limbaugh's program, a controversy fueled first by an analysis of presumed factual errors offered by the liberal media monitoring group FAIR (Fairness & Accuracy in Reporting) and then fanned by Al Franken's book *Rush Limbaugh Is a Big Fat Idiot*. What Limbaugh, Fox, and the *Journal*'s opinion pages do is increase the likelihood that their audiences will consider a "fact" that benefits the Democrats to be contested and as a result dismiss it.

By increasing or reinforcing the audience's adherence to the Republican view of contested facts and, in Fox's and Limbaugh's case, increasing the accuracy of background knowledge of uncontested facts, the conservative media contribute to a knowledge or opinion enclave. In the process, they either move their audience to a more extreme view of Democratic positions and policies than they otherwise would hold or attract an audience disposed to perceive Democrats as extreme and reinforce that view.

As with all of the survey data we offer in this book, these responses raise the question, Which came first, the exposure or the knowledge, attitudes, and beliefs? Our confidence in the causal direction is supported by the fact that the claims concerning the 2004 campaign were quite specific. If more general claims had been the object of study (e.g., reducing the size of government or positions on affirmative action) then inferences from party heuristics could easily guide the choices. Because this survey included questions that could not be answered by relying on party cues alone, we surmise that the audiences exposed to Limbaugh and Fox are more likely to be drawing their answers from the information on these programs than from other confounding factors.

Moreover, the experimental evidence of effects that we offered earlier in this chapter shows that exposure to one-sided partisan voices can affect the polarization of opinion within audiences (liberals and conservatives hearing the same message) and across channels (Limbaugh versus other sources). Findings such as these shore up the inference that the causal direction is, in part at least, from Fox and Limbaugh to the audience.

Summary

In chapter 7, we suggested that Limbaugh's audience believed that Democratic candidates (including Clinton in 1996, Gore in 2000, and Kerry in 2004) and potential Republican nominees that he opposes (such as Buchanan in 1996 and McCain in 2000) held positions far from its own. In this chapter and previous ones, we have drawn on survey data to show instances in which Limbaugh successfully framed an issue (e.g., interpretation of the Unabomber), induced emotion and attached it to a person or issue (e.g., Clinton and Dole), created distance between his audience's own positions and its perceptions of Democrats' positions (e.g., the positions of Clinton and Dole), and balkanized audience knowledge (e.g., on Bosnia, the Trilateral Commission, and balance of trade). To add to our case, we presented data from a field experiment to suggest that polarization effects result from exposure to Limbaugh's rhetoric (e.g., regarding racial groups and current social and political issues). After mapping the competing claims of the 2004 presidential general election and securing survey data on Limbaugh and Fox audience members' response to them, we also suggested that these programs increase audience adoption of the contested claims of the Republicans and decrease adoption of those of the Democrats. At the same time, we demonstrated that Limbaugh and Fox's audiences command uncontested fact as well as do consumers of traditional news sources, a phenomenon that should arm them effectively for political argument with those less knowledgeable. Taken together, these findings suggest that Limbaugh and Fox protect their like-minded audience members in an informational and attitudinal enclave.

14

Conclusion:
Echo Chamber: Cause for Concern or Celebration?

Throughout this book, we have argued that the impulse to absorb ideologically agreeable information draws conservative partisans to the protective shelter of the conservative media, where reassuring frames of argument decrease their susceptibility to other ideological points of view. When these partisans attend to nonconservative media or confront partisans of opposed political beliefs, this buffer insulates them from counterpersuasion. By reframing the mainstream outlets and journalists as "liberal" and untrustworthy, the conservative media massage their audiences' distrust in mainstream sources even as they continue to consume them. For example, the Pew Center for the People and the Press found in 2006 that 34% of Republicans regularly watch Fox while 20% of Democrats do so.[1] In 2004, another poll found that Republicans considered Fox the most credible news source, while Democrats considered it the least.[2] The same study found Republicans less likely than Democrats to rate a list of mainstream print and broadcast media as credible. The differences extended to print, with Republicans more likely than Democrats to report that they trusted the *Wall Street Journal*.

Within the conservative media, its audience finds a safe haven from the messages of those the hosts vilify as liberals, including the mainstream media. Listeners, viewers, and readers absorb a cogent, coherent view of the political world as well. This cognitive structure has the capacity to anchor the attitudes of these audience members at the same time that it prepares them to vigorously defend their point of view with sometimes legitimate and sometimes problematic means.

To the undoubted disappointment of those on the left, we have not argued that the conservative media menace the country's well-being; to the likely dismay of those on the right, neither have we championed the conservative media establishment. Our focus instead has been on understanding this cluster of media and the ways it functions. Before turning to the larger question—Is all of this a cause for celebration, concern, or some of each?—here we summarize the arguments we have advanced so far.

We opened this book by featuring the conservative opinion media adopting shared evidence, similar or compatible lines of argument, and common tactics, both in their defense of conservatism from the maladroit comments of a Republican leader and in their attack on the presumptive 2004 Democratic Party nominee. Our Lott and Kerry case studies featured a recurrent argument that constitutes a universally applicable rebuttal strategy the conservative media deploy against opponents: the argument that the mainstream media cover politics by employing a double standard that overlooks or forgives Democratic trespasses while magnifying those of Republicans. Hence any information in the mainstream that disadvantages conservatives can be discounted as the inevitable byproduct of the "bias" of the "liberal media."

By contrast, the conservative media portray themselves as trustworthy and reliable instructors who will guide audiences through the biases of the mainstream and arm them to critique "liberal" deception. This line of argument means that the conservative media will feature examples in which "liberals" have gotten away with a statement or action similar to one for which a conservative was chastised or punished. When conservative hosts find such an incident, they "turn the tables" on the "liberal" media and their "liberal" opponents.

Embedded in these two instances is the second recurrent move of the conservative media: attacking "liberals" and "liberalism" and advancing the cause of conservatives and conservatism. Taken together these two moves—the claim of media bias and double standard, and the combined vilification of "liberalism" and veneration of conservatism—contribute to the three effects we have examined in the final chapters of this book: the reframing of mainstream media to engender distrust of its content, the balkanization of conservative media audiences' knowledge and interpretation, and the polarization of their attitudes toward Democratic candidates.

The regularly repeated refrain "liberal media" and the menu of past sins of mainstream omission and commission are a central means of ensuring that what conservatives take away from exposure to nonconservative sources shores up their ideology. For audience members who embrace this "liberal media with a double standard" frame, counterattitudinal evidence from any source can more readily be dismissed. Rather than calling conservative beliefs into question, such material instead cushions conservative assumptions and confirms that "liberals" and the "liberal" media aggressively subvert and distort Reagan's ideology.

The message reinforced within the echo chamber by Limbaugh's radio show, the two programs on Fox, and the editorial page of the *Journal* establishes a second powerful frame that creates a Manichean dichotomy between "liberalism" and conservatism, "liberals" and conservatives. This structure and its embedded assumptions castigate "liberalism" and celebrate the philosophy and legacy of Ronald Reagan: a strong military combined with fiscal and social conservatism. Adding urgency to the conservative media's defense of the Gipper's brand of conservatism is the hosts' conviction that "liberals" and the "liberal media" are bent on undermining the Reagan years' vindication of his philosophy. As we have argued, the Reaganism espoused in these media is portrayed as largely blemish-free.

At the core of our analysis of these two frames is a troubling chicken-and-egg problem raised by the tendency of individuals to seek out content with which they are already disposed to agree. The phenomenon of selective exposure invites the question, Which came first, the attitudes of the host or those of the audience? In an effort to disentangle this concern, we displaced that dichotomous frame with one built on the notion of reciprocal influence. We also developed forms of experimentally derived evidence that permit causal inference. We blended our experimental data with insight obtained from surveys and content analysis.

The media on which we focus are important not only because they attract sizable audiences but also because these audiences' demographics match those of the core Republican base: middle-and upper-class white men who are more likely to be churchgoers and southerners than not. Without the loyalty of these groups, the prospects for the party of Lincoln and Reagan dim. One might expect that these outlets would as a result serve simply as a mouthpiece for the Republican Party. At times they do, but that function is not the one that interests us.

Instead, we are concerned about the ways the conservative media perform actual party functions. Accordingly, we have focused on the notion that Limbaugh and the *Journal* help vet candidates in Republican primaries for their loyalty to Reagan conservatism. Our surveys offer plausible evidence that Limbaugh's views about Pat Buchanan in the primaries of 1996, about John McCain in those of 2000, and about McCain and Governors Huckabee and Romney in 2008 affected his audience's dispositions toward these three contenders. Consistent with our notion of reciprocal influence, we also found suggestive evidence that when Limbaugh diverged from the dispositions of some, they recalibrated their affection for him. Importantly, consistent with our evidence from 1996 that Limbaugh listening primed the importance of party, our 2004 survey suggests that viewing Fox or listening to Limbaugh decreased the likelihood that one would defect from identification with the Republican Party during the 2004 election.

Consonant with the notion that the conservative media play roles expected of political parties, we found that Limbaugh in particular attaches negative emotions to Democratic candidates. He also attacks the problem-solving capacity of big government, without dampening his audience's disposition to participate in politics.

Where early in the book we introduced the notion that for the conservative media, the notion "liberal media" combined with "double standard" is a universal rebuttal frame; later we offered survey-based confirmation that the frame works. Specifically, in 1996 we isolated evidence that Limbaugh reframed his audience's perception of media treatment of the Unabomber. As just noted, evidence of successful framing is important, because if the audience sees the world through conservative frames, exposure to conflicting points of view—for example, by watching mainstream news—will reinforce rather than dislodge its conservative foothold.

Consistent with the "liberal media bias" frame, we also found in 1996 that Limbaugh was successful in engendering mistrust of the mainstream media. Importantly, in that election year his audience maintained a high level of consumption of mainstream broadcast media. However, by 2004 that broadcast exposure had shifted toward Fox News. We also note that interest in conservative programming can now be sated by content not simply on Fox but on CNN and MSNBC as well, an option available only recently and one testifying to the commercial success of the Fox model.

We are not arguing, however, that conservatives have barricaded themselves within the conservative media establishment. They demonstrably have not. Consumption of mainstream print remains high, for example, among Limbaugh listeners. Moreover, even ardent Fox viewers maintain contact with the broadcast mainstream. Our argument for an echo chamber is that there is sufficient exposure to these three sources and their kin, individually or in combination, to reinforce powerful conservative frames that then buffer the audience from counterattitudinal influence from other venues. If the two frames of media bias and double standard, and the combined vilification of "liberalism" and veneration of conservatism are well established in the audience, these ways of seeing politics will encourage the audience to reinterpret mainstream media in ways that reinforce the messages of the echo chamber.

Lurking in the assumptions of this book is an argument that we make explicit in its final chapters when we explore the discourse of in-group versus out-group that the conservative media use to create their interpretive community. Working from this model of in-group and out-group, we show that these media balkanize the knowledge and interpretations of the conservative audience and polarize their opinions about the Democrats and the main-stream media. For example, our post-2004 election data suggest that Fox viewers and Limbaugh listeners, more than other Republicans, regard facts that advantage the Democratic candidate as suspect, while embracing those advanced by the Republican incumbent's campaign. Despite their exposure to the mainstream, in a real sense these listeners, viewers, and readers exist in their own echo chamber.

If readers grant that we have made that case, they might well ask, should the existence of such a conservative echo chamber elicit concern or celebration or a bit of both? How healthy is this phenomenon for democracy?

Before we explore these important questions, we want to offer a reminder. The disposition to listen to Limbaugh, watch Fox, and read the *Journal* does not suggest that these audiences are locked exclusively in the fortress of any of these media, that those who consume one necessarily turn to the others, or that the conservative audience for politics has been seduced into a hermetically sealed conservative cocoon. Indeed, the notion that the audiences are umbilically tied to the programming is called into question by recent data suggesting drops in the audiences for Fox and Limbaugh. In 2006, as the popularity of the war in Iraq plummeted, taking with it the approval ratings of President Bush, for the first time since its inception, the audience for Fox News actually declined.[3]

Limbaugh's listenership may be down as well. In June 2007, *Talkers* magazine put Limbaugh's audience at 13.5 million. In 2004, the same industry outlet had estimated his audience at 14.75 million. These drops raise the circumstantial possibility that some who were drawn to these media channels because they reinforced their beliefs turned from them when Limbaugh and Fox's positive frames on the news clashed with public disenchantment with the Iraq war and conflicted with credible information telegraphed in other venues about Republicans' performance in office. Nonetheless, the outlets on which we have focused retain sizable audiences, particularly in a world of proliferating media channels.

Fox and Limbaugh are part of a world in which available channels have multiplied. We share a concern about this transformed world raised by media scholar James Hamilton, who notes that

> the added variety arising from the expansion of cable programing means that viewers uninterested in politics can more readily avoid it. In 1996 viewers with cable who had low levels of political interest (i.e., had low levels of political information) were much less likely to watch presidential debates than viewers who had broadcast channels.

Those who were not interested in politics but had only broadcast television did end up watching these debates, since their options were limited.[4]

This is worrisome, because we predictably see increases in actual knowledge across all educational levels of the viewing audience for debates.[5] Until recently, they also increased the respect audiences had for the candidates who participated in them. However, importantly, both Fox and Limbaugh's audience members are more, not less, likely than others of similar education and ideology to view presidential debates. In other words, gravitating toward conservative media does not produce a disposition to shun this rich source of political information.

Some scholars have suggested that as options within the media increase, so, too, will the drive toward selective exposure to congenial points of view.[6] That the balkanizing and polarizing effects we have described will become increasingly common and more widespread is likely, and probably inevitable. Although some have been quick to condemn the conservative media and the tendency for the like-minded to gravitate toward it, we are not convinced that this phenomenon is unrelievedly problematic for democracy, governance, social trust and tolerance, and civic engagement in the long run. Instead, we see pluses and minuses.

On the Positive Side

History sides with the notion that one-sided partisan communication produces engagement. Fervid partisans whose views were reinforced by one-sided broadsides and newspapers as well as parades and mass rallies were the "good citizens" of the late twentieth and early twenty-first centuries.[7] If voting is the measure, the republic flourished before the turn of the twentieth century when the press was partisan, not balanced. Consistent with that notion, in many other countries where presses are partisan, participation, measured by voting, is higher than in the United States.

For decades, scholars have lamented drops in political participation; the increased voting rates of the 2004 election did little to quiet the concerns. For almost as long, pundits have bemoaned declining newspaper readership, as well as diminished viewing of nominating conventions and general election presidential debates. For more than a quarter century, scholars have worried about the implications of the decline of the party as a source of coherent information about candidates. Yet the rise of a radio program that now attracts upward of 13.5 million likely voters to the discussion of ideologically coherent politics and coincides with high levels of basic factual knowledge about that which is uncontested in politics has elicited concern in some quarters. By making politics engaging and entertaining (and in so doing demonstrating the compatibility of the two), Limbaugh has shown that the link forged effectively in the nineteenth century remains possible today.

In a similar vein, during much of the mass media age, scholars have critiqued broadcast news for the lack of variety across major networks. Yet when Fox News, an outlet with a discernibly different focus, emerged and began attracting larger audiences than its cable competitors, it, too, was met with concerns that conservatives were more likely to gravitate toward it than to the mainstream.

The assumption that these venues give only one side of the argument is overstated. Although Fox, Limbaugh, and the opinion pages of the *Journal* privilege one political viewpoint over others, they do so in a context that, to varying degrees, presents alternatives. The fact that the opposing view tends to be framed to the advantage of conservatives and inconvenient facts aggressively contested, as is the case with Fox and Limbaugh, or offered in order to be rebutted (as is the case with the opinion pages of the *Journal*) does not obviate the fact that at least some representation of opponents' views is presented. Although the dominant assumptions are conservative and the frames more likely to be hospitable to conservatism than not, Fox does present multiple sides and even the occasional liberal host. And the *Journal* carries the occasional opinion piece taking issue with its editorial positions. From the beginnings of politics, one side has presented the alternative point of view selectively in order to rebut it. (As we will note shortly, concern rises, however, when that disposition to rebut veers instead into a tendency to disparage and ridicule.)

The conservatives' answer to the notion that the frame for Fox is conservative is that the frame of the mainstream is "liberal." Framing, of course, is an inevitable part of communication in general and news in particular. Whether we would call the frame of the mainstream news "liberal" or not aside, our comparative case studies suggest that the framing of the mainstream is different from that of Fox and, in sometimes subtle and sometimes obvious ways, more hospitable to Democratic than Republican points of view. The disadvantage of consistent framing from any ideological side is its capacity to block effective exposure to other frames or views.

However, there are advantages to consistently framed, ideologically coherent argument. Clear partisan structures should make it easier for those holding them to make sense of new information. Partisan communication also has the advantages that come from high levels of redundancy and a consistent point of view.

Importantly, behind Limbaugh's bluster and bombast, there is a substantive defense of a coherent political philosophy. The perspective offered by a conservative framing of issues does provide an alternative to that in the mainstream. At the same time, by monitoring each other for bias, the mainstream and the conservative media add an element of accountability to the system that was missing in the days when the three major network evening shows took their cues from the *New York Times* without disposition to examine the presuppositions in their own or others' coverage.

Among the positive effects we see is the likelihood that the conservative opinion media help their audience make sense of complex social issues on which elite opinion is divided. They accomplish this when they:

1. Consistently frame arguments from conservative assumptions
2. Build a base of supportive evidence for conservative beliefs and in the process distinguish them from "liberal" ones
3. Semantically and affectively prime key advocacy and attack points
4. Arm their audience to argue effectively
5. Minimize the likelihood of defection from conservatism by creating a sense of community among listeners who share a worldview, if not every political policy preference

The conservative opinion media produce three advantages for leaders and the party that share their ideology. First, they protect their audience from counterpersuasion by inoculating it against opposing messages; at the same time, they increase the likelihood that the audience will try to persuade others. Conservative viewers, readers, and listeners are told by these media outlets that they are part of a much larger community, a conviction that should prevent them from falling victim to the phenomenon Elizabeth Noelle-Neumann calls the spiral of silence.[8] The belief that they are part of an army of others of like mind should increase their disposition to talk politics with those with whom they disagree. Finally, they stabilize or anchor the conservative base. This effect is produced at a cost: Those in the fold see "liberals" and politicians as further from them—hence less worthy of support—than they actually are.

The Downside

We find other moves more problematic, including those that:

1. Insulate the audience from alternative media sources by casting them as untrustworthy, "liberal," and rooted in a double standard hostile to conservatives and conservatism

2. Protect their audience from the influence of those opposed to the conservative message by balkanizing and polarizing their perception of opponents and their arguments

3. Contest only the facts hospitable to opposing views

4. Invite moral outrage by engaging emotion. This produces one advantage and one disadvantage; emotional involvement invites action and engagement rather than distancing and lethargy. On the downside, a steady diet of moral outrage feeds the assumption that the opponent is an enemy.

5. Replace argument with ridicule and ad hominem.

6. Often invite their audiences to see the political world as one unburdened by either ambiguity or common ground across the ideological divide

Democrats are, of course, more likely to accept the contested facts offered by their party, and so are Republicans. We find it worrisome that the audiences for both Fox and Limbaugh were more likely than comparable conservatives to accept the Republican view of the contested facts in the 2004 election and more likely in the process to distort the positions of the Democratic nominee. But those who, with us, find the pro-Republican distortion among Limbaugh and Fox audiences problematic should, with us, find the pro-Democratic distortion equally troubling among NPR listeners and CNN viewers. Our reason for concern is straightforward: in a world without a shared account of what is, it is difficult to determine where and when a problem exists, its nature and scope, the elements within it worthy of remediation, and possible courses of action.

What the conservative opinion media do for the Right and CNN and NPR do for the Left is increase a tendency to embrace the arguments and evidence offered by those with whom their audiences already agree. Fox and Limbaugh have also created a commercially viable model of partisan media that has elicited the sincerest form of flattery. On the Left, *Air America* on radio and *Countdown with Keith Olbermann* on MSNBC are both experimenting with ways to translate their blend of entertainment and political advocacy into profits. Consistent with the model developed by the conservatives, Olbermann regularly features *Air America* hosts.

A problem with a proliferation of partisan media echo chambers is that democratic engagement at its best is characterized by fair presentation of the other side and fair rebuttal. Often that process does characterize the editorial page of the *Journal*. Our concern arises only when the other side is selectively or deceptively presented in order to ridicule it, disparage its proponents, and occasionally write its proponents out of American discourse by impugning their patriotism.

In the best moments in the echo chamber, the ideological suppositions of liberals and conservatives are accurately clarified; in the more problematic moments, the opposing party becomes the enemy party, morally defective, disloyal to the country's principles, menacing basic values. In the best moments, the other side is vigorously engaged, with evidence fairly presented and without ridicule or disdain.

A model deliberative democracy presupposes a world composed of people of good will and integrity who want the best for the country but differ in philosophy. When partisan difference becomes hyperpartisan disdain, audiences are invited to condemn those with whom they disagree. When this attitude is writ large into the legislative arena, it ensures election of those unwilling to compromise who will stalemate a legislative debate rather than incorporate the best from the alternatives being offered. Governance in the absence of commonality and cooperation may devolve to the tyranny of those in power.

There are consequences at the individual level as well. When one systematically misperceives the positions of those of a supposedly different ideology, one may decide to vote against a candidate with whom, on some issues of importance to both, one actually agrees. A polarized political world is one in which everyone is entitled to his or her own facts, the evidentiary grounds for political discussion are lost, and there is as a result no point in attempting to deliberate across ideological lines. In such a world, each side simply asserts its ideology. Neither is open to any good that may reside in the opposition's point of view. Compromise may become a lost art. And the forms of community that are created when those of divergent views find ways to meet on higher ground become the stuff of utopian novels.

It was for good reason that Thomas Jefferson's rules for the House of Representatives created sanctions for language that impugned the good will and integrity of others on the floor of that body. A person tagged as a liar or a traitor or both is no longer a person with whom one can productively talk, in part because the attacks undercut any assumption of mutual trust and in part because no one so characterized is likely to want to continue the discussion.

When they use ridicule and assaults on patriotism or character as vehicles to marginalize leaders of the other side, those we studied sow enmity and create enemies. These rhetorical moves undermine the assumption that it is possible to disagree while granting that the other is a person of good will and integrity. Philosophical differences become personal ones. Ad hominem attack is legitimized as a mode of argument. Ridicule invites ridicule, ad hominem, a rhetorical response in kind. When these rhetorical moves are harnessed to strong emotion, the result may be a sort of engagement that in the short term produces votes for one side but in the long term cultivates a political climate in which those who are elected find it difficult to effectively govern.

THE POSITIVE EFFECTS OF AN ECHO CHAMBER

So on the plus side, the echo chamber encourages engagement and increases the audience's ideological coherence; on the downside, its balkanization, polarization, and use of ridicule and ad hominem rhetoric have the potential to undercut individual and national deliberation.

Is there a way to salvage what is valuable, without undercutting the formula that attracts audiences to these media? If so, it would be a way to fairly present the opposing point of view and then fairly rebut it without use of ridicule or ad hominem. We see no reason one cannot meet these standards while also entertaining and framing from one ideological perspective rather than another.

In fairness, we can find many instances in which Limbaugh and the *Journal* do just that. However, deliberation requires more than that. It presupposes facts on which both sides can agree. It does not till under common ground. Ordinarily, one would turn to the press for such a function. However, if the press becomes partisan and abjures the ideals of fairness and balance and attempts to be objective, then instead of providing the ground on which deliberation can occur, it seeds the battlefield.

Those who read the demise of a healthy democracy into the rise of the conservative opinion media assume that each hour of Fox and Limbaugh is dense with ridicule and vitriol. While they are a part of the repertoire, these are seasonings in a complex stew of information and opinion.

Moreover, those who wring their hands over the rise of conservative media exaggerate their impact.[9] The numbers of readers, viewers, and listeners are not yet large enough to counterbalance the size of the mainstream outlets. Any one of the evening network broadcast newscasts attracts a larger audience than Fox. The NPR audience remains larger than Limbaugh's. And although impressive for a newspaper, the total audience for the *Journal* still falls below that of *USA Today,* and one suspects that at least some of those who subscribe do so not to read the opinion pages but for the front section of the paper.

The prospect that tit-for-tat practices will characterize the new media world is nonetheless possible. The disposition of audiences to seek reinforcing information is not, after all, limited to those of conservative bent. Whereas Fox is more likely to attract those who consider themselves conservative,

MSNBC's *Hardball with Chris Matthews* and *Countdown with Keith Olbermann* are more likely to attract those who consider themselves liberal.[10]

Indeed, as the increasing reach of programs such as *Countdown with Keith Olbermann* and the survival of *Air America* suggest, the emergence of a liberal media echo chamber with no pretense of balance is all but inevitable, if for no other reason than that the economics of such a move make sense for those of strong partisan bent. As media historians Michael Schudson and Susan Tifft note, "Just as the economic need to appeal to a broad audience in the nineteenth century encouraged the press to gradually wring political invective from the news, so the economic appeal of niche audiences in the twenty-first century has prompted the press to restore it."[11]

The overall impact on citizen involvement, engagement, collaboration, mutual understanding without serious distortion, and ultimately governance is as yet unclear. What we believe is apparent is that these developments do not have to shred the social and political fabric. Both in the not-so-distant past in the United States and in other contemporary democracies, partisan news offered by opposing sides has existed compatibly with higher levels of democratic engagement than that produced in the United States. We don't know whether the effects we describe and anticipate will lead to widespread social and political balkanization. What we do know is that—given trends in media segmentation and partisanship and pressures on the audience to manage their information environments—the partisan media world is a phenomenon that will continue to shape the ways at least some in the polity make sense of politics.

Preface

1. In an essay in the policy journal *Foreign Affairs*, Huckabee had characterized the foreign policy programs of the incumbent Republican as "arrogant."
2. Kim Strassel, "Leap of Faith," OpinionJournal.com, 21 December 2007.
3. David D. Kirkpatrick, "Shake, Rattle and Roil the Grand Ol' Coalition," *New York Times*, 30 December 2007, 4WK.
4. David J. Sanders, "Mike Huckabee's New Deal: More God, More Government," WSJ.com, 4 January 2008.
5. Jerry Bowyer, "FairTax Flaws," *Wall Street Journal*, 8 January 2008, A20.
6. Dave D'Alessio and Mike Allen, "Media Bias in Presidential Elections: A Meta-Analyis," *Journal of Communication* 50 (2000): 133–56.
7. Mark D. Watts et al., "Elite Cues and Media Bias in Presidential Campaigns: Explaining Public Perceptions of a Liberal Press," *Communication Research* 26 (1999): 144–75.
8. Robert P. Vallone, Lee Ross, and Mark R. Lepper, "The Hostile Media Phenomenon: Biased Perception and Perceptions of Media Bias in Coverage of the Beirut Massacre," *Journal of Personality and Social Psychology* 49 (1985): 577–85.
9. Researchers Talia J. Stroud, "Selective Exposure to Partisan Information" (Ph.D. diss., University of Pennsylvania, 2006), and Yariv Tsfati, "The Consequences of Mistrust in the News Media: Media Skepticism as a Moderator in Media Effects and as a Factor Influencing News Media Exposure" (Ph.D. diss., University of Pennsylvania, 2002), have also examined the role of exposure to media news sources with different slants. Stroud's work examines exposure to sources with different partisan slants, while Tsfati's explores the news media choices of those with different levels of trust in mainstream news sources.
10. Tony Blankley, "Rush's Show Goes On," *Washington Times*, 15 October 2001, 10.
11. Joseph N. Cappella, Joseph Turow, and Kathleen Hall Jamieson, *Call-in Political Talk Radio: Background, Content, Audiences, Portrayal in Main Stream Media*, Report by the Annenberg Public Policy Center, University of Pennsylvania, Philadelphia, 1996, 40, 43.

12. The NAES data from 2004 are available on an inserted disk in Daniel Romer et al., *Capturing Campaign Dynamics* (Philadelphia: University of Pennsylvania Press, 2006).

Chapter 1

1. Rush Limbaugh, "My Conversation with John Podhoretz," *Limbaugh Letter,* March 2004, 13.
2. Matt Bai, "Notion Building," *New York Times Magazine,* 12 October 2003, 84.
3. Josh Benson, "Gore's TV War: He Lobs Salvo at Fox News," *New York Observer,* 2 December 2002, 1.
4. 28 October 2004, B12. Because the words "news" and "media" are used to cover everything from the front pages of the *New York Times,* to its editorial pages, from network evening broadcast news to *The O'Reilly Factor,* and because there are both traditional news forms, such as the reporter-based hard news accounts and journalists' roundtables within the same program, we will specify which programs we are comparing when we talk about the conservative and mainstream media. We will also rely on a somewhat artificial distinction among three types of content: hard news, news analysis, and political opinion forms such as editorials, op-eds, political talk television such as CNN's now defunct *Crossfire* and Fox's *Hannity and Colmes,* and political talk radio. Most but not all of our analysis will focus on political opinion forms. When we turn to analysis of the content of news coverage on Fox, we will note that we are making that move.
5. For a more developed discussion of the effects of these two frames, see our *Spiral of Cynicism: The Press and the Public Good* (New York: Oxford University Press, 1997). Our argument is consistent with that of Jeffrey Bramson, who argues that Limbaugh's major rhetorical function is to frame issues in order to reinforce conservatives' beliefs; Bramson, "Radio of the Right: Limbaugh's Broadcasts Help Set Political Priorities," *Harvard Political Review* 32 (2005): 21.
6. Dan Rather, *CBS Evening News,* 15 March 2004.
7. Elizabeth Vargas and Linda Douglas, *World News Tonight with Peter Jennings,* ABC, 15 March 2004.
8. Brit Hume, "Political Headlines," Carl Cameron reporting, *Special Report with Brit Hume,* Fox, 15 March 2004.
9. Sean Hannity, "Are Foreign Leaders Really Backing Kerry?" interview with Cedric Brown, *Hannity and Colmes,* Fox, 16 March 2004.
10. Paul Farhi, "Kerry Challenged on Claim of Foreign Support; Powell Says Democrats Should Identify Officials with Whom He Spoke," *Washington Post,* 15 March 2004, final ed., A10.
11. James Taranto, "Are You a Republican?" *Wall Street Journal,* 16 March 2004, www.opinionjournal.com/best/?id=110004826.

12. Farhi, "Kerry Challenged," A10.

13. Matea Gold, "The Race to the White House: Kerry Maintains That World Leaders Want Bush to Go," *Los Angeles Times,* 15 March 2004, A13.

14. Mike Glover, "Kerry Talks Health Care in Two Battleground States," *Associated Press,* 14 March 2004.

15. Julie Mason, "Election 2004: Powell Challenges Kerry to Name 'Foreign Leaders,'" *Houston Chronicle,* 15 March 2004, A5.

16. Gold, "Race to the White House," A13.

17. Taranto, "Are You a Republican?"

18. Brit Hume, "Political Grapevine: Positive Poll for President Bush Is Underreported," *Special Report with Brit Hume,* Fox, 17 March 2004.

19. "Kerry's Foreign Legion," *Wall Street Journal,* 15 March 2004, A16.

20. James Taranto, "Kerry to Voters: Mind Your Business!" *Wall Street Journal,* 15 March 2004, www.opinionjournal.com/best/?id=110004823.

21. Sean Hannity, "Are Foreign Leaders Really Backing Kerry?"

22. To understand the difference in tone between Taranto and Limbaugh, contrast Taranto's statement "it's breathtakingly arrogant for Kerry to assert his putative promises to foreign leaders to change America's policies are not of the voters' business" with Limbaugh's "'I'm Senator Kerry. You're nothing but human debris. You challenge my word? Well, screw the hell out of you. You vote for Bush? I thought so, you SOB."

23. Fox News website, www.foxnews.com, 16 March 2004.

Chapter 2

1. Adam Clymer, "It's 1949: Meet President Strom Thurmond," *New York Times,* 15 December 2002, late ed., sec. 4, 5.

2. Thomas Edsall, "Lott Decried for Part of Salute to Thurmond," *Washington Post,* 7 December 2002, A6.

3. Tim Russert, interview with Soledad O'Brien. *Sunday Today, NBC,* New York, 22 December, 2002.

4. "Strom Thurmond's Lott," editorial, *Wall Street Journal,* 10 December 2002, A18.

5. Matthew Dowd, "Polling: Decisive Moments and Audience," in *Electing the President 2004: The Annenberg Election Debriefing,* edited by Kathleen Hall Jamieson (Philadelphia: University of Pennsylvania Press, 2006).

6. *NBC Nightly News,* 21 December 2002.

7. Edsall, "Lott Decried," A6.

8. Ibid.

9. Ibid.

10. Elijah Cummings, *CBS Evening News,* 10 December 2002.

11. Tim Cuprisin, "It's Lott vs. Talk Radio after Gaffe," *Milwaukee Journal Sentinel,* 12 December 2002, 8B.

12. Deborah McGregor, "Bush Rebukes Lott for Comments on Segregation," *Financial Times (London),* 13 December 2002, 13.

13. Harold Ford, interview with Bill Hemmer, *American Morning with Paula Zahn, CNN,* 13 December 2002.

14. "Strom Thurmond's Lott," A18.

15. Brit Hume, *Special Report with Brit Hume,* Fox, 10 December 2002.

16. Greg Meeks, interview with Sean Hannity, *Hannity and Colmes,* Fox, 11 December 2002.

17. Fox's Bill O'Reilly joins the chorus condemning Lott but is not in lockstep with Limbaugh, Hannity, or the *Journal*'s Taranto in the counterattack that turns the tables. O'Reilly is hearing from those armed with the Limbaugh argument. Max Tomasi, from Connecticut, writes: "Bill, your bias is showing. Why no mention of Robert Byrd? Could it be because he's a Democrat?" Reporting that he was getting 300 letters a day complaining that he was picking on someone when someone else was worse, O'Reilly noted, "Why criticize Trent Lott? Robert Byrd is worse.... By that standard, we could never report anything. We couldn't say Stalin was bad because someone would say, well, what about Hitler? Nero couldn't be criticized. What about Caligula? Unfortunately, that kind of thinking that dismisses wrongdoing because other things are worse is an epidemic in America.... No kid can be disciplined because they can always point to others who are worse. That kind of thinking...must be challenged." Importantly, the conservative media opinion leaders are not making the argument made by O'Reilly's audience member, Max Tomasi, in that they are condemning both Lott's comment and Byrd's. But the caller's move to use the argument against Byrd to exonerate Lott demonstrates the rhetorical utility of their position. To make the double standard argument, they must impose a single standard on themselves. Their audience is not similarly constrained.

18. Charles Krauthammer, interview with Brit Hume, *Special Report with Brit Hume, Fox,* 11 December 2002.

19. Alan Colmes, *Hannity and Colmes,* Fox, 10 December 2002.

20. "Strom Thurmond's Lott," A18.

21. John Fund, "The Weakest Link," *Wall Street Journal,* 12 December 2002, www.opinionjournal.com/diary/?id=110002756.

22. Why, one might wonder, did Nixon then gain only 30% of the black vote in 1960? The answer: whereas Kennedy had called King, who had been jailed, and worked to secure his release, Nixon had been silent. That set of actions prompted King's father to publicly state that he was voting for Kennedy.

23. Judy Woodruff, *Inside Politics,* CNN, 12 December 2002.

24. Dan Rather, *CBS Evening News,* Bob Schieffer reporting, CBS, 12 December 2002.

25. Illustratively, "How about a King Workday?" *Wall Street Journal,* 5 August 1983, 20. The *Journal* editorialized: "The question, in our view, is not whether

such a man should be honored. Clearly, he should be. It is how he should be honored. . . . The productivity lost to the country through this additional day of idleness will be significant. By some small factor, it will mean less creation of wealth. And the less production and wealth this country generates, the harder it becomes for those who are at the bottom of the economic totem pole to work their way up,"

26. James Taranto, "Empty Lott," *Wall Street Journal,* 17 December 2002, www .opinionjournal.com/best/?id=110002784.

27. Shelby Steele, "Of Race and Imagination: How Far Will Trent Lott Set Back Conservative Principles?" *Wall Street Journal,* 18 December 2002, www.opinionjournal.com/editorial/feature.html?id=110002787.

28. Trent Lott, *Herding Cats: A Life in Politics* (New York: HarperCollins, 2005).

29. Mike Allen and Dana Milbank, "Bush Won't Resist Leadership Change," *Washington Post,* 17 December 2002, A1.

30. James Taranto, "The New Dixiecrats?" *Wall Street Journal,* 19 December 2002, www.opinionjournal.com/best/?id=110002794.

31. Fund, "Weakest Link."

32. John McWhorter, "Not Fit to Lead," *Wall Street Journal,* 13 December 2002.

33. Bill Kristol, *Fox News Sunday,* Fox, 15 December 2002.

34. John Fund, "A Tale of Two Bubbas: What Do Trent Lott and Bill Clinton Have in Common? Not Enough for Lott to Survive," *Wall Street Journal,* 19 December 2002, www.opinionjournal.com/diary/?id=110002790.

35. Peggy Noonan, "Rent by Trent: Why We Mustn't Cast Our Lot with Lott," *Wall Street Journal,* 20 December 2002, www.opinionjournal.com/columnists/ pnoonan/?id=110002795.

36. Thomas J. Bray, "After Lott: Bush Must Reject the Racialism of the Left as Well as the Right," *Wall Street Journal,* 24 December 2002, www.opinionjournal.com/ columnists/tbray/?id=110002813.

37. Rep. Julius Ceasar (J. C.) Watts (R. Okla.), *NBC Nightly News,* NBC, 10 December 2002.

38. Rick Santorum, *NBC Nightly News,* NBC, 15 December 2002.

39. Pat Buchanan, *NBC Nightly News,* NBC, 12 December 2002.

40. Christopher Dodd, interview with Wolf Blitzer, *Late Edition with Wolf Blitzer,* CNN, 15 December 2002.

41. James Taranto, "Dodd-ering Old Byrd," *Wall Street Journal,* 5 April 2004, www.opinionjournal.com/best/?id=110004912.

42. Brit Hume, "The Political Grapevine," *Special Report with Brit Hume,* Fox, 7 April 2004.

43. Sean Hannity, *Hannity and Colmes,* Fox, 8 April 2004.

Chapter 3

1. Lowell Ponte, "Glenn Beck: Multimedia Talk Machine Refuses to Be Categorized," NewsMax.com, September 2007, 56.

2. David D. Kirkpatrick and Linda Greenhouse, "Justice Thomas Reportedly Has $1.5 Million Book Deal," *New York Times,* 10 January 2003, A19.

3. G. Gordon Liddy, interview, *Hannity and Colmes,* Fox, 20 November 2002.

4. Mike Hoyt, "Talk Radio, Turning Up the Volume," *Columbia Journalism Review* 31, 3 (1992): 45–50.

5. Michael Rust, "Tuning to America," *Insight on the News,* 17 July 1995, 11.

6. D. Petrozzella, "Hundt to Radio Show: Truth in Broadcasting," *Broadcast and Cable,* 17 October 1994: 11.

7. Blayne Cutler, "Mature Audiences Only," *American Demographics* (October 1989): 20–26.

8. Reid Bunzel, "Talk Networks Pursue Role of AM 'White Knight' (AM Radio)," *Broadcasting,* 27 August 1990, 40.

9. Ed Shane, "Modern Radio Formats: Trends and Possibilities," *Journal of Radio Studies* 3 (1995–96): 5.

10. Inquiry into Alternatives to the General Fairness Obligations of Broadcast Licensees, 102 F.C.C. 2d 143 (1985).

11. Syracuse Peace Council v. Federal Communications Commission, 867 F. 2d 654, 16 Media Law Rptr. 1225 (D.C. Cir 1989); cert. denied, 493 U.S. 1019, 110 S. Ct. 717, 107 L.Ed. 2d 737 (1990).

12. Ponte, "Glenn Beck."

13. Thomas E. Patterson, *The Vanishing Voter: Public Involvement in the Age of Uncertainty* (New York: Random House, 2001).

14. "The Talk Radio Research Project," www.talkers.com/talkaud.html.

15. In an Annenberg survey conducted in spring 2005 (Press and Public Survey, March 2005), 5% reported listening to Limbaugh daily; 19% of the adult population said it listened at least once a month. Since the U.S. census data indicated at that time that there were roughly 217,765,000 adults 18 and older in the United States, 5% would mean 10,888,250 listeners every day. Across our decade of surveys, an average of 7% reports regular listening, a percent that would put his regular audience at 15,243,550. In this 2005 survey, 9% listened almost every day or every week. These weekly figures are consistent with the report of a Limbaugh staff member who says that the number fluctuates between 16 and 20 million listeners, with numbers in the higher range in election years. In 2005, Limbaugh had an affiliate list of approximately 600 stations.

16. Representative Tom DeLay (TX), "A Tribute to Rush Limbaugh," Statement on floor of House, 16 October 2001, H6887. Retrieved from Thomas Congressional Library, http://thomas.loc.gov.

17. *NOW with Bill Moyers.* Bill Moyers, host. 17 December 2004. PBS (WHYY network). www.pbs.org.

18. Some studies have shown that attitudes toward Republican and Democratic political figures are more exaggerated among Limbaugh listeners, over and above what would be expected from their ideological leanings;

Diana Owen, "Talk Radio and Evaluations of President Clinton," *Political Communication* 14 (1997): 333–53; GangHeong Lee and Joseph N. Cappella, "The Effects of Political Talk Radio on Political Attitude Formation: Exposure versus Knowledge," *Political Communication* 18 (2001): 369–94.

19. See Kathleen Hall Jamieson and Karlyn Kohrs Campbell, *Interplay of Influence: News, Advertising, Politics and the Mass Media* (Belmont, Calif.: Wadsworth, 1992), 14–17.

20. "News Audiences Increasingly Politicized," Pew Research Center for the People and the Press, http://people-press.org/reports/display.php3?PageID=833, 8 June 2004.

21. Michael Learmonth, "Auds Droop at Cable Newsies," *Daily Variety*, 29 December 2004, 1.

22. Paul Farhi, "Everybody Wins," *American Journalism Review* 25, 3 (April 2003): 32.

23. "Fox News Claims Biggest Share of Viewership," *Business World,* 24 December 2004, 18.

24. Jacques Steinberg, "Fox News, Media Elite," *New York Times*, 8 November 2004, C1.

25. Alex Ben Lock, "Fox News Has Changed the Game," *Television Week,* 20 December 2004, 7.

26. For discussion see Clark Hoyt, "He May Be Unwelcome, but We'll Survive," *New York Times,* 13 January 2008, 12Wk.

27. Cal Thomas, "Liberals Keep Clucking about Fox in Media Henhouse," *Baltimore Sun*, 5 November 2003, 17A.

28. Robert B. Zajonc, "Mere Exposure: A Gateway to the Subliminal," *Current Directions in Psychological Science* 10 (2001): 224–28.

29. Fox's other identifying theme was "We Report. You Decide."

30. Richard A. Viguerie and David Franke, *America's Right Turn: How Conservatives Used New and Alternative Media to Take Power* (Chicago: Bonus Books, 2004).

31. Robert L. Bartley, "The Dawning Bush Establishment?" *Wall Street Journal,* 20 January 2003, www.opinionjournal.com/columnists/rbartley/?id=110002935.

32. John Fund, "Out-Foxing the Experts," *Wall Street Journal*, 9 February 2001, www.opinionjournal.com/diary/?id=85000566.

33. Brian C. Anderson, "We're Not Losing Anymore," *Wall Street Journal*, 3 November 2003, www.opinionjournal.com/extra/?id=110004245.

34. Bob Woodward, *Bush at War* (New York: Simon and Schuster, 2002).

35. Quoted by Paul Krugman, "In Media Res," *New York Times,* 29 November 2002, A39.

36. Ken Auletta, "Vox Fox; How Roger Ailes and Fox News are Changing Cable," *New Yorker,* 26 May 2003, 58.

37. Helen Thomas, *Watchdogs of Democracy? The Waning Washington Press Corps and How It Has Failed the Public* (New York: Scribner, 2006) 142.

38. "A Wall Street Legacy," *New York Times*, 1 August 2007, C8.
39. Martha Graybow, "U.S. Newspapers See Further Readership Declines," Reuters, 1 November 2004.
40. "Taking Aim," *New York Times*, 1 August 2007, C9.
41. L. Gordon Crovitz, "A Report to Our Readers," *Wall Street Journal*, 1 August 2007, A14.
42. Matthew Gentzkow and Jesse M. Shapiro, *What Drives Media Slant? Evidence from U.S. Daily Newspapers*, National Bureau of Economic Research working paper no. 12707, 2006, www.nber.org/papers/w12707.
43. Tim Groseclose and Jeff Milyo, "A Measure of Media Bias," *Quarterly Journal of Economics* 120, 4 (2005): 1191–237.
44. "Gotcha!" *Economist*, 4 August 2007, 30.
45. L. Gordon Crovitz, "A Report to Our Readers," *Wall Street Journal*, 1 August 2007, A14.
46. "Mr. Murdoch and *The Journal*," *New York Times*, 10 June 2007, 13Wk.
47. "Gotcha!" *Economist*, 4 August 2007, 30.
48. Godfrey Hodgson, *The World Turned Right Side Up: A History of the Conservative Ascendancy in America* (Boston: Houghton Mifflin, 1996), 195.
49. Boston: Houghton Mifflin.
50. Alan Murray, "Political Capital," *Wall Street Journal*, 28 October 2003, A4.
51. Charles Murray, *Losing Ground: American Social Policy, 1950–1980* (New York: Basic Books, 1984). Murray's argument was consistent with but not as apocalyptic as that in George Gilder's *Wealth and Poverty* (New York: Bantam Books, 1981).
52. Charles Murray, "The Coming White Underclass," *Wall Street Journal*, 29 October 1993, A14.
53. Newt Gingrich, *Winning the Future* (Washington, D.C.: Regnery, 2005), 197–98.

Chapter 4

1. James C. Dobson, "The Values Test," *New York Times*, 4 October 2007, A29.
2. David D. Kirkpatrick. "Giuliani Inspires Threat of a Third-Party Run," *New York Times*, 1 October 2007, A18.
3. The language in quotation marks is from John Micklethwait and Adrian Wooldridge, *The Right Nation: Conservative Power in America* (New York: Penguin Press, 2004), 252.
4. Edward G. Carmines and James A Stimson, *Issue Evolution: Race and the Transformation of American Politics* (Princeton, N.J.: Princeton University Press, 1989), 9.
5. Embargoed for release after 7 a.m. Monday, 4 June 2007, ABC hardcopy.
6. "In Praise of Huddled Masses," 3 July 1984, 1.

7. "Conservatives and Immigration," *Wall Street Journal,* 10 July 2006; "Immigration and the GOP," *Wall Street Journal*, 27 June 2007.

8. See John Fund, "Rush Limbaugh Issues a Warning to President Bush," *Wall Street Journal,* 31 January 2005. The *Journal*'s Paul Gigot noted the role of talk radio in "defeating the immigration bill," reporting: "We came in for a pounding in more than one talk radio show host's discourse about our support for some kind of immigration reform, or I guess more broadly for open immigration"; *Journal Editorial Report,* Fox, 2 July 2007, WSJ.com.

9. Peggy Noonan, "The Old Affection," *Wall Street Journal*, 15 June 2007. www.opinionjournal.com/columnists/pnoonan/?id=110010210.

10. In 1976, the Republican platform praised *Roe v. Wade*. In 1980, it came out for a constitutional amendment banning abortion. In an op-ed entitled "American Conservatism: Ronald Reagan, Father of the Pro-life Movement," in the *Journal*, Fred Barnes, executive editor of the *Weekly Standard,* noted the symbolic significance of President George W. Bush signing "the partial-birth abortion ban" in the Ronald Reagan Building, *Wall Street Journal*, 6 November 2003, A14.

11. "Policy and Law," *Wall Street Journal,* 5 July 1989, A10.

12. "Policy and Law." When *Roe* was decided, the *Journal* said it had "certain reservations about...[the] decision allowing women to have pregnancies aborted in their early stages, but on the whole we think the court struck a reasonable balance on an exceedingly difficult question; "Abortion and Privacy," *Wall Street Journal,* 26 January 1973, 12. The *Journal* invoked a second Republican principle by arguing that the fight over abortion belonged "not in Washington but in the state capitals"; "The Sun Still Rises," *Wall Street Journal*, 30 June 1992, A1.

13. "The Sun Still Rises," *Wall Street Journal,* 30 June 1992, A1.

14. Rush Limbaugh, *See, I Told You So* (New York: Pocket Books, 1994), 386.

15. William F. Buckley. *Up from Liberalism* (New York: McDowell, Obolensky, 1960).

16. Limbaugh, *See, I Told You So*, 387.

17. Ibid., 9.

18. "The Rest of Him," *Wall Street Journal,* 10 November 1994, A16.

19. Ralph Reed, "Conservative Coalition Holds Firm," *Wall Street Journal,* 13 February 1995, A14.

20. Limbaugh, *See, I Told You So,* 350.

21. "Dracula Liberalism," *Wall Street Journal,* 2 November 1992, A16.

22. Limbaugh, *See, I Told You So*, 43.

23. Ibid., 382.

24. See "Get the Fat Out," *Wall Street Journal,* 4 August 1994, A12.

25. "John Kerry, Supply-Sider?" *Wall Street Journal,* 29 March 2004, A18. Rather than saying that Reagan cut taxes as Kennedy did, Limbaugh noted: "Jack Kennedy cut taxes like Reagan did" (9 October 2007).

26. William G. Jacoby, "The Impact of Party Identification on Issue Attitudes," *American Journal of Political Science* 32, 3 (1988): 644.

27. Milton Lodge and Ruth Hamill, "A Partisan Schema for Political Information Processing," *American Political Science Review* 80, 2 (1986): 505–20.

28. Arthur Lupia, "Shortcuts versus Encyclopedias: Information and Voting Behavior in California Insurance Reform Elections," *American Political Science Review* 88, 1 (1994): 63–76; Arthur Lupia and Matthew D. McCubbins, *The Democratic Dilemma* (New York: Cambridge University Press, 1998).

29. Michael Tomz and Paul M. Sniderman, "Brand Names and the Organization of Mass Belief Systems," paper presented at the annual meeting of the Midwest Political Science Association, Chicago, 10 October 2005. See also James N. Druckman, "Using Credible Advice to Overcome Framing Effects," *Journal of Law, Economics, and Organization* 17 (2001): 62–82.

30. Keith Poole and Howard Rosenthal, *Congress: A Political-Economic History of Roll Call Voting* (New York: Oxford University Press, 1997); Robert S. Erikson and Gerald C. Wright," Voters, Candidates, and Issues in Congressional Elections," in *Congress Reconsidered*, 6th ed., edited by Lawrence C. Dodd and Bruce I. Oppenheimer (Washington D.C.: Congressional Quarterly Press, 1997), 132–61. As Stephen Ansolabehere, James M. Snyder, and Charles Stewart III, "Candidate Positioning in U.S. House Elections," *American Journal of Political Science* 45, 1 (2001): 136–59, report, "the two American parties diverge, nationally and locally" (153).

31. John L. Sullivan, James E. Pierson, and George E. Marcus, "Ideological Constraint in the Mass Public: A Methodological Critique and Some New Findings," *American Journal of Political Science* 22, 2 (1978): 233–49. The authors argue that the finding that "there was a greater tendency after 1964 for citizens to structure their political attitudes along liberal-conservative lines" (235) was due not to actual change but to changes in the survey items measuring "constraint."

32. Peggy Noonan, "Since You Asked: Questions and Answers on Bush and the War," OpinionJournal.com, 3 February 2003.

33. Speech, 27 October 1964, Los Angeles. www.reaganlibrary.com/reagan/speeches/rendezvous.asp.

34. "Liberal Face-Off," *Wall Street Journal,* 5 March 1992, A14.

35. Ralph Reed, "Conservative Coalition Holds Firm," 13 February 1995, A14.

36. "Liberal Fundamentalism," *Wall Street Journal,* 13 September 1984, 1.

37. "Select Quotes, 'The Way Thing[s] Ought to Be,'" RushLimbaugh.com, in "Essential Stack of Stuff."

38. James C. Dobson, "The Values Test," *New York Times,* 4 October 2007, A29.

39. "The Envy of Europe," *Wall Street Journal,* 10 May 2001, A18.

40. "Creating Common Ground," *Wall Street Journal,* 14 February 1996, A14.

41. Rush Limbaugh, *The Way Things Ought to Be* (New York: Pocket Books, 1992), 285.

42. Limbaugh, *See, I Told You So*, 121.

43. Ibid., 136.

44. "Reagan's Peers" (Part 2). www.ronaldreagan/rush2.html.

45. Sean Hannity, "Gray Davis on Reagan as a Governor," *Hannity and Colmes*, Fox, 9 June 2004.

46. *Fox News Sunday*, 6 June 2004.

47. Sean Hannity, "Former Attorney General Remembers Ronald Reagan," *Hannity and Colmes*, Fox, 7 June 2004.

48. Peggy Noonan, "Why We Talk about Reagan," *Wall Street Journal*, 8 February 2002, A18.

49. Mondale also carried the District of Columbia.

50. John Fund, "Here Is the Rest of Him," *Wall Street Journal*, 12 March 2000, A20.

51. Robert L. Bartley, "Thinking Things Over: The Question of Competency," *Wall Street Journal*, 23 October 2000, A39.

52. "The Rest of Him," *Wall Street Journal*, 10 November 1994, A16.

53. Arthur Schlesinger Jr., "Who Really Won the Cold War?" *Wall Street Journal*, 14 September 1992, A10.

54. Frank R. Kent, "The Great Game of Politics," *Wall Street Journal*, 14 November 1944, 6.

55. Rush Limbaugh,"Reagan Tribute," 7 June 2004. http://reagan2020.us/tributes/limbaugh.asp.

56. Limbaugh, *See, I Told You So*, 145.

57. Bartley, "Thinking Things Over," A39.

58. "Review and Outlook: The Reagan Legacy," *Wall Street Journal*, 17 August 1992, A6.

59. Ibid.

60. William C. Berman, *America's Right Turn: From Nixon to Clinton*, 2nd ed. (Baltimore: Johns Hopkins University Press, 2001), 88.

61. See Bruce Bartlett, "A Taxing Experience," *National Review Online*, 29 October 2003.

62. *Hannity and Colmes*, Fox, November 21, 2005. Liberals note that although revenues did increase during Reagan's time in office, they did not double. They suggest that the increases would have been greater without the tax cuts, and they state that receipts grew more rapidly after the Clinton increase in the top marginal rates than under Reagan. See "Hannity again falsely claimed that Reagan's tax cuts "doubled revenues'" at MediaMatters.org/items/200511122007.

63. "Reagan's Peers" (Part 2). www.ronaldreagan/rush2.html.

64. Ronald Reagan, *An American Life: The Autobiography* (New York: Simon and Schuster, 1990), 335.

65. Ibid., 336.

66. Ibid., 337.

67. Lee Edwards, *The Conservative Revolution: The Movement That Remade America* (New York: Free Press, 1999), 231–32.

68. Limbaugh, *See, I Told You So*, 128.

69. Ibid., 136. "Liberals then brilliantly took the natural cycle of recession and blamed it completely on the 1980s."

70. Greg Grandin, "The Imperial Presidency: The Legacy of Reagan's Central America Policy," in *Confronting the New Conservatism: The Rise of the Right in America*, edited by Michael J. Thompson (New York: New York University Press, 2007), 197.

71. "On the Make," *Wall Street Journal*, 28 September 1992, A12.

72. Sean Hannity, "Does the Reagan Mini-series Reveal a Secret Media Agenda?" *Hannity and Colmes*, Fox, 7 November 2003.

73. "Not Ready for Prime Time," *Wall Street Journal*, 5 November 2003, A20. The media-based conservatives also provided commentary on the adequacy of mainstream coverage of Reagan's death. On Fox, Brit Hume noted, for example, "The morning after Ronald Reagan died, the *Washington Post* ran a front-page banner headline saying, quote, 'Ronald Reagan Dies, 40th President Reshaped American Politics.' Four stories on Reagan were below it. The *Washington Times* devoted its entire front page with three stories to Reagan. In the *New York Times*, Reagan's death was only worth one three-column headline saying, quote, 'Reagan Fostered Cold War Might and Curbs on Government'"; Brit Hume, "Political Grapevine," *Special Report with Brit Hume*, Fox, 8 June 2004.

74. Paul M. Sniderman and Matthew S. Levendusky, "An Institutional Theory of Political Choice," in *The Oxford Handbook of Political Behavior*, edited by Russell J. Dalton and Hans-Dieter Kilngemann (New York: Oxford University Press, 2007).

Chapter 5

1. "What Ailes the Press?" *Wall Street Journal*, 22 November 2002, www.opinionjournal.com/editorial/feature.html?id=110002672.

2. *Limbaugh Letter*, October 2003, 10.

3. Robert L. Bartley, "Thinking Things Over: The Dawning Bush Establishment?" *Wall Street Journal*, 10 January 2003, A15.

4. Conservative leaders marvel at and take pride in the commercial success of the conservative media. "The marketplace has decided they want to give the conservatives a bigger microphone than they do the liberals," argues conservative direct mail guru Richard Viguerie. "The American people like the message they're hearing from the Rush Limbaughs, the Sean Hannitys of the world more than they do from the liberal commentators."

For decades, ABC, NBC, and CBS were the broadcast media establishment; Limbaugh now calls them "the partisan media" or the "drive-by" media.

Democrats respond in kind. "With the loss of the Senate, Democrats have suddenly spouted the droll complaint that the media is prejudiced against them," wrote Bartley in January 2003. "They want their own Rush Limbaugh. This is not quite as foolish as it sounds to most people and all conservatives. The media is an Establishment transmission belt, and it's true that liberal ideas no longer get automatic approval."

5. M. Stanton Evans, *The Liberal Establishment Who Runs America...and How* (New York: Devin-Adair, 1965).

6. "Liberal Face-Off," 5 March 1992, *Wall Street Journal*, A14.

7. Rush Limbaugh, *See, I Told You So* (New York: Pocket Books, 1994), 60.

8. Robert H. Wiebe, *Self Rule: A Cultural History of American Democracy* (Chicago: University of Chicago Press, 1995), 74.

9. Leon Festinger, *A Theory of Cognitive Dissonance* (Stanford, Calif.: Stanford University Press, 1957); J. L. Freedman and D. O. Sears, "Selective Exposure," in *Advances in Experimental Social Psychology*, edited by L. Berkowitz (New York: Academic Press, 1965), 2:57–97, and "Selective Exposure to Information: A Critical Review," *Public Opinion Quarterly* 31 (1967): 194–213.

10. S. S. Iyengar and D. R. Kinder, *News That Matters* (Chicago: University of Chicago Press, 1987); V. Price and D. Tewksbury, "News Values and Public Opinion: A Theoretical Account of Media Priming," in *Progress in Communication Sciences*, edited by G. Barnett and F. J. Boster (Greenwich, Conn.: Ablex, 1997), 13:173–212.

11. B. Berelson, P. F. Lazarsfeld, and W. N. McPhee, in their famous book *A Study of Opinion Formation in a Presidential Campaign* (Chicago: University of Chicago Press, 1954).

12. Vince Price and Scott Allen, "Opinion Spirals, Silent and Otherwise: Applying Small Group Research to Public Opinion Phenomena," *Communication Research* 17 (1990): 369–89. Michael Slater, "Reinforcing Spirals of Mutual Influence of Media Selectivity and Media Effects and Their Impact on Individual Behavior and Social Identity," *Communication Theory* 17 (2007): 281–303.

13. Slater, "Reinforcing Spirals," 282.

14. Respondents were assigned to listening groups on the basis of their identification of the host's political views as liberal, conservative, or moderate. The groups could have been determined in two other ways. The first alternative was the name of the show or its host along with its avowed—often published—political orientation. The second was the listener's own political ideology in combination with his or her assessment of the degree of similarity or dissimilarity with the host's views. The groups created by the three methods were all very similar, and results indicated little difference in assignment to group, regardless of which method was used to establish the groupings. The most direct method was used, thereby preserving the most observations. So listeners to conservative PTR are those who identify their host as conservative; listeners

to liberal/moderate PTR say their host's views are either liberal or moderate in orientation.

Although it would have been useful to separate the liberal and moderate PTR groups, the number of regular listeners identifying their host's views as liberal was too small (N = 86) to permit a separate group. The groups allow us to compare and contrast the audiences of Rush Limbaugh to those of conservative PTR and liberal/moderate PTR while comparing each to the nonlisteners.

15. D. Romer et al., *Capturing Campaign Dynamics 2000 and 2004* (Philadelphia: University of Pennsylvania Press, 2006), 14.

16. Ibid.; R. Johnston, M. G. Hagen, and K. Hall Jamieson, *The 2000 Presidential Election and the Foundations of Party Politics* (New York: Cambridge University Press, 2000).

17. Richard R. Miller, *Fact and Method* (Princeton, N.J.: Princeton University Press, 1987).

Chapter 6

1. Rush Limbaugh, "American Conservatism: Holding Court," OpinionJournal. com, 17 October 2005.

2. "A New Owner," *Wall Street Journal,* 1 August 2007, A14.

3. Edwin Black, "The Second Persona," *Quarterly Journal of Speech* 56 (1970): 109–19.

4. "America Votes 2004," www.cnn.com/ELECTION/2004/. Whereas Massachusetts Democrat John Kerry captured a majority of both those with postgraduate degrees and without high school diplomas, high school grads and those who completed some college or were college graduates favored Bush.

5. For a related argument see Tom Lewis, "Triumph of the Idol Rush Limbaugh and a Hot Medium," *Media Studies Journal* 7 (1993): 51–61.

6. In a survey we did in two stages in 1993–94, about 70% of the public reported ever listening to PTR, while about 17% said they were regular listeners. For those asked about Rush Limbaugh's radio program, 61% had never listened while 6% listened regularly, 20% sometimes, and 13% rarely. In 1996, the percentage of regular listeners (defined as at least two times per week) to some form of PTR was also 18%. Of these regular listeners, 7% were regular Limbaugh listeners, while the remaining 11% were regular listeners of some other program or of Limbaugh and a second program. By the 2000 presidential primary season, a survey supervised by Jamieson showed about 7.3% of the population said they had listened to Limbaugh in the previous week; NAES 2004 confirmed that about 8.3% had listened in the previous week.

7. Several other studies have described the audiences of PTR and of talk radio in general; Barry A. Hollander, "Political Talk Radio in the '90s: A Panel Study," *Journal of Radio Studies* 6 (1999): 236–45; Pamela Paul, "Opening Up the Conversation," *American Demographics* 23 (2001): 28–34. One of the most

comprehensive studies of demographics was completed by Stephen E. Bennett, "Predicting Americans' Exposure to Political Talk Radio in 1996, 1998, and 2000," *Harvard International Journal of Press/Politics* 7, 1 (2002): 9–22. His results are not as clear-cut as ours, in part because ours focus on Limbaugh listeners, not those listening to PTR more generally.

8. For details about each of the surveys, see the appendix to this chapter at our website, in the Political Communication section. www.annenbergpublicpolicycenter .org. However, the period of the survey reported in the charts in this chapter is the early primary period from January 1 until April 1. The definition of "PTR listener" in 1996 was someone who listened on at least two days per week in the typical week, and in 2000–2004, someone who had listened in the past week.

9. See "The Executive Branch: Public and Presidential Appointees Speak Out," a report prepared for the Annenberg Trust at Sunnylands by Princeton Survey Research Associates, November 2003. Data from the survey can be found at the Annenberg Public Policy Center website, Institutions of Democracy file. www.annenbergpublicpolicycenter.org

10. Ibid.

11. Rush Limbaugh, "Reagan's Peers" (Part 2), www.ronaldreagan.com/rush2. html.

12. Donald Reagan, "A Reaganomic 'GPS,'" *Wall Street Journal,* 11 June 2003, A16.

13. Sean Hannity, "Jack Kemp Recalls Working with Reagan," *Hannity and Colmes,* 9 June 2004.

14. Brit Hume,"Roundtable," *Fox News Sunday*, Fox, 6 June 2004.

15. US Bureau of Labor Statistics, *"Labor Force Statistics from the Current Population Survey* (6 February 2007). http://stats.bls.gov/.

16. Annette Bernhardt et al., *Divergent Paths: Economic Mobility in the New American Labor Market* (New York: Russell Sage Foundation, 2001).

17. Frank Levy, *The New Dollars and Dreams: American Incomes and Economic Change* (New York: Russell Sage Foundation, 1998), 50 ff.

18. David Leonhardt, "In a Wealthy Country Who Are the Truly Rich?" *New York Times,* 12 January 2003, 16.

19. NAES, 2000. Available on website of the Annenberg Public Policy Center, Political Communication Section, www.annenbergpublicpolicy.org.

20. "The Adoption Option," *Wall Street Journal*, 7 July 1989, A8.

21. "In the Name of Freedom," *Wall Street Journal,* 27 June 1962, 14.

22. "Say a Little Prayer," *Wall Street Journal*, 22 November 1994, A24.

23. Alex Ben Block, "Fox News Has Changed the Game," *Television Week* 20 (2004): 7.

24. *The Limbaugh Letter*, April 2004, 3; Limbaugh's speech accepting the Statesmanship Award, Claremont Institute, 19 November 2004.

25. Nolan McCarty, Keith T. Poole, and Howard Rosenthal, *Polarized America: The Dance of Ideology and Unequal Rights* (Cambridge, Mass.: MIT Press, 2006), 89.

26. "Uncivil Rights," *Wall Street Journal,* 7 November 2006, A12.

27. In 1956, women preferred Eisenhower over Adlai Stevenson; in 1960, more votes by women went to Nixon than Kennedy; and in 1984, Reagan carried the women's vote. By contrast, in 1992, 1996, and 2000, the women's vote was solidly in the Democratic corner. However, in 2004, the issue of national security substantially closed the gender gap for the Republicans among women in general. In that election, the party divide shifted with married women preferring the Republican Party and single women the Democratic Party. Overall, in 2004, women preferred Bush on the issue of national security/terrorism and Kerry on domestic issues. Overall, white men have been the mainstay of the Republican Party.

28. Rush Limbaugh, *See, I Told You So* (New York: Pocket Books, 1994), 222.

29. Ibid., 88.

30. *Wall Street Journal,* 26 March 1973, 12.

Chapter 7

1. Michael Pfau and his colleagues found evidence of Limbaugh's effect on the primary candidates in New Hampshire in 1996; Michael Pfau et al., "Influence of Communication during the Distant Phase of the 1996 Republican Presidential Primary Campaign," *Journal of Communication* 47 (1997): 626. Jones found no evidence of Limbaugh's impact in a Lafayette, Indiana, race in 1996; David A. Jones, "Political Talk Radio: The Limbaugh Effect on Primary Voters," *Political Communication* 15 (1998): 367–81.

2. Keynote address to the Democratic Leadership Council, Cleveland, 6 May 1991, quoted in John Micklethwait and Adrian Wooldridge, *The Right Nation: Conservative Power in America* (New York: Penguin Press, 2004), 103.

3. Rush Limbaugh, *The Way Things Ought to Be* (New York: Pocket Books, 1992), 288.

4. "Pat's Protesters," *Wall Street Journal,* 5 March 1992, A14.

5. "Review and Outlook: The Reagan Legacy," *Wall Street Journal*, 17 August 1992, A6.

6. Limbaugh, *The Way Things Ought to Be,* 286.

7. "Prime Time for Perot," *Wall Street Journal*, 2 October 1992, A14.

8. Limbaugh, *The Way Things Ought to Be,* 292–93.

9. Albert J. Menendez, *The Perot Voters and the Future of American Politics* (Amherst, N.Y.: Prometheus Books, 1996), 28.

10. "Democrats vs. Clinton," *Wall Street Journal,* 5 November 1992, A16.

11. Stanley B. Greenberg, *The Two Americas: Our Current Political Deadlock and How to Break It* (New York: St. Martin's Press, 2004), 64.

12. "McGovern Republicans," *Wall Street Journal,* 16 February 1996, A10.

13. "The Forbes Factor," *Wall Street Journal,* 15 March 1996, A10.

14. "Front-Runner Forbes," *Wall Street Journal,* 29 February 1996, A18.

15. "Status Quo Perot," *Wall Street Journal*, 20 August 1996, A10.

16. "Brownian Commotion," *Wall Street Journal*, 26 March 1992, A1.

17. "Forbes' Content," *Wall Street Journal*, 16 January 1996, A14.

18. Jones's panel survey in Lafayette, Indiana, in 1996 did find that "Limbaugh listeners were significantly cooler toward Ross Perot than nonlisteners," Jones speculates that "perhaps such feelings were partially the result of Limbaugh's frequent criticism of Perot during and since the 1992 election. The Limbaugh audience would presumably be predisposed to like Perot because of his conservative, probusiness political leanings. The fact that listeners are significantly cooler to Perot suggests that Limbaugh's criticism had an impact" (Jones, "Political Talk Radio," 378).

19. The *Wall Street Journal* editorialized that Buchanan was the only presidential candidate proposing a tax increase. "Mr. Buchanan's tax boosts reach up to 40%, the tariff he would apply to goods produced in China" (Buchanan's 40% Tax Increase," *Wall Street Journal*, 23 February 1996, A12). The same editorial calls "Mr. Buchanan's tariffs . . . a massive government intervention in the economy" and notes: "After New Hampshire, some are starting to catch on," The editorial continues: "One is Rush Limbaugh, who put it pretty well on his radio program this week: 'Buchanan wants to engage in policies that expand the role of government in people's lives. I find it a bit amazing that the same people who opposed Hillary Clinton's health care are now latching on to a candidate's promises that offer to do the same thing, only in the area of jobs. There's no government that can guarantee you your job.'"

20. *Talk Daily*, 1993, 27.

21. Eric Boehlert, "Politics 2000," 4 March 2000, www.salon.com/politics2000/feature/2000/03/04/rush.

22. The level of difference was P < .12.

23. P < .001.

24. This analysis was conducted by Annenberg graduate Danna Young.

25. Boehlert, www.salon.com/politics2000/feature/2000/03/04/rush.

26. Quoted by Joe Conason, "Rush's Defenders Ignore His Venom," *New York Observer*, 2 December 2002, 5.

27. See Matthew Dallek, *The Right Moment: Ronald Reagan's First Victory and the Decisive Turning Point in American Politics* (New York: Oxford University Press, 2000), 244.

28. Limbaugh, *Limbaugh Letter*, October 2003, 3.

29. Rush Limbaugh, "Moderate Myth," *Wall Street Journal*, 3 September 2005.

30. "Shades of Grey," *Wall Street Journal*, 18 January 2007, OpinionJournal.com.

31. John Fund, "Unhappy Days," *Wall Street Journal*, 22 January 2007, OpinionJournal.com.

32. Russ Buettner, "In Fox News, Led by an Ally, Giuliani has a Friendly Stage," *New York Times*, 2 August 2007, A12.

33. David Saltonstall, "Guiliani's Fox-y Pal Raises Money Questions," *New York Daily News*, 19 August 2007.

34. Research by Barker suggests that influence from Limbaugh may have substantial effects on voter preferences for Republican candidates (David C. Barker, "Rushed Decisions: Political Talk Radio and Vote Choice," *Journal of Politics* 61 (1999): 527–39.)

35. Mark O'Keefe, "Do Conservative Media Give GOP an Edge?" *Newhouse News Service,* 21 November 2002.

36. In chapter 12, we will present a case in which Limbaugh primed party as criterion for evaluating the presidential party candidates' performance more than did other PTR groups, even conservative ones.

37. As table 6.1 shows, both Fox and Limbaugh draw more than 1 in 3 of their audience members from the South. For an explanation of this model of processing, see Milton Lodge, M.R. Steenbergen, and S. Brau, "The Responsive Voter: Campaign Information and the Dynamics of Candidate Evaluation," *American Political Science Review* 89 (1995): 309–26.

38. Norman Nie, Sidney Verba, and John Petrocik, *The Changing American Voter* Cambridge, Mass.: Harvard University Press, 1979).

39. Ibid.

40. Annenberg Public Policy Center, NAES 2000, 2004. Available at the Annenberg Public Policy Center website, Political Communication section, www .annenbergpublicpolicycenter.org.

Chapter 8

1. Public Papers of the Presidents of the United States: Ronald Reagan, 1981 (Washington, D.C.: U.S. Government Printing Office, 1982).

2. Indeed, several other studies have found evidence of the association between listening to Limbaugh or PTR and lack of confidence in institutions, including the government in Washington: Barry Hollander, "The Influence of Talk Radio on Political Efficacy and Participation," *Journal of Radio Studies* 3 (1995): 23–31, and "Talk Radio: Predictors of Use and Effects on Attitudes about Government," *Journalism and Mass Communication Quarterly* 73 (1996): 102–13; Patricia Moy, Michael Pfau, and LeeAnn Kahlor, "Media Use and Public Confidence in Democratic Institutions," *Journal of Broadcasting and Electronic Media* 43 (1999): 137–58; Michael Pfau et al., "The Influence of Political Talk Radio on Confidence in Democratic Institutions," *Journalism and Mass Communication Quarterly* 75 (1998): 730–45.

3. Listeners to conservative talk radio—other than Limbaugh—were significantly different from Limbaugh listeners on mistrust of candidates' actions, with Limbaugh listeners more mistrustful.

4. Although some findings regarding PTR in general and Limbaugh listeners in particular are not always replicated in smaller samples or in particular contexts, studies of political efficacy and participation for PTR listeners are quite consistent. Other research paints the same picture of a politically engaged,

efficacious listenership: Stephen Earl Bennett, "Political Talk Radio's Relationships with Democratic Citizenship," *American Review of Politics* 19 (1998): 17; Diana Owen, "Who's Talking? Who's Listening? The New Politics of Radio Talk Shows," in *Broken Contract? Changing Relationships between Americans and Their Government*, edited by S.C. Craig and Lawrence C. Dodd (Boulder, Colo.: Westview Press); Barry A. Hollander, "Fuel to the Fire: Talk Radio and the Gamson Hypothesis," *Political Communication* 14 (1997): 355–70; Eric P. Bucy, P. D'Angelo, and J. E. Newhagen, "The Engaged Electorate: New Media Use as Political Participation," in *The Electronic Election: Perspectives on the 1996 Campaign Communication*, edited by L. L. Kaid and D. G. Bystrom (Mahwah, N.J.: Erlbaum, 1999); Louis Bolce, Gerald De Maio, and Douglas Muzzio, "Dial-in Democracy: Talk Radio and the 1994 Election," *Political Science Quarterly* 111 (1996): 457–82; Richard C. Hofstetter et al., "Political Talk Radio: A Stereotype Reconsidered," *Political Research Quarterly* 47 (1994): 467–79; C. Richard Hofstetter, "Political Talk Radio, Situational Involvement, and Political Mobilization," *Social Science Quarterly* 7 (1998) 9: 273–86; C. R. Hofstetter and Chris Gianos, "Political Talk Radio: Actions Speak Louder Than Words," *Journal of Broadcasting and Electronic Media* 41 (1997): 501–15.

5. See *The Executive Branch: Public and Presidential Appointees Speak Out,* report prepared for the Annenberg Sunnylands Trust by Princeton Survey Research Associates, November 2003. For the data from this survey, see the Annenberg Public Policy website in the Political Communication Section, Institutions of Democracy file, www.annenbergpublicpolicycenter.org.

6. Jack Citrin, "Comment: The Political Relevance of Trust in Government," *American Political Science Review* 68 (1974): 973–88.

7. Limbaugh had guest hosts during one of these weeks. Topics from the guests' shows were excluded from the Limbaugh summary even though the results for the guest hosts, when they were included, were virtually identical to those when the guests were excluded.

8. Joseph N. Cappella, Joseph Turow, and Kathleen H. Jamieson, *Call-in Political Talk Radio: Background, Content, Audiences, Portrayal in Main Stream Media,* Report by the Annenberg Public Policy Center, University of Pennsylvania, Philadelphia, 1996.

9. The rank order correlations between Limbaugh and the three mainstream channels are .10, .17, and .35, which are all nonsignificant. The rank order correlations among the mainstream channels are .85, .93, and .94, all highly significant.

10. Richard S. Lazarus and Bernice N. Lazarus, *Passion and Reason: Making Sense of Our Emotions* (New York: Oxford University Press, 1994); George E. Marcus, W. Russell Newman, and Michael Mackuen, *Affective Intelligence and Political Judgement* (Chicago: University of Chicago Press, 2000).

11. Arie W. Kruglanski and Wolfgang Stroebe. "Attitudes, Goals and Beliefs: Issues of Structure, Function and Dynamics," in *The Handbook of Attitude*

Research, edited by D. Albarracin, B. T. Johnson, and M. P. Zanna (New York: Guilford).

12. Antonio Damasio, "A Second Chance for Emotion," in *Cognitive Neuroscience of Emotion*, edited by Richard Lane and Lynn Nadel (New York: Oxford University Press, 1999), 12 ff.

13. Joseph LeDoux, *The Emotional Brain: The Mysterious Underpinnings of Emotional Life* (New York: Simon and Schuster, 1996).

14. See Richard Nadeau, Richard Niemi, and Timothy Amato, "Emotions, Issue Importance, and Political Learning," *American Journal of Political Science* 39, 3 (August 1995): 558–74; Thomas Rudolph, Amy Gangl, and Dan Stevens, "The Effects of Efficacy and Emotions on Campaign Involvement," *Journal of Politics* 62 (2000): 1189–97.

15. Joseph E. LeDoux and Elizabeth A. Phelps, "Emotional Networks in the Brain," in *Handbook of Emotions*, 2nd ed., edited by Michael Lewis and Jeannette Haviland-Jones (New York: Guilford, 2000), 157–72.

16. Antonio R. Damasio, *Descartes' Error: Emotion, Reason, and the Human Brain* (New York: Avon, 1994); Sheila T. Murphy and Robert B. Zajonc, "Affect, Cognition, and Awareness: Affective Priming with Optimal and Suboptimal Stimulus Exposures," *Journal of Personality and Social Psychology* 64 (1993): 723–39.

17. Robert B. Zajonc, "Feeling and Thinking: Preferences Need No Inferences, *American Psychologist* 35 (1980): 151–75; see also Joseph P. Forgas and Patrick T. Vargas, "The Effects of Mood on Social Judgment and Reasoning," in Lewis and Haviland-Jones, *Handbook of Emotions*, 2nd ed., 350–67.

18. Our concern is elicited when emotion is raised by forms of discourse that channel emotion in ways that counter thoughtful engagement, as we suspect is the cases with extreme supposition, ridicule, and character attack. It is raised as well when anger is directed not toward a desire to elect or defeat a position but toward individuals who hold opposing views.

19. John R. Hibbing and Elizabeth Theiss-Morse found that radio exposure was more responsible for emotional reactions to Congress than other news sources; Hibbing and Theiss-Morse, "The Media's Role in Public Negativity toward Congress: Distinguishing Emotional Reactions and Cognitive Evaluations," *American Journal of Political Science* 42 (1998): 475–98. R. Lance Holbert reported that emotional reactions among PTR listeners mediated their reactions to the outcomes of the highly contested 2000 presidential election; Holbert, "Political Talk Radio, Perceived Fairness, and the Establishment of President George W. Bush's Political Legitimacy," *Harvard International Journal of Press/Politics* 9 (2004): 12–27.

20. Marcus et al., *Affective Intelligence and Political Judgement*.

21. The correlation between emotionality and participation is .19 ($p < .001$). The unstandardized regression coefficient is .11 ($p < .001$) in the face of controls for PTR group and other demographic factors.

22. The correlations are small but significant: −.09 for emotionality and inefficacy (p < .01) and −.18 (p < .001) for emotionality and indifference.

23. GangHeong Lee, *Information Environment, Cognitive Appraisal, and Discrete Emotions in Citizens' Political Evaluation and Behavior: The 1996 U.S. Presidential Campaigns* (Ph.D. diss., Annenberg School, University of Pennsylvania, 2000).

24. Marcus et al., *Affective Intelligence and Political Judgement.*

25. For each candidate, four characteristics were presented: "would use good judgment in a crisis"; "personally likable"; "honest and truthful"; "has good ideas." Respondents indicated whether the characteristics described the candidate "very well," "somewhat," or "not at all," Scores could range from 0 to 8.

26. Issue similarity was assessed by asking two sets of questions about eight issues. The first set asked if Clinton or Dole favored each of the eight. The second set asked about the respondent's own support or opposition to the same eight issues. The issues included Medicare reduction, funding of anti-missile systems, funding of job training, across-the-board tax cuts, a ban on cigarette advertising, elimination of the Department of Education, allowing of late-term abortions, and legalization of same-sex marriages. For each issue, the respondent's view was compared to his or her perception of the candidates' position. A score of from 0 to 8 plotted a range from no perceived similarity to the highest perceived similarity. There was one score for each candidate.

27. G. Lee, J. N. Cappella, and B. Southwell, "The Effects of News and Entertainment on Interpersonal Trust: Political Talk Radio, Newspapers, and Television, *Mass Communication and Society* 6 (2003): 413–14.

28. Cappella, Turow, and Jamieson, *Call-in Political Talk Radio.*

Chapter 9

1. Rush Limbaugh, interview with Tim Russert, *Meet the Press,* NBC, CNBC, New York, 23 November 2000.

2. William A. Gamson and Katherine E. Lasch, "The Political Culture of Social Welfare Policy," in *Evaluating the Welfare State,* edited by Shimon E. Spiro and Ephraim Yuchtman-Yaar (New York: Academic Press, 1983); Thomas E. Nelson and Donald R. Kinder, "Issue Framing and Group-Centrism in American Public Opinion," *Journal of Politics* 58, 4 (1996): 1055–78.

3. William A. Gamson and Andre Modigliani, "The Changing Culture of Affirmative Action," *Research in Political Sociology* 3 (1987): 137–77; Donald R. Kinder and Lynn M. Sanders, *Divided by Color: Racial Politics and Democratic Ideals* (Chicago: University of Chicago Press, 1996).

4. Thomas E. Nelson and Zoe M. Oxley, "Issue Framing Effects on Belief Importance and Opinions," *Journal of Politics* 61 (1999): 1040–67; see also William G. Jacoby, "Issue Framing and Public Opinion on Government Spending," *American Journal of Political Science* 44 (2000): 750–67.

5. L. Stoker, "Political Value Judgments," in *Citizens and Politics: Perspectives from Political Psychology,* edited by J. H. Kuklinski (Cambridge: Cambridge University Press, 2001), 433–68. See also Donald R. Kinder and Lynn M. Sanders, *Divided by Color: Racial Politics and Democratic Ideals* (Chicago: Chicago University Press, 1996).

6. Vincent Price, David Tewksbury, and E. Powers, "Switching Trains of Thought: The Impact of News Frames on Readers' Cognitive Responses," *Communication Research* 24 (1997): 481–506.

7. Thomas E. Nelson, Rosalee A. Clawson, and Zoe M. Oxley, "Media Framing of a Civil Liberties Conflict and Its Effect on Tolerance," *American Political Science Review* 91 (1997): 567; for perspectives on framing, see Joseph N. Cappella and Kathleen H. Jamieson, *Spiral of Cynicism: The Press and the Public Good* (New York: Oxford University Press, 1997); Stephen D. Reese, Oscar H. Gandy Jr., and August E. Grant, eds., *Framing Public Life: Perspectives on Media and Our Understanding of the World* (Mahwah, N.J.: Erlbaum, 2001); Erving Goffman, *Frame Analysis: An Essay on the Organization of Experience* (Cambridge, Mass.: Harvard University Press, 1974); William A. Gamson and Andre Modigliani, "Media Discourse and Public Opinion on Nuclear Power: A Constructionist Approach," *American Journal of Sociology* 95 (1989): 1–37.

8. Vincent Price and David Tewksbury, "News Values and Public Opinion: A Theoretical Account of Media Priming and Framing," in *Progress in Communication Sciences: Advances in Persuasion,* volume 13, edited by G. A. Barnett and E. J. Boster (Greenwich, Conn.: Ablex, 1997), 173–212.

9. Thomas E. Nelson, Zoe M. Oxley, and Rosalee A. Clawson, "Toward a Psychology of Framing Effects," *Political Behavior* 19 (1997): 236; W. A. Gamson and K. E. Lasch,. "The Political Culture of Social Welfare Policy," in Spiro and Yuchtman-Yaar, *Evaluating the Welfare State,* 398.

10. Paul M. Sniderman and Sean M. Theriault, "The Structure of Political Argument and the Logic of Issue Framing," in *Studies in Public Opinion: Attitudes, Nonattitudes, Measurement Error, and Change,* edited by Willem E. Saris and Paul M. Sniderman (Princeton, N.J.: Princeton University Press, 2004), 148. For innovative work on credibility's role in framing and demonstration that counterframes and citizens' interpersonal conversations can undercut framing effects, see James N. Druckman, "On the Limits of Framing Effects: Who Can Frame?" *Journal of Politics* 63, 4 (2001): 1041–66; James N. Druckman and Kjersten R. Nelson, "Framing and Deliberation: How Citizens' Conversations Limit Elite Influence," *American Journal of Political Science* 47, 4 (October 2003): 729–45; and James N. Druckman, "Political Preference Formation: Competition, Deliberation, and the (Ir)relevance of Framing Effects," paper prepared for the summer 2003 Political Methodology meeting, University of Minnesota, Minneapolis, 17–19 July 2003.

11. Shanto Iyengar, "How Citizens Think about National Issues: A Matter of Responsibility," *American Political Science Review* 33 (1989): 878–900.

12. W. Russell Neuman, Marion R. Just, and Ann N. Crigler, *Common Knowledge: News and the Construction of Political Meaning* (Chicago: University of Chicago Press, 1992).

13. Cappella and Jamieson, *Spiral of Cynicism.*

14. Joanne M. Miller and Jon A. Krosnick, "News Media Impact on the Ingredients of Presidential Evaluations: A Program of Research on the Priming Hypothesis," in *Political Persuasion and Attitude Change,* edited by Dianna C. Mutz, Paul M. Sniderman, and Richard Brody (Ann Arbor: University of Michigan Press, 1996), 79–99; Shanto Iyengar, "The Accessibility Bias in Politics: Television News and Public Opinion," *International Journal of Public Opinion Research* 2 (1990): 1–15; Shanto Iyengar and Donald R. Kinder, *News That Matters* (Chicago: University of Chicago Press, 1987); Shanto Iyengar, Mark D. Peters, and Donald R. Kinder, "Experimental Demonstrations of the 'Not So Minimal' Consequences of Television News Programs," *American Political Science Review* 76 (1982): 848–58.

15. W. Lance Bennett, Regina G. Lawrence, and Steven Livingston, *When the Press Fails: Political Power and the News Media from Iraq to Katrina* (Chicago: University of Chicago Press, 2007), 42.

16. From January 1 to July 15, 2007, a study by the *Hotline* on interview time on the air given to presidential candidates found that, excluding time in news reports and on panels, whereas senators Joe Biden (D. Del.) and Chris Dodd (D. Conn.) garnered the most interview airtime in minutes on MSNBC (followed by Republican Mike Huckabee), on CNN the top two were Democratic governor Bill Richardson (N.M.), tied with Republican congressman Duncan Hunter (Calif.). On CNN, Democratic senator Barack Obama secured the third largest number of minutes of interview time. By contrast, the top two on Fox were former New York mayor Republican Rudy Giuliani and the then unannounced aspirant Fred Thompson, followed by former Massachusetts governor Republican Mitt Romney. "Tracking Face Time," *New York Times,* 2 August 2007, A12.

17. Paul F. Lazarsfeld, Bernard Berelson, and Hazel Gaudet. *The People's Choice: How the Voter Makes Up His Mind in a Presidential Campaign* (New York: Columbia University Press, 1948).

18. Eliju Katz and Paul F. Lazarsfeld, *Personal Influence: The Part Played by People in the Flow of Mass Communication* (New York: Free Press, 1955).

19. See, for example, Todd Gitlin, "Media Sociology: The Dominant Paradigm," *Theory and Society* 6 (1978): 205–53; W. Lance Bennett and Jarol B. Manheim, "The One Step Flow of Communication," *Annals of the American Academy of Political and Social Science* 608 (November 2006): 219. For a number of other provocative essays about the origins and impact of two-step flow, see Peter Simonson, ed., "Politics, Social Networks, and the History of Mass Communications Research: Rereading *Personal Influence,*" special issue, *Annals of the American Academy of Political and Social Science* 608, 1 (November 2006).

We agree with Bennett and Manheim that "conventional mass media [now] reach smaller audiences, while niche media attract increasing numbers, making it harder to send effective generalized messages but easier to target specialized appeals" (218), but we believe that Bennett and Manheim's notion of one-step flow fails to account for the ways Limbaugh, in particular, and the conservative media, in general, mediate the content of the mass media for their audiences.

20. Although *Personal Influence* was published in the early years of television, its finding were gathered before the dawn of that medium's role as a channel of mass communication. Katz and Lazersfeld concluded their synthesis of new research by saying that it warranted "increasing skepticism about the potency of the mass media"; Elihu Katz and Paul F. Lazersfeld, *Personal Influence: The Part Played by People in the Flow of Mass Communication* (Glencoe, Ill.: Free Press, 1955), 24.

21. Robert L. Bartley, "Consensus, the Enemy of News," *Wall Street Journal,* 27 November 1996, A10.

22. L. Brent Bozell III, "And the Networks' Whitewater Whitewash," *Wall Street Journal,* 17 December 1996, A22.

23. Data are missing for Limbaugh coverage of the ABC television network.

24. A16.

25. "The WMD Evidence," *Wall Street Journal,* 6 October 2003, A16.

26. Brit Hume, "Wartime Grapevine," *Special Report with Brit Hume,* Fox, 6 October 2003.

27. Tony Snow, Brit Hume, Mort Kondracke, Juan Williams, and Bill Kristol, "Below the Fold," *Fox News Sunday,* Fox, 1 June 2003.

28. Mort Kondracke, "All-Star Panel Discusses Bush's Success at G-8 Summit, Credibility in Finding WMD," *Special Report with Brit Hume,* Fox, 2 June 2003.

29. "Weapons of Mass Destruction," *Wall Street Journal,* 2 June 2003, A16.

30. Gary Cohn, Carla Hall, and Robert W. Welkos, "Women Say Schwarzenegger Groped, Humiliated Them," *Los Angeles Times,* 2 October 2003, 1.

31. Jill Stewart, "Why Wasn't Davis Investigated Too?" *Los Angeles Daily News,* 4 October 2003.

32. *Hannity and Colmes,* Fox News Channel, 6 October 2003, transcript no. 100601cb.253.

33. *The Big Story with John Gibson,* Fox News Channel, 6 October 2003, transcript no. 100604cb.263.

34. *Special Report with Brit Hume,* Fox News Channel, 6 October 2003, transcript no. 100605cb.254.

35. Bill Whalen, "Dirty Tricks: Gray Davis and the L.A. Times Go into Overdrive to Sink the Schwarzenegger Campaign," *Daily Standard,* 6 October 2003.

36. Jill Stewart, *Scarborough Country,* MSNBC, 6 October 2003.

37. "The Story behind the Story," *Los Angeles Times,* 12 October 2003, M5.

38. Howard Kurtz, "Daschle's Rush to Judgment," *Washington Post,* 29 November 2002, A23.

39. G. Gordon Liddy, interview, *Hannity and Colmes,* Fox, 20 November 2002.

40. Howard Kurtz, "Daschle's Criticism of Limbaugh Is Off the Mark," *Deseret News,* 24 November 2002, A04.

41. Rush Limbaugh, interview with Tim Russert, *Tim Russert,* CNBC, 30 November 2002.

42. Frank Rich, "Saving Private England: Sequel to a Hit," *New York Times,* 16 May 2004, A8.

43. Jonathan Alter, "The Picture the World Sees," *Newsweek,* 17 May 2004, 31.

Chapter 10

1. Spiro Agnew, speech in Des Moines, Iowa, 13 November 1969, transcript from audiotape.

2. Yariv Tsfati, "The Consequences of Mistrust in the News Media: Media Skepticism as a Moderator in Media Effects and as a Factor Influencing News Media Exposure" (Ph.D. diss., University of Pennsylvania, 2001).

3. Between 1996 and 2004, the media environment for news had changed radically, with the emergence of MSNBC, Fox News, and strong online presences for newspapers that had been available only in hard copy a few short years earlier. To compare media exposure questions in 1996 to those in 2004 is tenuous at best. We are continuing to probe the media exposure differences among Limbaugh listeners from 1996 through 2000 and 2004 to clarify whether consumption of mainstream news (NBC, CBS, ABC, and national print outlets) actually decreased or simply moved to the Internet.

4. Joseph Cappella and Kathleen H. Jamieson, *Spiral of Cynicism: The Press and the Public Good* (New York: Oxford University Press, 1997).

5. A study by Jones found similar results among conservative Republicans who listened to PTR. His data were from the year 2000 National Election Study; David A. Jones, "Why Americans Don't Trust the Media: A Preliminary Analysis," *Harvard International Journal of Press/Politics* 9 (2004): 60–75.

6. Note that "fair and balanced" was a standard for assessing the impartiality of news long before Fox News embraced that language.

7. The internal reliability for these two items was .72.

8. The interaction effect of three levels of ideology with five listening groups was significant: $F(10, 390) = 2.13$, $p < .03$.

9. The exception was for exposure to NPR and Public Broadcasting Service (PBS), both of which were used less by those with the greatest mistrust of mainstream news media. This pattern was consistent across listening groups, even in the presence of additional controls. Interestingly, in the mid-nineties conservative talk radio in general and Limbaugh in particular were arguing that both outlets were "liberal" and unworthy of taxpayer support.

10. At $p < .005$ at least.

11. Y. Tsfati and J. N. Cappella, "Do People Watch What They Do Not Trust? Exploring the Association between News Media Skepticism and Exposure," *Communication Research* 30 (2003): 1–26.

12. Yariv Tsfati and Joseph N. Cappella, "Why Do People Watch News They Do Not Trust? The Need for Cognition as a Moderator in the Association between News Media Skepticism and Exposure," *Media Psychology* 7 (2005): 251–71.

13. R. E. Petty and J. T. Cacioppo, "The Elaboration Likelihood Model of Persuasion," in *Advances in Experimental Social Psychology,* edited by L. Berkowitz (New York: Academic Press, 1986), 19:123–205.

14. James G. Webster, "Beneath the Veneer of Fragmentation: Television Audience Polarization in a Multichannel World," *Journal of Communication* 55, 22 (June 2005): 380.

15. Marcus Prior, *Post-broadcast Democracy: How Media Choice Increases Inequality in Political Involvement and Polarizes Elections* (Cambridge: Cambridge University Press, 2007), 157–58.

16. In a careful and thorough analysis of the public's selection of consistently liberal or conservative sources, Talia Stroud examined choices across multiple media sources—newspapers, talk radio, the internet, and television—and found evidence for ideological consistency in media selection. See Talia Stroud, "Selective Exposure to Partisan Information" (Ph.D. diss., Annenberg School for Communication, University of Pennsylvania, 2007).

17. Jonathan S. Morris, "The Fox News Factor," *Harvard International Journal of Press/Politics* 10, 3 (2005): 56–79.

18. Ibid., 74.

Chapter 11

1. Rush Limbaugh, *Limbaugh Letter,* "Democrats Implode," April 2005, 3.

2. D. T. Campbell, "Stereotypes and the Perception of Group Differences," *American Psychologist* 22 (1967): 817–29; Jordan M. Robbins and Joachim I. Krueger, "Social Projection to Ingroups and Outgroups: A Review and Meta-analysis," *Personality and Social Psychology Review* 9 (2005): 32–47.

3. Patricia W. Linville and Gregory W. Fischer, "Exemplar and Abstraction Models of Perceived Group Variability and Stereotypicality," *Social Cognition* 11 (1993): 92–125.

4. Jacques-Philippe Leyens et al., "Emotional Prejudice, Essentialism, and Nationalism: The 2002 Tajfel Lecture," *European Journal of Social Psychology* 33 (2003): 703–17.

5. M. Kent Jennings and Richard G. Niemi, *Generations of Politics* (Princeton, N.J.: Princeton University Press, 1981); Bertram Gawronski, Galen V. Bodenhausen, and Rainer Banse, "We Are, Therefore They Aren't: Ingroup Construal as a Standard of Comparison for Outgroup Judgments," *Journal of Experimental Social Psychology* 41 (2005): 515–26.

6. David Barker makes the general argument that the *Rush Limbaugh Show* creates a nontraditional social community along with pressures to conform and positive feelings of inclusion and efficacy; David Barker, "The Talk Radio Community: Nontraditional Social Networks and Political Participation," *Social Science Quarterly* 79 (1998): 261–73. Wayne Munson, following Joshua Meyerowitz's arguments about media and "place," suggests that talk radio (though not specifically Limbaugh) creates a space—or neighborhood—for participants to be together with one another separated from those outside; Wayne Munson, *All Talk* (Philadelphia: Temple University Press, 1993).

7. Kenneth Burke, *Language as Symbolic Action* (Berkeley: University of California Press, 1966), 45.

8. See David Zarefsky, "Definitions," in *Argument in a Time of Change: Definitions, Frameworks, and Critiques: Proceedings of the 10th NCA/AFA Summer Conference on Argumentation,* edited by James F. Klumpp (Annandale, Va.: National Communication Assoc., 1998), 1–11. For other important work on the rhetorical implications of definition see Chaim Perelman and Lucie Olbrechts-Tyteca, *The New Rhetoric: A Treatise on Argumentation,* translated by J. Wilkinson and P. Weaver (Notre Dame, Ind.: Notre Dame University Press, 1969); J. Robert Cox, "Argument and the 'Definition of the Situation,'" *Central States Speech Journal* 32 (fall 1981): 197–205; Edward Schiappa, *Defining Reality: Definitions and the Politics of Meaning* (Carbondale, Ill.: Southern Illinois University Press, 2003).

9. David Zarefsky, "Presidential Rhetoric and the Power of Definition," *Presidential Studies Quarterly* 34, 3 (September 2004): 612.

10. Ibid., 618.

11. Burke, *Language as Symbolic Action.*

12. Murray Edelman, *Constructing the Political Spectacle* (Chicago: University of Chicago Press, 1988.

13. Ibid.

14. R. E. Nisbett and L. Ross, *Human Inference: Strategies and Shortcomings of Social Judgment* (Englewood Cliffs, N.J.: Prentice-Hall, 1980).

15. S. E. Taylor and S. C. Thompson, "Stalking the Elusive 'Vividness' Effect," *Psychological Review* 89 (1982): 155–81; Dolf Zillman, *Exemplification in Communication: The Influence of Case Reports on the Perception of Issues* (Mahwah, N.J.: Erlbaum, 2000).

16. Kathleen Hall Jamieson, *Dirty Politics: Deception, Distraction and Democracy* (New York: Oxford University Press, 1992).

17. Charles Osgood, "Congress Vote to Ban Partial Birth Abortion Being Lauded and Condemned," *Osgood File,* CBS, 22 October 2003.

18. Katie Couric, Tim Russert reporting, *Today,* NBC, 22 October 2003.

19. However, in hard news pieces, including the news pages of the *Wall Street Journal,* the label "partial birth" is identified as the language of one side in the debate: "It is a hard won victory for opponents of abortion rights who

fought for eight years to ban what they call partial birth abortion" (*ABC News,* 21 October 2003). "The Senate gave final approval to a bill banning what critics call partial birth abortion" (*CBS Morning News,* 22 October 2003). "Ms. Lincoln was among 17 Democratic senators, many of them strong advocates of abortion rights, who voted to ban the procedure that critics call partial-birth abortion" (Sheryl Gay Stolberg, "Bill Barring Abortion Procedure Drew on Backing from Many Friends of Roe v. Wade," *New York Times,* 23 October 2003, A22). "Voting 64 to 34, the Senate joined the House in passing the measure to prohibit what abortion foes call a 'partial-birth' procedure and to punish doctors who violate the ban with fines and as many as two years in prison" (Helen Dewar, "Senate Passes Ban on Abortion Procedure; Bush Set to Sign Bill; Foes Plan Court Fight," *Washington Post,* 22 October 2003, A01). "The Senate joined the House Tuesday in passing a bill to ban what critics call partial birth abortion" (*NBC News,* 22 October 2003). "The Senate approved a ban on a procedure critics call partial birth abortion, fulfilling a top Republican priority and setting up a high-profile court fight over one of the nation's most emotional issues" (Ryan J. Foley, "Senate Approves Antiabortion Bill," *Wall Street Journal,* 22 October 2003, D2).

20. Jim Abrams, "House Passes Ban on Abortion Procedure," *Associated Press Online,* 3 October 2003.

21. Linda Douglas, "Ban on Partial-Birth Abortion," *World News Tonight with Peter Jennings,* ABC, 21 October 2003.

22. An editorial in the *Wall Street Journal* approvingly quotes President George W. Bush's statement that "'the best case against partial birth abortion is a simple description of what happens and to whom it happens. It involves the partial delivery of a live boy or girl, and a sudden, violent end to that life.' So spoke President Bush yesterday when he signed the Partial Birth Abortion Ban Act into law"; "The Daschle Abortion Ban," *Wall Street Journal,* 6 November 2003, A14."

23. "Daschle Abortion Ban."

24. "Challenging a Mendacious Law," *New York Times,* 6 November 2003, A32.

25. *Limbaugh Letter,* "Liberals' 'Theocracy' Paranoia," June 2005, 7, 4, 5.

26. Kevin Merida, "Role of House Women's Caucus Changes," *Washington Post,* 15 February 1995, final ed., A4.

27. *Limbaugh Letter,* April 2005, 14.

Chapter 12

1. Cass Sunstein, *Republic.com* (Princeton, N.J.: Princeton University Press, 2001).

2. Elihu Katz, "And Deliver Us from Segmentation," *Annals of the American Academy of Political and Social Science* 546 (1996): 22–33.

3. Joseph Turow, *Breaking Up America: Advertisers and the New Media World* (Chicago: University of Chicago Press, 1997), 7. See also Oscar Gandy, "Dividing Practices: Segmentation and Targeting in the Emerging Public Sphere," in *Mediated Politics*, edited by W. Lance Bennett and Robert M. Entman (New York: Cambridge University Press, 2001).

4. Others who have studied Limbaugh carefully offer characterizations of the Limbaugh experience as a nontraditional social network providing internal normative pressure to conform; C. Richard Hofstetter, "Political Talk Radio, Situational Involvement, and Political Mobilization," *Social Science Quarterly* 79 (1998): 261–72.

5. J. L. Freedman and D. O. Sears, "Selective Exposure," in *Advances in Experimental Social Psychology*, edited by L. Berkowitz (New York: Academic Press, 1965), 2:57–97; D. O. Sears and J. L. Freedman, "Selective Exposure to Information: A Critical Review," *Public Opinion Quarterly* 31 (1967): 194–213; N. Stroud, "Selective Exposure to Partisan Information" (Ph.D. diss., Annenberg School for Communication, University of Pennsylvania, 2006); C. S. Taber and M. Lodge, "Motivated Skepticism in the Evaluation of Political Beliefs," *American Journal of Political Science* 50, 3 (2006): 755–69; S. J. Best, B. Chmeielewski, and B. S. Kreuger, "Selective Exposure to Online Foreign News during the Conflict with Iraq," *Harvard Journal of Press/Politics* 10, 4 (2005): 52–70.

6. See appendix for this chapter at our website, www.annenbergpublicpolicy center.org, for proportions and rank order across media sources.

7. The rank order correlations between Limbaugh and the three mainstream channels are .10, .17, and .35, which are all nonsignificant. The rank order correlations among the mainstream channels are .85, .93, and .94, all highly significant.

8. For proportions and rank order across PTR and other media sources see the appendix to this chapter at our website.

9. Two of the others exhibited no significant differences at all across media groups (number executed for murder in U.S. each year and percentage of mothers on welfare for three years or more in a row). Three showed patterns of knowledge such that the four media-consuming groups had similar levels of knowledge and all were greater than the light MSMM group. (See the appendix to this chapter at the Annenberg Public Policy Centerwebsite, Political Communication Section, www.annenbergpublicpolicycenter.org.)

10. Carolyn W. Muzafer Sherif and Roger E. Nebergall, *Attitude and Attitude Change: The Social Judgment-Involvement Approach* (Philadelphia: Saunders, 1965).

11. The analyses summarized here were done separating the PTR groups into conservative and liberal and also with seven groups distinguishing heavy print consumers from heavy television news consumers. The results are no different with these other groupings.

12. The direction of distortion of Dole's and Clinton's positions is negative, suggesting contrast effects. However, this is a bit misleading, because people tend to project their own views onto others (both in the world of political and interpersonal judgment). This cognitive bias has the effect of producing more contrast than assimilation effects.

13. John Zaller, *The Nature and Origins of Mass Opinion* (New York: Cambridge University Press, 1992); Vincent Price and John Zaller, "Who Gets the News? Alternative Measures of News Reception and Their Implications for Research," *Public Opinion Quarterly* 57 (1993): 133–64.

14. Responses to this question are fewer (N = 715) than for the other questions (where N is closer to 815) because of a glitch in the early phases of interviewing that required the first 100 or so respondents to be dropped. The lower power may explain why the results for this question are not statistically significant, even though they are quite consistent with the other five questions in direction.

15. Joseph N. Cappella, Joseph Turow, and Kathleen H. Jamieson, *Call-In Political Talk Radio: Background, Content, Audiences, Portrayal in Main Stream Media,* Report by the Annenberg Public Policy Center, University of Pennsylvania, Philadelphia, 1996.

16. The list does help to account for perceptions of who did a better job in the debate. Regressions of perceptions of who did a better job were highly significant for the style factors. Demographics (party identification (with leaners), political ideology, sex, race (white v. nonwhite), age, and education accounted for .328 of the variance, while style judgments added .176 ($\Delta F(12,720) = 21.4$, $p < .0001$). The same regressions were run using perceptions of which candidate did a better job in the eyes of other listeners. The results were similar, although not as strong. Demographic factors accounted for a significant .077 of the variance, while the style factors contributed an additional 0.111. So style factors are consequential in judgments of debate performance.

17. In the charts in this section, the usual group of liberal/moderate PTR and conservative PTR are combined for simplicity's sake. In the appendix, the results are portrayed for the four media groups, where the same pattern of results obtains.

18. For analyses showing how these results are obtained, see the appendix to this chapter at our website, www.annenbergpublicpolicycenter.org.

19. B. Weiner, *Social Motivation, Justice, and the Moral Emotions: An Attributional Approach* (Los Angeles: University of California Press, 2006); S. Iyengar, *Is Anyone Responsible? How Television Frames Political Issues* (Chicago: University of Chicago Press, 1991).

20. For greater detail see also A. Hall and J. N. Cappella, "The Impact of PTR Exposure on Attributions about the Outcome of the 1996 Presidential Election," *Journal of Communication* 52, 2 (2002): 332–50.

21. These two regular groups were then subdivided into four subgroups in the same way as at wave 1. As a result, we have 149 people for the group consuming "regular newspaper only," 126 for "regular TV only," 180 for "both," and 393 for "neither," out of the total 858 of the nonregular PTR listeners at the wave 4.

22. B. A. Hollander, "Fuel to the Fire: Talk Radio and the Gamson Hypothesis," *Political Communication* 14 (1997): 355–69. D. A. Jones, "Political Talk Radio: The Limbaugh Effect on Primary Voters," *Political Communication* 15 (1998): 367–81. D. Owen, "Talk Radio and Evaluations of President Clinton," *Political Communication* 14 (1997): 333–53.

23. In data gathered during the height of the SBVT ads, August 2004, viewers of Fox News were more likely to say that Kerry did not earn his medals than were nonviewers, even in the presence of extensive controls; the same finding was not obtained for Limbaugh listeners. However, Limbaugh listeners, like Fox viewers, were more likely to deny that the Bush campaign was behind the SBVT attacks on Kerry. Besides being a Bush or Kerry supporter, the Limbaugh and Fox effects were the only ones that were statistically significant. Ideology and party identification were not predictors of this negative attribution to the Bush campaign.

Chapter 13

1. Carolyn W. Muzafer Sheriff and Roger E. Nebergall, *Attitude and Attitude Change: The Social Judgment-Involvement Approach* (Philadelphia: Saunders, 1965).

2. R. E. Petty and J. T. Cacioppo, "The Elaboration Likelihood Model of Persuasion," in *Advances in Experimental Social Psychology,* edited by L. Berkowitz (New York: Academic Press, 1986), 19:123–205.

3. C. G. Lord, L. Ross, and M. R. Lepper, "Biased Assimilation and Attitude Polarization: The Effects of Prior Theories on Subsequently Considered Evidence," *Journal of Personality and Social Psychology* 37 (1979): 2098–2109.

4. John R. Zaller, *The Nature and Origins of Mass Opinion* (New York: Cambridge University Press, 1992).

5. J. L. Freedman and D. O. Sears, "Selective Exposure," in *Advances in Experimental Social Psychology*, edited by L. Berkowitz (New York: Academic Press, 1965), 2:57–97; D. O. Sears and J. L. Freedman, "Selective Exposure to Information: A Critical Review," *Public Opinion Quarterly* 31 (1967): 194–213; N. Stroud, "Selective Exposure to Partisan Information" (Ph.D. diss., Annenberg School for Communication, University of Pennsylvania, 2006); C. S. Taber and M. Lodge, "Motivated Skepticism in the Evaluation of Political Beliefs," *American Journal of Political Science* 50, 3 (2006): 755–69; S. J. Best, B. Chmeielewski, and B. S. Kreuger, "Selective Exposure to Online Foreign News during the Conflict with Iraq," *Harvard Journal of Press/Politics* 10, 4 (2005): 52–70.

6. These six were reliable in both the pretest (alpha = .81) and the posttest (alpha = .86) and had a normal distribution. This index was scaled so that higher scores reflected more favorable attitudes toward the persons and groups.

7. The individual parameter estimates are somewhat unreliable, due to multicollinearity. However, the relative size of the t-tests is still a good indicator of where the real differences are to be found. The largest t-tests are located in comparisons between *Talk of the Nation* subgroups to the control and Limbaugh subgroups relative to the control.

8. Change in R^2 = .022, $F_{(5,379)}$ = 2.03, p = .07.

9. For an explanation of this concept, see Robert I. Barro, "Workfare Still Beats Welfare," *Wall Street Journal*, 21 May 1996, A22.

10. The interaction between PTR group and a measure of liberal-conservative ideology, $F_{(5,372)}$ = 2.72, p < .02, $\eta2$ = .035, along with a main effect for listening group, $F_{(5,372)}$ = 3.05, p < .04, $\eta2$ = .04.

11. Both differences are significant at p < .01.

12. Taber and Lodge, "Motivated Skepticism," 2006; M. Lodge and C. Tabor, "Three Steps toward a Theory of Motivated Political Reasoning, in *Elements of Reason: Cognition, Choice, and the Bounds of Rationality*, edited by A. Lupia, M. D. McCubbins, and S. L. Popkin (Cambridge: Cambridge University Press, 2000), 183–213.

13. For material similar to that in figure 13.5 along with statistical analyses, see the appendix to this chapter at our website. Listeners to conservative PTR favored the proposal as much as Limbaugh listeners by midseason in the primary, but sharp differences remained between the listeners to conservative PTR and other groups (listeners and nonlisteners).

14. The exact pattern of figure 13.5 is not replicated, but we do see that listeners to conservative and Limbaugh PTR are much more favorable toward conservative policies, and unfavorable toward liberal ones, than are listeners to liberal/moderate PTR. Similar patterns obtain for listeners to liberal/moderate PTR on liberal issues. For example, on the issue of vouchers, listeners to liberal PTR are much more unfavorable than any other media group, while the other four groups are quite similar in how much they favor vouchers. An exception to these trends is NAFTA, showing few differences among the media groups.

15. This procedure was different from that employed in the 1996 surveys, in which regular listeners to PTR were oversampled and regular listeners to Rush Limbaugh were specifically targeted.

16. I.e., p < .001.

17. For a report of more controlled analyses of perceived liberalness of the candidates using the full sample rather than just the sample of strong Republicans, see the appendix to this chapter at our website. The same results obtain under these broader, more controlled conditions as are represented by the simpler charts.

18. One other study of the impact of viewing Fox News focused on voting turnout and decision at both the local and national levels; S. DellaVigna and

E. Kaplan, "The Fox News Effect: Media Bias and Voting" (2005), available at the authors' website, http://ist-socrates.berkeley.edu/~ekaplan/foxnews.pdf. The authors report that in the 1996 and 2000 elections, Fox News had no effect on presidential vote in their sample (either turnout or more Republican votes cast) but did add a small percentage to votes for Republicans in local elections.

19. Other studies of political knowledge gain associated with PTR have made important distinctions between factual (nonideological) information and ideologically tinged information; C. Richard Hofstetter et al., "Information, Misinformation, and Political Talk Radio," *Political Research Quarterly* 52 (1999): 353–69, and between being informed and feeling informed; Barry A. Hollander, "The New News and the 1992 Presidential Campaign: Perceived vs. Actual Political Knowledge," *Journalism and Mass Communication Quarterly* 72 (1995): 786–98. Keith Stamm reports that substantial increments to knowledge can result when a source such as PTR takes up an issue intensely, as it did with the Contract with America in 1994; Stamm, Michelle Johnson, and Brennon Martin, "Differences among Newspapers, Television, and Radio in Their Contribution to Knowledge of the Contract with America," *Journalism and Mass Communication Quarterly* 74 (1997): 687–702.

20. I. Ajzen, "The Theory of Planned Behavior," *Organizational Behavior and Human Decision Processes* 50 (1991): 179–211. M. Fishbein and I. Ajzen, *Belief, Attitude, Intention, and Behavior: An Introduction to Theory and Research* (Reading, Mass.: Addison-Wesley, 1975).

21. Many previous studies have shown that exposure to television news has little to no association with increased levels of political knowledge. J. P. Robinson and D. K. Davis, "Television News and the Informed Public: An Information Processing Approach," *Journal of Communication* 40 (1990): 106–19.

22. Joseph N. Cappella, Joseph Turow, and Kathleen H. Jamieson, *Call-in Political Talk Radio: Background, Content, Audiences, Portrayal in Main Stream Media*, Report by the Annenberg Public Policy Center, University of Pennsylvania, Philadelphia, 1996.

Conclusion

1. "Online Papers Modestly Boost Newspaper Readership," 30 July 2006.
2. "News Audiences Increasingly Politicized," 8 June 2004.
3. "Viewership over the first eight months of the year was down 5 percent, compared to 2005, with a steeper 13% decline in prime time, according to Nielsen Media Research. For 12 straight months, Fox's prime-time audience has been smaller than the year before. Meanwhile CNN viewership inched up 5 percent this year through August"; David Bauder, "Fox News' First Slump May Be a Sign of the Times," Associated Press, 30 September 2006.
4. James T. Hamilton, "The Market and the Media," in *The Press*, edited by Geneva Overholser and Kathleen Hall Jamieson (New York: Oxford University Press, 2005), 366.

5. Kathleen Hall Jamieson and Christopher Adasiewicz, "What Can Voters Learn from Election Debates?" in *Televised Election Debates: International Perspectives,* edited by Stephen Coleman (New York: Macmillan, 2000), 25–42.

6. Diana C. Mutz and Paul S. Martin, "Facilitating Communication across Lines of Political Difference: The Role of Mass Media," *American Political Science Review* 95 (2001): 97–114.

7. Michael Schudson, *The Good Citizen* (Cambridge, Mass.: Harvard University Press, 1998).

8. Elizabeth Noelle-Neumann, *The Spiral of Silence*, 2nd ed. (Chicago: University of Chicago Press, 1984).

9. Morris P. Fiorina maintains that the polarization of American politics and the polity are exaggerated, while not denying that there are some splits in attitudes and ideologies. As the media environment becomes increasingly partisan in tone and segmented by its informational focus, we expect the disjunctures in American political and social milieu to widen; Fiorina, with Samuel J. Adams and Jeremy C. Pope, *Culture War? The Myth of a Polarized America* (New York: Pearson Longman, 2005).

10. Hamilton, "The Market and the Media," 352.

11. Michael Schudson and Susan Tifft, "American Journalism in Historical Perspective," in Overholser and Jamieson, *The Press,* 41.

balkanization (*continued*)
Limbaugh creating, 192
public deliberation undermined
by, 191
Barker, David, 273*n*6
Barnes, Fred, 33, 42, 48
Barone, Michael, 112
Bartley, Robert L., 49, 53, 68, 70,
77, 146
Bauer, Gary L., 56
Beck, Glenn, 43
Beckle, Bob, 49
Begala, Paul, 48
behaviors, 17
Belknap, George, 123
benign motives, 232–33
Bennett, Lance, 144
Berelson, Bernard, 82, 144
biased processing, 215–17
big government
fiscal conservatives aversion to, 60
Noonan discussing, 62–63
republican party/conservative
mistrust in, 127–28
Black, Edwin, 93
black leaders, 219*f*
Black, Roy, 76
Blankley, Tony, xiv
Bonior, David, 110
Bonjean, Ron, 22
Boxer, Barbara, 182
Bozell, Brent III, 146
brand names, 62
Braun, Carol Moseley, 187
Bray, Thomas, 36
Brown, Cedric, 5, 9, 18
conservative opinion media
characterization of, 13–14
Kerry's exchange with, 11–13
Brown, Jerry, 153
Brown, Ron, 213
Buchanan, Pat, ix, 37, 105
attitude changes toward, 112*f*

conservative opinion media on,
109–13
the *Journal* topic of, 265*n*19
Limbaugh at odds with, 109–11
PTR called by supporters of, 110
Buckley, William F., 59
budget cuts, 71
Burke, Kenneth, 179
Bush at War (Woodward), 50
Bush, George H.W.
conservatives betrayed by, 106–7
tax increases of, 97
Bush, George W., 262*n*4
campaign claims of, 234
DUI incident of, 50
Fox News/speech of, 149–50
Gore, Al, arguing about, 64
immigration proposal of, 57–58
the *Journal* backing, 17
Kerry's battle with, 9–10
perceived liberalness of, 228*f*, 229*f*
Lott and, 33–34, 36
as Lott arbitrator, 31–32
Lott's remarks problem for, 21–22
media audience beliefs about,
230–32
"partial birth abortions" statement
of, 276*n*22
Bush, Jeb, 33
"business conservatives," 93
Bustamante, Cruz, 188
Byrd, Robert, 25, 28, 184–85
King and remarks of, 39
mainstream media ignoring
comments of, 40–41
Taranto commenting on, 40
"white niggers" comment of, 36

cable networks, 102
cable news, 47
California recall campaign, 120
Cameron, Carl, vii, 9–11
campaign claims, 234

Campbell, Angus, 123
candidate-party relationship, 105
capital gains, 220*f*
Cappella, Joseph, 174
Carlson, Tucker, 43, 48
Carmines, Edward, 57
Carroll, John, 154
Carter, Jimmy, 185
CBS movie, 72–73
CBS News, 7, 32, 37, 170
character, 19
Cheney, Dick, 18–19, 46, 147
Christian conservative leaders, 56
Christian right, 65–66
Christmas, attack on, 101
churchgoers, 100–101
civics knowledge, 199–202
civil rights
    Dixiecrat Party and, 25
    Republican party pioneering, 29, 38
Civil Rights Act, 25–26
    Democratic/Republican vote
        on, 28–29
    Gore, Albert Arnold Sr., not
        supporting, 133
Clinton, Bill, xii, 26–27, 34, 72, 79
    conservative opinion media
        on, 106–7
    Dole defeated by, 166
    emotional reaction questions about,
        135, 135*f*
    Fulbright and remarks of, 27, 30
    as full-fledged liberal, 61–62
    Limbaugh listeners distortion on,
        199–203, 201*f*, 206
    mainstream media praising, 149
    New York Times endorsing, 170
    presidential debate with, 207, 208*f*
Clinton, Hillary, 56, 121, 184
"Clinton News Network"
    comment, 147
closed-ended responses, 210
closed systems, 84

Clymer, Adam, 31, 147
CNN News, 24, 40, 47, 49, 147,
    175–76
cold war, 68–69, 72
Coleman, Norm, 140
collective identity, communities,
    179–80
Colmes, Alan, 27, 43, 47
communication venues, 4
communism, 69
communities, collective identity,
    179–80
conflict frame, 6–7
Congress, 71
conservative echo chamber, 241
conservative message
    audience beliefs about, 230–32
    liberals exposed to, 222
    political involvement and, 126
    positive associations created
        through, 143
    safe haven for, 237
conservative opinion media, 78. *See also*
    Colmes, Alan; Fox News; *Hannity
    and Colmes;* Hannity, Sean; the
    Journal; Limbaugh, Rush
    Brown, Cedric, characterized
        by, 13–14
    on Buchanan, 109–13
    churchgoers and, 100–101
    on Clinton, Bill, 106–7
    complex social issues clarified
        by, 244
    connections binding, 42–43
    cross-promotion in, 43–44, 55
    Davis's battering issue and, 153
    Democratic leaders taking on, 3
    echo chamber of, 75–78
    elements of, ix
    emotionally charged vocabulary
        of, 179
    emotional voltage varied in, 79–80
    enemies-unifying force to, 59

conservative opinion media (*continued*)

in establishment, 77–78

extreme positions taken by, 15

on Forbes, 108–9

foreign leaders speculation of, 16–17

framing used by, 141–42

ideological identity function of, 123

immigration covered in, 57–58

informational/attitudinal enclave created by, 229–30

in-group bonds created by, 180–81

in-group language of, 189–90

insulating function of, 174–75

issues dividing, 58–59

Kerry-Brown exchange characterized by, 13–14, 19

knowledge enclave created by, 28–29

liberalism attacked by, 238

liberal media indicted by, xi

Lott's apologies inadequate to, 25

Lott's treatment from, 36–37

Lott target of, 32–34

mainstream media corrective information insulated through, 212

mainstream media relationship with, 140–41, 145

mainstream media v., 247–48

marketplace wanting, 260n4

message safe haven of, 237

Murdoch as financial godfather in, 43

opinion leaders with, 144–45

overtaxed/overregulated message of, 97

"partial birth abortion" rhetoric of, 182–83

on Perot, 107–8

political landscape importance of, 4–5

politics entertaining/engaging goal of, 242–43

politics navigated with, 142

presidential candidate's mistrust and, 266n3

as Reagan conservatism custodians, xii, 67

rebuttal strategy of, 238

reframing by, 151–52

Republican credentials of, 42–43

Republican leaders feedback loop of, 18–19

Republican party cover provided by, 22–23

Republican party functions performed by, 239

Republican party interests served by, 30–31

Republican party reinforced by, 20–21

Republican presidential contender and, vii

self-protective enclave of, x, 4–5

studying, 80–81

uncontested facts contribution of, 235

conservatives, 121

advertisers desiring, 99–100

audience percentage of, 96f

big government mistrust of, 127–28

Bush, George H.W., betraying, 106–7

Democratic southern centrists and, 61

demographics of, 92–93

distinctive common vocabulary of, 179–80

fiscal, 60, 117

Fox News seeking, 47–48

Hannity and Colmes for, 79

Huckabee's credentials lacking as, 121

as judgmental shortcut, 62

language/message reinforcing, 143

liberal media and, 41

liberals exposed to, 222

like-minded audience sought by,
47–48, 177–78
Limbaugh influencing, 219
mainstream media consumption
by, 240
mainstream media interpretation
and, x–xi
McClintock as true, 118
Murdoch's slant toward, 169
negative affirmations binding
together, 59–60
political information/opinion source
of, 175–76
politics with, 219*f,* 220*f*
PTR and, 86–87, 280*n*14
Reagan, Ronald, and, 67–68, 73–74
social, 60, 63
"unelected elite" intrusions and, 59
Consolidated Omnibus Budget
Reconciliation Act, 71
consuming groups, media, 277*n*9
content analysis
of Limbaugh, 132–34, 192–93
of media, 168–69
content distinction, media, 250*n*4
content mediation, 271*n*19
contested facts/opinions, 230–32
contrast, 215, 278*n*12
Countdown with Keith Olbermann, 248
country disloyalty, 15
Couric, Katie, 181
credibility issue
of Kerry, 8–11
in presidential campaign, 7
cross-promotion, 43–44, 55
Crovitz, L. Gordon, 52
Crowley, Monica, 43
Cubin, Barbara, 184
cultural elites, 64–66
culture of death, 65–66
Cummings, Elijah, 23
Cuomo, Mario, 89, 218
Cuprisin, Tim, 4, 24

Daily Standard, 153
Daschle, Tom, 40, 156–58, 187–88
data sources, on PTR, 85
Davis, Gray, 117, 153–54
Dean, Howard, 3, 17
Deficit Reduction Act of 1984, 71
DeLay, Tom, 46
deliberative democracy, 246
demeaning vocabulary, 185–86, 189
democratic engagement, 245
Democratic party
Civil Rights Act and, 28–29
Limbaugh attacking, 29
malignant motives of, 232–33
media's airtime for, 143–44
middle class position of, 64
southern centrists in, 61
democratic system, 160–61
democrats
character temperament assumptions
about, 19
conservative opinion media
challenged by, 3
Limbaugh's negative emotions
for, 240
demographics
of audiences, 239
of conservatives, 92–93
of Fox News, 92*t*
of the *Journal,* 92*t*
of Limbaugh, 92*t*
Dewey, Thomas, 21
differential exposure, 223–25
Dionne, E. J., 31
Dirksen, Everett, 28
distortion, 198
of candidate's stand, 199
defining, 214
of Limbaugh listeners, 199–203,
201*f,* 206
measures of, 198, 200*f,* 201*f*
Dixiecrat Party, 21, 25
Dobson, James C., 56

foreign leaders
  conservative opinion media
    speculating about, 16–17
  imaginary endorsements of, 16
  Kerry and, 5–11
  Limbaugh's ridiculous assertion
    about, 15
foreign policies, 69–70
Foster, Vince, xiv
Fox and Friends, 11
Fox News, viii, 47–52, 78, 175–76
  ABC news strategic frames different
    from, 10–11
  audience growing for, xv
  audience of, 93–96
  audiences insulated by, xiii
  Bush, George W., speech covered
    by, 149–50
  Bush-Kerry battle, 9–10
  conservative audience sought by,
    47–48
  demographics of, 92t
  emergence of, 164
  "fair and balanced" claim of, 49–50
  focus different of, 243
  Fund's comments on, 50
  mainstream media veiwership
    reduced by, 174
  other broadcasters influenced by, 51t
  presidential election called by, 50
  Republican party and, 51–52
  Republican party's defections
    and, 125
  similar ideology/education and,
    230–32
  southern audience of, 103
  uncontested facts perceptions after,
    233–35
  voter turnout focus of, 280n18
framing, 6–7, 141–42, 151–53,
    211, 243
free trade, 112–13
Frist, Bill, 182

Fulbright, J. William, 26–28, 30
Fund, John, 29, 34–35, 42, 68
  Fox News analyzed by, 50
  Schwarzenegger and objections
    of, 119

Garrett, Major, 181
Gaudet, Hazel, 144
gender-based attacks, 187
gender-based vulgarity, 188–89
Gephardt, Dick, 110, 187–88
Gibson, Mel, 101
Gigot, Paul, 257n8
Gingrich, Newt, xiv, 43, 51, 133,
    188
Giuliani, Rudy, vii, 56, 120
Goldwater, Barry, 29
Gorbachev, Mikhail, 72
Gore, Al, 3, 22, 133, 186
  Bush, George W., tax policies argued
    by, 64
  father's vote, 25–26
  perceived liberalness of, 228f
Gore, Albert Arnold, Sr., 28, 133
Gottfried, Jeffrey, 143
government. *See also* big government
  Limbaugh listeners' mistrust of,
    138–39
  mistrust of, 128f
  trusting, 127–29, 132
"government is the problem"
    quote, 126
Greeley, Horarce, 147
Greenberg, Stan, 108
group identity, 180
gubernatorial debate, 118

Hagel, Chuck, 35
Hall, Robert, 109
Hamblin, Ken, 89, 218
Hamilton, James, 241–42
Hannity and Colmes, 11, 17, 92, 143
  conservative/liberal host on, 79

liberal(s) (*continued*)

income inequality concern of, 98

as judgmental shortcut, 62

as Limbaugh enemy, 65–66

Limbaugh impugning, 187–88

Limbaugh influencing, 219

Limbaugh listeners' comparisons
with, 228–29

PTR and, 86–87, 280*n*14

Reagan, Ronald, revenues and,
259*n*62

in Republican party, 116

*The Liberal Establishment: Who Runs
America…and How* (Evans), 78

liberalism, 59

battle against, xi–xii

Bush, George W., perceived, 228*f*,
229*f*

Clinton, Bill, unabashed, 61–62

conservative media attacking, 238

conservative message exposure
to, 222

as culture of death, 65–66

Gore, Al, perceived, 228*f*

Kerry's perceived, 229*f*

media audience beliefs about,
230–32

presidential candidate's perceived,
228*f*, 280*n*17

untrustworthy casting of, 244

liberal media

conservatism and, 41

conservative media's indictment
of, xi

double standard frame of, 238–40

establishment, 78

Limbaugh's content differed from,
193–94

mainstream media as, 12, 145,
148–49, 161, 243

monitoring website, 160

"liberty and capitalism," 118

Liddy, G. Gordon, 44, 89, 157, 218

Lieberman, Joe, 188

Limbaugh Letter, 177, 184

Limbaugh listeners

Annenberg survey reporting on,
254*n*15

attribution differences of, 210–11

audience drop of, 241

Clinton, Bill, and distorted views of,
199–203, 201*f*, 206

distortion of, 199–203, 201*f*, 206

efficacy and, 130

government mistrust of, 138–39

language identification of, 184

less accurate, 197

liberal candidate's comparisons
of, 228–29

watching mainstream media, 174

mainstream media's mistrust by,
172–73

as mainstream news consumers, 171

media consumption patterns of,
194–95

middle class, 97–98

party affiliation judgments of, 209

Perot and attitudes of, 265*n*18

political party's perceptions of, 227,
254*n*18

PTR percentages of, 262*n*6

Republican view more accepted
by, 245

similar ideology/education and,
230–32

uncontested facts perceptions after,
233–35

Limbaugh, Rush, vii, 42, 44–47,
59–60, 67

attitude changes toward, 112*f*, 113*f*

audience of, 93–96, 99

audience's relationship with, xiii–xiv

balkanization created by, 192

Buchanan's issues at odds with,
109–11

Byrd's sound bite played by, 39

"Clinton News Network" comment
of, 147
content analysis of, 132–34, 192–93
Daschle's patriotism impugned by,
156–57
democratic candidates/negative
emotions from, 240
Democrats attacked by, 29
demographics of, 92*t*
disparaging remarks of, 18
double standard argument of, 25–26
environmental comments of, 186
feminism stand of, 103
flat tax favorable response of, 226
foreign leader/ridiculous assertion
of, 15
gender-based attacks of, 187
gender-based vulgarity of, 188–89
government mistrust likelihood
from, 138–39
Huckabee accused by, viii
in-group language reinforced by, 178
inoculation used by, 142
the *Journal* influenced by, 76
Kerry characterized by, 17–18
labels/ridicule used by, 183
liberal/conservative reactions to, 219
liberal elite enemy of, 65–66
liberal media differing from, 193–94
liberal media-monitoring website
responding to, 160
liberal men's masculinity impugned
by, 187–88
listener's affection drop for, 112
listener's efficacy feelings of, 130, 134
listener's income difference of, 99
listeners less indifferent of, 129–30
Lott's statement of, 24
Lott target of, 32–33
mainstream media and presence of,
158–59
mainstream media rank order
correlation between, 267*n*9

mainstream media's attacks of,
163–64, 169
mainstream media scrutinized by,
151–52
mainstream media's discussions of,
146–48
mainstream media's mistrust by,
166–67
male listeners of, 101–3
McCain bashed by, 113–15, 121
middle class listeners of, 97–98
moral outrage evoked by, 133–38
names/identities coined by, 185–86
nontraditional social network and,
277*n*4
NPR audience larger than, 247
as opinion leader, 144–45
polarized view from, xiv, 217
political involvement invited by,
126–27, 130
political philosophy defense by,
243–44
PTR and, 45–46
Reagan conservatism criteria used
by, 105–6
Reagan, Michael, pitted against,
110–11
Republican party defections and, 125
Republican party's leader role of,
46–47
Republican presidential candidates'
criteria of, 120–21
Republican presidential primaries
help from, 105
Schwarzenegger advised by, 117–18
Schwarzenegger not supported
by, 116
Schwarzenegger, Republican in
name only and, 118–19
as sharp-clawed entertainer, 157
southern audience of, 103
Taranto's tone different from,
251*n*22

names/identities, 185–86

National Annenberg Election Study (NAES), 85, 89, 96

national debt, 71

national defense, 72

national syndication, 45

negative affirmations, 59–60, 184

New Deal years, 69

news articles, 159f

News Corporation, 43

news media. *See* media

news sources, 165

New York Times, 122, 146–47, 170

Nickles, Don, 35

Nie, Norman, 124

Nixon, Richard, xii

nontraditional social network, 277n4

Noonan, Peggy, 35, 42, 57

    big government spending topic of, 62–63

    Reagan conservatism topic of, 67–68

North American Free Trade Agreement (NAFTA), 108

NPR audience, 247, 273n9

Omnibus Budget Reconciliation Act of 1987, 71

one-sided information, 214, 216, 218, 242

open-ended responses, 210

opinion leaders, 144–45

opinions, 215

oppositional judgments, 223

O'Reilly, Bill, 252n17

O'Reilly Factor, 79

Osgood, Charles, 181

out-group, 177–78, 240–41

overtaxed/overregulated message, 97

"partial birth abortion," 180–83

    bill banning, 275n19

    Bush, George W., statement on, 276n22

conservative media's rhetoric on, 182–83

detailed description of, 181

partisan differences, 246

partisan media, 213, 242

The Passion, 101

PBS. *See* Public Broadcasting Service

Pelosi, Nancy, 147

The People's Choice (Lazarsfeld/Berelson/Gaudet), 144

perceptions

    performance, 207–9

    about political party, 228

    in presidential debate, 207–9

    PTR influencing, 167–68

    regressions, 278n16

Perot, Ross, 106, 109, 133

    conservative opinion media on, 107–8

    Limbaugh listeners' attitudes toward, 265n18

"personal identity," 84

Personal Influence (Katz/Lazarsfeld), 144

persuasive message, 134–35

Petrocik, John, 124

Pinkerton, Jim, 43

Podhoretz, John, 3

polarization, 175, 183

    audience protection through, 245

    biased processing causing, 216–17

    differential exposure creating, 223–25

    "hot button" issues causing, 224–25

    Limbaugh creating, xiv, 217

    one-sided information in, 214, 216

    opinions/attitudes intensified through, 215

    policy proposals reactions of, 225–26

    political world, 246

    postexposure, 224

    PTR causing, 217–18

public deliberation undermined
by, 191
selective exposure causing, 216
polarizing perceptions
labels/ridicule with, 178–79
liberals target of, 189
of presidential candidates, 227–29
policy proposals, 225–26
political information
audience influenced by, 80–81
conservative source for, 175–76
political involvement
conservative message and, 126
Limbaugh inviting, 126–27, 130
from PTR, 131
political knowledge, 281*n*19, 281*n*21
political party
allegiance to, 124–25, 124*f*
audience percentages of, 94*f*, 96*f*
identification, 221–22
Limbaugh listeners' perceptions of,
227, 254*n*18
media airtime for, 143–44
media differences and, 230–32
oppositional judgments of, 223
perceptions about, 228
potential issues dividing, 57
political talk radio (PTR), xiv–xv
black leader attitudes and, 219*f*
Buchanan's supporters calling, 110
capital gains and, 220*f*
conservative/liberal, 86–87,
280*n*14
data sources on, 85
debate watched by, 206–7
defining, 263*n*8
EITC favorability of, 223*f*
emergence of, 44–45
emotions created by, 135–38, 135*f*
flat tax/assisted suicide issues
and, 224*f*
grouping, 277*n*11, 279*n*21
indifference of, 129*f*

institution confidence lacking from,
266*n*2
intolerant dangerous discourse of, xv
issue-oriented judgments by, 167*f*
knowledge levels and, 195–98
liberal/conservative, 86–87, 280*n*14
Limbaugh and, 45–46
Limbaugh listener percentages of,
262*n*6
listener's political involvement
and, 131
mainstream differences from, 196*f*
mainstream news mistrust by, 165*f*
media coverage of, 166*f*
news articles mentioning, 159*f*
people's perceptions influenced by,
167–68
polarization from, 217–18
political knowledge and, 281*n*19
political participation from, 266*n*4
political party identification and,
221–22
Republicans given edge by, 123
research project on, 87–89
separate group's of, 261*n*14
survey of, 85–86
politics
attacks in, 127
attitudes in, 258*n*31
conservatism in, 219*f*, 220*f*
conservative opinion media
importance to, 4–5
conservative opinion media
navigating, 142
entertaining/engaging goal for,
242–43
indifference of, 129–30, 129*f*
Limbaugh's philosophy defense in,
243–44
media framing of, 211
opinion forms in, 250*n*4
orientation in, 261*n*14
participation in, 130*f*, 266*n*4

regressions, perception, 278n16
Reich, Robert, 76
Reid, Harry, 177
"reinforcing spirals framework," 83
Renzi, Rick, 19
Republican candidates
    conservative opinion media and, vii
    Limbaugh assisting public with, 105
    Limbaugh's criteria choosing,
        120–21
    Republican party possibly destroyed
        by, ix
Republican in name only (RINO),
    118–19
Republican party
    audience demographics matching,
        239
    benign motives of, 232–33
    big government mistrust of, 127–28
    Civil Rights Act and, 28–29
    civil rights legislation pioneered
        by, 29, 38
    conservative media feedback loop
        with, 18–19
    conservative opinion media and, 239
    conservative opinion media cover
        from, 22–23
    conservative opinion media
        reinforcing, 20–21
    conservative opinion media's
        credentials in, 42–44
    conservative opinion media serving
        interests of, 30–31
    defection likelihood in, 125
    ERA opposed by, 102
    Fox News and, 51–52
    international enemy lost of, 66
    liberals in, 116
    Limbaugh leader in, 46–47
    Limbaugh listeners' judgments
        and, 209
    Limbaugh listeners more accepting
        and, 245

Lott distanced from, 23–25, 38–39
make up of, 91
media's airtime for, 143–44
PTR giving edge to, 123
racism and, 30
Republican candidates destroying, ix
rhetorical leaders for, 37
style/tone of, 91–93
research project, 87–89
rhetorical leaders, 37
Rich, Frank, 160
ridicule. See labels/ridicule
"right leaning." the Journal, 52
RINO. See Republican in name only
Rockefeller, Jay, 148
Roe v. Wade, 58, 101–2, 182–83, 257n8,
    257n10, 257n12
Romney, Mitt, vii, 122
Roosevelt, Franklin, xi, 59
Rothenberg, Stu, 22
Rush Limbaugh Show, 193–94, 273n6
Russert, Tim, 22, 42, 115, 140,
    158, 181

same-sex marriages, 225
Santorum, Rick, 37, 182
satellite dish, 45
SBVT. See Swift Boat Veterans for Truth
Scalia, Anthony, 58
Scarborough Country, 143
Scarborough, Joe, 43
Schlesinger, Arthur, Jr., 68
Schlesinger, James, 76
Schudson, Michael, 248
Schwarzenegger, Arnold, 106
    Fund's objections to, 119
    groping accusation of, 152–53
    ideology unknown of, 115
    Limbaugh conflicted toward,
        117–18
    Limbaugh not supporting, 116
    Los Angeles Times' bias against, 154
    as Republican in name only, 118–19

Van Susteren, Greta, 43
Vargas, Elizabeth, 7
Ventura, Jesse, 140
Verba, Sidney, 124
viewership, media, 281n3
Viguerie, Richard, 46, 49,
    260n4
vocabulary, common conservative,
    179–80
voter turnout, 280n18
Voting Rights Act, 34

Wallace, Chris, ix
Wall Street Journal. See the *Journal* (WSJ)
Walsh, Sean, 152
Wanniski, Jude, 53, 54
Washington Post, 22–23, 155
Watts, J. C., 37
*The Way the World Works: How
    Economics Fail—and Succeed*
    (Wanniski), 53
The Way Things Ought to Be (Limbaugh),
    42, 67
wealthy elites, 64–66

weapons of mass destruction, 148,
    150–51
Webster, James, 175
Weekly Standard, 150
welfare reform, 54
welfare system, 54
Wellstone, Paul, 140, 158
Weyrich, Paul, 3
white males, 101–3
"white niggers," 36
Whitewater, 146
Wiebe, Robert, 80
Will, George, 44
"The WMD Evidence," 148
Wolfowitz, Paul, 150
women's vote, 264n27
Wong, John, 170
Woodward, Bob, 50, 76, 101
World War II, 69
wrongdoing, dismissing, 252n17

Zaller, John, 199
Zarefsy, David, 179
Zhirinovsky, Vladimir, 111